Data Management

This guide illuminates the intricate relationship between data management, computer architecture, and system software. It traces the evolution of computing to today's data-centric focus and underscores the importance of hardware–software codesign in achieving efficient data processing systems with high throughput and low latency. The thorough coverage includes topics such as logical data formats, memory architecture, graphics processing unit (GPU) programming, and the innovative use of ray tracing in computational tasks. Special emphasis is placed on minimizing data movement within memory hierarchies and optimizing data storage and retrieval. Tailored for professionals and students in computer science, this book combines theoretical foundations with practical applications, making it an indispensable resource for anyone wanting to master the synergies between data management and computing infrastructure.

Xiaodong Zhang is Robert M. Critchfield Professor in Engineering and University Distinguished Scholar at the Ohio State University. He specializes in data management in computer and distributed systems. His influential research is broadly adopted in various sectors. He received the ACM MICRO Test of Time Award in 2020 and the VLDB Test of Time Award in 2024. He is a Fellow of both ACM and IEEE.

Rubao Lee is a distinguished computer scientist who has made significant contributions to GPU-accelerated database systems and data processing. His innovations, like RCFile and YSmart, are widely adopted in industry. He received the ICDCS Best Paper Award in 2011, the Lumley Research Award of The Ohio State University in 2018, and the VLDB Test of Time Award in 2024. He is a Senior Member of IEEE.

Data Management

Interactions with Computer Architecture and Systems

XIAODONG ZHANG

The Ohio State University

RUBAO LEE

The Ohio State University

 CAMBRIDGE
UNIVERSITY PRESS

CAMBRIDGE
UNIVERSITY PRESS

Shaftesbury Road, Cambridge CB2 8EA, United Kingdom

One Liberty Plaza, 20th Floor, New York, NY 10006, USA

477 Williamstown Road, Port Melbourne, VIC 3207, Australia

314–321, 3rd Floor, Plot 3, Splendor Forum, Jasola District Centre, New Delhi – 110025, India

103 Penang Road, #05–06/07, Visioncrest Commercial, Singapore 238467

Cambridge University Press is part of Cambridge University Press & Assessment,
a department of the University of Cambridge.

We share the University's mission to contribute to society through the pursuit of
education, learning and research at the highest international levels of excellence.

www.cambridge.org
Information on this title: www.cambridge.org/9781009123310

DOI: 10.1017/9781009122115

First published 2025

A catalogue record for this publication is available from the British Library.

A Cataloging-in-Publication data record for this book is available from the Library of Congress.

ISBN 978-1-009-12331-0 Hardback

Cambridge University Press & Assessment has no responsibility for the persistence
or accuracy of URLs for external or third-party internet websites referred to in this
publication and does not guarantee that any content on such websites is, or will
remain, accurate or appropriate.

To Ralph J. Slutz and Margret M. Slutz

Contents

Preface

The Data-Centric Computing Time

The computing field has undergone dramatic changes and rapid advancements. The initial stage of computing, which emerged in the 1930s, was primarily focused on scientific computation and number crunching. This stage saw the creation of the first two independent digital computers in the world: the ABC machine, developed by John Atanasoff and Clifford Berry at Iowa State University in the USA, and the Zuse machines, built by Konrad Zuse in Berlin, Germany [25, 31].

The subsequent development based on the core design of the ABC machine led to the creation of the ENIAC in 1943, which became the world's first operational computer [24]. This period introduced several key design ideas that shaped the field. Eventually, computer hardware design became standardized under the Von Neumann model [127]. Moreover, advancements in semiconductor and very-large-scale integration (VLSI) technologies resulted in the continuous growth of CPU chip performance, following Moore's Law until 2015 [23].

Throughout this period, operating systems, databases, and scientific computing libraries matured, enabling the support of essential applications in society. In the early 1970s, the second stage of computing began to emerge, which focused on networking. The phrase "The Network is the Computer," coined by Sun Microsystems in the mid-1980s, encapsulated the ambition and goal of this stage. Today, nearly every digital device is connected to the Internet, either directly or indirectly, facilitating a wide range of computing applications.

With significant achievements in computer hardware, system software, application software, and both wired and wireless networks, we have now entered the third stage of computing: data-centric computing. This stage is characterized by the central role of data and is exemplified by the title of the book *The Datacentre as a Computer* [11]. In this era, computing is driven by the processing and analysis of vast amounts of data, leading to new opportunities and challenges in various domains.

The Requirement of Understanding the Interactions

Over the course of more than 80 years of research and development in the field of computing, it has become evident that various subjects within computer science, such as algorithms and data structures, computer architecture, operating systems, databases, and networking, are highly interconnected and interdependent. However, this close interaction among key software and hardware components has remained hidden from most users, including computer science students, for two primary reasons.

First, multiple levels of programming abstraction have been developed to enable users to write machine-independent programs easily. These abstractions have attracted billions of users from various fields to utilize computers without requiring in-depth knowledge of the underlying system software and hardware.

Second, the continuous advancements in computing performance at the circuit level, driven by Moore's Law, have made machine-independent programming widely accepted. This rapid progress in hardware capabilities has allowed software to rely on the increasing computational power without being extensively optimized for efficiency.

However, as we enter the post-Moore's Law era, achieving highly efficient execution for applications, such as databases and machine learning, can no longer rely solely on the capabilities of software and hardware infrastructure. Instead, it necessitates insightful programming that carefully balances three critical factors: low algorithm complexity, minimal data movement, and high parallelism. These considerations are essential for achieving optimal performance in the absence of exponential hardware performance improvements.

As computer scientists, our primary focus today is on tailoring applications to effectively utilize the powerful and diverse resources provided by systems software and hardware architecture. To accomplish this goal, it is crucial to understand the intricacies of each of the three entities: applications, computer architectures, and system software. By doing so, we can identify the "sweet spots" where optimal and desirable performance effects can be achieved with an acceptable overhead and at a low cost.

However, despite the evolving landscape of computing, our current computer science classroom teaching often remains subject focused. For example, in an algorithm class, we typically teach students to analyze algorithm complexity using the Big-O notation, primarily focusing on counting the number of computing operations while assuming that data movement is cost free. In practice, a skilled programmer may not necessarily select the algorithm with the lowest complexity. Instead, they may choose an algorithm that exhibits high parallelism and data locality, allowing them to leverage the powerful and diverse architectural resources available and achieve the highest performance at a low cost.

Most textbooks on different subjects are written from specific "domain perspectives." For instance, database textbooks primarily focus on design and implementation at a logical level, while computer architecture and operating system textbooks describe hardware design and system software implementation, emphasizing critical path execution efficiency and effective resource management. This reflects the viewpoint of "infrastructure designers and builders."

In the post-Moore's Law era, where significant efforts are required to reshape the existing "one-size-fits-all" ecosystem, computer scientists must adopt an interactive approach that spans multiple areas, including applications, systems software, and hardware architecture. This approach necessitates breaking down subject barriers and promoting a holistic understanding of computing systems to address the challenges and opportunities of the evolving computing landscape.

The Goal of This Book

This book is written for senior undergraduate students and beginning graduate students who have completed entry-level courses in computer architecture, operating systems, and databases. Its aim is to explain the critical role of computer hardware infrastructure and networking in enabling highly efficient data management systems and data processing applications with the support of systems software.

The title of this textbook incorporates three crucial terms: *data*, *architecture*, and *systems*, which represent the primary objective of our writing: To break down the barriers among these three closely related subjects in classrooms. Throughout our years of teaching and conducting research in computer science, we have developed a keen interest in exploring the data movement behavior of various applications across computer architecture, software systems, distributed systems, and databases in real-time scenarios.

Together with our students and collaborators, we have proposed methods and techniques to maximize parallelism and minimize data movement by addressing critical issues that arise in these domains. Some of our fundamental research findings have been integrated into production systems, in both hardware and software. Interestingly, the foundational knowledge required for these research investigations largely falls within the scope of undergraduate classes in computer architecture, operating systems, and databases. However, the interactive thinking among these subjects is often overlooked in traditional teaching approaches.

For instance, the study of virtual memory management in operating system classes is often treated as somewhat independent from the cache structure discussed in computer architecture classes, even though they are closely related within the same physical memory address space. By bridging these two subjects and emphasizing the close connection between cache management in hardware architecture and memory management in operating systems, students would gain a deeper understanding of how the operating system can decide space allocation within the hardware cache on a per-process basis, thus mitigating data access conflicts in the last-level cache (LLC) of multicore processors.

Drawing from our teaching experiences and research endeavors, we have been motivated to write an unconventional book that interconnects these three areas in a linked and interactive manner. We hope to provide students and readers with a comprehensive resource that explores the intricate relationships and dependencies among applications, hardware architecture, and software systems. Our rich experiences and the lessons we have learned in these three fields give us a unique "latecomer advantage" in crafting this book, ensuring its relevance and value to those seeking a holistic understanding of the subject matter.

Outline of the Book

The book is structured in a way that aligns with the recommended order of teaching in class, as follows.

The first chapter, Introduction, will provide a historical perspective on the technical evolution, tracing it from the origins of "computing" to the emergence of "networking," and finally to the current era of "data-centric" computing. It will explore the fundamental hardware and system components that support data processing.

The primary goal of this chapter is to inspire readers to develop an interactive mindset encompassing these three domains. By understanding the interactions among hardware, software, and networking, readers will be encouraged to explore the synergies between them.

Additionally, Chapter 1 will present a road-map for the book, emphasizing the principle of hardware and software codesign and its vital role in constructing highly efficient data management systems. The ultimate objective is to achieve high throughput and low latency, which are critical goals in modern data processing.

Chapter 2 delves into data management from the foundational level of computing systems. It focuses on the exploration of logical data formats and physical allocations within storage systems. The chapter examines the interplay between the logical abstractions enabled by system software for data management and the physical placement of data.

A key aspect of this discussion is the analysis of data formats defined within software systems, as they directly influence the performance of data processing. This chapter emphasizes the importance of well-designed storage data formats, which aim to minimize unnecessary input/output (I/O) traffic and network communications. By optimizing data formats, efficient utilization of resources can be achieved, leading to improved performance in data processing.

Chapter 3 provides a comprehensive examination of main memory, considering both its architectural aspects and its role in system software. In the physical memory space, the cache is physically positioned between the central processing unit (CPU) and the main memory, serving as a repository for frequently accessed data by the CPU. This chapter explores the utilization of physical memory addresses as a linkage mechanism that connects a program in its virtual space to its corresponding execution space in the cache and main memory.

Numerous advancements in CPU and memory products are presented, highlighting their relevance to memory management. This chapter also introduces the concept of the operating system (OS) buffer cache, which serves as a repository for recently accessed I/O data, such as accessed disk blocks cached in memory. Additionally, at the user level, the development of a key–value store (KV-store) is discussed as an alternative approach for achieving the same objective.

Furthermore, this chapter revisits the log-structured merge-tree (LSM-tree), previously introduced in Chapter 2, to gain deeper insights into its interactions with the OS buffer cache and the KV-store residing in memory. By exploring these relationships, a more comprehensive understanding of the storage system is gained.

Chapter 4 centers around the diverse challenges and solutions associated with minimizing data movement within the memory hierarchy. This chapter explores both hardware and systems software approaches aiming at addressing this issue. Special attention is given to buffer management techniques that aim to optimize data movement and reduce access latency. Furthermore, the chapter delves into the significance of nonvolatile memory (NVM), particularly flash memory devices and their role in mitigating access latency within the memory hierarchy.

By examining these topics, readers will gain a deeper understanding of the strategies employed to minimize data movement and enhance overall memory performance.

Chapter 5 explores a crucial alternative to the main memory, offering a fast and direct data source for computing units, without relying on virtual memory support. This chapter focuses on the concept of in-memory data processing and its challenges, which involves storing large volumes of data in fast dynamic random-access memory (DRAM) as the primary working place, while using disk and solid-state device (SSD) storage mainly for backup and archival purposes.

By discussing in-memory data processing, this chapter sheds light on its significance and benefits, emphasizing its role in enabling efficient and rapid data access for computing tasks. The chapter also examines the implications of this approach for disk utilization, highlighting the shift towards utilizing disk and SSD storage as secondary storage mediums rather than primary data sources.

In Chapters 6, 7, and 8, we will learn about the dynamic interactions between data management and graphics processing unit (GPU) devices/accelerators. The focus of Chapter 6 will be a comprehensive introduction to the realm of GPU programming, with a particular emphasis on the utilization of sorting as a case study. Through this lens, we shall explore how parallel programming and architecture-oriented performance tuning are integral in unlocking the full potential of GPU as a powerful computing device. Our approach in this chapter will be comprehensive and gradual, taking readers through each step of the transformation process on how a sequential bubble sorting algorithm is systematically evolved into GPU-friendly bitonic sorting and odd–even merging sorting algorithms.

Building upon the foundational knowledge of GPUs established in Chapter 6, the ensuing two chapters will delve deeper into the realm of data management. In Chapter 7, our focus will be on the management of structured data using GPUs. Here, we will demonstrate how to construct a GPU-based structured query language (SQL) database engine that encompasses both hash-based and sorting-based relational operator algorithms. In particular, this chapter will explore how subqueries, a complex SQL concept, can be efficiently interacted with GPUs for optimal performance.

Chapter 8 shifts focus to the intricate world of spatial data management, offering an in-depth analysis of how spatial data management tasks, specifically in the context of pathology imaging applications, are approached and optimized on traditional CPU-based computing platforms versus GPU-accelerated platforms. Employing a case-study methodology, this chapter not only delves into the specifics of these applications but also extrapolates broader methodologies and strategies for leveraging advanced hardware to enhance application performance.

Chapter 9 delves into the transformative world of ray tracing, a technology that is reshaping the landscape of computational graphics and data processing. Bridging the gap between advanced graphical rendering and general computational tasks, it explores how ray tracing hardware, originally designed for stunning visual effects, is now being harnessed for diverse applications beyond graphics. The chapter employs Nvidia GPU RT Cores and the OptiX programming framework as conduits to explain ray tracing's fundamental concepts and practical implementations.

We conclude this book in Chapter 10. This chapter will not only consolidate the key learnings but also project future trends and emerging technologies in this dynamic field. We will explore how the convergence of advanced hardware, sophisticated algorithms, and artificial intelligence (AI)-driven solutions is shaping the next frontier of data management and computing. Emphasizing practical implications and future possibilities, this final chapter aims to equip readers with a comprehensive understanding and vision of how these integrated technologies will continue to transform the landscape of computing and data management.

As the book focuses on interactions among infrastructure hardware, system software, and running application programs in computer systems, each chapter maintains a certain level of autonomy. This allows readers to selectively explore chapters based on their individual interests. Similarly, classroom teaching can also follow a flexible approach based on the preferences and needs of both instructors and students.

Acknowledgments

We are deeply grateful to many people who have helped us to finally finish writing and publish this book. We would first like to acknowledge the students who took the class of Introduction of Computer Architecture at The Ohio State University in the 2023 and 2024 academic years, for their careful reading, doing homework, and their suggestions and comments on the draft of the book.

We would like to specially recognize several experts in the field who read the manuscript with passion. Professor Song Jiang of The University of Texas at Arlington and Professor Xiaoning Ding of the New Jersey Institute of Technology have meticulously reviewed numerous drafts of almost every chapter, each time enriching our work with their astute observations. We have been impressed by the debate between the two on several algorithms and concepts in the book. Their suggestions have been not merely helpful; they were pivotal, enabling the completion of this book.

Our gratitude is extended to Professor Feng Chen at Louisiana State University, whose expertise greatly enhanced the first five chapters. His insights, particularly on storage systems and cache replacement strategies, were invaluable. We also wish to express our appreciation to Professor Zhao Zhang and Professor Zhichun Zhu of the University of Illinois Chicago. Their feedback on the initial chapters, especially their detailed critique of the hardware discussion in Chapter 3, has been invaluable. Special thanks are due to Dr. Yuan Yuan at Google and Liang Geng at The Ohio State University for their valuable comments and suggestions on the GPU-related topics in Chapters 6 through 9.

The content of this book also reflects decades of research efforts on foundational research and teaching activities both at The College of William & Mary in Virginia and The Ohio State University. We have always learned more from our students than we taught them. The Athenian philosopher Plato (428 BC–347 BC) gives the following academic principle: A great teacher is measured by how many students have surpassed the teacher. We are far away from being great teachers; however, we have seen many students who have surpassed us. We are indebted to all our collaborators on various projects since the 1990s.

Finally, we extend our deepest gratitude to our friends and family. Their unwavering support over the years has been a constant source of strength and motivation in the journey of writing this book. Xiaodong Zhang, in particular, wishes to express his profound appreciation to his son, Dr. Simon Zhang, a young computer scientist who often updates him on the latest advancements in the field of AI; and to his wife Yan Meng, a seasoned software engineer whose industry-based problem-solving perspectives have influenced his academic thinking. Rubao Lee would like to convey his sincere thanks to all his family members, whose enduring support and encouragement have been the bedrock of his academic research career.

We cannot conclude our acknowledgments without sincerely expressing our deep appreciation for the invaluable assistance from Cambridge University Press. It was our pleasure to work with Arman Chowdhury, Laura Emsden, and Marijasintha Srinivasan, who guided us throughout the entire book-making process. In particular, we extend our deepest respect and gratitude to our copyeditor, Mrs. Beverley Lawrence, for her meticulous work in reviewing and polishing the entire draft. The book's production would not have been possible without Mrs. Lawrence's professional, valuable, and careful editing.

1 Introduction

A fundamental principle in the development of computer systems is the concept of *multilevel abstraction*. This principle involves each level of abstraction building upon a lower level that provides more-detailed functionality. In essence, each level hides the intricate operations of the level below it. The use of multilevel abstractions forms a hierarchical stack that enables increasingly detailed operations.

At the top of this stack, specific human expressions, such as structured query language (SQL) in databases, are used to make processing requests. These requests then traverse through multiple levels of software, eventually reaching the bottom level where they are executed through detailed hardware operations. For instance, a final executable program, which relies on a machine-dependent instruction set architecture (ISA), is represented by a set of binary code. This binary code directly drives the hardware to execute each instruction of the upper-level abstraction.

Overall, the concept of multilevel abstraction allows for the systematic organization of computer systems, with higher levels of abstraction providing more user-friendly and human-expressive interfaces while relying on lower levels for efficient and detailed execution.

During program execution on a computer, the central processing unit (CPU) tends to access a small subset of data and instructions repeatedly in both time and space. This subset is commonly known as the *working set*. The principle of *temporal locality* refers to the frequent access of a particular set of data or instructions within a relatively short time frame. In simpler terms, if a dataset is accessed once, it is highly likely that it will be accessed again in the near future. On the other hand, the principle of *spatial locality* states that data access often follows a pattern where nearby data objects are accessed in sequence. In essence, if a particular data object is accessed, it is expected that the neighboring data objects will be accessed next.

These observations of common data access patterns form the basis of the principle of locality [45]. To leverage this principle, computer architects have designed a crucial hardware hierarchy known as *the memory hierarchy*. The goal of this hierarchy is to store frequently used data in close proximity to the CPU, ensuring low-latency access. Additionally, the memory and storage systems are designed to organize data in a sequential or sorted manner to optimize spatial locality.

In Figure 1.1, the memory hierarchy is depicted as a pyramid-shaped structure. Each level in the hierarchy is ranked based on its access latency and capacity, with both increasing in a top-down direction. The hierarchy begins with registers, which

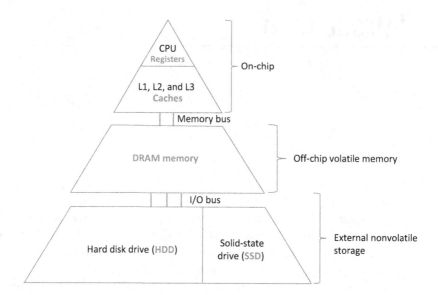

Figure 1.1 The memory hierarchy in computer architecture. At the top level of the hierarchy, we have the on-chip storage, which is located close to the CPU and includes registers as well as three levels of caches. Moving down the hierarchy, we encounter the middle level connected by a memory bus, which consists of off-chip DRAM memory. This type of memory is volatile, meaning it requires power to maintain the data that have already been stored. At the bottom level of the hierarchy, we have external storage devices that fall into the category of nonvolatile or persistent storage. These devices include HDD and/or SSD. They provide persistent storage for data and are not dependent on a continuous power supply to maintain the stored information.

are closest to the CPU, followed by on-chip caches spanning three levels. Next is the main memory, typically comprised of dynamic random-access memory (DRAM), and at the bottom level, we have persistent storage devices such as solid-state drives (SSD) and hard disk drives (HDD).

By implementing the memory hierarchy, computer systems can effectively exploit the principle of locality, optimizing data access patterns and improving overall system performance.

The implementation of software abstractions at multiple levels aims to enhance the productivity of software development by allowing developers to focus on each level without concerning themselves with the details of the subsequent levels. On the other hand, the hardware memory hierarchy is designed to reduce the latency gap between CPU-cycle-based computing and the growing volume of data movement.

The system design in multilevel abstraction and multilevel memory hierarchy in hardware are related and dependent on each other. Each layer of the hierarchy, including cache, main memory, and disk storage, has its own specific design and optimization considerations, which presents a challenge for achieving overall performance optimization across the entire system, particularly for different application execution patterns.

In this chapter, we will delve into these two stacks: the software levels of abstractions and the hardware memory hierarchy. Our objective is to examine the interaction between these software and hardware stacks, as they play a crucial role in determining the performance of data processing. By understanding these relationships, we can gain valuable insights into optimizing system performance. We will also present several cases that illustrate the challenge of achieving overall performance, serving as motivation to comprehend the dynamic interactions among applications, architecture, and software systems. By examining these interactions, we aim to gain a deeper understanding of how they influence system performance and explore potential avenues for improvement.

1.1 The Multilevel Software Abstraction and the Deep Hardware Memory Hierarchy

Computing applications, regardless of their nature, rely on a computer architecture with software management support. In this architecture, two primary tasks are performed: (1) executing arithmetic and logic operations, and (2) accessing data stored in the extensive memory hierarchy. Figure 1.2 illustrates the combination of two hierarchies – the multilevel software abstractions and the underlying hardware architecture, with a particular emphasis on the pivotal role played by the memory hierarchy.

Within Figure 1.2, the software stack is interconnected with the hardware stack through a machine-dependent ISA, which represents the final level of software abstraction.

1.1.1 Software Abstractions

In Figure 1.2, the highest level of software abstraction is represented by "executable apps." These apps provide a simplified interface to users, concealing intricate execution details related to both software and hardware. Each app is identified by a unique icon and application name, enabling users to easily execute them simply by tapping on the icon. This level of abstraction benefits billions of people who do not possess extensive computing backgrounds or knowledge.

The subsequent level of abstraction is referred to as the "user domain." Within this domain, users can write programs using high-level programming languages like Java. Various programming tools are available in this domain, including debuggers for tracing, testing, and correcting programs, compilers that translate machine-independent high-level code into machine-dependent assembly code, assemblers that convert assembly code to machine binary code, linkers that combine multiple object files into a single executable program, and more. The abstraction of executable apps builds upon the user working domain abstraction, as every app is developed through user programming.

To execute a program on a computer, well-prepared executable code in the user working domain requires resource allocations for CPU cycles and memory space.

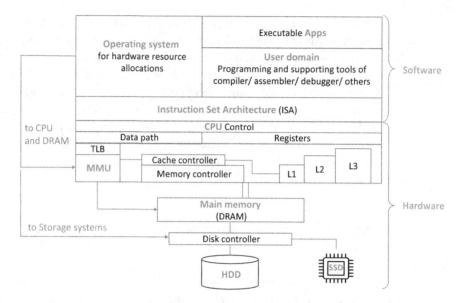

Figure 1.2 Key components in a general-purpose computer system. The highest level of abstraction in computing is the realm of executable apps, designed for billions of users to effortlessly run millions of applications without requiring any knowledge of the underlying computing system. Users simply need to touch the selected app icon on their screen using their finger. Moving down the hierarchy, we reach the programming environment. This level is developed for programmers, offering a variety of programming languages and tools that allow them to write programs. These programs can then be converted into assembly code and binary code, which are understood by the underlying computer hardware. The ISA forms the foundation for this assembly and binary code and is specific to the hardware platform. The OS plays a crucial role in the hierarchy by managing and allocating hardware resources to each executable program. It handles tasks such as scheduling CPU resources for computations, allocating memory space for data and instructions, and facilitating interactions with disk drives for reading and writing data. All of these components, including the OS, programming environment, and executable apps, reside within the software stack. The ISA serves as the crucial interface between the software and hardware layers, enabling communication and interaction between the two. The hardware layer provides a more-detailed illustration of the memory hierarchy, as depicted in Figure 1.1.

This allocation is facilitated by the operating system (OS), which acts as an agent between application programs and the hardware. The OS operates at another level of abstraction. It establishes critical connections with the computer hardware, specifically with the CPU, memory, and the storage system.

1.1.2   The Memory Hierarchy in Architecture

Within the hardware component depicted in Figure 1.2, a significant element is the memory hierarchy. However, there exists a fundamental distinction in the management approach between the OS and hardware architecture, primarily related to flexibility.

In the realm of the OS, management policies are designed and implemented in software, allowing for a wide range of variations and ideas. The OS has the flexibility to employ diverse algorithms and policies to optimize memory utilization and performance. For instance, the OS dynamically allocates data pages in DRAM and employs sophisticated algorithms to select victim pages for eviction when the memory space becomes full. These algorithms are often more complex and adaptive than the predetermined mapping schemes employed by the hardware. The flexibility in OS management stems from the dynamic nature of the software and the ability to adapt to varying workload conditions.

In contrast, the internal management of the hardware is predominantly predetermined and operates through automatic processes. For example, the hardware swiftly identifies the cache block associated with a given memory address using cache designs like set-associative caches, with limited choices available. Similarly, memory pages are automatically mapped to specific memory banks following predefined interleaving rules. These predetermined hardware mechanisms are designed to ensure efficient execution in the critical path of the system, where even minor increments in latency can significantly degrade overall performance.

The hardware's reliance on predetermined management processes is rooted in the need to maintain precise timing and minimize delays in critical operations. Altering these processes in real time can be challenging and may introduce unpredictable performance consequences. Therefore, the hardware often operates with fixed and automatic management procedures to ensure predictable and efficient execution.

Overall, while the OS enjoys flexibility in managing memory through dynamic allocation and advanced algorithms, the hardware implements predetermined mechanisms optimized for speed and efficiency, prioritizing strict timing requirements in critical system operations.

1.2 Interactions among Software Abstractions and the Memory Hierarchy

The concept of abstraction and its implementation form the foundation of software and hardware development, offering significant benefits to the computing ecosystem in terms of efficiency and productivity. However, achieving effective interactions and information sharing among different domains within existing computing systems, both in software and hardware, is often hindered by a lack of interoperability.

Interoperability refers to the capability of diverse computer systems and software to exchange and utilize information seamlessly across independent domains. Unfortunately, current computing systems suffer from limited interoperability, resulting in constrained interactions and information sharing between the abstractions and the memory hierarchy.

As a consequence, the full potential of the computing ecosystem remains untapped, as effective interoperability facilitates efficient data exchange and collaboration among different software and hardware components. Enhancing interoperability can unlock new possibilities for innovation, enabling more efficient and seamless interactions between software abstractions and the memory hierarchy.

1.2.1   The Merits of Multilevel Abstractions

The use of software abstractions is a widespread practice in the advancement of computing infrastructure across various applications. While Figure 1.2 illustrates some basic levels of abstraction, it is important to note that there are additional examples, such as remote procedure call (RPC) [19]. Remote procedure call offers users an abstraction that allows them to utilize computing services on a remote node, effectively hiding the intricate networking details. This abstraction provides users with a simplified interface, resembling a local procedure call, while transparently handling the complexities of remote execution.

The introduction of multilevel abstractions has significantly enhanced software development productivity. Different programming tasks can now be specialized, with focused attention given to specific computing domains. For instance, at the user level, developers can analyze and build application programs, while at the OS kernel level, they can work on system development. Similarly, networking programming can be accomplished by utilizing communication protocols, among other specialized tasks. Each level of abstraction defines a distinct computing domain, allowing programmers to concentrate on their specific tasks without being burdened by the details of lower levels.

This design approach aligns with the fundamental economic principle of "Division of Labor" or "Specialization of the Labor Force." By utilizing multilevel abstractions, a broad range of users in various domain areas can efficiently develop and run their programs on computers. This specialization not only enhances productivity but also enables users to leverage computing resources effectively within their respective domains.

> Economic growth is rooted in the increasing *division of labor*, which is primarily related to the *specialization of the labor force*, essentially the breaking down of large jobs into many tiny components. Each worker becomes an expert in one isolated area of production, increasing his efficiency.
>
> Adam Smith, *The Wealth of Nations*, 1776 (our emphasis).

Level-focused software development has historically demonstrated high efficiency, primarily due to the continuous performance improvements at the circuit level, as dictated by Moore's Law. This improvement has benefited all levels of abstraction within the computing ecosystem. Consequently, the performance loss resulting from inefficient interactions between levels and the underlying architecture has not been a significant concern.

However, as we approach the end of Moore's Law, the challenge of sustaining and further enhancing the performance of computing infrastructure to meet the increasingly high demands of various applications, particularly data-centric ones, has become a significant hurdle.

Data-centric applications, which rely heavily on processing large volumes of data, pose unique challenges in terms of performance. The traditional level-focused development approach may not be sufficient to address these challenges. Inefficient interactions and architectural limitations can become bottlenecks that impede the performance gains required for these demanding applications.

As a result, finding innovative solutions to continue raising the performance of computing infrastructure has become a major challenge for the industry. It requires exploring new avenues beyond traditional approaches and considering alternative strategies to optimize performance and address the demands of data-centric applications.

Efforts are being made to explore novel architectural designs, develop specialized hardware accelerators, leverage parallel and distributed computing paradigms, and invest in advanced memory and storage technologies. Additionally, optimizing software algorithms and leveraging machine learning techniques can also contribute to performance improvements.

Addressing these challenges necessitates a collaborative effort from researchers, engineers, and the computing community as a whole. By exploring new technologies, refining existing approaches, and embracing interdisciplinary solutions, we can tackle the performance demands posed by data-centric applications in a post-Moore's Law era.

1.2.2 Balancing Multiple Performance Objectives

The majority of programming tasks are carried out in the user working domain (as depicted in Figure 1.2), which operates at a logical and machine-independent level. Algorithmic complexity plays a crucial role in achieving high performance and is often represented using the Big-O notation, which quantifies the number of computing operations as a function of the data size. For instance, the bubble sort algorithm has a complexity of $O(n^2)$, where n represents the number of elements to be sorted. In the context of Big-O notation, algorithmic complexity assumes that data movement is cost free, with computing operations being the primary performance determinant.

However, in today's computing landscape, achieving highly efficient program execution relies on three critical factors: (1) attaining low algorithmic complexity, (2) minimizing data movement within the memory hierarchy, and (3) maximizing parallelism in both software and hardware. Table 1.1 characterizes the dynamics of program execution influenced by these three factors. The first row consists of all zeros, representing the rare scenario where none of the factors favor the program. Conversely, the last row contains all ones, indicating that all three factors align favorably for the program. These two extreme cases are infrequent in practical scenarios.

Below the row of three 0s, Table 1.1 comprises a set of three rows, each highlighting a single positive factor (value 1). However, a program's performance may still be uncertain in these cases, as relying solely on a single factor might not

Table 1.1 The performance of a program during execution is determined by three key factors: (1) algorithmic complexity, (2) data locality, and (3) parallelism. These factors interact to produce eight possible combinations of values. A value of 0 indicates that the program is not favored by that particular factor, representing high complexity, low locality, or low parallelism, respectively. Conversely, a value of 1 indicates that the program benefits from the factor, representing low complexity, high locality, or high parallelism, respectively.

Notes	Parallelism	Data locality	Complexity
Inefficient execution	0	0	0
Uncertain performance	0	0	1
	0	1	0
	1	0	1
Perfect sequential	0	1	1
Low locality	1	0	1
Possible high performance	1	1	0
Perfect execution	1	1	1

be sufficient for achieving acceptable execution efficiency. Additionally, there are three rows in Table 1.1 where two positive factors are present. Let us examine each case.

The row denoted by 0, 1, 1 represents a perfect sequential execution. In this case, the program parallelism is low ($=0$), but both data locality ($=1$) and complexity ($=1$) are favorable.

The row of 1, 0, 1 gives another uncertain case. When parallelism is high ($=1$) and algorithmic complexity is low ($=1$), but data locality is poor ($=0$), the question arises as to whether the benefits of high parallelism and low complexity can offset the overhead caused by data movement. Consequently, the program's performance may also be uncertain in such scenarios.

For the row of 1, 1, 0, despite the high complexity, studies have demonstrated that high-performance execution is still feasible in these scenarios due to the high strengths of both locality and parallelism [52].

In summary, while algorithmic complexity remains an important consideration, achieving efficient program execution in today's reality relies on a careful balance between low complexity, minimized data movement, and maximized parallelism. Various combinations of these factors can impact performance, and their interplay must be carefully evaluated to determine the most effective approach for a given program.

Considering the dynamic nature of execution performance influenced by the three factors, it becomes imperative for us to address effective interactions among software abstractions and the memory hierarchy. These interactions are crucial for sustaining high efficiency and performance during application execution. It is the responsibility of system and architecture professionals to tackle this challenge, alleviating the burden on application users. In Section 1.3, we will provide a concise overview of several case studies that highlight the importance of these interactions.

1.3 Case Studies: Performance Impact of Interaction Optimizations

This section highlights two data processing case studies that demonstrate the limitations of relying solely on user-level abstractions for efficient execution. It underscores the importance of interactive design between software and hardware to achieve high performance.

> What makes a programmer a good one, is mostly the ability to shift levels of abstraction, from low level to high level, to see something in the small and to see something in the large.
>
> A quote from Donald Knuth, *Dr. Dobb's Journal*, 1996.

1.3.1 Optimizations for Matrix Multiplication by Crossing Abstraction Levels

Matrix multiplication computations are extensively employed in machine learning and various scientific applications. In a paper [90] published in *Science*, the authors present a compelling case study showcasing the significant reduction in execution time for a 4096 × 4096 matrix multiplication. Through a series of concerted efforts involving effective interactions among software abstractions and leveraging parallelism and locality within the hardware architecture, the execution time was improved by an astounding factor of approximately 63,000. Initially, the program was written in Python, as shown here.

```
for i in xrange(4096):
    for j in xrange(4096):
        for k in xrange(4096):
            C[i][j] += A[i][k] * B[k][j]
```

These four lines of Python code have undergone a series of optimizations, building upon each previous implementation and resulting in cumulative performance improvements. The first optimization involves reimplementing the code in Java, a more-efficient programming language. This change alone leads to a reduction in execution time by a factor of 10.8. Subsequently, the matrix multiplication is implemented in C, a high-level language primarily designed for system programming. This modification further reduces the execution time by an additional factor of 4.4. These two optimizations, achieved through different programming language choices, operate at the logical level of abstraction and result in a remarkable 47-fold speedup compared to the original Python code.

The subsequent four optimizations involve cross-level interactions, harnessing the capabilities of the hardware. The first optimization involves parallelizing the loop using multiple cores (18 cores in this case). The second optimization exploits the memory hierarchy locality through a divide and conquer implementation. The third optimization focuses on vectorizing the parallel program. The final optimization

Table 1.2 A sequence of optimizations for matrix-multiplication of 4096 by crossing abstraction levels. "GFLOPS" is the billions of 64-bit floating-point operations per second. The baseline program is the Python implementation, and the speedup numbers are relative to that of the baseline program. The performance numbers in this table are quoted from [90].

Implementation	Execution time (s)	GFLOPS	Speedup
Python	25,552.48	0.005	1
Java	2,372.68	0.058	11
C	542.67	0.253	47
Parallel Loops	69.80	1.969	366
Divide and Conquer	3.8	36.180	6,727
Vectorization	1.10	124.914	23,224
AVX instructions	0.41	337.812	62,806

utilizes Intel's Advanced Vector Extensions (AVX) instructions, enabling direct interaction with the hardware architecture. Collectively, these four optimizations that leverage hardware features significantly reduce the execution time by a factor of 1300 compared to the optimized sequential C program. Table 1.2 illustrates the step-by-step reductions in execution time achieved through each optimization.

1.3.2 Sorting Algorithms and the Memory Performance

Sorting algorithms play a fundamental role in various data processing applications and are frequently utilized. Traditional algorithm analysis primarily focuses on counting the number of logical comparison operations performed during sorting to differentiate the complexities of different sorting algorithms. For instance, bubble sort requires n^2 comparisons, while merge sort requires $n \log(n)$ comparisons, where n represents the number of elements being sorted. However, in practice, the execution time for comparisons is significantly shorter compared to the time spent on data movement during sorting operations.

In particular, data movement refers to the loading of data from the DRAM memory to on-chip caches, assuming that all sorting operations are performed in memory. Researchers have recognized the importance of counting the number of memory requests and the amount of data loaded from memory during the execution of a sorting algorithm. These metrics have become integral components of algorithm analysis for sorting algorithms, as they shed light on the data movement and its impact on the overall performance.

The unconventional approach of analyzing algorithms based on data movement between memory and caches has gained increasing significance due to the dominant role of data-movement operations in overall execution time. It provides valuable insights into tailoring the design of sorting algorithms to align with the underlying cache organization, aiming to maximize cache hits by minimizing memory requests. This approach, often referred to as "algorithms design for memory hierarchies" [99],

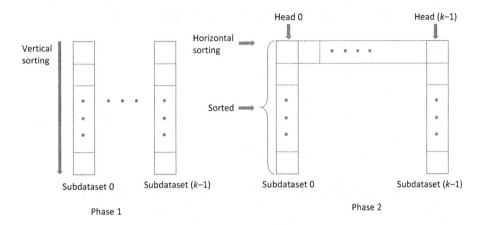

Figure 1.3 Two phases in a tiled merge sort: Each of the k vertical sorting in phase 1 is done in cache, and the iterative horizontal sorting in phase 2 is also in cache.

is dependent on the specific characteristics of the cache architecture. By considering the cache hierarchy during algorithm design, developers can optimize the utilization of caches and improve overall performance.

We will focus on implementing sequential sorting algorithms within a single node, using merge sort as our example. One technique we will explore is tiled merge sort, introduced in [83]. Tiled merge sort involves partitioning the dataset into multiple sub-datasets, denoted by k. The key idea behind this technique is to process two subdatasets at a time, assuming they can fit into the cache. Each subdataset is approximately half the size of the cache or smaller. By sorting each subset individually, we can effectively avoid cache capacity misses and make full use of the data loaded in the cache without interference. This allows us to perform the entire sorting process in the cache, incurring only compulsory (cold) misses.

The restructured merge sort algorithm consists of two phases. In the first phase (phase 1 in Figure 1.3), each subdataset is sorted vertically using the basic merge-sort algorithm. After sorting, each subset has a head pointer pointing to the smallest number within it.

In the second phase (phase 2 in Figure 1.3), a k-way merge method is employed to horizontally merge all the sorted subdatasets. This is achieved by creating a horizontal array that consists of the head elements of the sorted subdatasets. The horizontal array is then sorted. Similar to the first phase, the size of the horizontal array is chosen to be approximately half or smaller than that of the cache size. At the end of each horizontal array sort, the subdataset containing the selected winner contributes its next element from the head to the array. This iterative process continues until the last element (the largest number) in the last horizontal array is selected. A tournament sort [97] can be used within each horizontal merge sort. The tournament sort, also known as single-elimination tournament, is often used to select the winner in sports competitions and elections.

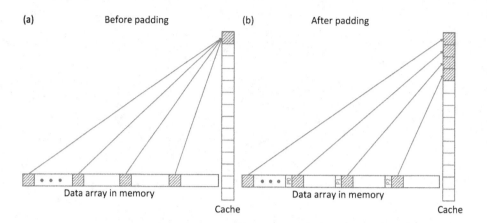

Figure 1.4 Effect of padding: (a) Before padding, a set of data elements maps to the same cache location; (b) after padding, the virtual memory addresses for the data elements are shifted by padding element p_i for $i = 1$ to $k - 1$, so that the same conflicting data elements are mapped to different cache locations.

Tiled merge sort ensures that cache capacity misses are avoided in each sorting phase. The reason for utilizing half the cache size for data is to allocate additional space for sorting-related operations, such as building a tournament tree in the second phase of horizontal sorting.

Cache capacity misses can be mitigated by partitioning the dataset, but addressing cache conflict misses is more complex. Cache conflict misses occur when multiple memory addresses map to the same cache location, resulting in cache misses. This is because the cache size is only a small portion of the main memory. Thus, only a small number of memory address bits is used for cache mapping. We will have more discussions on this issue in Chapter 3. One effective approach to tackle this issue is to modify the physical data layout to shift memory addresses. This can be accomplished at runtime by system software [17, 138]. Additionally, users can modify the data layout at the user level by inserting extra elements in specific locations within the dataset. By altering the virtual memory addresses of data elements, the base addresses of potentially conflicting cache locations are also changed. This technique is referred to as "padding" and has been successfully applied in the design of sorting algorithms [137].

Figure 1.4(a) illustrates an example of conflict mapping where multiple memory addresses of data elements are mapped to the same cache location in a direct-map cache (before padding). After applying padding, as shown in Figure 1.4(b), these conflicting memory addresses are mapped to different cache locations, effectively reducing cache conflict misses.

1.4 The PAPA Concept for Computing Interactions

The process of transforming a computing task, starting from its problem formulation by a human and ending with its execution in a machine, involves dynamic interactions among four key components or steps. We refer these components as PAPA, which stands for Premier, Algorithm, Program, and Advancement.

- *Premier* In computational problem solving, the Premier serves as a pivotal concept or methodological principle, steering the design and implementation of the computational process towards a viable solution. Unlike elementary arithmetic problems such as $1 + 1 = 2$, in practice, myriad problems do not readily decompose into a sequence of computational steps executable by a computer, a complexity that intensifies when parallel computing is employed. Therefore, Premier's foundational role is to "facilitate feasibility." It aligns more intimately with the domain knowledge or mathematical principles underlying the target problem rather than with the specifications of any particular computing system. For instance, consider the problem of calculating the area of a triangle given the coordinates of its three vertices (x_1, y_1), (x_2, y_2), and (x_3, y_3). A Premier-guided solution would involve employing the following formula: $area = \frac{1}{2} \cdot abs(x_1 \cdot (y_2 - y_3) + x_2 \cdot (y_3 - y_1) + x_3 \cdot (y_1 - y_2))$. This illustrates how the Premier component remains independent of the specific machine or computing system in use, focusing instead on the fundamental principles guiding the solution process.
- *Algorithm* An algorithm embodies a computational procedure characterized by a sequence of discrete steps or fundamental operations, each readily executable by a computer. Illustratively, in the aforementioned example of calculating the area of a triangle, the algorithm encompasses the systematic steps required to evaluate the right-hand side of the formula, involving a succession of elementary arithmetic computations. A vital aspect characterizing an algorithm is its complexity, which can encompass various dimensions such as time complexity, space complexity, input/output (I/O) complexity, and communication complexity. Among these, time complexity is the most important one that assesses the total number of computing operations (a function of the input size, e.g., $O(1)$ for the above example or $O(n^2)$ for bubble sort) required by the algorithm, offering insights into potential execution durations. Another pivotal concept within the realm of algorithms is recurrence, which refers to the repetitive occurrence or repetition of a specific operational pattern within the algorithm. This concept is prevalently employed within recursive algorithms, wherein a problem is segmented into smaller subproblems of identical nature, facilitating more manageable solutions. Notably, the algorithm maintains its independence from the underlying machine or computing system. Its design and attributes are not confined to any particular hardware configuration, thereby enabling implementation across diverse platforms.
- *Program* This component embodies the concrete implementation of the algorithm. Its design is shaped by various factors including the programming environment, system support, and the particularities of the machine or computing system in use. Consequently, the program can exhibit a high degree of dependency on these elements. Notably, even when based on the same algorithm, a program scripted in a high-level language (such as Python) can markedly differ in appearance from one crafted in assembly language. Illustratively, the following Python code, used in the preceding example, mirrors the original formula quite closely.

```
x1, y1 = 0, 0
x2, y2 = 5, 0
x3, y3 = 0, 4
area = abs(x1*(y2 - y3) + x2*(y3 - y1) + x3*(y1 - y2)) / 2
```

However, when utilizing a lower-level programming language, a myriad of intricate and complex programming concepts become more prominent, encompassing aspects such as memory management and register allocation (e.g., determining the storage location of a variable). The subsequent code showcases the same process, articulated in ARMv7 assembly language.

```
.data
x1:  .word 0
y1:  .word 0
x2:  .word 5
y2:  .word 0
x3:  .word 0
y3:  .word 4
area:  .word 0

.text
.global _start
_start:
        LDR R0,  -x1
        LDR R1,  =y2
        LDR R2,  =y3
        LDR R3,  [R0]
        LDR R4,  [R1]
        LDR R5,  [R2]

        SUB R6,  R4,  R5
        MUL R6,  R3,  R6

        LDR R0,  =x2
        LDR R3,  [R0]
        SUB R4,  R5,  R1
        MUL R4,  R3,  R4

        ADD R6,  R6,  R4

        LDR R0,  =x3
        LDR R3,  [R0]
        LDR R1,  =y1
        LDR R4,  [R1]
        SUB R5,  R4,  R2
```

```
MUL R5, R3, R5

ADD R6, R6, R5
MOV R7, #2
SDIV R6, R6, R7

STR R6, =area
```

For readers unfamiliar with assembly languages, the aforementioned R0-R7 denote CPU registers, while LDR/STR signify load/store instructions, and ADD/SUB/MUL/SDIV stand as arithmetic instructions.

- *Advancement* This focuses on optimizing the mapping of the Algorithm and Program to the unique hardware features of a machine as well as addressing potential corner cases during the Algorithm and Program phases. The Advancement is dependent on the machine and its system software. The final performance of any computing task is determined by interactive optimization methods that take into account the interplay between the Algorithm, its Program and the underlying software and hardware systems. This optimization process aims to improve the overall efficiency and effectiveness of the program's execution. It involves fine tuning various aspects, such as code optimization, resource allocation, and system configuration, to achieve optimal performance. For example, in the aforementioned example, we can find that the computation process for the area calculation actually contains three parts that have the same operations but only different inputs: $(x1*(y2-y3))$, $x2*(y3-y1)$, $x3*(y1-y2))$. Therefore, instead of executing them one by one as the previous assembly language code shows, we can use advanced vector instructions offed by the modern CPU to batch execute the three parts in a SIMD way (*single-instruction, multiple-data*). As we will introduce in later chapters for graphic processing unit (GPU) programming, we can see that such an Advancement step can be very difficult due to the complicated architecture of advanced computer hardware.

The PAPA process embraces the potential for iterative interactions across its four stages, wherein several cycles of redesign and implementation may be requisite. Generally, the PAPA process represents a multidisciplinary endeavor aimed at optimally solving practical problems through the utilization of modern hardware. This approach melds foundational mathematics, domain-specific knowledge, algorithm analysis, software engineering, and architectural optimizations into a cohesive strategy.

1.5   Summary

In this chapter, we have provided a brief overview of the interactions between software abstractions and the memory hierarchy in computer architecture. Achieving highly efficient program execution requires finding a balance among three critical factors: low algorithm complexity, low data movement, and high parallelism. To further enhance the performance of computing and data processing, it is essential to establish effective interactions among the virtual space of the user domain, the memory space of the operating system and architecture domains, and the storage space of external devices in both software and hardware.

These interactions often involve disruptive changes that may require adding, modifying, or bypassing conventional abstractions. As computer scientists, it is not practical to expect application users to be deeply involved in these long-term developments. Instead, our role is to provide tools and frameworks that enable users to automatically benefit from performance improvements in restructured ecosystems. For instance, ATLAS [131] is a software tool designed to automatically determine cache parameters through extensive testing of linear algebra algorithms during runtime. By automating the optimization process, tools like ATLAS would help users to effortlessly enhance the performance of their applications without requiring extensive manual intervention. By focusing on developing such tools and frameworks, we can pave the way for a more efficient and productive computing environment, where users can harness the benefits of effective interactions without the need for specialized expertise.

At the end of the chapter, we presented the concept of PAPA as a comprehensive framework encompassing the entire life cycle of any computing tasks. The PAPA concept and its implementation at various levels serve as central themes throughout the book.

2 Data Storage: Physical Allocation and Logical Format

We introduce two important concepts related to data storage, which reflect the interaction between software systems, such as databases and OS, and the disk drive architecture, such as HDDs and SSDs. The *data storage format* refers to how data elements in a data entity, such as a file and table, are logically organized for their allocations in storage. The *physical disk allocation* refers to how the logically organized blocks are placed in the storage drive. The reason for data format to be a logical view and data allocation to be a physical placement is due to logical and physical independence between the system software level and the storage hardware level. In this chapter, we first introduce physical data allocation methods, which depend on the storage hardware architecture and its interface with software systems. After that, we discuss the logical format for organizing applications' data in storage, focusing on relational tables and sorted LSM-tree data, which are two representative data formats in traditional databases and modern key-value stores.

For convenience of reading, Table 2.1 gives meanings of the prefixes we often use for data sizes. For example, Kilo (KBytes or KB), Mega (MBytes or MB), and others.

2.1 Basic Operations for Data Allocation in Storage Drives

To understand the basic interactions between an OS and external storage devices, let us use an analogy involving a customer and a moving company that has its own storage space. Imagine a scenario where a customer needs to move their belongings from their home to a public storage unit. The moving company offers a service to pack the items into standardized boxes, making it easier to manage transportation and storage operations. This analogy helps illustrate the abstractions involved in the interaction.

In this example, the specific location of each item in the customer's home is not relevant to the moving company. Similarly, the exact storage location within the company's storage unit is unknown to the customer. The key communication elements between the customer and the moving company include the customer's identification (ID), unique numbers assigned to each box in sequential order (e.g., 1, 2, 3, and so on), and the total number of boxes.

Once the moving company stores the boxes, the customer can request to retrieve specific boxes or all of them from the storage by providing the ID and box numbers to

Table 2.1 Commonly used data size labels and their values in decimal numbers to represent the amount of data in Bytes.

Data size label	Data size value in Bytes
Kilo (K)	$2^{10} = 1{,}024$
Mega (M)	$2^{20} = 1{,}048{,}576$
Giga (G)	$2^{30} = 1{,}073{,}741{,}824$
Tera (T)	$2^{40} = 1{,}099{,}511{,}627{,}776$
Peta (P)	$2^{50} = 1{,}125{,}899{,}906{,}824{,}624$
Exa (E)	$2^{60} = 1{,}152{,}921{,}504{,}606{,}846{,}976$
Zetta (Z)	$2^{70} = 1{,}180{,}591{,}620{,}717{,}411{,}303{,}424$
Yotta (Y)	$2^{80} = 1{,}208{,}925{,}819{,}614{,}629{,}174{,}706{,}176$

the company. As the moving company knows where each box is stored in the storage unit, it can quickly retrieve and return the requested boxes to the customer.

This simplified framework of moving goods between a home and an external storage unit can be applied to the movement of data between physical memory space and external storage space (e.g., hard drives or SSDs) in computer systems. The OS employs similar concepts, treating data as blocks and utilizing mechanisms to manage the movement and storage of these blocks between memory and external storage devices.

In software systems such as databases and OSs, the fundamental unit of interaction with the storage system is often referred to as the "block." This block size is independent of the physical data unit used by the underlying storage device, such as a sector on a hard disk, which is only 512 Bytes.

In software systems, a block is the smallest logical unit used to access a disk drive. A storage device that can be read from and written to in fixed-size blocks is known as a "block device." The block size serves as the basic unit of data transfer between the storage device and the computer's memory.

The choice of an appropriate block size is determined by the software system, taking performance considerations into account. For instance, in OS virtual memory, the block unit is typically referred to as the "page size," which is typically 4 KB. File systems often set the block size to be around 1–4 KB, while database systems may use an 8 KB block size. Additionally, the OS kernel may have its own block size, used for caching and buffering I/O data including disk data. For instance, the Linux kernel often employs a block size of 512 Bytes to 4 KB.

Both HDDs and SSDs utilize a common interface to provide an array of logical block addresses (LBAs) or logical block numbers (LBNs) for data entities. These LBAs or LBNs are then mapped to physical locations within the disk drive by the disk controller, allowing data retrieval or storage operations to be performed.

The two interactions described earlier, involving the moving company and the operating system, share common properties within a similar framework. The box sizes used by the moving company can be equated to the block sizes employed by the operating system. The box numbers assigned by the moving company align with the LBNs utilized in the operating system. Furthermore, the storing operations performed by the moving company can be likened to the mapping process that associates LBNs with physical storage locations by the disk controller.

Let us revisit Figure 1.2 in Chapter 1 for further clarification. In the memory stack, the management of memory data is handled by the operating system (OS) since the OS determines how data are stored and accessed in the memory space. This is done by the OS to directly interact with the memory management unit (MMU) within the CPU to place or/and replace applications programs' data in the physical memory. This allows the OS to control the allocation and deallocation of memory space resources to ensure efficient memory utilization.

On the other hand, disk data are not directly managed by the OS because it is in a different space, that is, disk space. Instead, presenting data access requests in a logical format, the OS interacts with the disk controller to establish communication with the disk drive. A disk controller serves as an agent between OS and the disk drive via the I/O bus for data communications between main memory and disks. Specifically, the disk controller utilizes LBAs or LBNs provided by the OS to locate the corresponding physical locations in the disk drive for data reads. Similarly, for data writes, the disk controller receives LBAs along with the data elements and determines the physical locations where the data should be stored in the disk. By employing this mechanism, the logical blocks managed by the OS are read from the disk and physically stored in the appropriate locations on the disk drive.

The storage architecture of a disk drive defines the basic unit of data allocation. Figure 2.1 provides a top view and a side view of an HDD to illustrate its structure. In the top view, a magnetic disk with a *platter* is depicted. The platter is divided into multiple circular tracks. Each track contains numerous *sectors* separated by small gaps.

The surface of the platter features a moving "read/write head" controlled by an "actuator arm." When accessing data in a specific sector, the read/write head first moves to the targeted track, a process known as *seek time*. Afterward, it waits for the

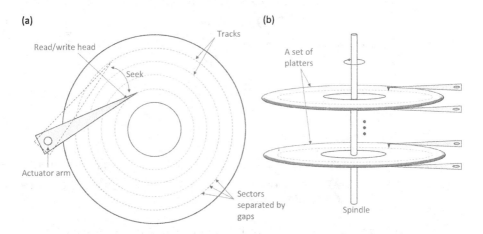

Figure 2.1 A top view (a) and a side view (b) of an HDD.

desired sector to rotate under it, which takes a *rotation latency* (half of the disk rotation time on average). The remaining time is utilized to read the data from the sector and transmit it via the I/O bus to the computer system.

In the context of a hard disk, a sector within a track represents the basic unit for physical data allocation. Typically, a hard disk sector size is 512 Bytes. The disk controller ensures that a sequence of sectors is utilized to store data blocks. For instance, an OS block size of 4 KB may be placed contiguously in eight disk sectors.

The side view of the HDD in Figure 2.1(b) shows that a hard disk drive comprises multiple platters. Both sides of each platter are employed to store data, and each side has its own dedicated read/write head. All the platters are held and rotated by a "spindle."

In contrast, an SSD utilizes nonvolatile flash memory as its storage media. The absence of mechanical moving parts in semiconductor-based flash memory results in significantly faster performance compared to traditional HDDs. Solid-state drives also offer several technical advantages over HDDs, including low power consumption, compact size, shock resistance, and high performance for random data accesses.

Figure 2.2 provides an overview of the structure of an SSD. The computer system connects to the SSD through a standard I/O bus interface. The SSD controller, a specialized and compact computer system, incorporates hardware management functions in firmware. On the hardware side, it consists of a processor (labeled as CPU in Figure 2.2) and memory, along with a buffer management facility. The primary functions of the SSD controller are carried out by the flash translation layer (FTL), which operates the hardware. In Figure 2.2, five major FTL functions are listed, which will be explained in detail later. The SSD controller communicates with multiple flash

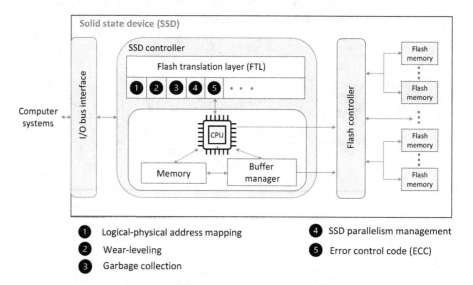

Figure 2.2 An overview of the SSD structure on how an I/O bus interface, an SSD controller, a flash memory controller, and the flash memory packages are integrated for an SSD.

packages in parallel through the flash controller. One of the FTL functions is SSD parallelism management (refer to FTL function 4 in Figure 2.2). For a comprehensive explanation of how internal parallelism is handled within an SSD, readers may refer to [34].

As depicted in Figure 2.2, FTL function 1 involves mapping logical blocks by software systems to a set of physical flash memory pages. In the context of an SSD, a crucial concept for resource allocation is the *flash memory block*. Each flash memory block typically consists of 64–128 *flash memory pages*. The flash memory page serves as the fundamental unit of storage in an SSD, typically with a capacity of 2–4 KB. Within a block, the flash memory pages are arranged in sequential order based on their address numbers. When writing data, the pages are written sequentially from the lowest address to the highest address within the block.

When a writing request involves a certain number of logical blocks, FTL function 1 in the SSD allocates a sufficient number of physical flash pages in one or more flash memory blocks to accommodate the data. Additionally, the FTL function keeps track of the logical-physical mapping information for future reading requests pertaining to these logical blocks. This mapping allows the SSD to efficiently locate and retrieve the corresponding physical flash pages when accessing the logical blocks.

It is worth mentioning that in computer systems and architecture, the term "block" is used in various contexts with different meanings. This can sometimes lead to confusion, so it is important to understand the specific context in which the term is being used. Different areas of computer systems and architecture, such as caching, storage devices, and memory management, may employ the term "block" to refer to distinct concepts and units of data. Therefore, it is essential to be aware of the specific context when encountering the term "block" in order to accurately interpret its meaning. It is important to understand these distinctions to avoid confusion. Here are a few examples.

- **Cache block** In CPU chips and hardware caches, a cache block refers to a fixed-size unit of data used for caching frequently accessed data. The cache block is the smallest unit of data that can be transferred between the main memory and the cache.
- **Block device** A block device is a term used to describe a storage device that transfers data in fixed-size blocks between the memory and external storage. This can include devices such as HDDs, SSDs, or even virtual block devices. The block size in this context refers to the fixed-size unit of data transferred between the memory and the storage device.
- **Flash memory block** In SSDs and flash memory storage, a flash memory block is a fixed-size set of pages. Flash memory works by erasing data blocks and reading/writing data in pages. The block size is determined by the specific flash memory technology used in the SSD.

For every writing request, irrespective of its data size, the SSD controller typically assigns one or more free (empty) flash memory pages. The SSD also tries to distribute writes evenly across all available blocks, rather than concentrating on a small subset of blocks. This technique is known as "wear-leveling" (FTL function 2 in Figure 2.2), and its primary purpose is to extend the overall lifespan of the flash memory.

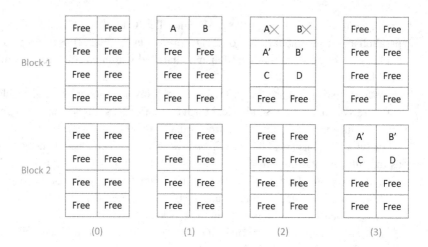

Figure 2.3 An example of SSD writes, explaining the concepts valid and invalid pages, and copying valid flash memory pages before erasing a SSD block. Stage (0): There are two empty SSD blocks, Block 1 and Block 2, each of which has eight flash memory pages. Stage (1): Datasets A and B are written to two pages in Block 1, and these two pages are valid. Block 2 remains the same. Stage (2): datasets A and B are modified. The original pages with A and B become invalid (the cross marks), and the updated datasets A' and B' are written to two new pages that are valid in Block 1. Datasets C and D are also written to the same block, which are valid. Block 2 remains the same. Stage (3): Before erasing Block 1, valid pages A', B', C, and D are copied to Block 2. After the erase, Block 1 becomes empty, and Block 2 has four available pages to write besides the four pages copied from Block 1.

By evenly distributing the write operations, wear-leveling helps prevent specific blocks from experiencing excessive usage, which can lead to faster wear and degradation.

In SSDs, there is a unique requirement that each flash memory block must be erased before it can be programmed (written) again. When a page is initially written, it becomes valid. However, if the content of that page needs to be modified, the updated content is written to a new page. This updated page becomes valid, while the original page becomes invalid. Erasing operations are performed at the block level. Before erasing a block, the valid pages within that block need to be copied to another empty block. For this reason, a flash memory block is also referred to as an "erase block."

The total number of program–erase (P/E) cycles a flash memory can endure determines the endurance of an SSD device. Figure 2.3 illustrates an example that demonstrates how valid and invalid pages are generated within a block and how the entire block is erased. In the initial state (0) shown in Figure 2.3, Block 1 and Block 2 are both empty, each containing eight free pages. The example follows the following writing sequence: (1) writing pages A and B in Block 1, (2) modifying pages A and B, and writing new pages C and D, (3) before erasing Block 1 to make it empty, valid pages A', B', C, and D are moved (or copied) to the empty Block 2.

The process of erasing a flash memory block to free up storage space is known as *garbage collection* (GC), which is represented by FTL function 3 in Figure 2.2. During garbage collection, the FTL seeks out blocks that have a high number of invalid pages for erasure. By targeting blocks with a significant number of invalid pages, the amount of valid pages that need to be copied before the block can be erased is minimized. It is important to note that copying valid pages to another block during garbage collection also involves data writing.

The additional writes resulting from garbage collection are referred to as "write amplification," which is a measure of the additional writes incurred due to garbage collection compared to the actual amount of data intended to be written. It can be calculated using the following ratio:

$$\frac{\text{the amount of data written in reality}}{\text{the objective amount of data for the write}}.$$

The write amplification factor provides insight into the efficiency of garbage collection operations and their impact on the overall lifespan and performance of the SSD. Let us consider an SSD with the following configuration: The flash memory page size is 4 KB, and a flash memory block consists of 128 pages (512 KB). Suppose we want to write a 4 KB page to a block where only one page is invalid, and the remaining pages are all valid.

In this scenario, the garbage collection process becomes necessary. To write the 4 KB page to this block, the garbage collection needs to copy the 127 valid pages, totaling 508 KB, to a free block. Afterward, the entire original block needs to be erased before the objective amount of data (4 KB) can be written to the new empty block. In practice, for this worst-case scenario, not only do we write the 4 KB page, but we also write an additional 508 KB to prepare for the write, resulting in a total of 508 KB + 4 KB = 512 KB being written. Consequently, the write amplification is 512 KB/4 KB = 128.

Thus, in this worst-case scenario, the write amplification is 128, indicating that for every 4 KB of user data written, an additional 128 times that amount (512 KB) is written due to the garbage collection process.

Figure 2.4 depicts the data flows involved in SSD writes, updates, and garbage collection, integrating all the operations mentioned above. For a write request, the SSD controller is provided with SSD blocks from the pool of free SSD blocks. These two operations are indicated by labels 1 in Figure 2.4. When an update request is made to existing blocks in the SSD, the SSD controller is provided with selected blocks from the pool of SSD blocks containing the data. These operations are denoted by labels 2 in Figure 2.4. After a new SSD block is written or an existing SSD block is updated, it is added to the pool of SSD blocks with data contents, as shown by label 3 in Figure 2.4. Label 4 in Figure 2.4 represents the garbage collection operations. Periodically, the garbage collection selects SSD blocks with the highest number of invalid pages to erase. These erased blocks are then returned to the pool of free SSD blocks.

Overall, Figure 2.4 provides an overview of the data flows involved in SSD writes, updates, and garbage collection, highlighting the interactions between the SSD controller and the different pools of SSD blocks.

Solid-state devices are typically constructed using an array of flash memory packages that are interconnected through multiple channels to flash memory controllers. This design enables independent and parallel data accesses. The parallelism inside SSDs offers two significant advantages. First, it has increased bandwidth.

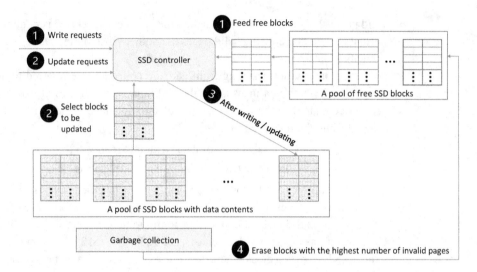

Figure 2.4 Data flow in SSD for writes, updates and garbage collection. There are two dynamically changed pools in an SSD system. One is the pool of free SSD blocks and another one is the pool of SSD blocks with data contents. The pair of labels 1 represent a write request operation done on free SSD blocks, while the pair of labels 2 represent an update operation done on a selected SSD block with data contents. Label 3 shows that newly written or updated blocks are put in the pool of SSD blocks with data contents. Label 4 is the garbage collection to supply new free blocks for the pool of free SSD blocks.

By transferring data from or to multiple flash memory packages in parallel, SSDs can achieve high aggregate bandwidth. This parallel data transfer capability enhances the overall data transfer rate of the SSD. Second, it has a latency hiding ability. The parallel design of SSDs allows concurrent operations to be executed simultaneously. This capability enables high latency operations to be effectively hidden behind other concurrent operations. As a result, the overall latency of the SSD is reduced, leading to improved performance. Therefore, the internal parallelism in SSDs is not only an inherent functionality but also a fundamental requirement for delivering high-performance storage solutions. FTL function 4 in Figure 2.2 plays the role of SSD parallelism management. For more information on SSD internal parallelism, readers may refer to [34].

Another critical function of the FTL in SSDs is error detection and correction during data communication. This functionality, referred to as function 5 in Figure 2.2, involves the use of an error correction code (ECC) mechanism. The ECC is responsible for detecting and correcting errors that may occur during data transmission and storage in the SSD. For details of ECC management in SSD, readers may refer to [143].

2.2   The File System and Data Allocation Management

A file serves as the fundamental unit of data for all computing applications. It contain data in various formats, including text, programs, tables, images, videos, and other data types. Nonvolatile storage devices like HDD and SSD provide permanent storage for files. In an operating system, a file system plays a crucial role by organizing files at a logical level using LBNs. It communicates with the disk controller through the generic block I/O layer to store files in physical storage devices. The file system creates management data structures (a.k.a metadata) that facilitate basic tasks, such as mapping logical files to physical storage space and enabling efficient user access and file manipulation. Above the file system layer, a layer of buffers is created in DRAM memory by OS to cache file data of disks and other I/O related data after their first accesses, optimizing and accelerating data accessing performance for the rest of accesses. In Chapter 3, we will delve into the study of this buffer cache used by OS. The directory structure within a file system provides essential information about all the files managed by the operating system and stored in storage devices. It acts as an interface between the logical space of OS management and the physical allocation space of storage devices. We will explore three major methods of data allocation management between logical file entities and their physical locations on disk drives: *contiguous allocation*, *linked allocation*, and *indexed allocation*. Each method has its own functionality and performance implications, affecting how it interacts with upper-level software systems (such as file systems and databases), its efficiency in utilizing disk space, and its impact on access latency.

2.2.1   Contiguous Allocation

In the contiguous allocation method, the data elements of a logical data entity are stored in a linear array that occupies a series of contiguous physical locations on a disk drive. These physical locations can be a sequence of aligned sectors on a hard disk or a collection of aligned flash memory pages within one or multiple SSD blocks. The contiguous allocation method provides a straightforward logical abstraction, consisting of the starting LBA and the length of the data entity. The disk controller maps the LBA to the corresponding location on the disk and determines the number of physical locations based on the length. Figure 2.5 illustrates an example of two files in a directory, displaying their logical views and their contiguous physical allocations on a disk drive. The directory entries, also known as a *file descriptors*, are stored on the disk drive along with the data entity. When the data entity is being accessed, its directory is kept in main

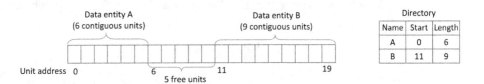

Figure 2.5 The six data units of data entity A are contiguously allocated in the disk drive from unit address 0 to unit address 5. The nine data units of data entity B are contiguous allocated in the disk drive from unit address 11 to 19. There are five free units in the disk drive between the two data entities. The directory keeps the name of each file, the starting unit address, and the number of data units.

memory. The contiguous allocation method is particularly advantageous for sequential read accesses, commonly referred to as "range queries" in databases, due to its high speed, especially on a hard disk.

However, the contiguous allocation method has several disadvantages. First, performing a sequence of random accesses on data elements requires individual logical-physical mappings, resulting in slow access times, particularly on a hard disk. However, this issue can be addressed by a very quick addition between the starting position of the file and an offset of the targeted block. Second, the method has inefficient space utilization. In the case of frequently updated data entities that require multiple versions with timestamps, the disk drive may need to allocate noncontiguous sections of space, leading to fragmented storage. Lastly, expanding a file within a contiguous space is challenging because file sizes change dynamically, and the disk drive cannot allocate a fixed-size contiguous space for file growth.

To overcome the limitations of the basic version of contiguous allocation, an extent-based file system has been developed and widely adopted. In this file system, an "extent" refers to a reserved contiguous space on a storage drive. A data entity can be allocated one or multiple extents. This allows dynamically changing files to be stored in a collection of extents, each of which represents contiguous space on a disk.

2.2.2   Linked Allocation

In the linked allocation method, the data elements of a given data entity are stored as a linked list of physical disk locations, without requiring contiguous allocation among the locations. These disk locations can be located anywhere on the disk drive. The logical representation provided by the linked allocation method is also straightforward, consisting of a pointer to the starting element and a pointer to the ending element of the data entity. Each location contains a pointer to the next location, enabling the linkage between elements of the data entity. Figure 2.6 illustrates an example of the logical view of data entity A in a directory and its six linked units on a disk drive. One implementation of the linked allocation method is the file allocation table (FAT), which maintains the linked list for the data entity and serves as a key index for disk accesses. One advantage of linked allocation over contiguous allocation is its effectiveness in managing space when expanding or shrinking a data entity.

However, the linked allocation method suffers from several performance issues. First, since the physical locations for a logical data entity are randomly allocated on

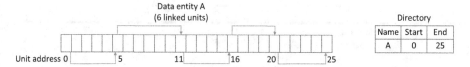

Figure 2.6 The six data units of data entity A are allocated in disk drive by a linked list starting from unit address 0. The directory keeps the name of data entity A, the starting unit address, and the ending unit address.

a disk drive, a large number of seek operations may be required, particularly on a hard disk. This significantly degrades data access performance. Second, regardless of whether the data access is sequential or random, the traversal through the linked list starts from the beginning of the element, resulting in inefficient access times. Finally, the pointer support for linked allocation, such as the FAT, incurs additional overhead.

2.2.3   Indexed Allocation

In the indexed allocation method, a logical data entity is mapped to a specific physical location on a disk drive known as the "index location." This index location contains all the necessary pointers to the actual data locations associated with the data entity. The logical representation provided by the indexed allocation method is even simpler compared to contiguous allocation and linked allocation, consisting solely of a pointer to the index location. All the location pointers related to a data entity are consolidated in one place. Figure 2.7 illustrates an example of the logical view of data entity A in the directory and the index location containing pointers to the data units on the disk drive. One advantage of indexed allocation is its ability to directly access data locations once the index location is accessed, thereby accelerating data retrieval speed. This method also effectively addresses the space efficiency concern present in contiguous allocation.

However, the indexed allocation method also has two significant limitations. First, due to the storage of all pointers in the index location, it incurs higher management overhead compared to the linked allocation method, which distributes pointers across multiple locations. Second, when dealing with very large data entities, a single index location may not have sufficient capacity to accommodate all the required pointers. Conversely, for very small data entities, the index location's capacity may not be efficiently utilized, resulting in wasted space. To address the issue of large data entities, a multilevel-index scheme can be employed to distribute a large number of pointers across multiple locations in a hierarchical structure. This allows for more efficient storage and management of index pointers.

The index node (inode) method, also known as the information node in some documents, is the most widely used approach. In this method, all the pertinent information items associated with a data entity, such as its name, size, and access permissions, are stored. A significant portion of the inode is dedicated to storing the disk locations that

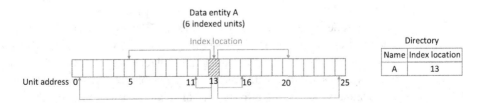

Figure 2.7 The addressed (or pointers) of the six data units of data entity A are stored in an index location (location 13). The directory only keeps the name of data entity A and its index location address.

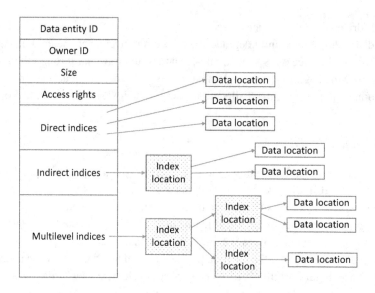

Figure 2.8 An example of inode structure. The data locations can be pointed by direct indexes, indirect indices, and multilevel indices.

hold the actual data or the locations within hierarchical levels. Figure 2.8 illustrates an example of the inode structure.

2.3   A Hybrid Storage System Consisting of Both HDD and SSD

During the early stages of SSD adoption in computer systems, the computer industry anticipated that SSDs would eventually replace HDDs due to their high performance, especially as SSD prices decreased. While the cost of small-capacity SSDs has become affordable, we have yet to witness a definitive shift towards widespread replacement. Solid-state device storage is commonly used in cell phones and laptops where write operations are light. However, large-enterprise computer systems still heavily rely on HDDs for several reasons.

First, the limited program/erase (P/E) cycles of SSDs make them less suitable for write-intensive workloads. Second, while SSDs exhibit significantly better performance than HDDs for random reads, the performance gap narrows for sequential reads. Considering the price difference between HDDs and SSDs, users of production systems often opt for HDDs for cost-effective and performance-effective sequential workloads. Finally, high-end SSD prices are still relatively expensive for high-capacity storage systems, making them less financially viable for widespread adoption.

In summary, despite the affordability of small-capacity SSDs and their prevalence in cell phones and laptops, the heavy reliance on HDDs in large-enterprise computer systems can be attributed to limitations in P/E cycles, comparable performance for sequential reads, and the higher cost of high-capacity SSDs.

Hystor [33] is a hybrid storage system that combines both HDD and SSD into a single block device. It was released as an open-source system in 2011 and gained significant attention. Notably, Hystor was adopted by Apple for their Fusion Drive in 2012.

In a typical setup, the file system is connected to a block device driver, which serves as a software agent between the operating system and a disk drive (e.g., HDD or SSD). In this configuration, the file system lacks knowledge of the specific allocation of its managed logical blocks, whether they reside on an HDD or SSD. This allocation is determined by the connection between the block device driver and either the HDD controller or the SSD controller.

The objective of Hystor is to proactively and dynamically allocate data to the most suitable storage devices. It aims to optimize data placement by effectively determining whether blocks should be stored on an HDD or SSD based on various factors such as access patterns, performance requirements, and available storage capacity. Hystor enhances the traditional environment by actively managing data allocation to leverage the benefits of different storage technologies within the system.

The Hystor system component is positioned between the file system and the block device driver. The file system communicates with Hystor using LBNs, similar to a conventional system. In the initial setup, all data blocks are stored on the HDD. Figure 2.9 illustrates the fundamental structure of Hystor, which incorporates the following three components to dynamically transfer data blocks between the HDD and SSD, optimizing their placement for optimal performance and efficiency.

1. **A data access pattern monitor** This periodically analyzes the data access patterns within the storage devices. It identifies frequently accessed data blocks of smaller

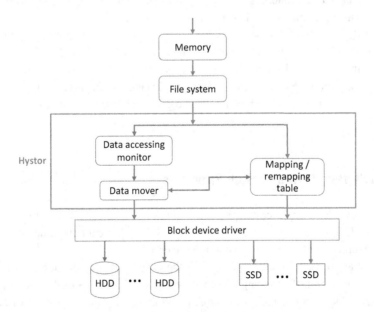

Figure 2.9 The basic structure of Hystor that is added between the file system and the block device drive within the OS.

sizes and labels them as optimal candidates for placement on the SSD. The frequency of access serves as an indicator of temporal locality, and smaller blocks are more likely to be associated with random access patterns. Additionally, the monitor prioritizes performance-critical data blocks, such as file system metadata, recognizing that these types of data are also best suited for SSD storage.

2. **A mapping/remapping table** This mapping table maintains the correspondence between the logical blocks managed by the file system and their corresponding physical locations in the storage devices. It is responsible for tracking the movement of data blocks between the HDD and SSD, based on the monitored data access patterns and any subsequent changes. Remapping is required when data blocks are relocated, and it involves modifying the entries in the mapping table to reflect the updated physical locations.

3. **A data mover** Once the decision is made based on the information provided by the data access monitor, the data mover proceeds to transfer the data blocks to the most suitable storage device, whether it be the HDD or SSD. It ensures that the data blocks are moved to the device that offers the best fit in terms of performance and efficiency.

Figure 2.9 also illustrates the relationships among the three components within Hystor. All disk access requests are directed to the data pattern monitor, which periodically analyzes the data and makes decisions regarding data allocation. These decisions are then communicated to the data mover. Additionally, disk access requests are also directed to the mapping/remapping table, serving as an index for storage accesses. The data mover and the mapping/remapping table interact with each other to update the table, ensuring it reflects the latest data reallocations.

The Hystor project demonstrates that a hybrid storage system, utilizing only a small percentage of SSD capacity, can achieve up to 85 percent of the performance offered by a fully SSD-based storage solution. This cost-effective approach maximizes the utilization of both SSD and HDD resources. This early study highlights the feasibility of hybrid storage systems, which have since gained widespread adoption in production systems.

2.4   Data Storage Format Design Principles

Now that we have explored the physical layout of storage for a data entity, let us delve into the data storage format, which encompasses the logical data structure governing the organization of data elements within the entity.

What are the crucial considerations in the design and implementation of different data storage formats? Drawing from observations and analyses of data access patterns in large-scale data processing systems, a collaborative team consisting of academia and industry has identified the following four requirements for an ideal data storage format [62].

1. *Fast data uploading* This requirement is fundamental for transactional or write-intensive data processing systems. In the realm of data-centric computing, large volumes of newly generated or modified data are consistently and promptly stored in diverse data warehouses. Fulfilling this requirement also bears significance for optimizing network and disk bandwidth utilization in cluster-based data centers.

2. *Fast query processing* This requirement primarily pertains to read-intensive data processing in analytical workloads. Numerous queries within such workloads demand fast response times to satisfy real-time online requests and the substantial load of decision-supporting queries. Therefore, it is essential for the data storage format to facilitate low-latency data accesses.

3. *Efficient memory and storage space utilization* With the ever-increasing data volumes in society, the availability of memory and disk space remains limited. Inefficient utilization of this space not only leads to higher power and hardware costs but also results in delayed data accesses. Hence, it is crucial to ensure optimal utilization of available space to mitigate these challenges.

4. *Adaptive to dynamic workloads* Datasets are subject to analysis by various application users, each with their unique purposes and approaches. Some data analytics involve routine processes executed periodically in a static manner, while others consist of ad-hoc queries to support both internal and external services. The majority of workloads lack regular patterns, requiring the underlying system to be highly adaptable to unforeseen dynamics in data processing, all within the constraints of limited storage space. Rather than being tailored to specific workload patterns, the system must demonstrate flexibility in handling diverse and unpredictable demands.

While it is feasible to address one or more of the aforementioned requirements within a specific data storage format, satisfying all four requirements simultaneously poses a challenge. In Section 2.5, we will examine various data storage formats and assess their effectiveness in meeting these requirements.

2.5 The Formats of Row-Store and Column-Store

In a table format, data elements are logically organized into a two-dimensional array structure consisting of rows and columns. Tables serve as predefined data structures with fixed specifications, including the column names, data types, element sizes, and any relevant restrictions. Examples of table formats can be seen in Table 1.1 and Table 1.2 in Chapter 1. In a relational database, tables form the fundamental data structure for storing, retrieving, and updating data in response to user queries.

A row in a table is commonly referred to as a record. In the table storage format, physical storage blocks are organized as a linear sequence or a continuous one-dimensional array. Each block contains one or more data elements from the table. For a table with n rows and m columns, there are two primary storage formats: *row-store* and *column-store*.

Class schedule

Name	Instructor	Class time
CSE-200	Smith	0900
Econ-100	Gupta	1200
Art-120	Wang	1600

Row-store format

CES-200	Smith	0900	Econ-100	Gupta	1200	Art-120	Wang	1600

Column-store format

CES-200	Econ-100	Art-120	Smith	Gupta	Wang	0900	1200	1600

Figure 2.10 The class schedule table can be placed in a disk drive either in row-store format or in column-store format.

In the row-store format, data records are stored sequentially in the order of rows, ranging from row 1 to row n. On the other hand, the column-store format stores data elements sequentially based on columns, from column 1 to column m. The logical view of these storage formats corresponds to their respective linear sequences in physical locations when the table is completely written to the storage device. Figure 2.10 provides a comparison between the row-store and column-store formats using the example of a "class schedule" table.

In practice, individual rows in the row-store format and individual columns in the column-store format can be treated as subtables, allowing for independent compression and indexing. When processing data in a cluster environment, columns or groups of columns can be distributed among different nodes for the column-store format, while rows or groups of rows can be distributed among different nodes for the row-store format. This distribution strategy enables efficient data processing in a distributed computing environment.

2.5.1   Merits and Limits of the Row-Store Format

The row-store format [132], is a fundamental method for storing tables. In this format, data are written sequentially, row by row. Each row represents a complete record consisting of related fields (columns) that contain elemental data items. For instance, a student record or a patient record contains predefined entries for the respective entity. A student file or a patient file may comprise numerous records of students or patients, respectively. Physically, the record data are stored sequentially in the storage medium.

The row-store format is record-based and assumes that data processing is performed in a row-centric manner. When workloads align with this assumption, the data processing system can efficiently retrieve records from storage. One advantage of the

Adding record (Sci-210, Jones, 1400)
in row-store format

CES-200	Smith	0900	Econ-100	Gupta	1200	Art-120	Wang	1600	Sci-210	Jones	1400

Adding record (Sci-210, Jones, 1400)
in column-store format

CES-200	Econ-100	Art-120	Sci-210	Smith	Gupta	Wang	Jones	0900	1200	1600	1400

Figure 2.11 Adding a new record (Sci-210, Jones, 1400) in the class schedule table. The new record (or the new row) is simply appended in the row-list in row-store format. But each of the three items of the new record has to be inserted in the proper place in the column-list in column-store format.

row-store format is its fast data-uploading capability (requirement 1). As updates or modifications are made to entries in a table, they can be done on a record-by-record basis. For example, to update the GPA entries in a student file, the modifications must be made on a per-student basis. In Figure 2.10, if we add a new class entry (Sci-210, Jones, 1400) to the class schedule table, the row-format in Figure 2.11 demonstrates how the record is easily appended to the existing row-store list.

Another advantage of the row-store format is its adaptability to dynamic workloads (requirement 4). The format ensures that a complete record will be allocated in the same computing node, facilitating efficient processing and analysis of the data.

In summary, the row-store format offers fast data uploading and is well-suited for dynamic workloads. However, it may not be as efficient for read-intensive analytical workloads or optimal space utilization (requirements 2 and 3). We will explore other data storage formats to evaluate their effectiveness in meeting these requirements.

The row-store format has limitations when it comes to large-scale data processing. One major disadvantage is its impact on I/O efficiency. In this format, all the columns of a row must be read, even if only a few columns are actually used in practice. This becomes especially problematic for very wide tables, which are common in database applications. Many data analytics applications involve column-centric operations, such as aggregation-like analysis. For example, computing the average GPA of a class, department, or college is a column operation that is independent of individual records. However, the row-store format does not facilitate such operations efficiently.

Another drawback of the row-store format is its suboptimal data compression for values of different types in multiple columns. Since row-based data compression treats the entire row as a unit, it may not effectively utilize storage space when different columns have distinct compression characteristics.

In summary, the row-store format does not offer the advantage of fast query processing (requirement 2) due to the need to read all columns for each row. It also falls short in terms of efficient memory and storage space utilization (requirement 3), as it may not effectively compress values in multiple columns.

2.5.2   Merits and Limits of the Column-Store Format

The column-store format addresses the disadvantages of the row-store format and offers two distinct advantages [1]. First, it optimizes I/O bandwidth and memory utilization by reading only the required columns during query selection. This improves I/O efficiency and allows for efficient operations within columns, such as aggregation-type operations. Second, the column-store format enables high compression rates by leveraging the similarity of data types within each column.

In summary, the column-store format excels in query processing (requirement 2) as it focuses on retrieving and processing only the necessary data from the relevant columns, which is common in many data analytics queries. Additionally, it provides efficient memory and storage space utilization (requirement 3) by enabling effective compression methods at the column level.

The column-store format, while offering its own advantages, also has two disadvantages that align with the advantages of the row-store format. First, when a query involves operations across multiple columns that may be stored in different disk tracks or computing nodes connected through networks, significant processing delays can occur due to random disk accesses or remote network accesses. Second, the column-store format is not well suited for interactive transaction workloads that involve frequent additions, deletions, and updates of records. For instance, when adding a new class entry (Sci-210, Jones, 1400) to the class schedule in Figure 2.10, the column-format in Figure 2.11 illustrates that each element of the new record must be individually inserted into its proper position in the column-list, resulting in additional overhead compared to the same operation in the row-store format.

Therefore, the column-store format does not possess the advantages of fast data updating (requirement 1) and adaptability to dynamic workloads (requirement 4).

2.6   The Format of Record Columnar File (RCFile)

The advantages of the row-store format and the column-store format are independent and complementary to each other because they aim to address two different key issues in a table. The row-store format focuses on the record-centric organization, while the column-store format prioritizes the selected content-centric organization. Both perspectives are crucial in efficient table processing. By combining the representation of records and columns in a storage format, the complementary effect can be achieved in table processing. The record columnar file (RCFile) [62] was specifically developed for cluster-based parallel data processing. The acronyms "R" and "C" in RCFile represent records and columns, respectively, and "File" signifies a table entity. Owing to its effective resolution of limitations present in both the R-storage format and the C-storage format, RCFile has emerged as a standard storage format in many large-scale data processing systems.

The RCFile is a hybrid data format designed to store a table using a sequence of row groups. Each row group consists of multiple rows, and within each row group, the data

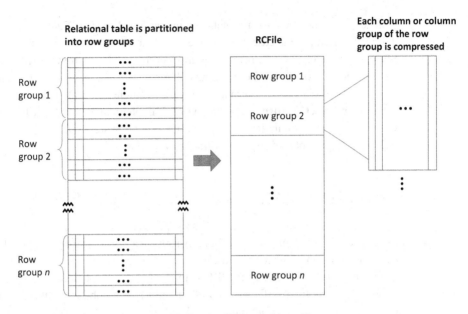

Figure 2.12 Three basic steps in RCFile: A table is partitioned into row groups.

are partitioned into columns. This unique structure allows an RCFile entity to combine the advantages of both the row-store and column-store formats, making it highly suitable for big data processing in cluster environments. In RCFile, contiguous rows form a "row group," and contiguous columns form a "column group." The overall RCFile structure is depicted in Figure 2.12, illustrating how a relational table is partitioned into multiple row groups to create a basic RCFile. Each column or column group within a row group is compressed, resulting in a basic storage unit that encompasses both records and their corresponding columns.

2.6.1 Variations of the Hybrid Format

A hybrid storage format has gained its recognition in both academia and industries as a means to strike a balance between the row-store and column-store formats. Each format possesses desirable features and merits that are incompatible with the other, necessitating a compromise. This compromise involves horizontally partitioning rows within a table to create row groups, and subsequently partitioning columns within each row group. The hybrid format can vary based on three factors: (1) the method used to form a horizontal logical subset of a table and its size (measured by the number of records in a row group), (2) the method used to form a vertical logical subset within a row group (referred to as a column group) and its size, and (3) the strategy employed to allocate columns or column groups within a row group to physical blocks on disks.

For instance, RCFile offers users the opportunity to reorder records in a table before forming row groups, enabling affinity processing and locality considerations. As a row group becomes an independent entity in a computing node, users possess the best knowledge to select records for inclusion in a group. The size of a row group is a pre-defined constant. In the case of column groups, the default size is 1 (a single column). Since all columns within a row group are encompassed within the partitioned entity, the specific method and size of forming column groups are less critical in a distributed system. It is crucial for a row group to fit within a single physical block on a disk drive, although the exact size depends on the system's implementation. The RCFile has found widespread utilization in the Hadoop Distributed File System (HDFS) [121], where an HDFS block is allocated for one or more row groups.

2.6.2   Optimized RCFile (ORC)

An enhanced iteration of RCFile, known as optimized record columnar file (ORC), has been developed and implemented in numerous data processing systems [69]. It introduces several significant advancements in data structures and optimization techniques.

One notable improvement in ORC is the inclusion of integrated indexes, enabling efficient seeking to specific rows based on their row numbers. Unlike RCFile, ORC maintains information about the physical locations of rows. Consequently, the reader of an ORC file does not need to perform a file scan to determine the starting point of a record.

In terms of optimization techniques, ORC employs a two-level compression approach. Firstly, the writer automatically applies encoding methods tailored to each column's data type. This type-specific encoding helps to reduce the size of the encoded data streams. Additionally, ORC offers the option to further compress the encoded data streams using an optional code.

Overall, ORC provides significant improvements over RCFile, incorporating integrated indexes for efficient row seeking and employing advanced compression techniques to optimize storage efficiency and data processing performance.

2.7   The Evolution of Data Storage Format

The concept of a page in the field of databases shares similarities with the memory pages used in the OSs, as both represent fixed-size spaces for storing data. However, there are two significant differences between OS pages and database pages.

First, an OS manages pages through memory addresses, directly mapping to physical and cache memory locations via hardware. In contrast, a database page is a logical concept representing a contiguous space of storage, commonly referred to as a disk page. It is the responsibility of the database management system (DBMS) to determine the placement of database pages on disk. The OS itself cannot dictate where a database page should be located on disk.

Second, the page sizes in OSs and databases differ: the OS typically employs default page sizes of 4 KB or 8 KB, while the default page size for a database is commonly 16 KB. In the context of databases, a page serves as a container for multiple records.

To differentiate one record from another, each page is divided into multiple slots, with each slot containing a record. This organization is commonly referred to as a "slotted page."

The default data storage format for a table in a relational database is known as the N-ary storage model (NSM). In NSM, records are stored contiguously within disk pages, and a table consists of multiple disk pages. Thus, NSM can be considered an early version of the row-store format and is still utilized in many systems today.

To overcome the limitations of the NSM, a model called the decomposition storage model (DSM) was introduced in 1985 [39]. This model involves vertically partitioning a table into multiple independent columns, with each column having its own row identification attached. This approach aligns with the concept of a column-store.

The decomposition storage model offers efficiency in accessing specific column data when only those data are required. However, when operations involving multiple columns are necessary, such as joining columns together, nonsequential disk activities can result in slower data accesses.

Another storage format, called partition attributes across (PAX) [5], builds upon the NSM model where a sequence of records is stored in each slotted page; PAX takes the vertical partitioning approach further by grouping the values of each column into separate entities within each page. These column entities, residing within the same disk page, are referred to as mini-pages.

Experiments conducted on PAX and its improved version [60] demonstrate that the dual partitioning of rows and columns enhances cache performance in database applications. The concept of PAX has been extended by RCFile for managing data processing in large-scale clusters.

2.8 Sequential Disk Allocations for Sorted Data Structures

In our daily lives, we often organize information items to facilitate quick lookups. Consider the following examples: a dictionary sorted alphabetically, an index at the end of a book, athletic competition results ranked by numerical values (e.g., seconds, weights, and heights), and storm warning levels ordered by predefined colors. Sorted datasets, whether numerical, alphabetical, or following other predefined orders, provide a fundamental structure in data processing that enables efficient lookup operations.

A logically sorted data structure should also be physically organized in a consistent order on a disk drive to enable fast access. In this section, we will discuss two sorted data structures, namely the B+tree and LSM-tree, with a focus on the data movement involved in interactions between logical data structures and their physical placement in storage.

2.8.1 B+tree: An In-Place Updating Structure

The B+tree is a widely used data structure for storing sorted data elements efficiently. It is based on the B-tree [13, 14, 37], which is a multilevel tree structure comprising a

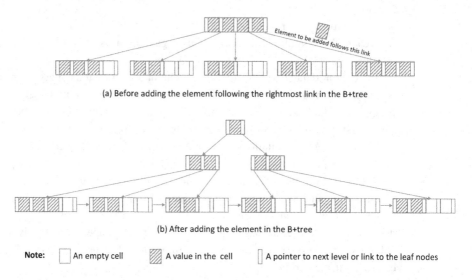

(a) Before adding the element following the rightmost link in the B+tree

(b) After adding the element in the B+tree

Note: ☐ An empty cell   ▨ A value in the cell   ▯ A pointer to next level or link to the leaf nodes

Figure 2.13 This example of B+tree before and after adding a data element shows the in-place updating of B+tree frequently changes the tree structure, causing disk writes to timely maintain a sorted data list in the leaf nodes.

root node, internal nodes (also known as index nodes) at intermediate levels, and leaf nodes at the bottom level to store data elements.

In a B+tree, the leaf nodes, which are stored on a disk drive, are linked together to form a single sorted data list. This enables fast retrieval of data, especially for operations that involve a range of sorted data elements, such as range queries in databases. The B+tree is designed for in-place updating, allowing quick and direct data transactions without requiring additional memory space or computing support. Updates to the logical data structure are directly reflected in the physical locations on the disk drive, ensuring that the B+tree is always up-to-date and accessible to users.

Building a B+tree can be time-consuming due to the frequent interactions between updates to the logical data structure and the corresponding physical placements in the disk's leaf nodes. Figure 2.13 illustrates an example of how a B+tree is dynamically updated after a data insertion operation. In this example, the maximum number of elements in a node (whether it is the root, an index node, or a leaf) is set to four.

Initially, as shown in Figure 2.13(a), the root level is fully occupied with four elements, which are directly linked to five leaf nodes. The rightmost leaf node is also full with four elements. When a new element needs to be added, it will be inserted into the rightmost leaf node by following the rightmost link from the root.

After the insertion operation, as depicted in Figure 2.13(b), the B+tree undergoes a transformation with the root node being split and a new level of middle index nodes being created. This results in a three-level tree structure.

To maintain the integrity of such a dynamically updated B+tree, the data structure needs to be frequently reorganized, and the disk drive must also be managed to ensure the timely maintenance of a sorted list of data elements.

2.8.2 LSM-tree: An Out-of-Place Updating Structure

Unlike in-place updating data structures, *out-of-place updating* data structures require additional space and computing support for data writing. They update data structures using auxiliary memory and disk space, along with additional computational operations. This approach reduces the frequency of interactions between the logical data structure and its physical placement on the disk drive.

One example of an out-of-place updating data structure is the LSM-tree. The LSM-tree is a sorted data structure that utilizes delayed disk writes in a batch and cascading manner. The original design of the LSM-tree was introduced in the paper by O'Neil et al. [110], and a comprehensive survey of the LSM-tree can be found in the paper by Luo and Carey [94].

Figure 2.14 illustrates the basic structure of an LSM-tree, where data elements are stored in sorted order across different levels of a data hierarchy. The top level (C_0) resides in DRAM memory, while the remaining levels (C_1 to C_{k-1}) are stored on disk. The capacity ratio between any pair of levels remains constant, facilitating exponential growth in capacity as we move down the hierarchy. For instance, if the ratio is 10, the data size at level i is ten times larger than at level $i-1$. This design allows for concurrent batch-mode data writing and sorting at different levels.

As each LSM-tree level becomes full, starting from level C_0, the sorted data elements in that level are merged into the next level to create a newly sorted data element list. This process, known as compaction, leaves the level empty and ready to accept merging data from the upper level. The sorted data structure in each level can be efficiently organized using methods such as B+tree.

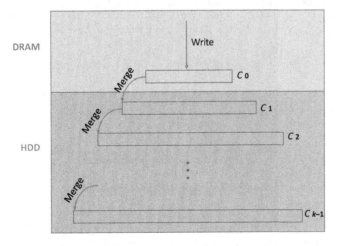

Figure 2.14 The basic structure of LSM-tree: Data elements are written to hierarchical data levels, each of which is a sorted data list. The data sorting and writes always start from the top level C_0 in DRAM memory. As a level of data is full, it will merge to the next level to create a newly sorted data list there. The LSM-tree makes disk writes in a batch and cascading way, and eliminates frequent data structure updates in disks.

Compared to a B+tree, an LSM-tree performs compaction (merging and sorting) in a batch mode using sequential disk operations. Data is written to the disk in a log fashion and continuously merged with the next level to create another sorted structure. The name "log-structured merge-tree" reflects this unique property. By deferring and consolidating disk writes, the LSM-tree minimizes the number of random disk accesses required by an in-place updating structure. Instead, it maximizes sequential disk operations during compaction.

In a B+tree, the single sorted data element list is always maintained in the linked leaf nodes. However, in an LSM-tree, the presence of a single sorted data list across all levels depends on the number of data elements and the capacity of each level. In an extreme case where the number of data elements is smaller than the capacity of the top level (C_0), the single sorted data list can be stored entirely in C_0 or in C_1 after writing it to disk.

In general, for the LSM-tree, sorted data lists can be distributed among different levels. Each level contains a portion of the overall sorted data. Therefore, when performing data retrieval, especially for retrieving specific data or a range of data, a search across multiple levels of the LSM-tree is required. The search operation involves accessing and examining data from various levels until the desired data are found or the search range is satisfied.

In Figure 2.14, the storage component is represented by an HDD, which aligns with the original design of LSM-tree. However, it is important to note that LSM-tree's compaction operations involve numerous writes, which can lead to garbage collection and write amplification issues when implemented on SSDs. For more details on these issues, please refer to Section 2.1 in this chapter. While LSM-tree is specifically designed for write-intensive scenarios and optimized for long-term usage, it may not be the most suitable choice for implementation on SSDs [114].

3 Main Memory: The Physical Space

Main memory, also known as DRAM memory, plays a crucial role in the memory hierarchy by providing physical space for the execution of application and management programs. While hardware caches are typically located on CPU chips, they use the same address space as the main memory. Therefore, it is important to study caches and main memory together as closely related topics. In this chapter, we will delve into various aspects of memory systems. First, we will review the organization of cache and memory based on memory addresses. Second, we will explore how data elements are transferred between the virtual memory space and the physical memory space, as well as their storage mechanisms based on storage physical space. Third, we will examine three unconventional memory system techniques commonly employed in standard memory systems. Finally, we will gain an understanding of the interactions involved in data exchange between the memory and the storage.

3.1 Byte-Addressable Memory

In a computer system, DRAM memory can be conceptually viewed as an array of Bytes. The fundamental unit of data in memory is a Byte, which consists of 8 bits. Each unique memory address corresponds to a specific Byte location. This memory addressing scheme is known as *byte-addressable memory*. The memory addresses begin from 0 and extend up to an upper limit determined by the length of the memory address. For instance, if the memory address is 8 bits long, there are 256 distinct memory locations, with each location capable of storing a single Byte. The memory addresses span from 00000000 (0) to 11111111 (255). Consequently, the 8 bit memory address provides a memory space of 256 Bytes. The majority of computer architectures employ byte-addressable memory.

The choice of using a Byte as the basic unit in memory is motivated by its suitability for character representation. ASCII, short for the American Standard Code for Information Interchange, is a widely used character-encoding standard in electronic communication. Therefore, a Byte is employed to represent a single character. In the original ASCII character set, each binary value ranging from 0 to 127 corresponds to a specific character. Subsequently, the ASCII character set was expanded to encompass the full range of 256 possible characters. Within the extended ASCII character set, binary values between 128 and 255 accommodate approximately 128 additional characters, primarily comprising accented characters from European languages.

A processor possesses a collection of registers that serve the dual purpose of supplying the arithmetic and logic unit (ALU) with input for basic computational operations and storing the computed results. Each register is assigned a unique address, distinct from memory addresses. Furthermore, registers typically have a word length of 4 Bytes or double words (8 Bytes). Now, let us consider the order in which a computer reads 4 Bytes from a register and writes them into four memory locations, each corresponding to a single Byte. We will also explore the reverse process of data communication from four memory locations to a register.

In many human languages, words are conventionally read from left to right, following a left-to-right script. However, certain languages, such as Hebrew and Arabic, adopt a right-to-left script, where words are read and written in the opposite direction. This distinction between left-to-right and right-to-left ordering is significant when transferring data between a word-based register and a byte-addressable memory. The order of reading and writing data is governed by the concepts of "Big-endian" and "Little-endian."

In Big-endian format, the data sequence commences from the "big end," which corresponds to the high-order portion of the sequence (left-to-right). Conversely, Little-endian format dictates an opposite order, commencing from the "little end" or the low-order section of the data sequence (right-to-left). Figure 3.1 depicts a comparison between Big-endian (a) and Little-endian (b) schemes for communication between a 4 Byte register and a byte addressable memory. In this scenario, four consecutive memory locations located at addresses adr, adr $+$ 1, adr $+$ 2, and adr $+$ 3 are utilized.

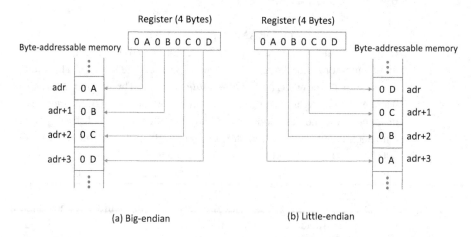

(a) Big-endian   (b) Little-endian

Figure 3.1 Big-endian vs. Little-endian. The content of the 4-Byte register is a sequence of eight hexadecimal values, and each of the two values form 1 Byte. For Big-endian in (a), the 4 Bytes in the register from high order to low order (from left to right) are stored to the four memory locations. In contrast, for Little-endian in (b), the 4 Bytes in the register from low order to high order (from right to left) are stored to the four memory locations.

Assembly programs, based on a machine-dependent ISA, are converted to executable programs in the format of machine code by a utility software tool called *assembler*. In the case of reduced instruction set computer (RISC) architectures, the length of each instruction is fixed. For instance, in an early version of the MIPS processor, each instruction occupies a storage space of 4 Bytes. When an instruction is fetched from memory, the program counter (PC) is automatically incremented by 4 to indicate the location of the next instruction in memory. This systematic increment allows the processor to sequentially fetch and execute instructions in the program.

3.2 Virtual Addresses of a Program and Physical Memory Allocation to Its Process

A *program* is a static concept that consists of a sequence of different code formats, starting from the source code in a chosen programming language, to the machine-dependent assembly code, and finally, the executable code. The executable code, along with its associated datasets, is stored as a file on a disk drive. On the other hand, a *process* is a dynamic concept that refers to a running program. When a program becomes a process running on a computer, it receives runtime support from the CPU and the entire memory hierarchy stack, with the OS playing a major role in allocating hardware resources.

To facilitate the execution of a program, two address spaces are used: a virtual address space and the physical memory address. The virtual address space represents the capacity in terms of absolute Bytes from a programmer's perspective, and it is bound at the time when the executable code is generated. Typically, the starting virtual address is 0, with a contiguous range of addresses. Each process has its own dedicated address space. The size of a computer's virtual address space is determined by the number of bits in the CPU's hardware address space. For example, a 32-bit CPU provides a virtual address space ranging from 0 to $2^{32} - 1$, which equals 4 GB. In contrast, a 64-bit CPU offers a virtual address space of 2^{64} Bytes, which is equal to 16 EB. The virtual address space is divided into fixed-sized units called pages, with a standard page size of 4 KB. In physical memory, the basic data allocation unit is also a page, and to differentiate it from logical pages, physical pages are referred to as page frames. The sizes of logical pages and physical pages are always the same.

Figure 3.2 illustrates a 32-bit virtual address space (4 GB) and an 30-bit physical memory address space (1 GB), where the page size is set to 4 KB. When preparing the execution of a program, either all or a part of the virtual pages will be placed into physical memory. The address mapping between the two spaces is achieved through a translation process, depicted in Figure 3.2, which will be explained in detail later. In a multiprogramming environment, the virtual address space of a computer is independently used by multiple programs, but their physical address mappings by OS are conflict free among the running programs, as will be elaborated upon shortly.

When a programmer requests memory space allocation for running a program, they define a virtual address space, which doesn't actually exist in physical memory.

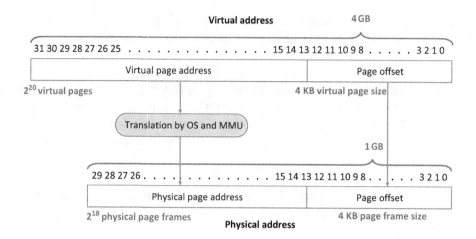

Figure 3.2 The 32-bit virtual address space has a capacity of 4 GB, and the 30-bit physical address space has only 1 GB capacity. The 4-KB page size is the basic unit in both spaces. The address mapping between virtual space to physical space is managed by OS and translated by MMU.

The program's execution, however, takes place in the physical memory address space. In cases where the demanded memory size of the virtual space is always smaller than the available physical memory capacity and the computer is dedicated to running one program at a time, the virtual address space will be equivalent to the physical address space. The starting address may shift from the virtual starting address (e.g., 0) to the starting physical address in memory, depending on user requirements.

The virtual memory system is designed to support the simultaneous execution of multiple programs in a multiprogramming environment. In such scenarios, some programs may request a memory allocation larger than the available physical memory capacity, and it is crucial to isolate the memory space allocated to each running program from others. To address this, we can draw parallels with common solutions we encounter in daily life. For example, a popular restaurant often has more customers than available seats. To accommodate them, customers need to make reservations by specifying the number of participants. The restaurant's service center physically assigns seats based on the requests of reservations, and an usher guides customer groups or individuals to their assigned seats. In the context of virtual memory, the number of virtual pages for each program corresponds to the number of participants in a reservation, and the corresponding physical pages are akin to the seats assigned to the customers with a page table for the book-keeping purpose. The service center and usher can be seen as playing the role of the operating system, creating a page table for each running program on allocating physical pages to hold requested virtual pages.

In practice, multiple programs, each with its own dedicated virtual address space, undergo a virtual-to-physical address translation process. This process ensures that their virtual pages are mapped, either fully or partially, to physical pages within a single memory address space. Figure 3.3 illustrates the concept of "reservation and ushering" to allocate a complete or partial space in physical memory for each program.

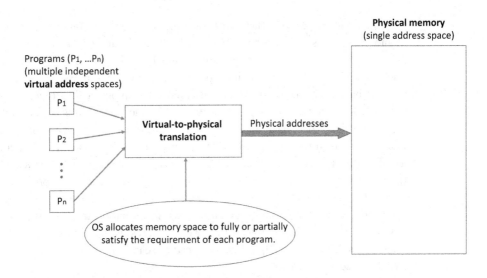

Figure 3.3 The "virtual-to-physical translation" mechanism allocates physical locations in a single address memory space for multiple programs represented by their independent virtual addresses.

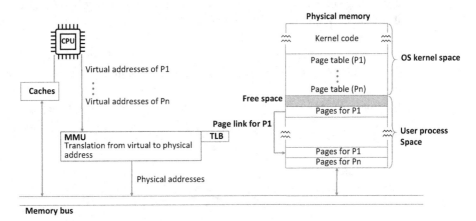

Figure 3.4 The virtual addresses of multiple programs are issued from CPU. The OS uses MMU to translate the virtual addresses to physical addresses and creates a page table for each running program. The page tables are allocated in the OS kernel space and the physical pages for each running program are allocated in user process space in the physical memory. Physical memory pages for each running program can be allocated contiguously, for example, Pn, or in separate regions, for example, P1. The pages in two separate memory regions for P1 are marked in page table (Pn). The page link in the figure is used for an explanation only. The physical memory addresses are also used to map to cache blocks by CPU. The hardware components of CPU, MMU, and caches are all on-chip.

Figure 3.4 illustrates the mapping between virtual addresses of a program and its physical addresses during execution in a computer system. To run a program, the OS component known as the *process loader* accesses the executable file and sets up the program's virtual address space. In Figure 3.4, the CPU generates a set of *n* virtual memory addresses for *n* programs (P1, . . ., Pn). The OS utilizes the MMU, an on-chip hardware device responsible for monitoring the dynamic state of physical memory, to translate each virtual address to its corresponding physical address.

For a basic system environment, a reserved space in physical memory is allocated for the OS kernel, which is typically known as "kernel space." It is a protected region of memory that is dedicated to the OS and its core components. Each running program maintains its own *page table*, which tracks the translations between virtual addresses and their physical counterparts. The OS creates a separate page table for each program (page table (P1), . . ., page table (Pn)) using the physical addresses provided by the MMU. These page tables are stored in the OS kernel space within the physical memory. To expedite memory page accesses during program execution, the translation lookaside buffer (TLB) cache, located within the MMU, stores the most recently used address translations. This cache helps avoid the need to search the page table in memory for frequently accessed pages.

The OS allocates pages for each running program within the user process space of the physical memory, which can be either contiguous or noncontiguous. In Figure 3.4, the physical pages for P1 are allocated in two separate memory locations, with links connecting them to the pages in two distinct physical memory regions dedicated to this running program. On the other hand, the physical pages for Pn are allocated contiguously.

Each program's page table is accessed through a dedicated register known as the page table base register PTBR. This register allows independent data allocations in physical memory for multiple programs. When the CPU performs a context switch from one process to another, the OS switches the PTBR to access the page table of the

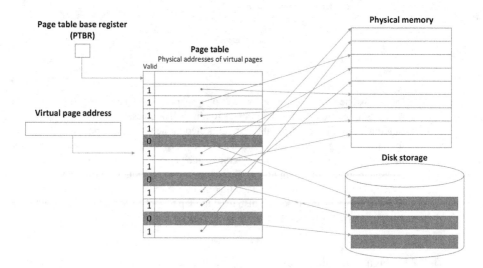

Figure 3.5 The basic structure of a page table, where the valid bit = 1 in each entry indicates that the page is in the physical memory, and valid bit = 0 means the page is still in the the disk.

corresponding process. This ensures that each process has its own isolated memory allocation.

To effectively utilize limited physical memory space for multiple running programs, a technique called *demand paging* is employed in virtual memory management. With demand paging, the OS brings virtual pages into physical memory only when they are required for program execution. Consequently, not all virtual pages are present in physical memory during program execution. Figure 3.5 provides an example of a page table pointed to by a PTBR. In this example, a valid bit of 1 indicates that a virtual page has been loaded into physical memory, and the corresponding table entry stores the specific memory address of the page. On the other hand, a valid bit of 0 signifies that the virtual page, identified by its virtual address, remains on disk. In Figure 3.5, the dark-colored entries in the page table point to disk locations, with their valid bits set to 0. The remaining entries in the page table point to specific physical memory addresses, and their valid bits are set to 1.

During the execution of a process, if a requested page is not found in physical memory, it results in a *page fault*. The OS handles this by loading the virtual page from disk, placing it into memory, and updating the page table accordingly. If the physical memory is already full, the OS selects a victim page to evict in order to make space for the new page. The victim page is typically chosen based on a prediction that it is least likely to be accessed in the future. Replacement policies for selecting victim pages will be covered in Chapter 4.

Figure 3.6 illustrates the step-by-step operation flow, involving the CPU, MMU, TLB, page table, and memory, when processing a CPU-issued virtual page address

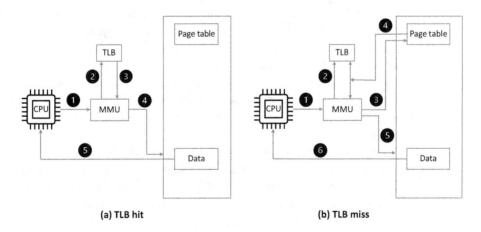

(a) TLB hit   (b) TLB miss

Figure 3.6 (a) The operation sequence for a TLB hit: (1) CPU issues a virtual page address, (2) MMU checks TLB, (3) TLB hit, (4) MMU accesses the memory by the physical page address, (5) the requested physical page is delivered to CPU. (b) The operation sequence for a TLB miss: (1) CPU issues a virtual page address, (2) MMU checks TLB, (3) TLB miss and MMU accesses the page table in memory by the virtual page address, (4) the physical page address is sent to MMU and TLB is updated, (5) MMU accesses the memory by the physical page address, (6) the requested physical page is delivered to CPU.

request and delivering the requested page to the CPU. The figure includes two scenarios: (a) a TLB hit and (b) a TLB miss, which requires an additional memory access to the page table compared to a TLB hit. Please note that Figure 3.6(b) does not take into account page faults.

3.3   Memory-Address-Based CPU Caches

During program execution, users are unaware of locations in the memory hierarchy where their executable code and datasets are allocated. The CPU executes instructions and accesses data by initially searching for them in hardware caches. The cache search is performed using the same memory addresses assigned by the OS for the program's instructions and data in the memory. These memory addresses are used by a *cache controller* to search within the hardware caches. Consequently, users are also unaware of the specific cache locations where their code and data are allocated during execution. The cache controller is located on a CPU chip too, which manages and monitors data accesses in CPU caches for several major activities, determining which data to keep, which data to evict, and how data are organized in the cache.

Hardware caches are smaller and faster memories that are located close to the CPU. They store copies of frequently used data from the main memory. The three main types of caches are the instruction cache, data cache, and TLB cache, which were studied in Section 3.2. The shared data unit between virtual addresses and physical memory addresses is a "page." However, when transferring data between the memory and a cache, the basic unit is a "cache block" or "cache line" of a fixed size. The cache block will be delivered to the CPU from a page. The main component of a cache block belongs to the basic unit of the "cache storage," which typically ranges from 4 Bytes to 64 Bytes or more. A cache block also contains additional bits, such as a valid bit and a tag, which will be explained further.

From a user's perspective, when referring to the cache block size, we are primarily referring to the basic unit size in the cache storage (e.g., 16 Bytes). However, it is essential to consider the other bits present in a cache block from a computer architecture standpoint.

The cache controller is a hardware component located on the CPU chip that handles the automatic data flow from memory to cache. This process is designed to be fast and efficient, allowing for minimal flexibility. There are three main mapping methods used to map a memory address to a cache location: direct-mapped cache, set-associative cache, and fully associative cache.

3.3.1   Direct-Mapped and Set-Associative Caches

The design of a cache relies on the mapping from a large memory address space to a smaller cache space. This mapping is based on a common framework that will be explored in this section, along with its variations.

Direct-Mapped Cache

The concept of the direct-mapped cache was introduced as early as 1965 [133]. Let us focus on the cache block index in the memory address only to explain the cache mapping. We will later explain how a memory address is divided into three regions for the cache address mapping. In a direct-mapped cache, each block index of the memory address is mapped to a single cache block location. This mapping is determined by a straightforward formula:

$$(\text{block index}) \bmod (\text{number of cache blocks}).$$

In direct-mapped cache, a mathematical observation is that a sequence of contiguous memory addresses, larger than the number of cache blocks, will exhibit a repeated pattern of access. Specifically, a single cache block will be mapped by multiple memory addresses, where the address differences or distances among these addresses are factors of the cache size by the number of cache blocks. However, it is important to note that the actual mapping between a memory address and its cache block address is not computed using a modulo operation by the CPU.

Figure 3.7 illustrates a simple example of a direct-mapped cache. In this example, 5-bit block index in the memory address are mapped to eight cache blocks, each with a 3-bit address space. A key advantage of direct-mapped cache is that the cache location is determined by the low-order $\log_2$(the number of cache blocks) bits in the memory address, which allows for fast circuit operations. In Figure 3.7, the cache location is determined by the low-order 3 bits of the 5-bit memory addresses. For instance, memory addresses ending in 111 are all mapped to cache block 111. These low-order bits are commonly referred to as the "cache index bits." When multiple block indices

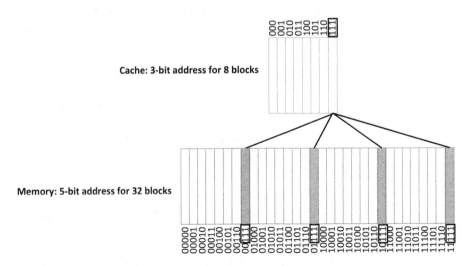

Figure 3.7 A simple example for direct-mapping between a 5-bit memory space for an index of 32 blocks to a 3-bit cache space of 8 blocks. The low-order bits in the memory address directly map to the cache block. The length of the low-order bits is the number of bits for the cache address space.

are mapped to the same cache block, it is called "cache mapping conflict." For example, Figure 3.7 shows that block indices of 00111, 01111, 10111, and 11111 are all mapped to the same cache block 111.

   To resolve cache access conflicts, the remaining bits of the memory address are added to each cache block as a "tag." In the example shown in Figure 3.7, the two remaining bits in the memory address are used as the tag. The tag in each cache block corresponds to a unique memory location. During a direct-mapped cache access, after locating the cache block using the cache index from the memory address, the cache controller also compares the tag portion of the memory address with the tag stored in the cache block. If the comparison is successful, it indicates a cache hit; otherwise, it is considered a cache miss. The tag is initially stored in the cache block when the block's content is first written into the cache. Additionally, each cache block includes a "valid bit" that indicates whether the block contains valid content (valid bit = 1) or not (valid bit = 0).

   Figure 3.8 illustrates an example of the design of a direct-mapped cache with a cache storage of 128 KB and a cache block size of 16 Bytes. In Figure 3.8(a), the 32-bit memory address is divided into three parts: (1) the byte offset bits for the block size, (2) the cache index bits, and (3) the tag bits. Since the cache storage consists of 8192 cache blocks, each 16 Bytes in size, the cache index requires 13 bits. The remaining 15 bits are used for tags. Figure 3.8(b) depicts the organization of a cache block, with the bits arranged from low order to high order. The cache block storage comprises 128 bits for the 16 Bytes of data, 15 bits for the tag, and 1 bit for the valid bit. Consequently, the total number of bits in a cache block is $128 + 15 + 1 = 144$ bits. With 8192 cache blocks, the total number of bits required for the cache is $8192 \times 144 = 1,179,648$ bits. This exceeds the storage capacity of the 128 KB cache, which corresponds to 1,048,576 bits. The total number of cache bits amounts to 12.5 percent more than the cache storage capacity. In practical cache designs, additional bits are employed in each cache block,

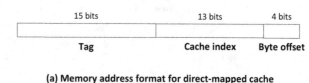

(a) Memory address format for direct-mapped cache
(1) Cache storage size = 128 KB, and (2) cache block size = 16 Bytes

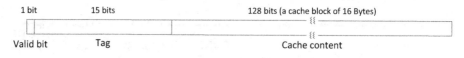

(b) One cache block only

Figure 3.8 The cache size is 128 KB and the cache block size is 16 Bytes. (a) The memory address format for direct-mapped cache, and (b) the organization of the single cache block.

such as a dirty bit to handle cache writes for data consistency between the cache and memory, an access bit to track recent accesses for replacement considerations, and bits for other management purposes. In practice, the number of bits in the cache space is limited, both for content storage and for management operations.

During a direct-mapped cache access, after indexing the cache block using the cache index bits, the tag in the cache and the corresponding tag portion in the memory address are compared. Simultaneously, the cache block is dispatched to a buffer for CPU acceptance. If the tag comparison succeeds, indicating a match, the CPU accesses the cache block in the buffer, resulting in a cache hit. Conversely, if the tag comparison fails, indicating a mismatch, the CPU receives a cache miss signal. The direct-mapped cache offers the lowest latency for cache hits due to the parallel operations of tag comparison and cache block placement in the buffer. However, its hit ratio is relatively low due to the occurrence of direct-mapped conflicts for multiple addresses mapping to the same cache block, which can lead to cache conflict misses.

Set-Associative Cache

The set-associative cache is designed to mitigate conflict misses and improve the cache hit ratio. It is also referred to as an N-way set-associative cache, where each memory block index in the memory address maps to a set of N cache blocks. The value of N represents the cache's associativity, with larger values indicating higher associativity. After indexing the set, the CPU performs tag comparisons across the N blocks, aiming for a cache hit. This mapping mechanism follows the same framework as a direct-mapped cache but with a reduced number of cache index bits. The remaining bits are used for the tag. The term "set index" is more general because a direct-mapped cache can be considered a special case of a set-associative cache, specifically a one-way set-associative cache (with one cache way or block per set).

To illustrate a four-way set-associative cache with the same size of 128 KB cache storage and a cache block size of 16 Bytes as shown in Figure 3.8, we divide the 32-bit memory address into three parts: (1) the 4-bit byte offset for the block size, (2) the 11-bit set index, and (3) the 17-bit tag. In Figure 3.9(a), the cache storage consists of 2048 sets, with each set containing four cache blocks, and each block holding 16 Bytes. Figure 3.9(b) illustrates the organization of the four cache blocks within each set, from low order to high order. In each block, there are 128 bits allocated for the cache block storage of 16 Bytes, 17 bits for the tag, and 1 bit for the valid bit. Thus, the total number of bits for a cache block is $128 + 17 + 1 = 146$ bits. For a set of four blocks, we require 584 bits. With 2048 sets, the total number of bits used for the cache amounts to $2048 \times 584 = 1196032$ bits. Comparatively, the 128 KB cache storage requires 1,048,576 bits. Therefore, the total number of cache bits for this four-way set-associative cache is 14.1 percent greater than the cache storage. Owing to the utilization of additional tag bits per cache block, a set-associative cache necessitates more bits compared to a direct-mapped cache.

Compared to a direct-mapped cache, a set-associative cache offers a reduced number of mapping conflicts due to the presence of multiple cache blocks within a set, resulting in an improved hit ratio. However, the advantage of quickly determining a

(a) Memory address format for four-way set-associative cache

(1) Cache storage size = 128 KB, and (2) Cache block size = 16 Bytes

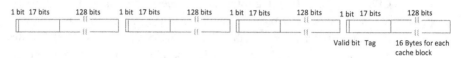

(b) Four cache blocks in each set

Figure 3.9 The cache size is 128 KB and the cache block size is 16 Bytes. (a) The memory address format for four-way set-associative cache, and (b) the organization of the four blocks in each set.

cache hit or miss, as seen in the direct-mapped cache, is not present in a set-associative cache. In a set-associative cache, once the set is indexed, each cache block within the set needs to undergo tag comparisons to determine a hit or miss. If the tag comparison succeeds, the cache block is dispatched to the buffer, indicating a cache hit. Unfortunately, the multiple comparison operations and the subsequent dispatching of the correct cache block cannot be executed concurrently. Consequently, the latency of a set-associative cache is relatively higher, particularly in the case of a cache hit.

Fully Associative Cache

While a direct-mapped cache can be considered as a one-way set-associative cache, a fully associative cache is a special case where all the cache blocks are contained within a single set. We will use the same cache design example to illustrate how the memory address is divided and how the cache is organized for a fully associative cache. In this example, the cache size remains 128 KB with a cache block size of 16 Bytes.

In Figure 3.10(a), the 32-bit memory address is divided into two parts: (1) the 4-bit Byte offset for the block size, and (2) the tag bits. The Byte offset remains 4 bits for the 16-Byte blocks. The remaining 28 bits are used for the tag. The 128 KB cache storage consists of 8192 cache blocks, each with a size of 16 Bytes.

Figure 3.10(b) illustrates the organization of a fully associative cache with 8192 blocks. In each cache block, 128 bits are allocated for the storage of 16 Bytes of data, 28 bits are dedicated to the tag, and 1 bit is reserved for the valid bit. Thus, the total number of bits for a cache block is $128 + 28 + 1 = 157$ bits. With a total of 8192 blocks, the fully associative cache requires $8192 \times 157 = 1,286,144$ bits. Since the 128 KB cache storage requires 1,048,576 bits, the fully associative cache utilizes 22.7 percent more bits than the cache storage. The fully associative cache requires the highest number of tag bits among the three cache structures since the eliminated index bits are added to the tag region.

A unique advantage of a fully associative cache is that the entire cache space can be fully utilized. However, since there is no index, the entire cache must be searched in the worst case scenario. The search involves comparing the tag portion of each cache block with the tag region in the memory address. This comparison is performed from one valid block to another until a match is found for a cache hit. If all valid blocks are checked without finding a match, it results in a cache miss.

While a fully associative cache achieves the lowest miss rate due to its optimal space utilization, it also incurs the highest access latency. This is because the entire cache must be searched sequentially, making it slower compared to direct-mapped or set-associative caches where the search can be narrowed down to a specific cache block or set.

Summary of the Cache Mapping Framework

The three cache designs, direct-mapped cache, set-associative cache, and fully associative cache, are variations within a common address mapping framework. This framework maps block indices to cache blocks in different ways: one-to-one (direct-mapped cache), one-to-many (set-associative cache), and one-to-all (fully associative cache). Figure 3.10 illustrates the address mapping framework, where the placement of the dividing line between the tag region and the set index region determines the cache associativity for a given cache block size.

By moving the dividing line one bit to the right, the cache associativity is increased by a factor of 2, doubling the number of blocks per set (or ways). Conversely, moving the dividing line one bit to the left decreases the associativity by a factor of 2, halving the number of blocks per set (or ways). Figure 3.11 showcases the two extreme cases: a

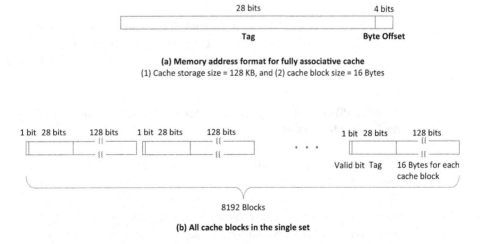

Figure 3.10 The cache size is 128 KB and the cache block size is 16 Bytes. (a) The memory address format for a fully associative cache, and (b) the organization of all the cache blocks in the single set.

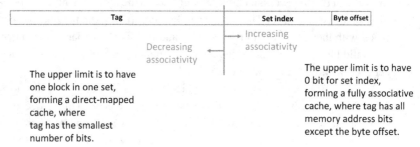

A general memory address format for cache mapping

Required parameters: (1) cache storage size in Bytes and (2) cache block size in Bytes

Tag	Set index	Byte offset

→ Increasing
associativity

Decreasing ←
associativity

The upper limit is to have
one block in one set,
forming a direct-mapped
cache, where
tag has the smallest
number of bits.

The upper limit is to have
0 bit for set index,
forming a fully associative
cache, where tag has all
memory address bits
except the byte offset.

Figure 3.11 The memory address format for three types of cache mapping is determined by the dividing line between the set index region and the tag region.

fully associative cache with 0 set-index bits and a direct-mapped cache with the highest number of set-index bits.

In the concluding part of this section, we will briefly explain how a cache controller handles a memory address to determine a cache hit or miss. When a data access request is received, the cache controller divides the memory address into three regions: the byte offset region for cache block storage size, the set index region, and the tag region, in a low-to-high order.

First, the cache controller uses the set index bits to locate the corresponding cache set. Within the set, the cache controller examines each block and checks the valid bit to determine if the block contains valid content. Then, it compares the tag bits in the cache block with the tag region bits in the requested memory address. If both the validity check and tag comparison are successful, it signifies a cache hit. The cache controller transfers the content of the cache block from the cache to a buffer, which the CPU can then access.

On the other hand, if the valid bit check or tag comparison fails, it indicates a cache miss. In the event of a cache miss, the CPU utilizes the same memory address to request the corresponding block from the memory location and load it into the cache.

3.4 Multicolumn Caches: A Hybrid Cache Mapping for Both Low Latency and Low Miss Ratio

Increasing cache associativity can effectively reduce the miss ratio, but it also leads to increased hit latency. However, the impact of changing the associativity is not proportional to the changes in miss ratio and latency. Research has indicated that the steepest reduction in miss ratio occurs when transitioning from a direct-mapped cache to a two-way set-associative cache. Beyond a four-way associative cache, the miss ratio tends to plateau, yielding diminishing returns for improving the hit ratio [64, 67].

Despite the higher conflict miss ratio in direct-mapped caches, they still remain appealing due to their low latency [66]. On the other hand, higher associativity caches

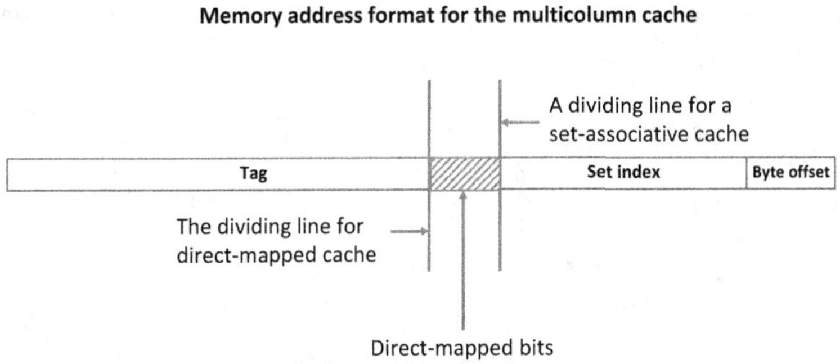

Memory address format for the multicolumn cache

Figure 3.12 The direct-mapped bits in multicolumn cache memory address format enable one-to-one mapping in a set-associative cache.

have the advantage of reducing competition for block replacement within a set. The address mapping framework for caches depicted in Figure 3.11 demonstrates that associativity primarily determines the tradeoff between latency and hit ratio. Considering the significance of both low latency and high hit ratio, a natural question arises: Is it possible to achieve both simultaneously?

Indeed, it is possible to achieve both low latency and high associativity simultaneously through a hybrid cache design known as multicolumn cache [140]. The underlying principle of this cache design follows the address mapping framework depicted in Figure 3.11. The key distinction between a direct-mapped cache and a set-associative cache lies in the position of the dividing line between the set index region and the tag region in the memory address. In a set-associative cache, some bits from the set-index region are allocated to the tag region, allowing for increased associativity.

The multicolumn cache takes advantage of the unused region of bits between the dividing line of a direct-mapped cache and that of a set-associative cache. This region, called the *direct-mapped bits*, is explicitly highlighted in Figure 3.12. In the multicolumn cache, these direct-mapped bits are utilized for cache mapping. The set index is used to determine which set to go to, while the direct-mapped bits determine which way within the set to access. In other words, the mapping in the multicolumn cache not only points to a set using the set index but also directly selects a specific way within the set based on the direct-mapped bits.

In the multicolumn cache, the set index and its direct-mapped bits map to both a set and a cache block within a specific way, its corresponding cache block is referred to as being in the *major location*. If a tag comparison in the major location succeeds, it is referred to as a *major location hit* or the *first hit*. Figure 3.13 provides a comparison of the memory address mapping among a basic direct-mapped cache, a four-way set-associative cache, and a four-way multicolumn cache for a cache with eight blocks. For simplicity, this example focuses solely on the 3-bit address mapping, excluding the byte offset and tag region.

Figure 3.13(a) illustrates a direct-mapped cache with eight blocks, where the 3-bit cache index 101 in the memory address directly maps to cache block address 101.

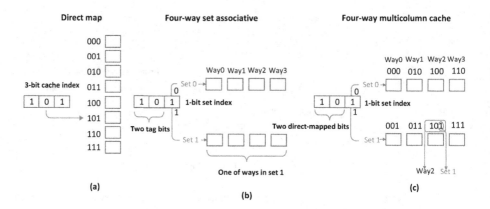

Figure 3.13 Memory address format comparisons among (a) direct-mapped cache, (b) four-way associative cache, and (c) four-way multicolumn cache.

In Figure 3.13(b), a four-way set-associative cache is shown, where only the least significant bit of the cache index bits is used for the set index, while the remaining 2 bits are allocated to the tag region. For the same index 101, the set index maps to set 1, and one of the four cache blocks in that set is selected after tag comparisons.

Figure 3.13(c) depicts a four-way multicolumn cache with eight cache blocks. The cache index is divided into a 1-bit set index and two direct-mapped bits. For the address 101, the multicolumn cache directly maps to cache block 10, determined by the direct-mapped bits, within set 1 determined by the set index. Each cache block is represented by its set index in the low order and direct-mapped bits in the high order.

While a set-associative cache uses set-based mapping, pointing to a row of cache blocks, as shown in Figure 3.13(b), the multicolumn cache derives its name from its ability to directly map to multiple columns (ways) within a row (set), as depicted in Figure 3.13(c).

The multicolumn cache design offers a significant improvement over conventional set-associative caches by reducing mapping conflicts through the distribution of direct-mapped accesses across multiple cache blocks in a set. Experimental results have shown that the first hit ratio in major locations can be as high as 90 percent [140], indicating that the latency of the majority of hits in the multicolumn cache is equivalent to that of a direct-mapped cache. This is a notable advantage compared to traditional set-associative caches.

However, the challenge lies in handling the remaining 10 percent of conflict misses. A straightforward solution is to adopt a direct-mapped cache management approach, where the cache block causing the conflict is evicted and replaced by loading the requested cache block from memory. This simple approach proves to be highly cost effective, as the utilization of the direct-mapped bits incurs no additional hardware cost. Thus, this approach holds practical value.

For instance, in ARM Cortex R series processors, memory-address-based cache mapping allows direct access to one of the ways in a set, aligning with this approach.

However, it does not fully exploit the resources of a set-associative cache, especially in the case of high associativity caches where numerous cache blocks are available within each set.

The multicolumn cache addresses the issue of the 10 percent miss conflicts by providing additional hardware support at a low cost. When a cache block in the major location is identified as a conflict miss after tag checking, it is swapped with an unused cache block in the set. The cache location of this unused block is referred to as a *selected location*. The newly loaded cache block from memory is then placed in the major location. This ensures that the cache block in the major location is always the most-recently used (MRU), capitalizing on temporal locality – the tendency of recently accessed blocks to be accessed again soon. In cases where no unused cache block is available in the set as a selected location, a replacement is performed, similar to a direct-mapped cache. Fortunately, the multicolumn cache can support a high associativity, providing an ample number of cache blocks as selected locations. The multicolumn cache makes the best effort to keep the cache blocks in cache either in the major location or in a selected location, aiming to improve hit ratios and to reduce the latency.

To efficiently locate the cache block when a conflict miss occurs in the major location, an index of bit vectors is maintained for each cache block. Figure 3.14 illustrates the basic structure of the bit vector index, which tracks the selected locations for each cache block in a four-way multicolumn cache. In Figure 3.14, the bit vector "1" for cache block in major location 1 (way 1) indicates that it has two selected locations in way 0 and way 2, respectively. The other bit vectors in Figure 3.14 show that cache blocks in ways 0, 2, and 3 do not have any selected locations.

When a cache miss occurs in a major location, the cache controller searches the bit vector to find potential selected locations. If a selected location is found, the cache block in the selected location is swapped with the cache block in the major location to ensure that the block in the major location remains MRU. If a selected location is not

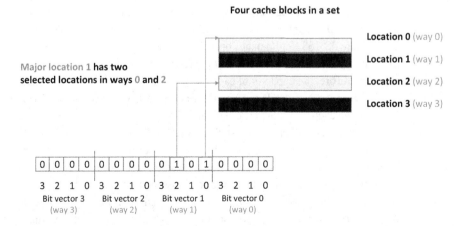

Figure 3.14 A bit vector is associated with each major location cache block to link its selected locations.

found, the cache block is swapped with an unused cache block, and the newly loaded cache block from memory is placed in the major location. Whenever the selected locations for a cache mapping to a major location change, the corresponding bit vector is updated accordingly.

The authors of the multicolum cache [140] also address the scenario of cache misses occurring when all the cache blocks in a mapped set are occupied. To accommodate a new selected location, a straightforward replacement operation is employed, evicting the least-recently used (LRU) block. Chapter 4 will give a comprehensive examination of replacement algorithms. Additionally, in their paper [140], the authors present parallel and sequential techniques for searching selected locations following a miss in the major location.

3.5   The Effect of Cache Accesses on DRAM Performance

Dynamic random-access memory is a critical component in computing systems of various types. It was invented in 1968 by Robert Dennard at IBM [43]. In DRAM, each bit of data is stored in a memory cell that consists of a tiny capacitor and a single transistor. The term "dynamic" is used because the capacitor needs to be timely charged in a few dozen milliseconds. In contrast, hardware cache uses static random-access memory (SRAM), where each cell has six transistors. Once a cell is written, it retains its value as long as the power is on, hence the name "static" RAM; SRAM is utilized for on-chip caches due to its high speed and limited capacity, while DRAM is used as off-chip memory due to its higher capacity and lower cost. Researchers and practitioners have continuously worked on improving memory performance. A significant concern is how DRAM memory can efficiently allocate and return cache blocks to the CPU after a cache miss occurs.

A basic component of a memory system is memory chips that are composed of transistors and capacitors. Furthermore, a memory chip is organized into multiple "memory banks." In Figure 3.15, a 2 GB memory chip consists of 16 memory banks, with each bank having a capacity of 128 MB. Within each bank, the 128 MB is further divided into 32,768 (32 K) pages or rows, with each page size set at 4 KB. Each page or row is comprised of 256 columns, which represent the cache blocks within the memory page. Therefore, the capacity of each memory bank shown in Figure 3.15 is calculated as 32,768 (pages) × 4 KB = 128 MB. Each memory bank features a *row-buffer* that serves as the cache for that particular bank. The size of the row-buffer typically matches the physical memory page size, such as 4 KB in Figure 3.16.

When a cache miss occurs, the CPU sends a request to the memory controller using the same memory address to fetch the cache block from the memory into the cache. The memory controller is an additional circuit component within the CPU chip. Whether it is the CPU or disks for getting data from the DRAM memory, requests are made to the memory controller. The memory controller performs several key functions.

First, it is responsible for timely charging (refreshing) specific areas of the capacitor-based DRAM core. This ensures that the stored data remains intact.

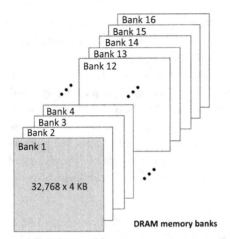

Figure 3.15 A 2 GB memory module consists of 16 memory banks, each of which has the capacity of 128 MB. The 128 MB space is further divided into 32,768 (32 K) pages, which are also called rows in DRAM.The page size is 4 KB. Each page contains 256 cache blocks, and the block size is 16 Bytes. Corresponding to the term of row, the cache block is called column in DRAM. Each memory bank has a row-buffer as large as a page of 4 KB.

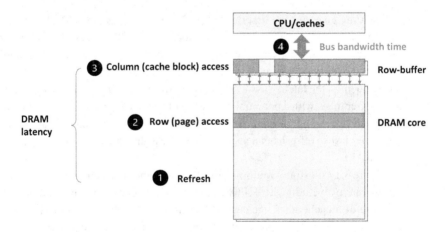

Figure 3.16 To respond a cache miss, the DRAM in a memory bank needs four basic steps to deliver the cache block to CPU/caches, assuming that a row-buffer miss occurs.

Second, the memory controller translates memory access requests into appropriate DRAM operations. It converts the requests into commands that can be executed by the DRAM modules.

Third, the memory controller handles scheduling and reordering of memory access sequences, if necessary. This optimization aims to increase the number of row-buffer hits and maximize the utilization of the memory bus bandwidth. Additionally, it implements page distribution policies among memory banks to enhance memory access efficiency.

Finally, the memory controller manages the power consumption of the DRAM modules through various power management techniques. For more-detailed information on this topic, readers can refer to [70] and [147].

In addition to the page offset region, the memory address also requires a bank index region to map the appropriate bank before locating the requested page. In the case of a cache miss, if the missed cache block is present in the row-buffer of the mapped bank, it can be quickly delivered to the CPU via the memory bus. However, if the missed cache block is not in the row-buffer, resulting in a row-buffer miss, the memory controller takes the necessary steps to retrieve it from the memory bank. The process of delivering a missed cache block from a memory bank to the CPU/caches involves four steps, as illustrated in Figure 3.16.

1. **Refresh** Capacitors in the relevant area of the DRAM are charged timely.
2. **Row access** A row access is performed to select the corresponding page and place it into the row-buffer after the memory cells are fully charged.
3. **Column access** A column access is made within the row-buffer to select the specific cache block.
4. **Transfer** The selected cache block is transferred to the CPU/caches via the memory bus.

The time taken for the first three steps is referred to as the "DRAM latency," while the time required to deliver the cache block to the CPU/cache through the memory bus is known as the "bus bandwidth time." Although bus bandwidth has significantly improved over time, the improvement of DRAM latency has been at a very slow pace. Consequently, the latency associated with a row-buffer hit is much lower than that of a row-buffer miss, with a potential difference of up to 67 percent [142]. It is worth noting that each refresh operation covers multiple memory rows (pages), and the memory controller issues refresh at an average rate of less than 8 µs due to frequent accesses to the DRAM.

Figure 3.17 illustrates multiple operation sequences that encompass the entire memory hierarchy, including MMU/OS, TLB, hardware caches, main memory, and disk. In the case of a cache miss, the cache block is always delivered from the row-buffer of the main memory. If the physical memory address is not present in the page table, the OS initiates its page fault handler to request the data from the disk.

In Figure 3.17, the hardware cache is referred to as a "physically indexed cache" because its cache mapping is based on the physical memory address. Specifically, the cache is positioned between the TLB and the main memory. An alternative cache design option is the "virtually indexed cache," which stores data in the virtual address space. A virtually indexed cache is situated between the CPU and the MMU/OS. With a virtually indexed cache, the CPU can directly access data from the cache without undergoing the virtual-to-physical address translation performed by the MMU. However, in this book, our focus is solely on the physically indexed cache.

Reducing DRAM latency is a crucial objective, and it can be achieved by maximizing row-buffer hits during memory accesses. From a DRAM architecture perspective, a row-buffer hit occurs when the requested data are already present in the row-buffer,

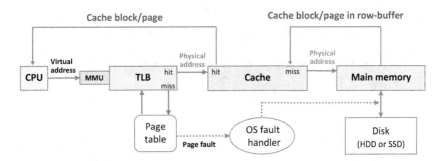

Figure 3.17 Data flows in the entire memory hierarchy starting from virtual addresses are controlled and passed through several critical hardware and software components including MMU, OS, TLB, page table, hardware caches, main memory, and hard disks. The cache is a physically indexed cache because it is in the physical memory address space.

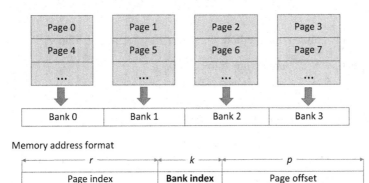

Figure 3.18 The bank index bits are located between the page index and the page offset for the conventional memory page interleaving. For the page interleaving in this four-bank memory, bank index bits $k = 2$.

eliminating the need for precharging and row access operations. On the other hand, a row-buffer miss happens when the requested data resides in a different page within the same memory bank, requiring the memory controller to perform refresh and row access operations to fetch the data.

When a sequence of memory accesses repeatedly targets the same page in the row-buffer, it results in a series of row-buffer hits. This situation is advantageous as it avoids the overhead of precharging and row access, significantly reducing DRAM latency. In contrast, row-buffer misses occur when the memory accesses are directed to different pages within the same memory bank, necessitating the retrieval of data from the memory cells, leading to increased DRAM latency.

The allocation of memory pages in multiple memory banks is determined by a memory page interleaving method. In the conventional approach illustrated in Figure 3.18, four memory banks (0, 1, 2, and 3) are utilized to store the memory pages. A subset of the memory address, represented by k bits, is designated as the bank index. In Figure 3.18, k is set to 2.

(a) Memory address format for page interleaving in memory banks

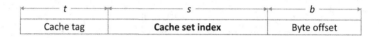

(b) Memory address format for cache mapping

Figure 3.19 Comparing the memory address format for page interleaving in memory banks in (a), and the memory address format for cache mapping in (b), we determine a conflict symmetry between the last-level cache and the row-buffer in DRAM memory.

With this interleaving method, the pages are allocated as follows.

- Pages 0, 4, 8, . . ., are assigned to bank 0.
- Pages 1, 5, 9, . . ., are assigned to bank 1.
- Pages 2, 6, 10, . . ., are assigned to bank 2.
- Pages 3, 7, 11, . . ., are assigned to bank 3.

The bank index is crucial for identifying the appropriate bank when multiple banks are present. However, if there is only one bank available, the bank index is not necessary, and the page index bits will be represented by $r + k$ in Figure 3.18.

The memory address format for page interleaving in Figure 3.19(a) provides insights into the conditions for row-buffer hits or misses. Considering the condition changes of both bank index and page index for a sequence memory accesses, we obtain the following four results.

1. If both the bank index and the page index in the memory addresses remain unchanged, the accesses consistently hit the same memory page in the row-buffer of the same memory bank.
2. If the memory bank index changes, while the page index remains the same, the memory accesses hit row-buffers in different memory banks. This enables concurrent access among the memory banks.
3. On the other hand, if the bank index remains unchanged, but the page index changes from one access to another, the page in the row-buffer of the same bank is consistently replaced in each access, leading to row-buffer misses.
4. If both the bank index and the page index change across the sequence of memory accesses, row-buffer misses may occur in different memory banks. Owing to the uncertain dynamics in this situation, we will specifically focus on the condition of row-buffer misses in a single memory bank.

Figure 3.19(b) illustrates the memory address format for cache mapping, allowing us to compare it with the memory address format for memory page interleaving in

Figure 3.19(a). By examining these two address formats, we can understand the behavior in both the cache domain and the DRAM memory domain for a given memory address.

In cache mapping, a cache conflict occurs when multiple memory addresses share the same cache index but have different tags. On the other hand, a row-buffer conflict leading to a miss happens when multiple memory accessing addresses share the same bank index but have different page indices.

By comparing Figures 3.19(a) and (b), we can observe that the bank index bits are a subset of the cache set index bits, and the cache tag bits are a subset of the page index bits. Consequently, if two addresses experience a conflict miss in the cache, they will also encounter a row-buffer conflict miss. This implies the presence of conflict symmetry between hardware caches and the row-buffer in DRAM memory through conventional memory page interleaving.

The conflict symmetry between hardware caches and the row-buffer in DRAM memory can be disrupted by employing a permutation-based page interleaving technique [142]. Figure 3.20 illustrates this approach, which utilizes a bit-wise "exclusive or" (XOR) gate to combine the low-order k bits of the cache tag and k bits of the bank index as inputs, resulting in a new bank index of k bits. The XOR gate performs a bit-wise comparison, generating a "1" if the corresponding bits are different and a "0" if they are the same. By using the low-order k bits of the tag to modify the bank index, the XOR gate introduces variation in the bank index, addressing the conflict source arising from cache conflicts based on tag differences. Moreover, XOR operations are highly efficient and have minimal associated latency and hardware costs. For further information on the unique properties of XOR operations, readers may refer to [126].

It is important to note that the memory addresses themselves are not modified; only a new bank index is generated for each memory access. The XOR gate is implemented within the memory controller to permute the memory page interleaving scheme across

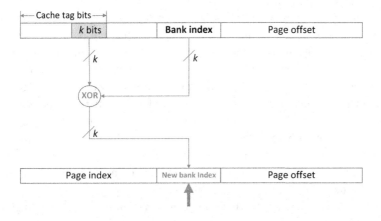

Figure 3.20 The permutation-based page interleaving technique uses a bit-wise XOR gate to generate a new memory bank index for each memory access, breaking the symmetry of conflicts between the last-level cache and the row-buffer in each memory bank.

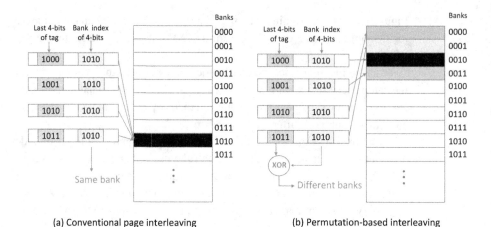

(a) Conventional page interleaving   (b) Permutation-based interleaving

Figure 3.21 A comparison between the conventional page interleaving in (a) and the permutation-based interleaving in (b) explains property 1 of the permutation method: The bit-wise XOR operations redistribute a sequence of conflicting page addresses to different memory banks.

memory banks. The overhead introduced by the XOR operation, both in terms of latency and hardware cost, is negligible. As a result, this technique has become widely adopted in memory controllers for both general-purpose and embedded processors.

The permutation-based interleaving technique exhibits three unique properties. Property 1 can be illustrated by considering the same sequence of four memory accesses. Figures 3.21(a) and (b) provide an explanation. In this scenario, the 4-bit bank index remains constant for each access, while the low-order 4-bit cache tags differ for each access. With conventional page interleaving, all of these accesses are mapped to the same memory bank, and each access corresponds to a distinct page. Consequently, row-buffer conflicts occur, resulting in access misses, as depicted in Figure 3.21(a).

By employing the permutation-based interleaving, the conflicting addresses are distributed across different memory banks, thereby satisfying property 1, as shown in Figure 3.21(b). This redistribution of conflicting addresses helps alleviate row-buffer conflicts and reduces the number of access misses. In other words, under conventional page interleaving in Figure 3.21(a), memory accesses within a page are confined to a single memory bank. This arrangement can lead to potential bottlenecks and limited bandwidth when multiple memory accesses occur concurrently. However, by employing the permutation-based interleaving in Figure 3.21(b), pages are distributed across different memory banks. As a result, memory accesses within a page can be performed concurrently across multiple banks, leveraging the full memory bandwidth and ensuring the completeness of memory accesses within each page.

Figures 3.22(a) and (b) provide an explanation of property 2, which highlights the preservation of the completeness of memory accesses within a page through the use of permutation-based interleaving. In this context, "completeness" refers to the ability to access all the data within a given memory page without missing any elements.

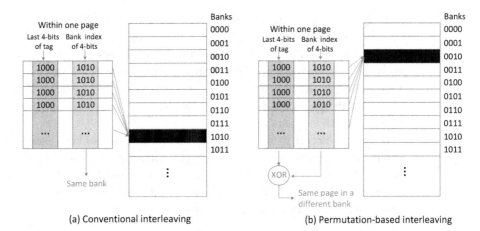

(a) Conventional interleaving   (b) Permutation-based interleaving

Figure 3.22 A comparison between the conventional page interleaving in (a) and the permutation page interleaving in (b) explains property 2 of the permutation method: The bit-wise XOR operations do not change the completeness of a page, but distribute it to a different memory bank.

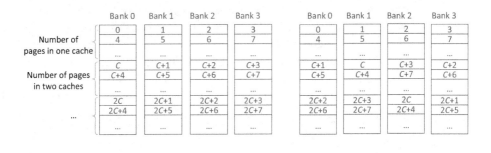

(a) Conventional interleaving   (b) Permutation-based interleaving

Figure 3.23 A comparison of the page interleaving orders between the conventional page interleaving in (a) and the permutation page interleaving in (b) explains property 3 of the permutation method: Both interleaving methods uniformly interleave pages among all the memory banks. Variable C is the cache capacity in a unit of page.

Thus, property 2 ensures that the permutation-based interleaving technique preserves the completeness of memory accesses within a page by redistributing pages to different memory banks.

We can illustrate property 3 by comparing conventional interleaving and permutation-based interleaving in Figures 3.23(a) and (b). Property 3 highlights that despite the different page orders in memory banks between the two interleaving methods, both methods uniformly distribute pages among all the memory banks. In the figures, the variable C represents the capacity in pages of the last-level cache (LLC).

In Figure 3.23(a), which represents conventional interleaving, the pages are allocated to memory banks in a contiguous manner. Each memory bank contains a consecutive set of pages, ensuring a linear mapping between the page indices and the memory bank indices. This results in a straightforward and evenly distributed allocation of pages across the memory banks.

In contrast, Figure 3.23(b) represents the permutation-based interleaving, where the pages are distributed using the XOR permutation technique. As a result, the page orders in the memory banks differ from the conventional interleaving. However, it is important to note that the permutation-based interleaving still achieves a uniform distribution of pages among all the memory banks.

Therefore, property 3 emphasizes that both conventional interleaving and permutation-based interleaving techniques uniformly interleave pages across all memory banks, albeit with different page orders in the banks. The ultimate goal is to ensure efficient and balanced utilization of the memory system, especially in the context of the LLC with a capacity denoted by variable C.

3.6   Managing the Shared Last-Level Cache by OS in Multicores

A multicore processor, comprising two or more independent computing cores on a single integrated circuit, is widely used in various applications, including general-purpose computing, embedded systems, and specialized systems [21]. Figure 3.24 illustrates a four-core processor, where each core has its own private L1 and L2 caches and operates autonomously. The LLC, which is the L3 cache, is shared among all the cores. With the availability of affordable DRAM and a 64-bit memory address space, computers can accommodate a large main memory capacity. However, the per-formance bottleneck in modern platforms has shifted from slow I/O devices to high

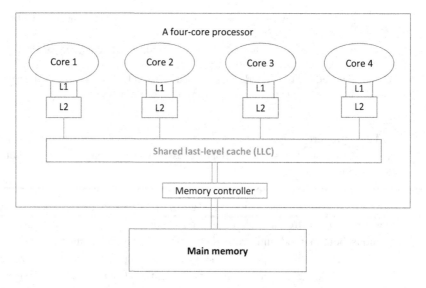

Figure 3.24 Four independent computing units are in this four-core processor, each of which has its own L1 and L2 caches. The LLC is shared by all the 4 cores.

memory access latency. In the presence of cache misses in the LLC caused by multiple independent or dependent processes, all processes require the memory bus to load the requested datasets from DRAM memory, resulting in a memory access bottleneck. Thus, the LLC plays a critical role in multicore systems, particularly for data-intensive applications.

Operating systems ensure conflict-free memory space allocation through the use of a page table per process. The cache controller automatically handles memory-address-based cache mapping. However, the management of hardware cache space by the OS, as implied by the section title, is a separate consideration. In this section, we will explore how the OS manages the allocation of hardware cache space and will present a relevant case study to illustrate this concept.

3.6.1   Memory Address: The Mapping between Memory and Cache Spaces

Figure 3.25 illustrates the relationships among the virtual address space, the physical memory address space, and the cache space. At the top of Figure 3.25, a program is composed of multiple virtual pages, represented by the virtual address format. In an OS class, we often discuss virtual memory and how these virtual pages are translated by the MMU and OS into their corresponding physical page addresses, as depicted in the middle of Figure 3.25 using the physical address format.

In this context, we want to introduce the cache space, which is represented at the bottom of Figure 3.25. Although it belongs to the domain of architecture rather than the OS class, understanding cache space is crucial. For a physically indexed cache, the physical memory address is also used for cache mapping. Figure 3.25 includes

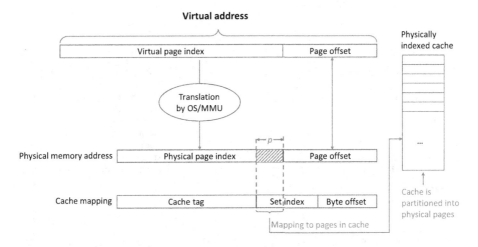

Figure 3.25 The relationships among a virtual address space, the physical memory address space, and the memory-address based cache mapping are presented, where the p bits in the memory address can be used by the OS to determine the memory page allocations in cache regions. In this way, the OS can assign each process with a set of memory pages in an independent cache region without any conflict with others.

two vertical dot-lines. The right dot-line starts from the end of the page offset and extends vertically down to the set-index region of the cache mapping space. This dot-line suggests that the cache block size should match the memory page size, resulting in a uniform page size across virtual space, physical memory space, and the physically indexed cache space.

The left dot-line in Figure 3.25 begins at the end of the cache set index and extends vertically up to the physical memory page index region in the memory space. This dot-line represents the cache capacity in bytes without considering byte offset bits, in blocks with byte offset bits, or in pages with page offset bits. As a result, the bits between the two dot-lines directly map each of the 2^p cache sets into the cache space, where p denotes the number of bits between the two dot-lines, and each set corresponds to an n-way set-associative cache.

While the OS cannot directly allocate the LLC, it can control the allocation of pages in memory through virtual-to-physical address translation. Since the OS assigns physical memory pages to each process, it can group these pages into independent cache regions and assign them to different processes. By systematically partitioning the shared LLC, the OS eliminates cache space conflicts among multiple processes. The p bits between the two dot-lines are also referred to as page color bits, which assign cache sets different colors [80] in early works on multiprogramming in a uniprocessor. The OS assigns a unique set of colors to each process, ensuring that the colors are not shared among processes.

Figure 3.26 presents an illustration of the LLC-aware page allocation method employed by the OS to partition the LLC into two regions, each assigned to a specific process along with its corresponding physical pages. Operating system kernels for multicore processors have implemented both static and dynamic page allocation methods [92].

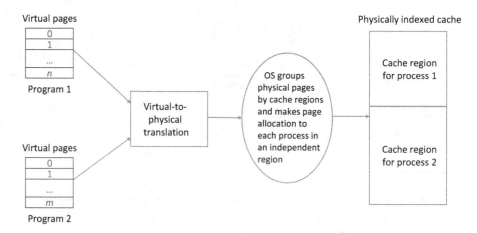

Figure 3.26 The added function in an OS is to group physical pages by cache regions and make page allocation to each process in an independent region. In this example, the OS is able to allocate a group pages to process 1 in cache region 1 and another group of pages to process 2 in another region.

In the static allocation method, each process is allocated a fixed number of pages within a cache region before its execution. On the other hand, the dynamic allocation method allows the OS to adjust its page allocation policy during execution. By observing the memory access patterns, the OS can adaptively allocate more pages for frequently accessed data, while allocating only a small number of pages for one-time or infrequently accessed data. This dynamic adjustment ensures efficient utilization of cache resources based on the specific needs of different processes and their memory access behaviors.

3.6.2 The Shared Cache Awareness in Query Optimization on Multicores

The shared LLC in multicore processors can be considered a double-edged sword for DBMS transactions. On the positive side, the LLC provides a shared space where multiple queries can access common data. When concurrent queries access shared tuples and index data in a database, the LLC enables efficient data sharing among multiple cores, optimizing cache utilization and reducing unnecessary memory accesses. This allows queries to benefit from cached data loaded by other queries, improving overall performance.

However, on the negative side, the LLC can also become a source of conflicts among multiple queries. Private data structures specific to each query, such as a hash table used in the hash join operator, are not shareable among queries. As a result, different queries may contend for cache space, leading to cache conflicts and evictions in the LLC. These conflicts are particularly problematic for frequently accessed data structures during query execution, as they can result in a large number of cache misses and increased access latency.

Therefore, while the shared LLC offers opportunities for data sharing and performance gains, it also presents challenges related to cache conflicts and eviction, especially for private data structures that cannot be shared among queries. Efficient management of cache space and minimizing conflicts are crucial for optimizing DBMS transaction performance in multicore processors.

Although hardware caches are not capable of understanding data access patterns during query execution, a DBMS operating at the user level has a clear understanding of the access patterns for a given query execution plan. However, the DBMS does not have direct control over hardware cache allocation. To address this challenge, a system for minimizing cache conflicts for databases (MCC-DB) has been designed and implemented [87]. This system focuses on effective interactions among three levels of abstraction: (1) the DBMS at the user level, (2) the operating system (OS) at the resource allocation level between the DBMS and the hardware architecture, and (3) the hardware cache management.

By leveraging these three levels, MCC-DB aims to minimize cache conflicts and optimize cache utilization for database systems. The DBMS provides insights into data access patterns and query execution requirements. The OS plays a crucial role in managing resource allocation, including page-level allocation and cache partitioning, to mitigate cache conflicts among concurrent queries. Finally, the hardware cache management, guided by the information provided by the DBMS and OS, can make informed decisions on cache eviction policies, replacement strategies, and cache coherence mechanisms to improve overall performance.

By integrating these three levels of abstraction, MCC-DB seeks to bridge the gap between the user-level DBMS, the resource allocation level of the OS, and the hardware cache management. This enables more-effective cache utilization and reduces cache conflicts in database systems, ultimately improving their performance.

Data blocks in queries exhibit varying levels of locality, which can be measured by how frequently they are reused during query execution. For instance, a hash table used in a hash join operation demonstrates strong locality, as the data it contains is repeatedly accessed. On the other hand, tuples accessed during a sequential table scan exhibit weak or no locality, as they are typically accessed only once. Owing to these differences in locality strength, the impact of cache space allocation varies across different queries.

To address this issue, the cache allocation policy for a query process needs to take into account its locality strength. The challenge lies in enabling a DBMS in the user domain to effectively utilize the shared LLC of a multicore processor, which is managed by the on-chip hardware controller operating at a lower level of abstraction. In this context, MCC-DB, a database system, leverages the knowledge of query execution patterns possessed by the DBMS to guide the OS in making informed decisions regarding LLC space allocation at runtime.

An enhanced OS mechanism is employed by MCC-DB to allocate LLC space among concurrent queries based on their locality strengths. It relies on the collaboration between the DBMS and the OS to manage hardware cache space allocations through two separate software components. By utilizing the information provided by the DBMS about query execution patterns, the OS can dynamically allocate LLC space to queries, prioritizing those with stronger locality. This approach allows for more efficient utilization of the shared LLC and helps mitigate cache conflicts, ultimately improving overall performance in data-intensive workloads.

DBMS Guidance

Given the DBMS's ability to predict data access patterns during query execution, it becomes possible to identify the locality strengths of data blocks. To effectively utilize this information, the DBMS incorporates a query optimizer and an execution scheduler. The query optimizer selects query plans and categorizes them as either having strong or weak locality, forming a distinction between the two. Subsequently, the scheduler determines a combination of corunning queries based on their locality strengths, with the aim of minimizing LLC conflicts.

It is important to note that running strong locality queries alongside weak locality queries can have a negative impact on the performance of the former, which is not desirable. To address this issue, MCC-DB recommends grouping all the weak locality queries together, allocating each of them a limited space. By doing so, the performance impact is minimized since weak locality queries have less influence on each other. On the other hand, strong locality queries are grouped together to corun, enabling them to fit within the LLC space allocated to them. This approach effectively reduces cache misses and optimizes performance for queries with strong locality.

In summary, MCC-DB leverages the DBMS's predictive capabilities to distinguish the locality strengths of data blocks. By grouping queries with similar locality characteristics, it optimizes LLC utilization, ensuring that weak locality queries do not significantly impact strong locality queries. This approach enhances the overall performance of data-intensive workloads by minimizing cache misses and improving data access efficiency.

OS Actions

After concurrent queries are scheduled to run on a multicore processor, MCC-DB employs an enhanced OS mechanism for the partitioning of the LLC cache [92]. This mechanism ensures that each query receives the necessary cache allocation, taking into account the locality strengths of the queries. Strong locality queries are allocated a larger space in the LLC cache, while weak locality queries are allocated with a minimum amount of space.

By allocating cache space according to the locality strengths of the queries, MCC-DB maximizes the utilization of the LLC cache and effectively reduces cache misses. Strong locality queries, which benefit from frequent data reuse, are granted a larger cache space to minimize cache evictions and improve overall performance. On the other hand, weak locality queries, which exhibit minimal or no data reuse, are allocated a smaller cache space to mitigate the impact of their cache misses.

Through this approach, MCC-DB optimizes the cache allocation within the LLC cache, ensuring that each query receives an appropriate cache space based on its locality characteristics. By minimizing cache conflicts and enhancing cache utilization, MCC-DB significantly improves the efficiency and performance of concurrent query execution in data-intensive workloads.

3.7   Buffer Caches in Memory

In computer systems, an OS-managed "cache" in memory is utilized to enhance disk performance. As discussed in Chapter 2, the storage system operates on a block-level granularity. Data transfers between memory and storage are performed in fixed-size units called "blocks." In physical memory, the space allocation to user programs is managed using pages as the basic unit. On the other hand, blocks serve as the disk access units.

When a user process requests to read a sequence of logical blocks from a disk drive, the OS interacts with the disk controller to locate the corresponding physical blocks on the disk and load them into memory for the executing process. The OS designates a dedicated region known as the *buffer cache* to manage the disk blocks that are loaded into memory. The purpose of the buffer cache is to store recently and frequently accessed data blocks, aiming to reduce the reliance on slower disk accesses.

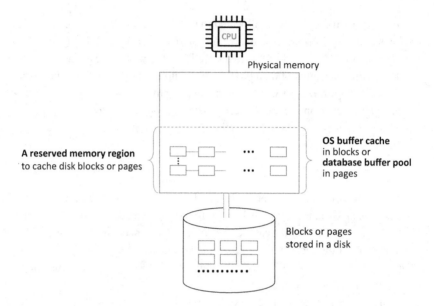

Figure 3.27 The concept of an OS buffer cache or a database buffer pool is presented. There is a one-to-one relationship between a data block in the disk and its block copy in the buffer cache, or a page in the disk and its page copy in the buffer pool.

Ideally, the OS maintains a buffer cache that effectively retains storage data that is likely to be reused in the near future. Similarly, in a database system, a *buffer pool* is a reserved memory region used to cache table and index data after retrieving them from disks. There are two key distinctions between a database buffer pool and an OS buffer cache. First, the buffer pool is managed by the database system, whereas the buffer cache is under the purview of the OS. Second, the granularity of the buffer pool is typically defined in terms of pages, such as 8 KB, 16 KB, or 32 KB in systems like IBM DB2, while the buffer cache operates at the block level as determined by the OS and its file system. For instance, a common configuration in Linux employs a 1–4 KB as the buffer cache block size.

Figure 3.27 visually illustrates the concept of a buffer cache or buffer pool, high-lighting their respective roles in managing disk blocks and enhancing data access performance.

In the context of the buffer cache managed by the OS, the buffer cache holds disk blocks that are mapped from requested logical blocks. Essentially, the buffer cache serves as a temporary storage location in memory for copies of disk blocks. Another term used in the buffer cache is called *block buffer* that is a specific area of memory region within the buffer cache allocated to hold a single block of data. The manage-ment of the buffer cache involves keeping track of each block using a linked structure consisting of multiple block buffers.

Each block buffer comprises two crucial components: the buffer header and a pointer within the header to the data content of the corresponding data block. When the OS receives a request to read or write disk data, such as a file, it initially reads the inode into memory. The inode provides the necessary metadata about a disk block, including the disk device ID, the block number, the file size, and the indexing structure for loading file blocks from the disk. This information is then used to fill the buffer header, which holds the metadata of the disk block.

The buffer header also maintains the status of the data block, indicating whether it is valid, whether it is being accessed by other processes, and other relevant information. Additionally, the header includes pointers that link to other block buffers in both forward and backward directions within the linked structure. These pointers facilitate efficient navigation and management of the buffer cache.

When a read request for data blocks on disks is received, the OS begins by searching the buffer cache for the requested data blocks. If the data blocks are found in the buffer cache, the request can be quickly fulfilled without the need for a slow disk access. However, if a buffer cache miss occurs and the data blocks are not present in the cache, the OS will communicate with the disk controller to load the data blocks from the disk into the buffer cache.

In the case of writing data blocks to the disk, the OS first checks the buffer cache to determine if the blocks are already available. If the blocks are found in the buffer cache, they are updated accordingly. In a "writethrough" policy, the changes made to the blocks in the buffer cache are immediately propagated to the disk as well. Conversely, in a "writeback" policy, the updated data blocks in the buffer cache are marked as "dirty" and kept in memory. The actual write to the disk occurs later, either when the blocks are evicted from the cache or when a specific write operation to disk is triggered. This delayed write allows for efficient management of the buffer cache, as the blocks can be written to the disk in batches.

In cases where the requested data blocks are not found in the buffer cache, they need to be read from the disk into the buffer cache first. Subsequently, any modifications made to these blocks are overwritten in both memory and the disk, ensuring consistency between the two storage locations.

3.8   Key–Value Store in Memory

After discussing OS buffer caches, we would like to introduce a user-managed software solution that can also serve as a cache. This solution is based on a data structure called a key–value store (KV-store), which is managed by a hash table of a fixed size. The hash table stores keys, each of which is associated with a corresponding value. A hash function is used to directly map each key to a specific location in the hash table. This mapping is not order-preserving but occurs in a random manner within the scope of the hash table. This data structure is also called *key–value pair record file*.

The value associated with each key can represent the desired content itself or serve as an address pointing to the location of the content. This straightforward data structure provides an average time complexity of O(1) and has found extensive use in various data processing applications for storing, retrieving, and updating data. In a KV-store, each key must be unique, while the values can be of different types, including integers, strings, or even complex data structures such as sets of data or files. One notable advantage of KV-stores is their flexibility in accommodating different data types for the values they store.

Let us now discuss the three fundamental operations supported by a KV-store.

- GET (Key): to retrieve the value of the Key;
- SET/PUT/ADD/REPLACE (Key, Value): write the key–value pair in the hash table; and
- DELETE (Key): delete the key–value pair in the hash table.

Currently, the prevalent approach is to store large hash tables and extensive amounts of value contents in DRAM memory, which can also be extended to distributed clusters. This practice is commonly known as in-memory computing. In a KV-store, data retrieval is typically performed through an exact match on the key, ensuring equal treatment for each individual read and write operation. However, when it comes to range queries that aim to retrieve all keys with values falling between specified upper and lower boundaries, such as in a column access operation on a database table, conventional KV-stores do not offer efficient support for these types of operations.

3.9   LSM-Tree vs. In-Memory Buffer Caches

Figure 3.27 illustrates a one-to-one mapping relationship between data blocks in an OS buffer cache and the corresponding disk blocks. In Chapter 2, we explored the LSM-tree data structure, which is designed independently by storing data in a sorted order across multiple levels. The top level (C_0) resides in memory, while the lower levels are stored on disk. It is important to note that this top level C_0 in memory is unrelated to the buffer cache or buffer pool. Now, let us delve into the implications of using buffer caches when the underlying storage engine is based on the LSM-tree, particularly considering the frequent occurrence of compaction operations. In this case study, we only consider that the LSM-tree is constructed on the foundation of the file system, and the buffer cache plays a crucial role in caching the data blocks retrieved from various layers of the LSM-tree, which are stored on disk.

3.9.1   LSM-Tree-Induced Buffer Cache Invalidation

Figure 3.28 depicts a four-level LSM-tree structure (C_0 to C_3) along with a buffer cache. The LSM-tree's levels C_0 and the buffer cache reside in memory, while the remaining three levels of the LSM-tree are stored on disk. In this scenario, the data blocks a, b, and c located at levels C_1, C_2, and C_3 of the LSM-tree, respectively, are accessed by a user process and cached in the buffer cache. Subsequent requests for these data blocks will be serviced through in-memory accesses directly from the buffer cache. The OS buffer cache contains cached data blocks/pages that are indexed to their respective data sources on the disk.

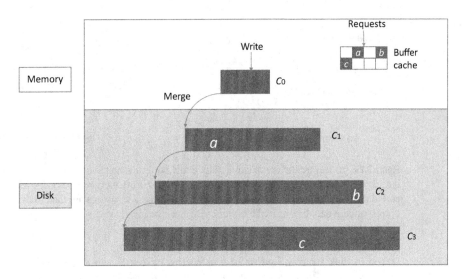

Figure 3.28 A four-level LSM-tree and a buffer cache are presented. The buffer cache has block copies of a, b, and c from C_1, C_2, and C_3 in the disk, respectively.

As an LSM-tree level reaches its capacity, the sorted data blocks in that level undergo a compaction process, resulting in the creation of newly sorted data blocks in the next level. Owing to the frequent occurrence of data writes, compaction operations are performed regularly. During compaction, the disk data are initially loaded into memory for sorting and then written back to the disk. The OS buffer cache is utilized as a temporary storage space for the loaded data blocks during compaction.

One significant challenge posed by LSM-tree structures to the buffer cache is their competition for the limited capacity of the buffer cache with other application processes. In the worst-case scenario, the data blocks requested by application processes can be easily evicted from the buffer cache to make room for the data blocks loaded during a compaction operation. Consequently, LSM-tree compaction operations may lead to capacity misses in the OS buffer cache. To mitigate this issue, a database system named BigTable, which is built upon LSM-tree, implements an application-level database buffer cache exclusively designed to serve queries [32].

As we are aware, compaction operations in LSM-trees frequently reorganize the data blocks stored on disk. Owing to the relocation of source data blocks on the disk, the links to their corresponding copies in the buffer cache become invalid. Consequently, the affected data blocks in the buffer cache are invalidated, resulting in what is known as "LSM-tree compaction induced cache invalidation." This phenomenon leads to a high miss rate in the buffer cache, thereby impacting the performance of the system. This issue arises from the original design of LSM-trees, where the buffer cache was not taken into consideration.

The occurrence of read/write conflicts can be avoided if the LSM-tree is constructed in a dedicated environment where data reading requests from other processes do not occur simultaneously. Essentially, separating the reading operations on the LSM-tree

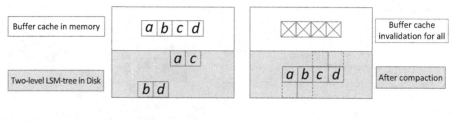

(a) Before the compaction   **(b)** After the compaction

Figure 3.29 (a) Before the compaction, data in the buffer cache have direct links to the source data in the disk. (b) After the compaction, the two levels are merged into one level, and newly sorted data blocks are placed in different locations. The dot squares are the old locations. The correspondent data blocks in the buffer cache must be invalidated.

stored in disk from the writing (constructing) process would eliminate this conflict. To draw an analogy, during the day, a library remains open for readers to borrow books, while in the evening, when the library is closed, new books can be brought in to reorganize the positions of the existing books on the shelves. However, in practical scenarios where LSM-tree construction involves data writes and data access through the buffer cache, it becomes necessary to address this issue if the OS buffer cache continues to be involved in this process.

To illustrate the issue, consider the example depicted in Figure 3.29(a). The frequently requested data blocks a, b, c, and d belong to two LSM levels stored on the disk, with their corresponding disk blocks residing in the buffer cache. However, when these two levels are compacted into a single level, as shown in Figure 3.29(b), the compacted data blocks are written to new locations on the disk. Consequently, although the data contents remain unchanged, the cache data blocks holding a, b, c, and d need to be invalidated by the system because the underlying disk blocks have been relocated. Upon subsequent requests for these data blocks, buffer cache misses occur. The system is then required to load data blocks a, b, c, and d from their new locations on the disk. Additionally, the access information for these blocks is lost due to the changes in their referencing addresses. Compounding the problem, since compaction writes are performed in batches, the resulting buffer cache invalidation and data reloading may occur in bursts, leading to significant periodic performance degradation [124].

3.9.2   Key–Value Caches for LSM-Tree

One solution to address the issues caused by LSM-tree compaction is to bypass the OS buffer cache and use an in-memory KV-store as a cache for reading data blocks of the LSM-tree. This KV-store functions as an independent cache in memory, decoupled from any address indexing to the data source on the disk. When a read access is requested, the KV cache is checked first. If the data are found in the cache, a low-latency read can be performed, resulting in improved performance. In the case of a KV-store cache miss, the data will be retrieved from the LSM-tree on the disk.

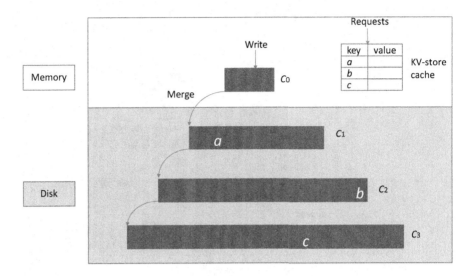

Figure 3.30 A KV-store cache on top of the LSM-tree do not have an indexing relationship to each other: LSM-tree compaction can be done independently without interfering the KV-store cache. As long as the contents of a, b, and c remain the same in the disk, their copies in the KV-store are valid. However, range query performance in KV-store is low.

By utilizing an in-memory KV-store as an independent buffer for the LSM-tree, it remains unaffected by the frequent reorganizations caused by compaction. Figure 3.30 illustrates the absence of an indexing relationship between the KV-store cache and the data source on the disk. Consequently, the cached data in the KV-store is not impacted by LSM-tree compaction operations.

However, it is important to note that the KV-store may not be efficient for range queries, as discussed in Section 3.8 of this chapter. While there are proposals to enhance the support for range queries in a KV-store, they typically come with additional software costs in terms of data structure complexity and increased computing overhead [113].

3.9.3   Lazy Compaction in LSM-Tree

To mitigate the impact of compaction-induced cache invalidation in the buffer cache, another approach is to reduce the frequency of data reorganization activities in the disk. This can be achieved by employing a lazy compaction method [71]. In this method, instead of fully sorting the data blocks in a tree level in disk, they are segmented into multiple sorted datasets.

Figure 3.31 illustrates the lazy compaction approach. Data blocks a, b, and c are cached in the buffer cache, and their corresponding data sources reside in LSM-tree levels C_1, C_2, and C_3, respectively. When level C_1 becomes full, the data in this level are sorted and combined into a single dataset. However, instead of performing a compaction operation with level C_2, the sorted dataset from C_1 is appended to the existing

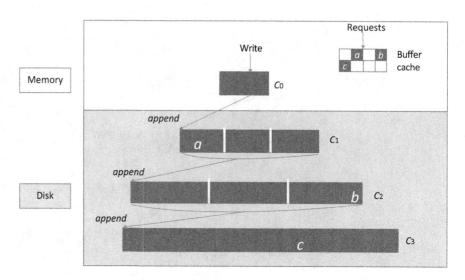

Figure 3.31 With a lazy compaction, each disk level consists of segmented sorted datasets. As level C_1 is full, the segmented sorted datasets are merged into a single sorted dataset, which is appended to the existing datasets in level C_2. After then, level C_1 is empty, the cached a in the buffer cache is invalidated, but b remains valid.

datasets in C_2. This results in each level, except for C_0, containing segmented datasets rather than a single sorted dataset.

After the append operation from C_1 to C_2 is completed, level C_1 is once again ready to accept data from C_0. Since the location of data block a has changed on the disk, the cached copy of data block a in the buffer cache becomes invalidated. However, data block b in level C_2 remains in the same position, and its cached copy b in the buffer cache remains valid. In summary, when level C_i is full (where $i > 0$), the data blocks are sorted into a single dataset and appended to the existing datasets in level C_{i+1}. The cached data blocks in the buffer cache from level C_i will be invalidated, while those from level C_{i+1} will remain unaffected. This reduces the frequency of buffer cache invalidation caused by LSM-tree compaction.

However, the performance improvement in the buffer cache comes at the cost of performance degradation in two other aspects. First, because the data blocks within each level are not fully sorted, range queries conducted within any level may require multiple disk seeks, negatively impacting the range query performance of the LSM-tree with lazy compaction. Second, the the full compaction process also eliminate redundant data blocks. Thus, for workloads with a large proportion of repeated data, the lazy compaction method may not eliminate redundant data in a timely manner.

3.10   Log-Structured and Buffered-Merge-Tree: LSbM-Tree

The RUM conjecture [8] addresses the design of a storage system considering three critical parameters: read latency (R), update overhead or write performance (U), and memory and storage cost (M). Each parameter represents an area of optimization: minimizing read latency, maximizing write throughput, and minimizing memory/storage space, respectively. According to the conjecture, optimizing any two of these parameters comes at the expense of the third one.

The lazy compaction approach in the LSM-tree retains the high write throughput and keeps the storage cost unchanged. While it reduces the read latency in the buffer cache by mitigating compaction-induced cache invalidation, it increases the read latency for range queries on the disk. The question arises: Can we reduce read latency in the buffer cache, maintain range query performance in LSM-tree on the disk, and preserve the high throughput of LSM-tree by utilizing additional disk space?

This question is addressed by the log-structured buffer-merged-tree (LSbM-tree) [124], which employs extra disk space for compaction operations. The LSbM-tree aims to achieve all three objectives simultaneously. It reduces read latency in the buffer cache, preserves range query performance in the LSM-tree on the disk, and maintains the high throughput of the LSM-tree, albeit at the cost of additional disk space utilization.

The LSbM-tree introduces the concept of a compaction buffer in addition to the foundation LSM-tree. The compaction buffer is an on-disk component that works in conjunction with the buffer cache in memory. The LSbM-tree structure consists of two main parts: the foundation LSM-tree and the compaction buffer. The buffer cache directly indexes the cached data to the data sources in the compaction buffer.

In Figure 3.32, the LSbM-tree data structure is illustrated. The buffer cache holds data blocks a, b, and c, which correspond to their root data sources in LSM-tree levels

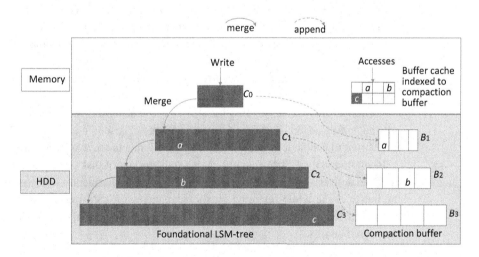

Figure 3.32 The basic structure of the LSbM-tree. The foundation LSM-tree is retained, and a compaction buffer in the disk is added. After a compaction in the LSM-tree between levels C_i and C_{i+1}, the sorted dataset in level C_i is appended to compaction buffer B_{i+1}. Buffer cache in the memory is indexed to the compaction buffer where lazy compaction reduces the frequency of data location changes, improving buffer cache hit rates. Range queries will be served in the foundation LSM-tree.

C_1, C_2, and C_3, respectively. The compaction buffer is an integral part of the LSM-tree and stores the data blocks a and b as well, as depicted in the example. The foundation LSM-tree is constructed independently, following standard merging and compaction operations from level C_0 to the other levels, without interacting with the buffer cache.

The focus is on the creation of the compaction buffer. The size of the compaction buffer at level B_i corresponds to the size of level C_i in the foundation LSM-tree, where $i \geq 1$. When level C_0 becomes full, in addition to the standard merging and compaction operations that move the single sorted dataset to level C_1 in the foundation LSM-tree, it also appends the sorted dataset to the compaction buffer at level B_1. Similarly, when level C_1 is full, the sorted dataset from C_1 is appended to the compaction buffer at level B_2, in addition to the merging and compaction operations to level C_2.

The key difference between the data appending operations for C_0 to B_1 and C_1 to B_2 lies in the data movement. The former involves moving data from memory to disk, while the latter does not require any data movement. This is because the sorted dataset in C_1 is already present on the disk, and B_2 only needs a pointer, such as an inode, to reference the dataset. Consequently, B_2 consists of multiple pointers to the sorted datasets from C_1, forming the appended datasets.

To summarize, the compaction buffer in the LSbM-tree is created without any data movement, except for the top-level B_1, which requires additional space to accommodate the pointers and references.

The LSbM-tree effectively utilizes disk space by maintaining frequently accessed data in the compaction buffer while evicting inactive data blocks. The goal is to minimize data movement at each level, thereby significantly reducing buffer cache invalidation operations.

When accessing data in the LSbM-tree, the buffer cache is checked first, and a cache hit allows for fast in-memory access. If there is a cache miss, the search proceeds to the compaction buffer on the disk, where frequently accessed data are stored. The accessing record within each appended dataset is tracked for replacement purposes, ensuring that the actively and recently accessed data blocks are retained in the compaction buffer.

For range query accesses that miss the buffer cache, the foundation LSM-tree is utilized, taking advantage of the fully sorted dataset present in each level. This allows LSbM-tree to handle long sequences of range queries in the disk efficiently.

In summary, the LSbM-tree utilizes a small amount of disk space as a compaction buffer to deliver high and stable performance. It serves frequently accessed data from the buffer cache while retaining all the advantages of LSM-tree for write-intensive workloads, including efficient handling of long sequences of range queries in the LSM-tree stored on disk.

3.11   Summary

Each program in a computer system has its own isolated virtual address space in a storage region, which is connected to its corresponding physical memory space and cache space through physical memory addresses. The cache, positioned between the CPU and main memory, stores recently used data to expedite memory access. Typically, more than 80 percent of a processor chip is dedicated to caching mechanisms. When the CPU needs to access data, it first checks the cache for its availability.

In this discussion, we focus on physically indexed caches, where cache mapping is based on memory addresses. We introduce three advancements in memory systems, all of which share the same starting point: the memory address.

The multicolumn cache operates within the framework of a set-associative cache. It utilizes the *direct-mapped bits* in the tag section to perform a direct-mapped access within one of the ways in a set. With additional hardware support, the multicolumn cache achieves an average latency as low as that of a direct-mapped cache while maintaining a low miss rate characteristic of a set-associative cache.

The conflict symmetry between the LLC and the row-buffer in DRAM arises due to the intersection between the page index bits in the memory address format, which facilitate page interleaving among memory banks, and the tag bits used for cache mapping based on the same memory address. This symmetry is broken by employing the XOR permutation to generate a new bank index for each memory access. As data accesses from multiple processes to the LLC in multicore systems start conflicting with each other, it becomes crucial to have control over cache allocation for each process.

Another approach in memory systems involves enabling the OS to allocate cache space. Since cache usage and cache mapping can indirectly be controlled by the OS, which manages the memory address space, it becomes possible to assign a group of pages in an independent cache region to each process. This allows the OS to manage data movement in both cache and memory at a page granularity.

Memory access latency has remained relatively constant over the years, and the three technical approaches in memory systems discussed in this chapter aim to reduce latency by leveraging various memory address formats.

We have studied the basic structure of buffer caches and KV-stores, which are both managed in memory but by different entities: the OS and users, respectively. To demonstrate the impact of this independent storage structure on the performance of the two in-memory caches, we present the LSM-tree as a case study. Subsequently, we introduce the LSbM-tree, which utilizes additional disk space to mitigate conflicts between the LSM-tree and the buffer cache. This approach allows us to retain the advantages of both the LSM-tree and the buffer cache.

4 Buffer Replacement Algorithms

In Chapters 1 and 2, we examined the memory hierarchy within a general-purpose computer system. This hierarchy comprises various small storage buffers, such as the TLB and three levels of caches within the CPU chip, row-buffers within each DRAM bank, a limited space region in the physical memory for storing data and instructions for running multiple programs, a buffer cache in memory for holding disk data blocks, and a cache in the disk controller for buffering data to and from the disk.

When any critical yet small storage component within the memory hierarchy becomes full, the system must decide which data entries to evict in order to make room for newly accessed blocks. In this chapter, the term "data blocks" encompasses cache lines in hardware caches, pages in virtual memory, device blocks for buffer cache, and other similar entities. To facilitate an effective replacement decision, we need to address the following questions.

- What data entries should be selected for eviction?
- Why are these entries chosen?
- How can a replacement policy be implemented based on the "what" and "why" considerations at different levels of the memory hierarchy?

To address these questions, we will examine representative *replacement algorithms* that guide data eviction decisions when a buffer reaches its capacity. In this chapter, the term *buffer* encompasses various types of caches in both hardware and software, serving a general-purpose function. The effectiveness of these replacement algorithms directly impacts data access latency, which plays a crucial role in the overall performance of data-intensive applications. The importance of accessing hits in caches, in row-buffers, in buffer caches, in physical memory, and other buffers are studied in chapter 3.

The design of replacement algorithms is largely machine independent and general purpose, as the nature of data access locality is primarily determined by load and store operations in algorithm design. The implementation of a replacement policy relies on its design, incorporating necessary approximations based on the specific level within the memory hierarchy. Replacement decisions for various components, such as CPU caches, virtual memory, and buffer caches, can be made either in hardware or in software. Hardware-based replacement methods typically involve simple operations and may employ approximations to make efficient decisions. On the other hand, software-based replacement methods offer more flexibility for algorithm optimizations, allowing for more-sophisticated and fine-tuned approaches.

4.1   Least-Recently Used (LRU) Replacement

The study of replacement algorithms can be traced back to L. A. Belady's seminal paper in 1966 [16]. In this paper, Belady defines the replacement problem, establishes the objective of solving this problem, and presents a solution. Later on, other researchers coined the term "least-recently used" (LRU) algorithm to refer to the solution proposed in the paper. The name LRU reflects the algorithm's goal of prioritizing the eviction of blocks with the least likelihood of being accessed in the near future.

Additionally, Belady's paper introduces three categories of replacement algorithms based on assumptions regarding data access patterns and the recording of data access information.

- *Class 1* In the context of the discussed replacement algorithms, it is assumed that data accesses are evenly distributed among all the data blocks throughout the execution of a program. Furthermore, these algorithms do not rely on or require knowledge of the specific data access history.
- *Class 2* Accesses on data blocks are classified into most recently used and others during a program execution. The replacement algorithm is based on the historical records, focusing on protecting the most recently used blocks.
- *Class 3* To maintain the access history of each data block, a record in a separate data structure is kept. Following each access, the accessing records of data blocks are sorted based on their usage order, with the most-recently used (MRU) block at the forefront and the least-recently used block at the end. When the buffer reaches its full capacity, the least-recently used blocks are evicted to accommodate new arrivals.

The Class 1 algorithm, although inconsistent with reality, is primarily used for simulation purposes to evaluate the relationship between the statistical distribution of data accesses during program execution and the corresponding replacement algorithm. On the other hand, the Class 2 algorithm focuses on prioritizing the most-recently accessed blocks, assuming that they are likely to be accessed again in the near future. Building upon Class 2, the Class 3 algorithm serves as an extension and forms the foundation of the LRU algorithm.

The LRU algorithm introduces an additional data structure called an "LRU stack" to dynamically record the access history of each data block, which is crucial for making replacement decisions. The LRU stack maintains a list of accessed blocks in temporal order, with the MRU block at the top and the LRU block at the bottom. When a new block is brought from a lower-level memory hierarchy, it is pushed into the LRU stack as the MRU block, causing other blocks to move down one position. The LRU block at the bottom of the stack becomes the candidate for eviction, and once replaced, it leaves the stack. If a block in the buffer is accessed again, it is promoted to the top of the LRU stack, becoming the new MRU block.

To illustrate the operations of the LRU algorithm, Figure 4.1 provides an example. The LRU stack depicted in Figure 4.1 has four entries, representing the size of the buffer. In the first part of the access sequence, blocks A, B, C, and D are accessed in temporal order. Initially, as shown in Figure 4.1(a), the LRU stack is empty, indicating

The first part of accessing string in its temporal order of blocks A, B, C, and D

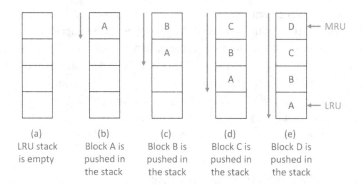

(a)
LRU stack
is empty

(b)
Block A is
pushed in
the stack

(c)
Block B is
pushed in
the stack

(d)
Block C is
pushed in
the stack

(e)
Block D is
pushed in
the stack

Figure 4.1 An LRU stack is a supporting data structure to make replacement decisions for a buffer. The LRU stack is used to represent the equivalent number of blocks in the buffer. The example here is a four-block LRU stack to manage a four-block buffer. As a string of data blocks A, B, C, and D are accessed, each is pushed in the LRU stack.

The second part of the accessing string in its temporal order of blocks B and E

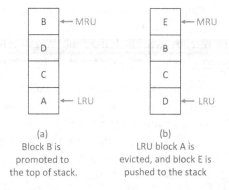

(a)
Block B is
promoted to
the top of stack.

(b)
LRU block A is
evicted, and block E is
pushed to the stack

Figure 4.2 As block B is accessed, it is hit in the buffer. Block B in the LRU stack is promoted to the top, becoming the MRU block. As block E is accessed, it is missed in the buffer. Based on the temporal order of LRU stack, block A is evicted before block E is brought in the buffer. Same operations happen in the LRU stack.

an empty buffer. When block A is brought into the buffer, it is pushed onto the LRU stack, as illustrated in Figure 4.1(b). Subsequently, blocks B, C, and D are successively brought into the buffer, and the LRU algorithm pushes them into the stack in the same temporal order, as seen in Figures 4.1(c), (d), and (e), respectively. At this point, the LRU stack becomes full, indicating that the managed buffer is also full.

In the second part of the access sequence, blocks B and E are accessed in temporal order. When block B is hit in the buffer, it is promoted to the MRU position at the top of the stack, as depicted in Figure 4.2(a). However, the subsequent access to block E is a miss in the full buffer. In order to bring block E into the buffer, the LRU algorithm evicts the LRU block A and pushes block E into the MRU position of the stack, as shown in Figure 4.2(b).

The LRU algorithm incorporates a crucial concept known as "recency" to capture the unique nature of each block's locality within the buffer after every data access. Recency refers to the distance between the current position of a block and the top entry of the MRU block in the LRU stack. For instance, in Figure 4.1(e), the MRU block D has a recency of 0, block C has a recency of 1, block B has a recency of 2, and the LRU block A has a recency of 3. A higher recency value indicates that the block has been accessed less recently. Notably, the LRU block at the bottom of the stack has a recency value of $L-1$, where L represents the total number of data blocks within the buffer.

4.1.1   What Can and Cannot LRU Do?

The LRU algorithm can be implemented in an accurate or approximate manner, offering simplicity in both cases. The LRU stack data structure automatically monitors data accesses, determining the recency of each block based on its position within the stack, such as the MRU block, the LRU block, or blocks in between. The LRU algorithm requires only a constant number of operations to respond to each data access, such as moving a data block to the top of the stack for a buffer hit, pushing a newly fetched block into the stack after a miss, or evicting the LRU block from the bottom of the stack for replacement. Consequently, the computational complexity of the LRU algorithm is $O(1)$.

The LRU algorithm is also adaptive, as the recency value of each data block can change after each access to the buffer, as indicated by the updates in the temporal order within the LRU stack. However, the LRU algorithm relies on a strong assumption of temporal locality for every data block, assuming that once a block is accessed, it will be accessed again in the near future. As a result, the LRU algorithm proves effective for data accesses exhibiting high locality. It is also tolerant to low locality accesses, as a block will remain in the LRU stack until its recency reaches $L - 1$, where L represents the length of the stack. In modern memory systems, L can be very large, causing infrequently accessed data blocks to persist in the buffer for extended periods. However, the LRU algorithm struggles to distinguish between different types of data accesses due to its inherent uncertainty. The LRU author acknowledges this weakness, describing it as "an inherent uncertainty about the occurrence of block usage."

In summary, the LRU algorithm encounters the following three challenges when handling three specific data access patterns due to its inherent uncertainty, leading to suboptimal caching performance.

1. **LRU cannot prevent a stream of low-locality data accesses from "polluting" a buffer** The LRU algorithm exhibits a vulnerability to cache pollution, which occurs when a burst of accesses to infrequently used data blocks replaces frequently used data blocks within the buffer. This can happen, for example, during sequential scan

operations on a large dataset. As a result, a significant number of misses occur in the buffer when these frequently accessed data blocks are subsequently requested again.

On the other hand, infrequently accessed data blocks that have been cached by the LRU algorithm will remain in the LRU stack until their recency gradually increases, pushing them towards the bottom of the stack. This behavior contributes to cache pollution, which poses a significant concern for various data processing applications. The accumulation of infrequently accessed blocks in the buffer leads to reduced effectiveness and efficiency of the cache, potentially impacting overall system performance.

2. **LRU cannot properly handle loop-like accesses in a buffer** Consider the following double loop written in C, which is executed within a buffer of size 4. In the case of a cyclic pattern of accesses to a dataset, where the loop length is slightly larger than the buffer size, the LRU algorithm tends to incorrectly evict blocks that will be reaccessed soon within the loop. This behavior can have a significant impact on the caching efficiency and overall performance.

```c
for (int i = 1; i <= n; i++) {
    for (int j = 1; j <= 5; j++) {
        A[j] = A[j]+1;
    }
}
```

Consider the given code snippet with a double loop in which the five elements of Array A are sequentially accessed and updated from 1 to 5 within each inner loop. The outer loop repeats the inner loop n times. In this scenario, if the buffer size is limited to four blocks, the LRU algorithm exhibits specific behavior.

Figure 4.3 illustrates the first iteration of the outer loop ($i = 1$). During this iteration, each of the five blocks (A(1) to A(5)) in the inner loop is brought into the buffer one by one from a lower level of the memory hierarchy. However, before A(5) is loaded into the buffer, A(1) is evicted.

Figure 4.4 depicts the second iteration of the outer loop ($i = 2$). During this iteration, all the accesses to the five blocks are missed in the buffer. This occurs because, according to the temporal order maintained in the LRU stack, each of the upcoming elements is evicted from the buffer. As a result, all accesses to the elements of Array A will miss in the buffer. This pattern persists for subsequent iterations of the outer loop ($n - 2$ times), leading to all accesses to Array A being missed in the buffer for the same reason.

3. **LRU cannot recognize different accessing localities among data blocks in a timely manner, causing an unfair competition among data blocks for the limited buffer space** To illustrate this, let us consider tree-based indexing structures as an example. In a data retrieval system that employs tree-based structures such as B-trees [14] and R-trees [15], the process of searching for a data record involves traversing and indexing a tree structure in multiple steps. It is common for both the indexing structures and the actual records to share the same buffer.

The first outer loop, $i = 1$

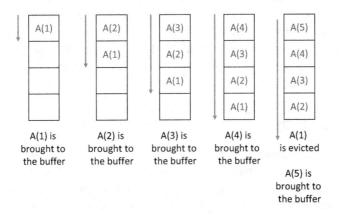

Figure 4.3 In the first outer iteration for $i = 1$, four array elements are brought in the buffer. Before the last element A(5) is brought in the buffer, the LRU element A(1) is evicted.

The second outer loop, $i = 2$

A(1)	A(2)	A(3)	A(4)	A(5)
A(5)	A(1)	A(2)	A(3)	A(4)
A(4)	A(5)	A(1)	A(2)	A(3)
A(3)	A(4)	A(5)	A(1)	A(2)

A(2) is evicted · A(3) is evicted · A(4) is evicted · A(5) is evicted · A(1) is evicted

A(1) is missed in the buffer · A(2) is missed in the buffer · A(3) is missed in the buffer · A(4) is missed in the buffer · A(5) is missed in the buffer

Figure 4.4 In the first outer iteration for $i = 2$, every access to array A is a miss in the buffer.

In practice, the frequency of access to the indexing structure is significantly higher than that of the records, primarily due to two reasons. First, a tree-index structure is typically lightweight and comprises a relatively small number of data blocks, whereas the total number of records can span a large file consisting of numerous data blocks. Moreover, locating a specific record often requires multiple accesses within the index structure. Second, the indexing structure is constantly accessed during searches for all records, making it a frequent and essential component of the system. In contrast, many of the cached records are infrequently accessed or even accessed only once.

The LRU algorithm tends to retain these infrequently accessed records, which can occupy a considerable amount of space within the buffer for an extended period. This leads to a competition for limited buffer space between the frequently accessed indexing structure, which typically occupies a smaller space, and the infrequently accessed records, which may be numerous and larger in size. As a result, the buffer space utilization may become suboptimal, impacting the overall performance of the system.

4.1.2   Improvement of LRU

The LRU algorithm, along with its variants, has been extensively employed at various levels of the memory hierarchy in both hardware and software systems. This is primarily due to its effectiveness in handling high locality accesses, its ease of implementation, and its low computational complexity of O(1).

However, researchers have recognized the limitations of LRU and have dedicated significant efforts to address its weaknesses through various approaches. For instance, some approaches utilize accessing frequencies to inform replacement decisions [116]. Others combine both recency and frequency information to make more informed decisions [86, 98]. Additionally, there are methods that focus on evicting infrequently accessed data blocks before they reach the bottom of the LRU stack [76, 109, 122]. These alternative techniques have proven effective in certain scenarios. However, it is important to note that some of these methods come with higher execution overhead compared to LRU, making them less suitable for general-purpose applications.

In summary, while researchers have made notable progress in addressing the limitations of LRU, there is no universally superior replacement algorithm that can fully overcome its constraints in all scenarios. The choice of an appropriate replacement algorithm depends on the specific characteristics and requirements of the system at hand.

4.1.3   Approximation of LRU

Maintaining an accurate LRU stack requires updating recency after each access, including promoting the MRU block. This overhead is considered to be high. In order to mitigate this overhead, a commonly employed approach, both in hardware and software, is to assign an *reference bit* to each data block. The access-bit is set to 1 when a block is accessed and to 0 when it is not. While this method may not provide precise access records, it offers a more affordable implementation.

The first approximation method for LRU, known as Clock, was developed by F. J. Corbato in 1968 [40]. Clock replaces the LRU stack with a circular array, where each cell stores an access-bit indicating whether the corresponding block is accessed (1) or not accessed (0) in the buffer. Clock utilizes a single hand that continuously sweeps through the cells, pointing to one cell at a time.

For a data access request that hits in the buffer, the hardware automatically sets the access-bit of the corresponding block to 1, requiring no additional operations. In the case of a miss in the buffer, if the buffer is full, the clock hand sweeps through the circular array and selects the first block with an access-bit of 0 as the replacement block. During the sweeping process, the clock hand resets the access-bit of each block to 0 if it was previously 1. This sweeping operation resets the status of many blocks from "accessed" to "not accessed." Consequently, a recently accessed block needs to be accessed again soon, or it may be reset to "not accessed" by the clock hand and become a candidate for replacement. Numerous studies, both through analysis and experiments, have demonstrated that Clock provides a close approximation to LRU, with similar operational characteristics. Therefore, all the performance merits and limitations discussed thus far regarding LRU can be applied to Clock as well. In Clock, the major overhead is incurred upon buffer misses by sweeping the clock hand. Compared to LRU that needs to update LRU stack upon every access, the overhead of Clock is much lower, since misses are usually much less frequent than hits.

Figures 4.5 and 4.6 provide an example to illustrate the operations of the Clock algorithm. In this example, the buffer contains 10 blocks, and the corresponding circular array also has 10 cells, each representing the access-bit for a data block.

Figure 4.5(a) depicts the initial state of the clock, where blocks B, C, D, X, Y, and Z have been accessed (access-bit $= 1$), while blocks A, E, O, and P have not been accessed (access-bit $= 0$). The clock hand is positioned at block X.

Next, in Figure 4.5(b), there is a request to access block A, resulting in a hit in the buffer. The hardware automatically sets the access-bit of block A to 1 without requiring any additional operations.

Following that, there is another request to access block L, which is not present in the buffer and the buffer is already full. In Figure 4.6(a), the clock hand sweeps through the circular array and reaches block E, which is the first block with an access-bit of 0. Block E is selected as the replacement block. As the clock hand sweeps, it sets the access-bits of blocks X, Y, Z, A, B, C, and D to 0.

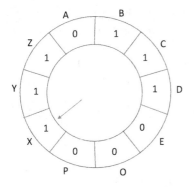

(a) Initial Clock status:
Blocks B, C, D, X, Y, Z have been
accessed and blocks A, E, O, P
have not been accessed. Clock
hand points to block X.

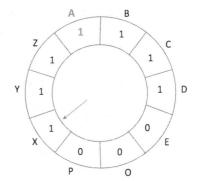

(b) Accessing block A that is a
hit. Access-bit of block A is
set to 1 automatically by
hardware without other
operations.

Figure 4.5 (a) The initial clock status. (b) Setting the access-bit after a buffer hit.

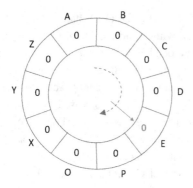 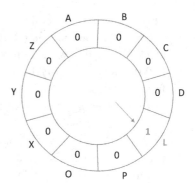

(a) Accessing block L that is a miss. The clock hand sweeps to block E that is selected for replacement. On the way of sweeping, the clock hand sets access-bits of blocks X, Y, Z, A, B, C and D to 0s.

(b) Block E is evicted, and block L is in. Access-bit of blockLis set to 1.

Figure 4.6 (a) The clock hand sweeps through cells to find a replacement block. (b) Block E is replaced by block L whose access-bit is set to 1.

Finally, in Figure 4.6(b), block E is evicted from the buffer, and it is replaced by block L. The access-bit of block L is set to 1 to indicate its recent access.

This example demonstrates the basic operations of the Clock algorithm, where the clock hand sweeps through the circular array, selecting replacement blocks based on the access-bits and resetting the access-bits along the way.

Can Clock always find a block for replacement? Yes, because even if the access-bits of all blocks are set to 1, during the first sweeping loop, the clock hand sets them to 0s and eventually selects a block at the beginning of the second loop for replacement.

What does it mean if the clock hand moves slowly? If the clock hand moves slowly, it indicates that there have been many hits in the buffer. Consequently, the clock hand is not actively searching for blocks to replace since there is a high likelihood of accessing recently used blocks.

What does it mean if the clock hand moves quickly? If the clock hand moves quickly, it means that there have been numerous cache misses in the buffer. In such cases, the clock hand actively searches for blocks to be replaced as there is a higher demand for new data.

In summary, the Clock algorithm does not necessarily evict the LRU block but instead selects a not-recently used block for replacement. The algorithm aims to approximate LRU behavior by considering the access-bits and effectively evicting blocks that have not been recently accessed.

4.2   Low Inter-reference Recency Set (LIRS) Replacement

After thoroughly examining the strengths and limitations of the LRU algorithm, an important question arises: How can we overcome its limitations while preserving its advantages? To tackle the limitations of LRU in a comprehensive manner, we need to explore alternatives outside the framework of recency-based replacement decisions. However, it is crucial to develop new algorithms that retain the effectiveness of LRU by keeping frequently accessed data, are easy to implement, and maintain the low complexity of operations in O(1) as seen in LRU.

In this section, we will introduce a replacement algorithm that utilizes a different measure of locality for making effective replacement decisions. We will also delve into how this approach fundamentally addresses the "inherent uncertainty" inherent in LRU. By adopting an effective locality measure, this algorithm aims to provide a solution that addresses the limitations of LRU while preserving its merits.

4.2.1   Measuring Data Locality by Reuse Distance

Let us introduce the concept of *reuse distance* as an alternative locality measurement for data blocks. The reuse distance of a data block is defined as the number of distinct memory accesses that occur between the last access to the block and the current access to it. Figure 4.7 provides an example to compare the reuse distance and the recency for each data block in a sequence of 10 data accesses.

There are several significant differences between these two locality measurements. First, the reuse distance for the first access to a block is considered infinite, whereas the recency for the same block is 0 and it is placed in the MRU position. By utilizing the reuse distance, a replacement algorithm can establish a timing threshold for blocks with infinite distance, allowing for early eviction of one-time accessed or infrequently accessed data blocks. In contrast, with the recency-based approach, the same data block will not be evicted until it reaches the bottom of the LRU stack, which can take a considerable amount of time, particularly for a deep stack. In reality, blocks that are evicted from the LRU stack after a long waiting period could have been evicted much earlier to better utilize the limited buffer space.

Second, the recency changes dynamically for each data block as it represents the distance between a block and the MRU block at the top of the stack. After each data access, the recency of many data blocks is likely to change. On the other hand, the

Temporal order

Access time	1	2	3	4	5	6	7	8	9	10
Data blocks	A	B	C	A	B	B	A	D	B	A
Reuse distance	∞	∞	∞	2	2	0	1	∞	2	2
Recency	A:0	B:0 A:1	C:0 B:1 A:2	A:0 C:1 B:2	B:0 A:1 C:2	B:0 A:1 C:2	A:0 B:1 C:2	D:0 A:1 B:2 C:3	B:0 D:1 A:2 C:3	A:0 B:1 D:2 C:3

Reuse distance and recency for each block in temporal order

Figure 4.7 A comparison between reuse distance and recency for a sequence of data accesses.

reuse distance refers only to the distance between the two most-recent accesses to the same block, involving only the data blocks that are directly relevant.

Finally, the LRU stack organizes the positions of data blocks based on their recency in a straightforward manner. Consequently, it is relatively easy to implement an LRU or LRU-like algorithm in the LRU stack framework. In contrast, effectively monitoring the reuse distance for each block, dynamically ranking all blocks based on their reuse distance, and making efficient replacement decisions at a low cost of O(1) present significant challenges in both software and hardware implementations.

The concept of reuse distance, originally referred to as "stack distance" in [95], has been studied extensively. In relation to the recency measurement used in LRU algorithms, the concept was named "inter-reference recency (IRR)" in [73]. However, the term "reuse distance" has gained widespread acceptance and is considered the most understandable and intuitive name for this concept, as seen in studies such as [18] and [46].

In a buffer with limited capacity, LRU focuses on retaining frequently accessed data blocks while allowing one-time and infrequently accessed data blocks to remain in the buffer for an extended period. However, due to its inability to promptly evict data blocks that only require short-term storage, LRU often results in the eviction of data blocks that could have been beneficial from remaining in the buffer. Consequently, buffer pollution frequently occurs with the LRU algorithm.

4.2.2   The Basis of an Optimal Replacement Algorithm

If we know in advance a complete access trace of a program execution, we can construct an optimal replacement algorithm based on this trace information. This algorithm, known as OPT in [4] and MIN in [16], aims to achieve the minimum buffer miss rate. However, since the optimal algorithm requires access information unavailable at runtime, it is not practical for real-world usage. Nevertheless, the results obtained from this algorithm can serve as an ideal benchmark for comparing the performance of other proposed algorithms, highlighting how closely they can approach the optimal performance.

The primary distinction between the optimal algorithm and other algorithms lies in their approach to locality measurement for each data block. In the optimal algorithm, the locality of a data block at any given time, referred to as the "current time," is defined by the distance between the current time and when the block is accessed. The distance to the next access, denoted as D_{next}, determines the strength of the locality for that particular data block. A longer D_{next} implies a weaker locality.

To illustrate the concept of D_{next}, we follow the format presented in [144] and refer to Figure 4.8. In Figure 4.8, the timing order is depicted from left to right on the horizontal bar, starting from 0. We focus on a specific data block, denoted as block A. For the optimal algorithm, D_{next} of block A is determined as the number of distinct blocks between the current time and when it is accessed. This accurate measurement allows the optimal algorithm to consistently select blocks with the weakest localities for eviction, resulting in optimal performance.

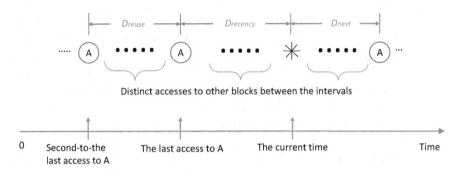

Note: the data accesses beyond the current time (✳) are offline traces that are not available at runtime.

Figure 4.8 Comparisons of the locality measures of D_{next} for the optimal replacement algorithms, $D_{recency}$ for LRU and D_{reuse} for LIRS. Block A is the target for a locality measure at the current time by three types of distances.

Figure 4.8 also introduces two other measures of locality: recency ($D_{recency}$) for LRU and reuse distance (D_{reuse}) for LIRS. Recency ($D_{recency}$) represents the distance between the last access to block A and the current time, while reuse distance (D_{reuse}) represents the distance between the last access to block A and the second-to-last access to block A. These measures are utilized in LRU and LIRS replacements, respectively, to predict the locality of a block.

Observing Figure 4.8, we can see that there is little relationship between $D_{recency}$ and D_{next}. Furthermore, as the current time progresses, $D_{recency}$ increases accordingly, indicating its highly dynamic nature. On the other hand, the reuse distance of block A, which is used to predict its locality (D_{next}), exhibits a strong relationship with the actual locality. While the absolute values of D_{reuse} and D_{next} may differ, the rank orders of the locality of all data blocks measured by both variables remain consistent in practice. This consistency is the reason why the reuse distance measure is widely employed to predict the locality of data blocks in various applications.

4.2.3 The LIRS Algorithm

The abbreviation LIRS [73] stands for "low inter-reference recency set," indicating its goal of maintaining a high-locality data block set in the buffer, where each block has a low inter-reference recency or reuse distance. The LIRS algorithm employs the reuse distance to predict the locality of each data block and dynamically ranks their localities in the buffer from high to low. By storing blocks with high localities in the buffer and evicting those with low localities (often represented as infinity or long reuse distances), LIRS makes effective replacement decisions.

However, there exists inherent uncertainty in the algorithm. Consider the scenario where a block, initially cached in the buffer due to its high locality, is infrequently accessed later on. How can such a block be evicted? To address this issue, LIRS introduces a measure called the "maximum" of the reuse distance and the recency:

$$\text{max(reuse distance, recency)}.$$

This measure takes advantage of the timely changes in recency for each block. After the reuse distance is measured for a block, its recency begins to increment by 1 after each subsequent data access within the buffer (assuming no repeated accesses to the same block). If the recency surpasses the reuse distance, it indicates that the block has not been accessed within an interval greater than the previously measured reuse distance. In such cases, LIRS employs the recency as the locality measure for the block and potentially moves it to the replacement candidate group.

The LIRS Data Structure

The LIRS algorithm dynamically categorizes data blocks into two types: low inter-reference (LIR) blocks and high inter-reference (HIR) blocks. It efficiently manages the changing status of blocks, transitioning them between LIR and HIR based on their inter-reference behavior. In this section, we will explain how the dynamics of the LIRS algorithm are implemented at a low cost.

To illustrate the organization of the buffer space, Figure 4.9(a) is presented. The buffer is divided into two sections: a larger space dedicated to storing LIR blocks (referred to as LIRS) and a smaller space for housing HIR blocks (referred to as HIRS). Figure 4.9(b) depicts the LIRS data structure, consisting of two stacks: the LIRS stack (representing the larger space) and an LRU stack specifically for resident HIR blocks. Within the LIRS stack, three types of data blocks are managed:

1. all LIR blocks that are currently resident in the buffer,
2. a small number of HIR blocks that are resident in the buffer, and
3. some nonresident HIR blocks that have been evicted from the buffer.

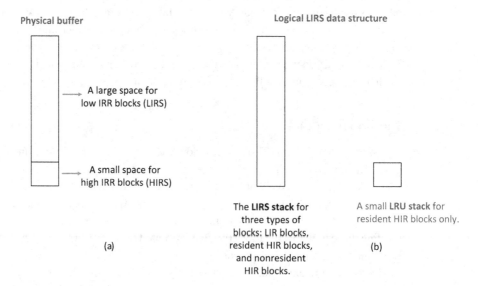

Figure 4.9 (a) The physical buffer is divided into a large space for low IRR blocks, and a small space for high IRR blocks. (b) The logical LIRS data structure consists of a large LIRS stack for three types of data blocks, and a small LRU stack for resident HIR blocks only.

The inclusion of nonresident HIR blocks in the LIRS stack serves the purpose of measuring the inter-reference recency or the reuse distance of data blocks at runtime.

At the beginning of the LIRS algorithm, all referenced blocks are assigned an LIR status until the available physical LIR block space is fully utilized. Once the LIR block space reaches its capacity, the first-time accessed data blocks are labeled as HIR blocks and managed using a small LRU stack. This marks the starting point of the LIRS algorithm.

The LIRS algorithm ensures the maintenance of a low-reuse distance block set (LIRS) by adhering to the following data management rules.

1. When an LIR block is accessed and it is a hit, it is promoted to the top position of the LIRS stack. The LIRS stack is organized in such a way that the bottom block is always an LIR block with the highest recency among the LIR blocks. As a result, it is necessary to perform pruning operations to evict both resident and nonresident HIR blocks from the bottom of the LIRS stack. This ensures the effective management of the LIRS block set.

2. When a resident HIR block is accessed and it is a hit in both the LIRS stack and the LRU stack, its status is changed to an LIR block, and it is moved to the top of the LIRS stack. This is because the reuse distance of this block after the access is smaller than the recency of the LIR block at the bottom of the LIRS stack. If the LIR block set is already full, the LIR block at the bottom of the LIRS stack is demoted to the LRU stack, and its status is changed to a resident HIR block. This demotion may result in an eviction in the LRU stack if the HIR block set is also full. If the demoted block is not accessed soon, it will be physically evicted from the HIR block set (HIRS) in the buffer.

   The exchange of status between the two blocks follows the locality measurement rule for max(reuse distance, recency). This rule ensures that the block with the highest locality, as determined by the maximum of its reuse distance and recency, is retained in the LIRS stack, while blocks accessed less frequently are demoted to the LRU stack or evicted if necessary.

3. Upon an access hit to a resident HIR block, if this block is only present in the LRU stack, its status remains the same. According to the LRU rule, it is moved to the top of the small LRU stack. Additionally, the same block is pushed to the top of the LIRS stack. The reason for keeping the HIR status of the block is that the reuse distance of this block after the access is larger than the recency of the block at the bottom of the LIRS stack. However, if this block is accessed again before it is pruned or evicted from the LIRS stack, it will become an LIR block by following rule 2.

4. Upon an access miss to an HIR block, it is brought into the buffer. If the block is not found in the LIRS stack, it will be placed at the top of both the LRU stack and the LIRS stack, with a status of resident HIR. If the LRU stack is full, the bottom block in the LRU stack will be evicted to make room for the new HIR block.

5. Upon an access miss to an HIR block, if its nonresident block is found in the LIRS stack, it will be moved to the top of the LIRS stack and its status will be changed to

LIR. This is because its presence in the LIRS stack indicates that its reuse distance after this access is shorter than the recency of the LIR block at the bottom of the LIRS stack. This operation may require adjustments in the LIRS stack, such as demoting the bottom LIR block to the LRU stack and changing its status from LIR to HIR, as well as other necessary pruning operations.

An Example to Explain the LIRS Algorithm

In this example, the physical buffer has a capacity of five blocks and is divided into two parts: the LIRS stack and the LRU stack. The initial conditions are shown in Figure 4.10(a). The LIRS stack contains three LIR blocks (A, D, and H), two resident HIR blocks (C and E), and three nonresident HIR blocks (B, F, and I). The LRU stack contains two resident HIR blocks (C and E).

Figure 4.10(b) illustrates a sequence of data accesses in temporal order: D, H, C, E, G, I, and E. This sequence is used to trace the operations of the LIRS algorithm starting from the initial conditions depicted in Figure 4.10(a).

To demonstrate the operations of the LIRS algorithm for a sequence of seven data block accesses, three figures are used to track the updates in the LIRS stack and the LRU stack. Figure 4.11(a) illustrates the changes in the LIRS stack after accessing blocks D and H, which result in two LIR block hits. Both blocks are moved to the top of the LIRS stack in the order of their access. To maintain an LIR block at the bottom of the LIRS stack, pruning operations are performed, resulting in the eviction of nonresident blocks F and I from the LIRS stack. The LRU stack remains unchanged. Figure 4.11(a) highlights the application of data management rule 1 in the LIRS algorithm.

Figure 4.11(b) illustrates the updates in both the LIRS stack and the LRU stack after accessing block C, which corresponds to a hit on a resident HIR block. Since block

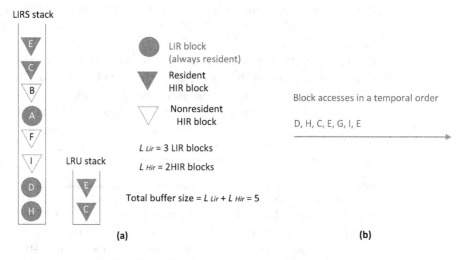

(a)   (b)

Figure 4.10 (a) The initial conditions of the LIRS stack and the LRU stack of the example. (b) A string of blocks to be accessed in the example in a temporal order.

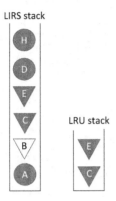

(a) Accessing blocks D and H are hits to LIR blocks. They are moved to the top of the LIRS stack. Pruning operations evict nonresident blocks F and I.

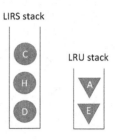

(b) Accessing block C is a hit to a resident HIR block. It is in both LIRS stack and LRU stack. Its status is changed to LIR. Block A in the bottom of the LIRS stack is demoted to the LRU stack. Pruning operations evict HIR blocks E and B from the LIRS stack.

Figure 4.11 (a) Accessing blocks D and H. (b) Accessing block C.

C is also present in the LIRS stack, it is moved to the top of the LIRS stack and its status is changed to LIR. As the LIRS stack is already full, block A at the bottom is demoted to the top of the LRU stack, transitioning its status to HIR. Pruning operations are then performed, resulting in the eviction of resident HIR block E and nonresident HIR block B from the LIRS stack. Figure 4.11(b) exemplifies the implementation of data management rule 2 in the LIRS algorithm.

Figure 4.12(a) depicts the modifications in both the LIRS stack and the LRU stack following the access of block E, representing a hit on a resident HIR block. However, since block E is not present in the LIRS stack, it will be moved to the top of both stacks without any change in its status. Figure 4.12(a) demonstrates the implementation of data management rule 3 in the LIRS algorithm.

Figure 4.12(b) illustrates the outcomes in both the LIRS stack and the LRU stack following the access of block G, which represents a miss to a nonresident HIR block. The block will be fetched into the buffer. Since it is not found in the LIRS stack, it will be placed at the top of both stacks as a resident HIR block. To accommodate block G, block A is evicted from the LRU stack. Figure 4.12(b) provides an explanation of the implementation of data management rule 4 in the LIRS algorithm.

Figure 4.13(a) illustrates the resulting configurations of the LIRS stack and the LRU stack following the access of block I, which represents a miss to a nonresident HIR block. The block will be fetched into the buffer. Since it is not found in the LIRS stack, it will be placed at the top of both stacks as a resident HIR block. To accommodate block I, block E is evicted from the LRU stack. Additionally, the status of block E in the LIRS stack is changed from resident HIR to nonresident HIR. Figure 4.13(a) demonstrates the execution of data management rule 4 in the LIRS algorithm.

LIRS stack

LRU stack

(a) Accessing block E is a hit to an HIR block, which only exists in the LRU stack. Thus, placing it on the top in both the LIRS stack and the LRU stack without changing the status.

LIRS stack

LRU stack

(b) Accessing block G is a miss to an HIR block, and it is not found in the LIRS sack. It is placed in the top of both the LIRS stack and the LRU stack with a status of resident HIR. Block A in the bottom of the LRU stack is evicted.

Figure 4.12 (a) Accessing block E. (b) Accessing block G.

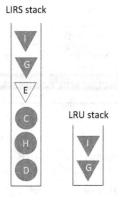

(a) Accessing block I is a miss to a nonresident HIR block. HIR block E is evicted from the LRU stack, and HIR block I is in as a resident. HIR block E in the LIRS stack becomes a nonresident block.

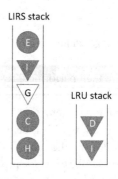

(b) Accessing block E is a miss to a nonresident HIR block. Since it is found in the LIRS stack, it becomes an LIR block after it is brought in the buffer. Block D is demoted to the LRU stack by changing its status to LIR. Block G is evicted from the LRU stack, and its status in the LIRS stack is changed to nonresident.

Figure 4.13 (a) Accessing blocks I. (b) Accessing block E.

Figure 4.13(b) illustrates the final configurations of the LIRS stack and the LRU stack after the access to block E, which corresponds to a miss for a nonresident HIR block. The block will be brought into the buffer. Since it is present in the LIRS stack, it will be positioned at the top of the LIRS stack with a status change to LIR. As a result, block D, located at the bottom of the LIRS stack, will be demoted to the top of the LRU stack and its status will change to HIR. Block G will be evicted from the LRU stack to create space for block D. Additionally, the status of block G in the LIRS stack will change from resident HIR to nonresident HIR. Figure 4.13(b) elucidates the implementation of data management rule 5 in the LIRS algorithm.

The Complexity of LIRS

The LRU algorithm is well known for its simplicity of implementation and low complexity, achieving a time complexity of O(1). The LIRS algorithm, while maintaining the same complexity as LRU, also preserves its merit by employing a double-stack data structure. However, additional operations such as pruning, block pushing, and eviction are involved in LIRS due to the management of three types of data blocks: LIR blocks, resident HIR blocks, and nonresident HIR blocks. As a result, the space requirement for the LIRS data structure is higher than that of LRU.

Despite the increased space requirement, modern computer systems can easily accommodate it. The LIRS algorithm leverages the larger data access history scope in the LIRS stack and the double-stack structure to efficiently measure both the reuse distance and recency of each data block, enabling more effective replacement decisions compared to LRU. In practice, the size of the LIRS stack is typically reasonable, as pruning operations are commonly used to retain an LIR block at the bottom of the LIRS stack. The authors of the LIRS algorithm have demonstrated that limiting the LIRS stack size to 1.5 to 3 times the buffer size still yields expected performance, making it a practical and efficient choice for buffer management [73].

One important parameter in the LIRS algorithm is the allocation of buffer space between the LIR block set (LIRS) and the HIR block set (HIRS). By default, the LIRS algorithm allocates 99 percent of the buffer size to LIRS and 1 percent to HIRS. However, a sensitivity study has shown that the performance of LIRS remains unaffected when adjusting the size of HIRS within a range of 1 percent to 30 percent of the buffer size. This flexibility allows system administrators to fine-tune the LIRS algorithm based on their specific workload characteristics and memory requirements.

Summary

From an algorithm design perspective, LRU can be considered a special case of LIRS; LRU uses a single stack to keep track of resident blocks in the buffer, without distinguishing between LIR and HIR blocks. On the other hand, the LIRS algorithm introduces a more sophisticated replacement decision process while maintaining the same computational complexity as LRU. Although the LIRS data structure requires a slightly larger space, it addresses the critical limitations of LRU by utilizing the reuse distance as a measure of locality for effective replacement decisions. This enhancement in the LIRS algorithm allows for better utilization of the buffer and improved overall performance compared to LRU.

The LIRS algorithm has undergone extensive evaluation, testing, and implementation in various industry products, such as [50, 72, 98, 125, 128, 135], as well as in numerous academic research projects. In a comprehensive trace-driven simulation conducted by Butt et al. [27], LIRS was compared against other popular replacement algorithms including 2Q [76], ARC [98], LRU [44], LRU-2 [109], LRUF [116], MQ [145], and the optimal replacement algorithm (OPT) [16]. The evaluation utilized workloads comprising sequential, random, and regular data access patterns.

The results of the experiments demonstrated that, in most cases, the performance of LIRS in terms of hit ratios and execution times closely approached those of OPT as the buffer size increased. This finding validates the effectiveness of the reuse distance metric and the efficiency of the LIRS algorithm design in achieving improved cache replacement performance.

4.2.4   An Approximation of LIRS

The maintenance of double stacks in the LIRS algorithm to accurately measure the reuse distance and recency for each data block after every access incurs a significant runtime overhead. To make the LIRS algorithm more feasible for system implementations in both software and hardware, an efficient approximation of LIRS is required to reduce the overhead while preserving the core principles of LIRS. In response to this need, an approximation called Clock-pro for LIRS was developed, drawing inspiration from the Clock algorithm for LRU [74]. Clock-pro aims to provide a more efficient implementation of LIRS, enabling practical adoption in various computing systems.

The Clock-pro Structure

Clock-pro is developed within the framework of the Clock algorithm, where each resident data block is assigned a reference bit to indicate whether it has been accessed or not (1 for "accessed" and 0 for "not accessed"). However, Clock-pro introduces three significant modifications to the original Clock structure. These differences are outlined as follows.

1. Similar to LIRS, Clock-pro also manages three types of data blocks: LIR blocks, resident HIR blocks, and nonresident HIR blocks. By default, Clock-pro allocates 99 percent of the buffer size to LIR blocks and 1 percent to resident HIR blocks, adhering to the same default configuration as LIRS. However, Clock-pro imposes an upper limit on the number of nonresident HIR blocks that can be stored.
2. In contrast to Clock's single clock hand, Clock-pro introduces three independent clock hands.

    $Hand_{LIR}$ This hand is responsible for selecting a block from the LIR block group to be demoted to the resident HIR block set, thereby creating space to accommodate a new LIR block.

    $Hand_{HIR}$ The $Hand_{HIR}$ is used to identify a resident HIR block for eviction, making room for a newly fetched block. It also promotes an HIR block to become an LIR block when necessary.

    $Hand_{test}$ This hand is employed to handle the elimination of nonresident HIR blocks in Clock-pro once the upper bound is reached. Additionally, it determines whether a newly fetched block should be designated as an LIR block or not.

    Each clock hand moves in the clockwise direction.

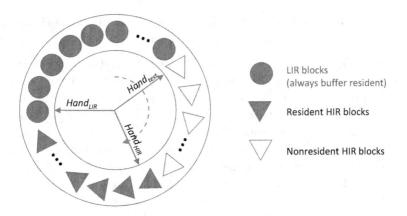

Figure 4.14 The structure of the Clock-pro algorithm.

3. Handling a data access miss in Clock-pro involves more dynamic operations compared to Clock, primarily due to the presence of three distinct groups of data blocks. This increased complexity allows Clock-pro to effectively manage LIR blocks, resident HIR blocks, and nonresident HIR blocks in a more intricate manner.

Figure 4.14 depicts the Clock-pro structure. The initial state of Clock-pro resembles that of the LIRS algorithm. Initially, all referenced blocks are assigned an LIR status until the available physical space for LIR blocks is fully utilized. Subsequently, a restricted number of HIR blocks are utilized to accommodate newly arrived data blocks, which are designated as HIR blocks. Clock-pro employs several approximations to uphold the LIRS principle, which are governed by the following data management rules.

1. When an LIR block is accessed and there is a hit, its reference bit is simply set to 1 without any additional operations.
2. When a resident HIR block is accessed and there is a hit, its reference bit is set to 1 without any other operations.
3. When there is an access miss to an HIR data block and the buffer as well as the Clock-pro circular list are both full, Clock-pro performs the following operations to handle the miss.

   If the missed block is identified as a nonresident HIR block by $Hand_{test}$, the newly accessed block will be considered a LIR block. Otherwise, it is classified as an HIR block.

   The $Hand_{HIR}$ is used to sweep through the resident HIR blocks. Clock-pro evicts the first encountered HIR block with a reference bit of 0 to make room for the newly fetched block. As $Hand_{HIR}$ progresses, it resets the reference bit of each block it encounters from 1 to 0.

   The evicted HIR block, which was replaced by the new block, transitions into a nonresident HIR block.

By running $Hand_{test}$, Clock-pro identifies the specific block to be replaced with the evicted HIR block. This block is then substituted with the evicted HIR block.

4. Before $Hand_{HIR}$ locates a resident HIR block for replacement, if it encounters a resident HIR block with a reference bit of 1, that HIR block will be promoted to the LIR block group. This promotion allows the HIR block to be treated as an LIR block, enhancing its chances of remaining in the buffer for longer periods.
5. In rules 3 and 4, a resident HIR block has the possibility of being changed to an LIR block. To facilitate this change, $Hand_{LIR}$ is employed in Clock-pro. It scans the buffer to locate an LIR block with a reference bit of 0, which can be demoted to the HIR group. During this scanning process, $Hand_{LIR}$ also resets the reference bit of each block it encounters from 1 to 0 if necessary.
6. When an LIR block is demoted to the HIR group, Clock-pro follows rule 3 to select a replacement. This task is performed by $Hand_{HIR}$, which scans the resident HIR blocks to identify a suitable block for eviction and replacement.

For an access hit to any block in the buffer, Clock-pro handles it in the same way as Clock, by simply setting the reference bit without any additional operations. The status changes among the three types of blocks (LIR, resident HIR, and nonresident HIR) only occur when an access miss takes place. The inclusion of nonresident HIR blocks in Clock-pro allows for the approximation of the reuse distance measure for each block. Despite the presence of nonresident HIR blocks, the number of operations after each miss in Clock-pro remains constant. As a result, Clock-pro retains the advantages of Clock while also making more effective replacement decisions by considering the approximate reuse distance.

An Example to Explain the Clock-pro Replacement
We will use the same example to explain the Clock-pro algorithm. In this example, the physical buffer consists of three LIR blocks and two HIR blocks, with a total capacity of five blocks. Figure 4.15(a) shows the initial condition in Clock-pro, where the buffer stores three LIR blocks (A, D, and H), two resident HIR blocks (C and E), and three nonresident HIR blocks (B, F, and I). The reference bits for all five resident blocks in both the LIR and HIR groups are set to 0. Nonresident blocks do not have reference bits. Each group of data blocks is monitored by a dedicated clock hand: $Hand_{LIR}$ for LIR blocks, $Hand_{HIR}$ for HIR blocks, and $Hand_{test}$ for nonresident HIR blocks.

Figure 4.15(b) presents a string of data accesses in temporal order: D, H, C, E, G, I, and E. We will trace the operations of the Clock-pro algorithm, starting from the initial condition depicted in Figure 4.15(a).

Similarly to the case study of the LIRS algorithm, we will use two additional figures to trace the operations in Clock-pro for the string of data accesses. Figure 4.16(a) shows the results after accessing blocks D, H, C, and E, which include two LIR block hits and two HIR block hits. In each case, the reference bits of the accessed blocks are set to 1 without any other operations. Figure 4.16(a) explains data management rules 1 and 2 of Clock-pro.

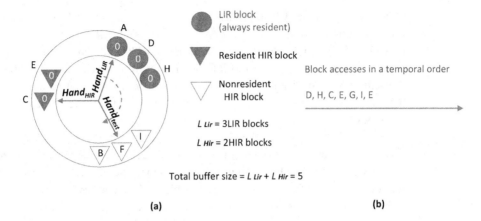

(a)   **(b)**

Figure 4.15 (a) The initial condition of the data blocks managed by Clock-pro. (b) A string of data accesses in a temporal order.

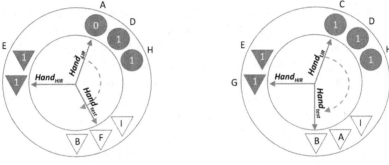

(a) Accessing blocks D, H, C, and E are hits to both HIR and LIR blocks, whose reference bits are set to 1.

(b) Accessing block G is a miss, which is not in the nonresident block group (detected by *Hand*test). *Hand*HIR is used to search for a replacement block in the HIR group. Since the reference bit of HIR block C is 1, it is promoted to the LIR block group. *Hand*LIR is used to find a LIR block with the reference bit of 0. Thus, block A and C are exchanged. Block A is replaced by block G and becomes a non-resident HIR block. *Hand*test moves to the next position.

Figure 4.16 (a) The Clock-pro results after accessing data blocks D, H, C, and E, which are hits in the buffer. (b) The Clock-pro results after accessing data block G, which is a miss in the buffer.

Figure 4.16(b) illustrates the Clock-pro results after accessing block G, which results in a miss in the buffer. When handling a miss, Clock-pro first uses $Hand_{test}$ to determine if the missed block is a nonresident HIR block. In this case, block G is not a nonresident HIR block. Then, $Hand_{HIR}$ is employed to find a block to evict and make space for block G. During the sweeping loop, the first block checked by $Hand_{HIR}$ is HIR block C, which has a reference bit of 1. According to data management rule 3, HIR block C needs to be promoted to the LIR group.

To accomplish this, Clock-pro uses $Hand_{LIR}$ to find a suitable LIR block for demotion, and LIR block A with a reference bit of 0 is identified. Blocks A and C are exchanged between the two groups. Since HIR block A's reference bit is 0, it can be replaced by the newly fetched block G, and it is moved to the nonresident HIR group, replacing nonresident HIR block F, as indicated by $Hand_{test}$. Afterwards, $Hand_{test}$ moves to the next position. Figure 4.16(b) explains data management rules 3, 4, 5, and 6 of Clock-pro.

Figure 4.17(a) illustrates the Clock-pro results after accessing block I, which is a miss in the buffer. Block I is identified as a nonresident HIR block by $Hand_{test}$ and will be promoted to the LIR block group. $Hand_{LIR}$ is then used to find a suitable LIR block for demotion, and after one sweeping loop, block C is identified.

Next, $Hand_{HIR}$ is employed to find an HIR block to evict in order to accommodate the demoted block C. After one sweeping loop, HIR block G is selected for eviction. Once block G is moved to the nonresident HIR group, $Hand_{test}$ moves to the next position.

In summary, the newly fetched block I replaces block C in the LIR group. The demoted block C, in turn, replaces HIR block G, which is evicted and joins the nonresident block group. Figure 4.17(a) provides an explanation of data management rules 3, 4, 5, and 6 of Clock-pro.

Figure 4.17(a) depicts the Clock-pro results after accessing block I, which results in a miss in the buffer. Block I is identified as a nonresident HIR block by $Hand_{test}$ and will be promoted to the LIR block group. To accommodate block I, $Hand_{LIR}$ is utilized to find a suitable LIR block for demotion. After one sweeping loop, block C is identified as the demoted block.

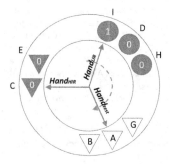

(a) Accessing block I is a miss, which is in the nonresident HIR group (detected by $Hand_{test}$). It will join the LIR group. $Hand_{LIR}$ is used to search for a LIR block to demote. After one sweeping loop, block C is selected. $Hand_{HIR}$ is used to search for a HIR block to leave space, and block G is evicted for block C. Block G is placed in the nonresident HIR block group. $Hand_{test}$ moves to the next position.

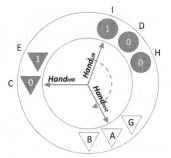

(b) Accessing block E is a hit to a resident HIR block. Its reference bit is set to 1 without other operations.

Figure 4.17 (a) The Clock-pro results after accessing data block I, which is a miss in the buffer. (b) The Clock-pro results after accessing data block E, which is a miss in the buffer.

Next, $Hand_{HIR}$ is used to find a HIR block to evict in order to accommodate the demoted block C. After one sweeping loop, HIR block G is chosen for eviction. Once block G is moved to the nonresident HIR group, $Hand_{test}$ advances to the next position.

In summary, the newly fetched block I replaces block C in the LIR group. The demoted block C, in turn, replaces HIR block G, which is evicted and moved to the nonresident block group. Figure 4.17(a) provides an illustration of data management rules 3, 4, 5, and 6 of Clock-pro.

When comparing the final results of the LIRS algorithm in Figure 4.13(b) with the final results of its approximation, Clock-pro, in Figure 4.17(b), we observe that all the resident blocks in the buffer are the same: C, D, E, H, and I. This example demonstrates the effectiveness of the approximation, as both LIRS and Clock-pro cache the same set of data blocks in the buffer after a sequence of seven block accesses. However, there are differences in the composition of the LIR group and the resident HIR group between LIRS and Clock-pro. In LIRS, the LIR group consists of blocks E, C, and H, while the resident HIR group includes blocks D and I. On the other hand, in Clock-pro, the LIR group consists of blocks D, I, and H, and the resident HIR group includes blocks C and E. These differences arise due to the approximations made in Clock-pro.

Summary

In the case of a buffer hit, both Clock and Clock-pro incur the lowest cost of resetting the reference bit without any additional algorithmic operations. However, when it comes to a buffer miss, Clock requires only a single clock hand to search for a replacement block by examining the reference bits in a sweeping process. On the other hand, Clock-pro involves up to three clock hands and performs several operations. Therefore, the number of operations for both Clock and Clock-pro remains constant. Overall, Clock-pro maintains the O(1) complexity of Clock while achieving comparable effectiveness in replacement decisions to the LIRS algorithm.

Clock-pro has undergone extensive evaluation, testing, and implementation across multiple system infrastructure platforms. It has been integrated into various operating systems such as NetBSD [28], Linux [96], and the Rust system environment [29]. Additionally, there have been numerous academic research projects related to Clock-pro.

One notable study is a comprehensive trace-driven simulation in [3]. In this study, a simplified version of Clock-pro that excludes the storage of nonresident HIR blocks was compared with Clock, LRU, and FIFO [42]; FIFO is a simplified version of LRU that uses the same LRU stack but does not perform any operations on buffer hits. Despite this additional approximation in Clock-pro, where only two clock hands, $Hand_{HIR}$ and $Hand_{LIR}$, are utilized without measuring the reuse distances of data blocks using nonresident HIR blocks, the experimental results demonstrated Clock-pro's superior performance compared to other algorithms across several benchmark workloads. These findings confirm the effectiveness of the Clock-pro approximation for the LIRS algorithm.

4.3   Spatial-Locality-Aware Replacement Algorithms

All the replacement algorithms studied in this chapter are based on a temporal locality prediction of each data block. Specifically, the concepts of recency, the reuse distance, and the frequency are accessing time related. However, the spatial locality is not considered, which is particularly important when random accesses and sequential accesses in storage locations make a big difference in performance. We will give a case study in this section showing the significance of data block replacement algorithms by considering spatial locality at the level of hard disks.

4.3.1   Disk-Spatial Locality Awareness for Buffer Cache Management

In Section 3.7 of Chapter 3, we introduced the concept of a buffer cache. The buffer cache is a dedicated region in the DRAM memory that is used to cache disk data. Its purpose is to store frequently accessed data so that subsequent accesses can be served from memory, eliminating the need to fetch the data from the disk again. The management of the buffer cache is handled by the OS.

Locality, both temporal and spatial, plays a crucial role in the effectiveness of the buffer cache. Temporal locality refers to the tendency of a data object that has been recently accessed to be accessed again in the near future. Spatial locality, on the other hand, suggests that if a particular data object is accessed, it is likely that other data objects located in a nearby space location will also be accessed.

The OS operates with a logical disk geometry, which represents the linear layout of data on the disk in the form of logical blocks. The OS manages these logical blocks, which are the units of data storage on the disk. However, the OS is unaware of the actual physical storage locations of these logical blocks on the disk.

Given this limitation, the OS primarily manages the buffer cache based on temporal locality. It maintains a consistent view between the logical blocks and the sequence of their access times. By doing so, the OS can make informed decisions about which data to cache in the buffer based on the frequency of its access.

In summary, the buffer cache is a specialized region in the DRAM managed by the OS. It leverages temporal locality to cache frequently accessed disk data, while the OS maintains a logical view of the disk's data layout. By exploiting temporal locality, the buffer cache aims to improve the overall system performance by reducing disk access latency.

In Chapter 2, we discussed the architecture of a hard disk and the characteristics of data access. Sequential data accesses on a disk involve minimal seek time and head rotation time, making them very fast. However, in the case of random accesses, each access requires a seek time and a rotation time, resulting in significantly higher access latency compared to sequential accesses.

Once the buffer cache is filled, the OS needs to decide which data blocks to evict in order to accommodate newly loaded disk data blocks. This decision is made using replacement algorithms. To optimize buffer cache management, the OS also employs data prefetching, where it predicts the data blocks that are likely to be needed in the near future and loads them from the disk in advance.

Data replacement and prefetching are two critical mechanisms in buffer cache management. The effectiveness of these mechanisms can be limited without knowledge of the disk layout and spatial data locality. For instance, a replacement algorithm that considers spatial locality would prioritize keeping random blocks in the buffer cache, as retrieving them from the disk would incur significant latency, while giving lower priority to sequential blocks, which can be loaded quickly.

Considering both temporal and spatial locality in a replacement algorithm proves to be particularly effective. However, there are two important considerations for data prefetching. Firstly, the sequential logical block accesses from the perspective of the OS's file abstraction may not correspond to sequential accesses in the physical layout of disk data. Secondly, file-level prefetching in the OS view involves a sequence of sequential accesses across contiguous files, which may not align with the actual data layout on the disk.

By leveraging knowledge of spatial locality, a prefetching algorithm can determine an effective prefetching order that maximizes sequential data accesses on the disk. This helps minimize the latency associated with disk accesses and improves overall system performance.

Researchers have made significant efforts to exploit spatial locality in data management by speculating and inferring the disk layout for operating systems. One proposal, outlined in [118], suggests aligning the file system block size with the track size of hard disks. By aligning these sizes, data placement within the disk would follow a track-by-track pattern, minimizing the seek time required by the disk read/write head for future accesses to the file.

Taking advantage of speculated disk data layout information, the DULO (dual localities) approach proposed in [75] enables the operating system to make data replacement decisions in the buffer cache while considering both temporal and spatial localities. By incorporating this speculated disk data layout information, data prefetching can also be optimized to maintain sequential access patterns on the disk, as discussed in [47].

These research efforts aim to leverage knowledge of the disk layout to enhance data management in operating systems. By aligning file system block sizes with disk track sizes and using speculated disk data layout information, both data replacement decisions and prefetching strategies can be improved, leading to better utilization of spatial locality and enhanced system performance.

Currently, disk controllers in disk products do not provide an interface to disclose dynamic disk layout information. This limitation may arise due to concerns such as overhead, cost, and security. However, it is anticipated that future storage systems will be designed to interact more with the operating system, enabling information sharing and leading to significant improvements in storage system performance and efficiency.

By establishing a communication channel between storage systems and the operating system, valuable information about the disk layout can be exchanged. This enhanced interaction would allow the operating system to have a more accurate and up-to-date understanding of the disk's internal organization. With this knowledge, the operating system can make more informed decisions regarding data placement, data replacement, prefetching, and other data management strategies.

The improved performance and efficiency of storage systems, facilitated by information sharing between the operating system and storage devices, would lead to enhanced system responsiveness, reduced latency, and optimized resource utilization. As storage technology continues to advance, it is expected that closer integration between the operating system and storage systems will become a standard practice, enabling more effective management of disk resources.

5   In-Memory Data Processing in Large Data Centers

Having comprehensively studied the entire memory hierarchy, we know that a conventional computing ecosystem relies heavily on disk storage, as the disk serves as a permanent repository for various types of data. During program execution and data processing, the OS, equipped with virtual memory and file systems, manages the movement of data bytes, words, blocks, pages, segments, and other data chunks up and down in the memory hierarchy. Nonetheless, the true execution platform resides in the main memory, situated close to the CPU and featuring fast on-chip caches. As applications handle increasingly large volumes of data, the existing disk-based systems are increasingly incapable of meeting the demands for low data access latency and high processing throughput. Consequently, in-memory data processing has evolved from an emerging technology to a mature necessity. In-memory data processing involves dynamically allocating data in a distributed environment, where fast and volatile DRAM memory serves as the permanent storage location, while slow nonvolatile disk drives are solely used for data archival purposes. In simpler terms, when a program executes, its datasets are loaded from disks only once, with the subsequent processing occurring primarily in the main memory. To achieve significant improvements in latency and throughput often surpassing hundreds or even thousands of times over those of disk-based systems, a suite of systems and application software has been developed to efficiently manage data in memory across a cluster of computing nodes. This chapter delves into the imperative nature and feasibility of in-memory data processing, with a specific focus on critical techniques of achieving low latency for remote memory access and minimizing random memory accesses.

5.1   Why Is In-Memory Data Processing Necessary?

As we have studied in Chapters 1, 2, 3, and 4, the primary objective of constructing a deep memory hierarchy in a system is to minimize data access latency by leveraging and exploiting data locality. However, when application programs exhibit limited locality, it poses challenges for the memory hierarchy's effectiveness. In-memory computing is primarily driven by the objective of achieving low latency across all applications. It is well understood that the latency of data access varies significantly among DRAM, SSD, and HDD. For instance, random accesses on HDD are exceptionally slow, while they are more acceptable for SSDs. On the other hand, sequential accesses on HDD offer a cost-effective and performance-efficient solution. Additionally, the latency for both read and write operations differs across these storage devices. To simplify the comparison of latency levels among DRAM, SSD, and HDD without being tied to specific products, a general rule of thumb can be applied. Assuming a DRAM data access latency of 1, SSDs can be estimated at 10^3, and HDDs at 10^6. By considering this approximation, even in the case of a 0.1 percent DRAM miss rate for page faults or storage data updates to maintain data consistency, transitioning from a traditional HDD-based system to an in-memory computing system would result in a 1000-fold reduction in runtime latency.

In 1987, Jim Gray and Gianfranco Putzolu introduced the Five-Minute Rule [57], an economic model that guided decisions to store data in either DRAM or HDD. The Five-Minute Rule states that "pages referenced every five minutes should be memory resident." This is based on the ratio between the cost effectiveness of hard disk (i.e., the price paid on a unit of disk bandwidth, or $ per MB/s) versus the cost effectiveness of DRAM (i.e., DRAM price per MB). With a cost-effective disk, the system may choose to leave frequently accessed data on disk and read it on-demand. With a cost-effective memory, the system may choose to buffer the data in memory even if it is not frequently accessed. By incorporating the disk accessing time and DRAM accessing time per MByte, the delay for disk data access or the time spent accessing data in DRAM can be determined using the following formula:

$$\text{memory time} = (\text{disk price} \times \text{disk time}) / \text{DRAM price per MByte}, \qquad (5.1)$$

where memory time is the interval between disk data accesses, representing the inverse of access frequency, aimed at keeping frequently accessed data in memory, disk time represents the accessing latency per MByte to disk, and disk price refers to the cost of the entire disk drive. Four decades ago, HDDs were expensive, had a small capacity, and had relatively low access latency due to the much slower CPUs at the time. Therefore, the choice between accessing DRAM or HDD was primarily driven by cost rather than performance. For instance, in the 1980s, accessing 1 KByte of data on a disk would cost around $2000, while the same amount of data in DRAM would only amount to $5. To provide context, the average cost of a typical disk drive in 1987 was approximately $20,000. Given an average disk bandwidth of 15 KBytes per second during that time, the disk time required to access 1 MByte of data was approximately 66.7 s. Additionally, the price of DRAM per MByte was $5000. Substituting these values into the Five-Minute Rule formula (5.1), the following result was obtained for the year 1987:

$$\text{memory time} = (\$20,000 \times 66.7 \text{ s}) / \$5000 = 266.8 \text{ s} \approx 5 \text{ min.}$$

The price of DRAM has experienced a significant decrease over the past 40 years. As an example, the cost per MByte of DRAM in 2022 was approximately $0.01. Simultaneously, the capacity of disks has witnessed a remarkable increase, thanks to the discovery of giant magnetoresistence (GMR) [9], leading to a significantly higher HDD density. Moreover, the I/O bandwidth has seen an improvement of over 1000 times. In today's context, at the time of writing, a $20,000 disk would provide a substantial amount of storage space. However, the latency associated with disk access has not seen significant improvements due to the persisting bottlenecks of mechanical seek and rotation times. Data centers require substantial and ongoing investments in disk drives with progressively larger capacities, given the era of data explosion and the need for extensive data archiving. When accessing data on a disk today, the primary latency arises from both seek and rotation times, averaging around 15 ms. Considering a combination of random and sequential disk accesses, the estimated average data accessing latency per MByte on a disk is approximately 0.07 s. Compared to the 66.7 s in 1987, this improvement is primarily attributed to enhancements in I/O bandwidth. A budget of $20,000 for HDD devices is very modest for a data center today, which will be used for the calculation. Substituting disk price = $20,000, disk time = 0.07 s, and DRAM price per MByte = $0.01 into the Five-Minute Rule formula (5.1), we obtain the following result:

$$\text{memory time} = (\$20,000 \times 0.07 \text{ s}) / \$0.01 = 140,000 \text{ s} \approx 39 \text{ h}.$$

The current technology trend, characterized by very low memory prices and ever-expanding storage capacities, indicates that increasingly large datasets should be primarily stored in DRAM for a long time, while disks are primarily utilized for backup purposes.

5.2   In-Memory Computing for High Scalability and Throughput

Scalability in a data center involves the ability to serve an increasing number of users by connecting more computing nodes and consistently updating each node's computing power and memory capacity to achieve sustained performance. Another crucial performance factor in data centers is throughput, which measures the number of major operations or tasks completed within a given time frame, such as the number of key-value store operations per second. High scalability and throughput are fundamental requirements for achieving high performance in data centers. In-memory computing enhances scalability and throughput through three key mechanisms.

First, the reduced latency in accessing in-memory data decreases execution time, thereby improving both scalability and throughput. Second, the elimination of data movement between disk and memory during program execution eliminates the overhead associated with such movement, which is a significant bottleneck limiting scalability and throughput. Finally, in-memory computing enables extensive parallel processing on data, allowing for the distribution of data processing tasks across multiple nodes in clusters. This parallelism can substantially enhance throughput and scalability by leveraging the power of concurrent processing across a large number of nodes.

5.3   The Limit of Memory Caching in Large-Scale Data Processing

As discussed in Chapter 3, memory caching has served as a solution to mitigate the long disk latency. This solution relies on the assumption of high data access locality, meaning that the majority of accesses are concentrated on a small set of data blocks. When this condition is met, memory caching can deliver in-memory computing performance at a cost comparable to disk-based systems. However, the limitations of memory caching solutions are often overlooked due to their maturity and standardization.

There are three significant issues to consider. First, even with a small miss rate, such as 1 percent, memory caching solutions can experience significant performance degradation due to the substantial performance gap between memory and disk, which is around 1000 times. Second, when data replacement operations occur, the updated data blocks in the memory must be written back to disk to maintain data consistency. This data transaction incurs significant overhead and introduces delays. Finally, for workloads with low data locality in many data-intensive applications, effective memory caching solutions require a substantial memory space. Therefore, in-memory computing solutions are better suited to handle both high and low locality workloads effectively.

5.4   The Advantages of In-Memory over SSD Data Processing

Is it possible to use SSD as the primary platform for data processing, creating an in-SSD computing system? This idea may seem to be reasonable and appealing since SSDs have lower latency compared to HDDs. However, in practice, employing SSDs as the main data processing platform is not feasible for achieving low latency and high throughput. An SSD is not a byte addressable device. Under current OS management, data still has to be loaded into the memory before processing, increasing data accessing latency. Additionally, there are three other key reasons for this limitation.

First, the latency of SSDs is still significantly higher than that of DRAM, which has a detrimental impact on scalability and throughput. Despite the lower latency compared to HDDs, SSDs are not able to match the performance levels offered by DRAM.

Second, SSDs are I/O devices with a complex device controller managing its internals. Similar to HDDs, SSDs function as block devices. The OS prepares SSD data block access requests for read or write operations and transfers them to the SSD via the I/O bus. The SSD controller then performs the read and write actions on the SSD. This process incurs unavoidable additional overhead due to device drivers and interrupt handlers, which further adds latency to accessing the SSD.

Finally, SSD's flash memory cells have a limited number of program and erase cycles, commonly known as P/E cycles. Because of this physical limitation, SSDs are not suitable as working devices for highly interactive and dynamic transactions. However, they can serve as relatively low latency storage devices for data archiving purposes.

In summary, while SSDs offer lower latency compared to HDDs, they are not suitable for serving as the main data processing platform due to their higher latency compared to DRAM, the processing overhead associated with device drivers and interrupt handlers, and their physical limitations in handling highly interactive and dynamic transactions.

5.5   Necessary Mechanisms for In-Memory Data Processing

When designing and implementing disk-based systems, computer system architects and developers did not need to address certain issues that are crucial for in-memory computing. However, these issues become significant considerations in the context of in-memory computing.

First, the price of DRAM is higher compared to disk storage. Consequently, building an in-memory computing system can be more expensive than a disk-based system. This cost difference must be taken into account when considering the feasibility and affordability of an in-memory computing solution.

Second, the capacity of DRAM memory sets a limit on the amount of data that can be processed simultaneously. This limitation can impact the scalability and throughput of an in-memory computing system. The available memory capacity must be carefully managed and optimized to ensure efficient data processing.

Third, as discussed in Chapter 3, datasets in DRAM devices are organized and stored in three dimensions: banks, rows (pages), and columns (cache lines) [115, 142]. Consequently, the performance of memory access is closely tied to the access patterns of the application's data. For instance, if each memory access accesses only a single page and the subsequent access is to another page within the same memory bank, it will miss the DRAM row-buffer for each access, leading to increased latency. This kind of accessing patterns is called "random accesses" among many pages in DRAM memory. This issue needs to be addressed by application users who are aware of the memory system architecture.

Finally, it is important to note that in-memory computing systems are volatile, meaning that data are lost when power is turned off or in the event of a system crash. This characteristic can pose challenges for applications that require persistent storage and data durability. Strategies for data persistence, such as regular backups or employing nonvolatile memory technologies, need to be considered to ensure data integrity and continuity.

It is widely recognized that DRAM is more expensive than disk storage. However, this cost difference has been relatively insignificant in the context of in-memory computing due to the significant performance gains it offers. The benefits of in-memory computing far outweigh the additional costs associated with DRAM.

Nevertheless, when implementing in-memory computing, the challenge lies in addressing the need for a large and fast storage. This requirement often involves connecting many DRAM memory devices across networks to enable remote memory accesses. As the demand for memory space continues to grow, the latency of remote memory access becomes a critical factor impacting the scalability of an in-memory computing system. Efforts must be made to minimize this latency and ensure efficient and timely access to remote memory.

We will also examine a case that explores the reduction of random accesses in DRAM memory through the introduction of external acceleration forces.

Another major concern in in-memory computing is data reliability and consistency. Since data resides in volatile memory, ensuring its integrity and consistency becomes a significant challenge. It is essential to establish a robust set of system mechanisms that effectively address these concerns. These mechanisms are crucial for enabling in-memory computing in various large-scale data processing applications within data centers.

In summary, while the higher cost of DRAM is a well-known fact, it has been overshadowed by the substantial performance gains of in-memory computing. However, the challenges of providing a large memory space, minimizing remote memory access latency, reducing random memory accesses, and addressing data reliability and consistency are crucial aspects that must be tackled to fully leverage the benefits of in-memory computing in diverse large-scale data processing applications within data centers.

5.6   Communication Protocols for Remote Memory Accesses

This section introduces three communication protocols that are essential for enabling remote memory accesses in the context of in-memory computing. These protocols play a crucial role in facilitating efficient and reliable data transfer between distributed memory nodes.

5.6.1   Remote Procedure Calls (RPC) for In-Memory Computing

With the continuous advancement of networking technologies, such as Terabit Ethernet (TbE) [6], the bandwidth available for accessing and transferring data remotely within a large-scale data center has reached levels comparable to the internal bandwidth within a single node. This remarkable progress has enabled data centers to leverage the vast capacity of remote memory resources for in-memory computing. In a data-center environment, numerous microservices [49] from remote nodes are interconnected using remote procedure calls (RPC) [19].

To illustrate, we can say that a computing task is always "outsourcing" multiple RPC services from remote nodes, with each computing node serving others in a similar manner; RPC enables "computing globalization" within data centers, delivering high performance at increasingly affordable costs. By providing a request-response protocol, RPC abstracts away the complexities of communication and allows remote procedure calls to be executed seamlessly, being just like local function calls. It serves as an easy and architecture-independent programming interface, empowering developers to efficiently build applications within sophisticated distributed systems.

Furthermore, this "computing globalization" across networks has become a fundamental pillar of modern system infrastructure. According to a Google data-center report, the number of RPCs per second has surpassed 10 billion [55], highlighting the widespread adoption and importance of RPC in contemporary computing environments.

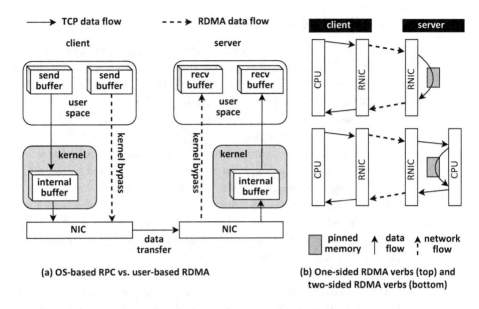

Figure 5.1 A data- and execution-flow comparison between RPC and RDMA and the two internal communication primitives in RDMA. (a) In OS-based RPC, the data are copied from a user buffer to a kernel buffer before being transferred to a buffer in the NIC for delivery to the server's NIC. On the server side, the data are once again copied from the NIC buffer to a kernel buffer and then moved to the receive (recv) buffer in the user space. In contrast, in user-based RDMA, the data are directly moved from the user buffer to the buffer in the NIC for delivery to the server's NIC. Similarly, on the server side, the data from the NIC buffer is directly moved to the receive (recv) buffer in the user space. (b) Please note that in this figure, the user buffers inside the CPUs are omitted, and "RNIC" refers to RDMA NIC. It is important to mention that one-sided RDMA enables direct access to pinned memory without involving the server CPU. On the other hand, two-sided RDMA requires the involvement of the server's CPU.

However, traditional RPC implementations rely on a transmission control protocol (TCP)-based transport layer, which introduces inherent latency issues when accessing remote nodes due to data copying between user space and kernel space, as well as the significant overhead caused by frequent OS kernel interrupts. In Figure 5.1(a), the solid lines depict the OS-based RPC communication protocol. When a client initiates an RPC request to a remote server, it first prepares the necessary arguments and variables related to the procedure in its "send buffer" located in the user space, which is simplified as "data." Subsequently, an interruption occurs in the OS to copy the data from the client's "send buffer" to the "internal buffer" residing in the kernel space. Simultaneously, the OS sets up a TCP communication channel between the client's network interface card (NIC) and the server's NIC. Once the data reaches the server's NIC, another interruption takes place in the OS on the server side to copy the data from the NIC to the "internal buffer" within the kernel space. The OS then facilitates the transfer of data from the "internal buffer" to the "receive buffer" in the user space on the server side. Once the client-to-server data transfer is complete, the server can proceed to execute the requested procedure call.

5.6.2   Remote Direct Memory Access (RDMA)

In contrast to RPC, the remote direct memory access (RDMA) protocol, along with its specialized NICs, enables direct remote memory accesses without involving OS kernels on either the client or server side. The RDMA protocol achieves low latency in data communication by managing data operations within the user space, eliminating the need for data copies between the user space and kernel space, as well as the overhead of CPU interruptions for OS services. Figure 5.1(a) illustrates the RDMA communication protocol using dotted lines, which signifies its user-based nature. When a client initiates an RDMA request to a server, it prepares the data in its "send buffer" within the user space. Subsequently, the data in the "send buffer" is directly transmitted to the NIC, initiating an RDMA communication from the client's NIC to the server's NIC. Upon arrival at the server's NIC, the data are directly copied from the NIC to the "receive buffer" within the user space on the server side. At this point, the server can proceed to execute the requested data accesses.

Remote direct memory access is a communication protocol that allows applications to directly read from and write to specific memory regions across a network, facilitating efficient data transfer between nodes. To utilize RDMA, users must register or pin the memory regions and specify the attributes of these regions. These attributes define how the memory regions can be accessed by local or remote nodes and provide instructions to the RDMA NIC. Once the registration is complete, the RDMA client and server can exchange data stored in their respective memory regions through the designated RDMA NIC. Both the client and server "pin" their specified RDMA memory regions to inform the kernel that the registered memory is intended for RDMA communication. This pinning process establishes a channel between the NIC and the registered memory.

Remote direct memory access programming is facilitated through an application programming interface (API) known as "verbs" [54]. The communication primitives of RDMA can be classified into two categories: one-sided verbs and two-sided verbs. One-sided verbs, depicted in the upper part of Figure 5.1(b), enable direct access to remote memory without the need for remote CPU involvement. On the other hand, two-sided verbs, illustrated in the lower part of Figure 5.1(b), require CPU involvement on both the sender and receiver sides to facilitate remote memory accesses.

5.6.3   Achieving Low-Latency Memory Accessing under RPC

Both RPC and RDMA have their own merits and limitations. On one hand, RPC provides a general-purpose programming interface that allows for easy programming for various applications. However, its high-latency remote data accesses can hinder scalability and throughput in in-memory computing scenarios. On the other hand, RDMA offers low-latency data accesses, which is advantageous for efficient data transfer. However, its user interface is more specialized and may not be as user friendly for a wide range of users, thus limiting its applicability.

By integrating RPC and RDMA into a single system, we can leverage the unique advantages of both approaches. Such a system would exhibit two key benefits. First, it would provide a broad user scope similar to that of RPC, allowing for the development of general-purpose systems to support many and diverse applications. Second, it would harness the low-latency advantage of RDMA, enhancing overall system performance.

In summary, an integrated system that combines RPC and RDMA would offer an easy programming interface while leveraging the low-latency benefits of RDMA, resulting in improved scalability and performance for in-memory computing applications.

5.7   Data Reliability and Availability in In-Memory Computing

Given that DRAM memory is a volatile device, the risk of data loss and disruptions to computing operations due to power outages is a significant concern. To mitigate these risks and ensure data reliability and availability, several system mechanisms have been developed. In this section, we will discuss five commonly used techniques that address this issue.

1. **Uninterruptible power supply (UPS)** is a commonly used power device in all data centers. In-memory computing systems often employ UPS devices to provide short-term power backup during power outages. These UPS systems typically have batteries that can keep the servers running for a limited time, allowing for a controlled shutdown of the system or transferring the workload to alternative power sources.

2. Another approach is to facilitate **redundant power supply** devices. In-memory systems usually have redundant power supplies in each server. If one power supply fails or experiences a power outage, the other power supply takes over to ensure continuous operation of the server.

3. In-memory computing systems also **replicate data across multiple servers or even sites** to ensure high availability and durability. Specifically, each data block stored in an in-memory system is typically replicated across multiple server nodes. In the event of a power outage or failure of a server, the data can still be accessed from other replicas, ensuring data durability and availability. Although the replication approach is expensive in both space and time, timely data availability during a regional power outage in a data center is guaranteed.

4. **Checkpointing** is a conventional system mechanism used to ensure fault tolerance for long-running applications. It involves periodically saving the state of the running application to nonvolatile storage devices. The checkpointing mechanism works by persistently storing the in-memory data onto nonvolatile storage and maintaining a log of all the changes made to the data since the last consistent data update between the in-memory data and the stored data.

   In the event of a power outage or system failure, the checkpointing mechanism plays a crucial role in recovering and restoring the data to a consistent state. It does this by restoring the last consistent checkpoint, which represents the data state at the time of the most recent storage update. From there, the mechanism replays the subsequent changes recorded in the log, applying them in the order they occurred. This process ensures that the in-memory data are brought up to date with the latest modifications made before the power outage, thereby achieving data consistency and preserving the integrity of the application.

5. When power is restored after an outage, in-memory computing servers need to be restarted. Upon a **restart**, the servers go through a recovery process to restore their state. This typically involves contacting other servers in the cluster to retrieve missing or outdated data and syncing up with the latest state of the system.

Some of the above-mentioned techniques are described in the RAMCloud project [111], which is a distributed in-memory storage system designed for high-performance and low-latency applications.

5.8   Fast Indexing for In-Memory Key–Value Stores

The KV-store utilizes a data structure consisting of a *key–value pair record*, where each key is associated with a corresponding value. The keys are directly mapped to specific locations in the record using a *hashing function*. This mapping is not order preserving, but rather random within the scope of the record file. The associated value of a key can represent the actual content or serve as an address pointing to the content's location. This straightforward data structure allows for efficient storage, retrieval, and updating of data in various data processing applications, typically achieving an average time complexity of $O(1)$.

However, in practical implementations, the KV-store has a more-complex data structure to handle collision events that occur when multiple keys are mapped to the same location in the record. A search in a KV-store generally involves two stages.

The first stage is indexing, which involves calculating the hashing function and managing collisions if they occur. The goal of the indexing stage is to determine the location of the value within the key–value pair record file.

Once the location is found, the second stage involves accessing the value and delivering it from the server to the requesting client.

Three basic KV-store operations of GET (key), SET/ADD/REPLACE (Key, Value) and DELETE (Key) have been described in Chapter 3.

In an in-memory computing environment, large key–value pair record files are stored and operated in the DRAM memory, serving many clients. Figure 5.2 illustrates a basic execution flow of a conventional KV-store. The clients' keys are transmitted to the server's NIC via networks, where they are processed by the CPU of the in-memory computing server. By employing a hashing function, the CPU locates the corresponding value for each key, which is a fundamental operation in any KV-store and is commonly known as *indexing*. To deal with hashing collisions in a key–value pair record, different data structures are developed, such as trees or linked lists. Thus, indexing is not just a hashing function calculation, but often operates a sophisticated data structure, which demand multiple random memory accesses in the key–value

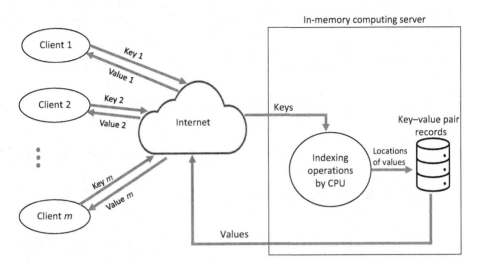

Figure 5.2 A data and execution flow for a conventional KV-store.

pair record. Once the indexing is complete, the content of the value can be retrieved from the record. Both the indexing and value content retrieval operations are carried out in the DRAM memory. The size of the key–value pair record file has grown considerably in various applications, resulting in indexing memory accesses that are highly random due to the inherent nature of hashing functions and hashing collision management. In Chapter 3, the randomness phenomenon is further explored and we make a brief review based on indexing operations of a hash table. The DRAM memory contains a cache known as the "row-buffer" [70]. Before processing, a memory page is always fetched from the row-buffer. If a row-buffer miss occurs, the page needs to be loaded from the DRAM core to the row-buffer, which significantly increases the DRAM latency. This internal DRAM operation is referred to as *row access*. Since key–value indexing memory accesses are rarely concentrated on a single page, but rather spread across multiple pages due to several indexing steps before reaching the location of the value, each memory access to a new page results in a row-buffer miss, causing the existing page in the row-buffer to be replaced by the new page. Random memory accesses contribute to a high row-buffer miss rate due to the structure of the DRAM. Although a commonly used technique called "XOR permutation" [142], implemented in the memory controller for general-purpose processors, can reduce the row-buffer miss rate, the high volume of indexing remains a bottleneck for KV-stores. For instance, a study [141] indicates that 50 percent to 75 percent of the execution time in a KV-store is dedicated to indexing operations. The indexing operations are effectively accelerated by parallel processing of GPUs in Mega-KV.

Mega-KV: GPU Accelerations for Indexing

A KV-store system called Mega-KV [141] was developed to address architectural issues related to the interactions between KV-store and DRAM memory. Figure 5.3

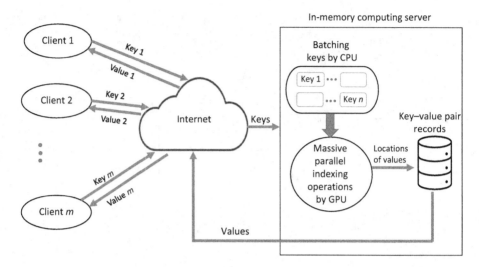

Figure 5.3 A data- and execution-flow for a GPU-accelerated KV-store.

illustrates the basic execution flow of Mega-KV. The system's software environment remains unchanged, but instead of immediately performing indexing operations, the CPU in the server first batches the requests for values based on keys to accumulate a sizable amount. This prepares for massively parallel indexing operations by the GPU in the subsequent step. The GPU performs these indexing operations concurrently and in a super-fast mode, breaking the bottleneck of random memory accesses in DRAM. By avoiding random memory accesses in server's main memory during indexing operations and employing massive parallelism on the GPU, Mega-KV achieves significant indexing acceleration.

In 2015, Mega-KV demonstrated a throughput of over 160 million key–value operations per second, which was the highest record by then. Subsequently, through further optimization and the use of more advanced GPUs, a collaboration between NVIDIA and Oak Ridge National Laboratory pushed Mega-KV to a new high record of 888 million key–value operations per second in 2018 [35]. The indexing acceleration framework of Mega-KV can easily scale it to the Giga-KV level or even higher, as the speed and memory capacity of GPUs continue to increase over time.

RDMA-Based KV-Stores

To enable the deployment of KV-stores at scale in large clusters, a shared key–value pair record architecture is utilized, where the record file is distributed among multiple nodes and accessed by clients. Remote direct memory access has been employed as a method for implementing these KV-stores, as demonstrated in previous work [48].

In this architecture, the keys submitted by clients are directly connected to the hash table residing in a registered region of the DRAM memory of a remote node, bypassing the OS kernel. The indexing operations required for key-value retrieval are performed by client computing facilities located remotely. The retrieved value is then delivered directly to the registered memory regions in clients, bypassing the client CPU. This approach ensures high throughput and low latency.

Overall, the use of RDMA and distributed key–value pair records allows for efficient and scalable deployment of KV-stores in large clusters, facilitating fast and direct access to key–value pairs with minimal involvement of the servers' CPUs and operating systems.

KV-Direct: Parallel Indexing in NIC

Conceptually, KV-Direct [91] combines the strengths of both Mega-KV and RDMA-based KV-stores by leveraging parallel indexing in the server and bypassing the OS kernel on both sides. In KV-Direct, a specialized NIC is utilized that incorporates a field-programmable gate array (FPGA) for parallel processing. The system's software environment is customized to enable bypassing the host CPU and OS kernel, while the NIC is programmable with FPGA capabilities for parallel processing.

In the KV-Direct architecture, the keys submitted by clients are directly connected to the key–value pair in DRAM memory through the NIC, effectively bypassing the host OS kernel. The FPGA embedded in the NIC handles the indexing operations within the server. Once the value is retrieved, it is delivered directly to the NIC for subsequent transmission to the clients, bypassing the CPU. This approach enhances the basic RDMA functions by enabling parallel indexing operations within the NIC using the FPGA.

By combining the benefits of parallel indexing and bypassing the OS kernel, KV-Direct offers an optimized solution for key–value storage. The integration of an FPGA within the NIC enhances performance and allows for efficient processing, resulting in improved throughput and reduced latency in the KV-Direct system.

6 GPU Computing: A New Algorithm-to-Architecture Interaction

> You think you know when you can learn, are more sure when you can write, even more when you can teach, but certain when you can program.
>
> Alan Perlis, *the first recipient of the Turing Award.*

We have entered a new era of computing where domain-specific hardware accelerators, such as graphics processing units (GPUs) [102], tensor processing units (TPUs) [77], and data processing unots (DPUs) [26], are becoming increasingly crucial in supporting a range of critical applications. These applications include graphic processing, high-performance computing, machine learning, network data processing, and many other computing tasks. The architecture and programming interfaces of hardware accelerators, such as GPUs, TPUs, and DPUs, differ from those of traditional general-purpose CPUs like x86 or ARM processors. As a result, existing applications and software systems need to be modified or redesigned to fully take advantage of the hardware's capabilities. This interaction between algorithms, systems, and hardware accelerators is a significant challenge in this new era of computing.

This chapter highlights the GPU, the trailblazer of hardware accelerators, which initially served graphics applications but has since become a leading platform for high-performance computing and deep learning. The widespread popularity of GPUs, such as the Nvidia GPU, can be attributed to both hardware and software advancements. The hardware side boasts numerous parallel processing cores, high-performance memory systems, and specialized hardware, such as tensor and ray tracing cores. For example, Figure 6.1 shows an architectural diagram of the Nvidia Ada Lovelace GPU. This comprehensive hardware setup enables the acceleration of various compute-intensive tasks. On the software front, GPU manufacturers offer parallel computing platforms and libraries, such as the Nvidia CUDA toolkit [104], to assist developers in utilizing the GPU through a general-purpose programming interface. With continuous improvement of the software platform in areas like memory management, the Nvidia GPU and CUDA have become the dominant ecosystem for accelerated computing.

Despite the advancements in GPU programming platforms, developers still face challenges in effectively implementing their applications on GPUs due to the presence of two key difficulties.

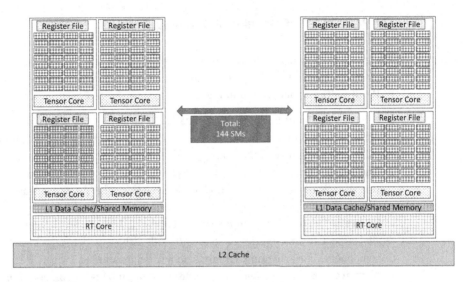

Figure 6.1 The redrawn architectural illustration of the full-chip block diagram of the Nvidia Ada GPU (AD 102) according to the Nvidia Ada Lovelace Architecture whitebook [107]. Inside each SM (Streaming Multiprocessor), there are 128 CUDA cores, 4 tensor cores, and 1 RT Core (for ray tracing).

- **Difficulty of auto parallelization** The GPU's computational power advantage stems from its numerous parallel processing units. For instance, the latest Nvidia ADA GPU depicted in Figure 6.1 has 18,432 CUDA cores [107]. Efficient parallel algorithms are crucial to fully utilize all the cores. However, developing parallel algorithms and programs, either from scratch or from sequential versions, is challenging, both for human developers and even automatic programming tools.
- **Difficulty of auto optimization** High-performance GPU programs heavily rely on optimal utilization of hardware features, such as GPU core organization, thread scheduling and synchronization, memory hierarchy, and other hardware parameters and limitations. Moreover, rapid advancement in GPU hardware often results in diverse features across generations of hardware. Automatically optimizing a GPU algorithm to account for these rich hardware features is a challenging task.

This chapter is not meant to serve as a tutorial on high-performance GPU programming. Readers are encouraged to consult Nvidia CUDA programming books (e.g., [82]) for that purpose. Additionally, this book is not a parallel algorithm book. Instead, this chapter focuses on exploring the interaction between algorithms and GPUs using a case study approach. Sorting algorithms are used because they are fundamental computer algorithms and foundational algorithms for GPU-based data management applications. The journey will start with a well-known sequential sorting algorithm and end with efficient GPU sorting algorithms. Along the way, we will introduce a principle methodology of GPU parallel programming based on PAPA (Premier, Algorithm, Program, and Advancement), which was introduced in Chapter 1.

6.1   The PAPA of GPU Parallel Programming

The process of using GPU parallel programming to solve a computing problem involves the interaction of four key components or steps, which are referred to as the PAPA of GPU parallel programming.

- **Premier** The central concept or underlying principle that drives the design and implementation of a parallel algorithm solution is referred to as the "premier." The premier is machine independent.
- **Algorithm** The algorithm encompasses both a sequential version and a parallel version specifically designed for GPU implementation. The algorithm is again machine independent.
- **Program** The program comprises both GPU-side kernels, which represent the parallel aspect of the solution, and a CPU-side driver, which serves as the control component. The program is highly machine dependent.
- **Advancement** The advancement focuses on optimizing the mapping of the algorithm and program to the unique hardware features of the GPU, as well as addressing potential corner cases during the design and implementation phase. The advancement is machine and its system software dependent.

The PAPA process encompasses the possibility of iterative interactions among the four steps, particularly during the advancement step, where multiple rounds of redesign and implementation may be necessary. This section will utilize detailed examples to illustrate these components and their interactions.

6.1.1   Premier

> We can't solve problems by using the same kind of thinking we used when we created them.
>
> Albert Einstein, *one of the greatest scientists in human history.*

An abstract and mathematical foundation that allows a problem to be broken down into manageable tasks, making a parallel solution both possible and efficient, is referred to as the "premier." It is important to note that the premier is not an algorithm itself, but rather a general-purpose methodology, or *meta-algorithm*, such as a dynamic programming approach, or a specific principle or property that pertains to the target problem.

The concept of premier will be demonstrated using the problem of generating the Fibonacci sequence. The nth number in the sequence is determined by the sum of the two preceding numbers, as described by the following equation:

$$F(0) = 0, F(1) = 1, F(n) = F(n-1) + F(n-2).$$

Regardless of whether the program for solving this problem will be written in a recursive or nonrecursive form, the equation implies a *dependency* between the calculation of the nth number and the calculations of the $(n - 1)$th and $(n - 2)$th numbers. This dependency dictates that the numbers in the sequence must be generated in a sequential manner, such as 0, 1, 1, 2, 3, 5, 8, and so on. The challenge is to find a way to parallelize this process.

Before a parallel algorithm can be designed to generate the Fibonacci sequence, it is necessary to identify the parallelism opportunities through the use of a premier. The premier has a significant impact on the degree of parallelization and ultimately on the performance of the solution.

To start, let us consider the most basic premier that regards $F(n - 1)$ and $F(n - 2)$ as two independent subproblems that can be executed in parallel prior to calculating $F(n)$. However, this premier does not effectively reveal any parallelism within the Fibonacci sequence as the calculation of $F(n)$ still relies on $F(n - 1)$. Essentially, it only parallelizes two redundant calculations of $F(n - 2)$ that are not truly necessary. As a result, this premier creates only *"no parallelism."*

Given that the first n numbers in the sequence have already been calculated, what kind of parallelism can be identified? By repeatedly applying the formula $F(n) = F(n-1) + F(n-2)$, the following equation can be derived, which serves as our second premier:

$$F(n + i) = F(n) \times (F(i) + F(i - 1)) + F(n - 1) \times F(i), i > 1.$$

The equation indicates that if the values of $F(0)$ through $F(n)$ are already known, then each number between $F(n+1)$ and $F(2n)$ can be calculated independently. Hence, the generation of the Fibonacci sequence can be considered as a series of stages, where the number of independently calculable numbers in each stage doubles that of the previous stage. This type of parallelization, enabled by the second premier, is referred to as *"staged parallelism."*

Essentially, the second premier has successfully converted the dependency between two consequent numbers into the one between two consecutive stages. However, we can go further if we know more about mathematical properties of the Fibonacci sequence. Actually the numbers have a closed-form expression according to the following equation (called *Binet's formula*) [68]:

$$F(n) = \frac{\varphi^n - (1 - \varphi)^n}{\sqrt{5}}, \varphi = \frac{1 + \sqrt{5}}{2}.$$

Here, we do not delve into the derivation of this analytical expression. Rather, we emphasize that it renders the generation of the Fibonacci numbers devoid of dependencies, as each $F(n)$ is only linked to n and no other numbers in the sequence. This equation allows us to calculate the nth number in the Fibonacci sequence directly and in a parallel way. Hence, we refer to the parallelization created by this premier as *"max parallelism."*

By exploring the three premiers and the parallelism they uncovered, we can conclude that the design and implementation of a parallel algorithm heavily depend on the premier. Different premiers can lead to different degrees of parallelism and different levels of performance. Choosing the right premier is crucial for solving a computing problem effectively and efficiently in a parallel way. The example also highlights the fact that the opportunities for acceleration are closely tied to a developer's understanding of the application-specific domain knowledge.

6.1.2   Algorithm and Program

After the premier step, we move away from the mathematics and application domains and return to the realm of computer science and engineering to discuss algorithms and programs. While a premier can be abstract in one's mind, both algorithms and programs have strict definitions. An algorithm must be capable of being printed on paper so that a programmer can comprehend it and convert it into a program. Furthermore, a program must be able to be compiled, interpreted, or executed by a tangible computer.

Writing a parallel algorithm for GPUs based on a premier can still be challenging. In many cases, a recursive process can obscure the parallelism. Consequently, while it may be relatively easy to obtain a recursive sequential algorithm, a programmer must still derive an equivalent nonrecursive sequential algorithm before converting it to a parallel one for the GPU.

In addition, developers must be able to analyze the space and time complexity of a parallel algorithm. Two extreme scenarios for analysis include (1) when a parallel algorithm is reduced to a sequential one due to a lack of parallel computing resources (such as a single CPU core), and (2) when a parallel algorithm has an unlimited number of parallel computing resources or when the number of parallel units equals the problem size, denoted by n. For example, in the case of the Fibonacci sequence, if we develop three GPU algorithms based on the three premiers, we can obtain their time complexities with unlimited parallel units as $O(n)$, $O(\log n)$ (due to the doubling expansion in stages), and $O(1)$.

Writing a GPU program with a given GPU algorithm is a relatively straightforward task. However, unlike the conventional thinking that "Algorithms + Data Structures = Programs" [134], a GPU platform can often involve more specific implementation details due to the variations in different generations of GPU hardware and software. For instance, diverse Nvidia GPU devices can have highly intricate hardware feature descriptions, which are defined using the concept of *compute capability* [104]. As a result, any concrete programs must be constructed with consideration of these practical factors.

6.1.3   Advancement

This step mainly pertains to GPU hardware-oriented optimizations, which may necessitate redesign and reimplementation of all previous steps. Real GPU hardware devices are intricate, and there are multiple performance-critical factors that require explicit usage in GPU programs.

For instance, if we examine the Nvidia Ada GPU architecture in Figure 6.1, we may initially perceive it as two separate abstractions of programmable devices.

- **Ideal PRAM** A GPU consists of a single-layered set of parallel processors and a global memory. All processors can access any part of the global memory with uniform performance, and they can communicate with each other in a coordinated manner. Usually, such a parallel device abstraction is called a parallel random-access machine, or simply a PRAM [61].
- **Practical network** A GPU comprises a two-layered set of parallel processors, which are first organized into multiple local groups (e.g., streaming multiprocessors in Nvidia GPU) and then a global group. The same task executed on processors within the same local group and processors across different local groups can have vastly different performance behaviors.

Thus far, we have only discussed parallelism, which essentially applies only to the first abstraction. However, as the following sections will explain, when targeting the second abstraction, more-complex factors must be considered, such as locality, synchronization, coalesced memory access, and others. Furthermore, when considering these factors, all of the previous steps may need to be reevaluated in an iterative manner.

6.2 Parallelizing Bubble Sort: Where Can We Go?

In this section, we provide an overview of parallel sorting algorithms and their implementations in GPUs. We begin by presenting a well-known sequential sorting algorithm, namely bubble sort [7], and demonstrate why this simple algorithm is not suitable for parallel processing. Next, we utilize a sorting network approach, which provides a higher-dimensional view to analyze various sorting algorithms, and explain how bubble sort can be parallelized into a form of the so-called odd–even sorting algorithm (simply called odd–even sort) [59]. We then demonstrate that while such a parallel sorting algorithm is effective, its efficiency can be further improved by utilizing two more advanced sorting networks, including Batcher's bitonic sorting network and Batcher's odd–even sorting network [12].

6.2.1 Bubble Sort

Our sorting journey begins with bubble sort, which is commonly regarded as one of the simplest sorting algorithms in various teaching materials. Its main idea is straightforward: to sort an array in ascending order, the algorithm sequentially compares and swaps (if necessary) each element with its adjacent element in the array. Larger elements are then moved to their correct positions through multiple rounds or passes of these operations, until the array is finally sorted.

The following C-language code illustrates how bubble sort works. It is designed to sort a length-n array a in ascending order. Here, we omit the implementation of the swap function. It is often to use a single operation (or function), *CompareAndSwap*, to represent the combination of the comparison operation and the swap operation, as shown by the commented line in the code.

```
for (int i = 0; i < n - 1; i++)
{
    for(int j = 0; j < n - 1 - i; j++)
    {
        // CompareAndSwap(a[j],a[j+1]);
        if(a[j] > a[j+1]) swap(a[j], a[j+1]);
    }
}
```

The code consists of a two-layer for loop. The outer loop defines the $n-1$ executions of the inner loop, which processes each element from the beginning to its corresponding position. In the inner loop, the stop condition $j < n - 1 - i$ is an improved version that is more efficient than simply using $j < n - 1$, since comparisons for the elements whose indexes are after $n-1-i$ are unnecessary. From the code, according to its double loop nature, we can observe that the average complexity of bubble sort is $O(n^2)$.

The question now arises as to how we can parallelize the execution of bubble sort using multiple processors (e.g., n). Unfortunately, upon an initial examination of the code, its highly sequential nature becomes evident. Firstly, the code consists of multiple passes, and before each pass (an execution of the inner loop) can begin, the previous pass must have already ended. Secondly, during each pass, the comparison and swaps are sequential, that is, processing of the next element can only start after the previous element has been processed. This absolute ordering between two operations creates a dependency, which renders the parallel execution of two operations impossible. Consequently, even with multiple processors, the presence of both intrapass and interpass dependencies results in all operations being executed sequentially during bubble sort.

Fortunately, the analysis above is too conservative because there is actually potential parallelism within bubble sort. This parallelism can be exposed by utilizing a higher-dimensional view to examine the dependencies of the algorithm.

6.2.2   Parallel Bubble Sort: From a Higher-Dimensional View

When navigating inside a complex building with multiple rooms, it can be challenging to grasp the overall structure of the entire building. However, if you possess the floor plan of the building, you can quickly understand its structure because you are viewing the building from a different dimension. Similarly, if we can create a floor plan for an algorithm, we can reexamine the relationships among the operations within the algorithm.

In computer science, a *sorting network* can be considered as a floor-plan tool for analyzing various sorting algorithms. For the aforementioned bubble-sort algorithm, which sorts n elements, we can create a visualization such as the following.

- **Horizontal line** A horizontal line is drawn for each array position from left to right.
- **Vertical line** For each comparison and swap operation between elements at two array positions, a vertical line is drawn to connect the two corresponding horizontal

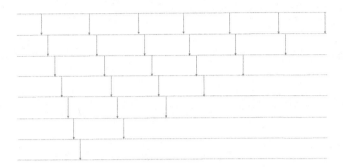

Figure 6.2 A sorting network diagram to illustrate the operation of comparison and swap during the execution of a bubble sort algorithm. Each horizontal line represents an element to be sorted, and the time line is shown by from left to right. Each vertical line (with arrow) represents that the two elements at the endpoints need to be compared and swapped. The arrow direction shows where the larger element goes.

lines. If an operation occurs after another one, it should be on the right side of the earlier one.

A vertical line can be accompanied by an arrow to explicitly indicate the direction of the compare and swap operation. If the arrow points downwards, it indicates that between two elements, the larger one should be swapped down and the smaller one should be swapped up. In this book, if no arrow is explicitly drawn for a vertical line, we treat the compare and swap operation it represents as downward. Figure 6.2 illustrates such a picture of a sorting network for the aforementioned bubble sort.

The image clearly depicts the execution sequence of operations expressed by the two-layer loop mentioned earlier. The outer loop determines the major passes that progress from left to right in the picture, while the inner loop defines the operations that occur within each pass from top to bottom. Unfortunately, all the operations depicted in the picture are sequential and ordered in terms of absolute timing. As a result, the total number of executions of the comparison and swap operation from left to right is given by the sum $(n - 1) + (n - 2) + \cdots + 2 + 1$, which simplifies to $(n^2 - n)/2$, resulting in a time complexity of $O(n^2)$.

You might be wondering why it is necessary to use a visual representation of the algorithm since they are identical. However, the visual representation offers the advantage of showing the relationship among operations in terms of their positions on both the horizontal and vertical lines. We describe bubble sort as sequential due to two characteristics. First, as dictated by the outer loop, the major passes must be sequential. Second, as governed by the inner loop, the operations within each pass must also be sequential. Nevertheless, the picture illustrates that two operations from different passes may not be dependent on each other, which means they can be executed simultaneously.

Figure 6.3 illustrates such opportunities. The dashed line connects two circled arrows, such as the one near the top left corner, indicating that the two comparison and swap operations are completely independent of each other (because they process

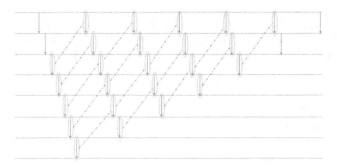

Figure 6.3 Unlock the potential for parallelism in bubble sort with this illustrative diagram. The circled vertical lines denote comparison and swap operations, with dotted lines connecting independent operations that can be executed in parallel. By visualizing the potential for parallelism, we can gain a deeper understanding of how bubble sort can be optimized for efficient sorting.

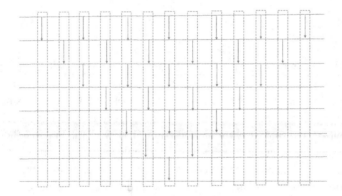

Figure 6.4 Illustration of a parallel bubble sort algorithm. This diagram illustrates the concept of "pass" in the algorithm, where the entire execution is comprised of multiple sequential passes, and within each pass, all processors can work independently.

two nonoverlapping element pairs). Although they originate from different outer loops in the aforementioned bubble sort code, their executions can be arranged to occur simultaneously if two available processors are present. Likewise, there are several other parallelism opportunities depicted by the other dashed lines in the image.

Thus, efficient utilization of such parallelism involves rescheduling the execution of independent operations (even across outer loops) to occur simultaneously within a redefined pass. Figure 6.4 illustrates this execution, which clearly depicts that during one pass, there could be several independent operations, as illustrated by the dashed lines in Figure 6.3.

Figure 6.4 demonstrates the functioning of a parallel bubble sort. Firstly, it does not alter the number of operations (comparisons and swaps) used in the sequential version. Instead, it modifies the organization of operations to enable parallel execution. This represents the first parallel sort algorithm discovered thus far. It comprises multiple passes, and within each pass, there may be several independent operations that can be assigned to different processors.

Figure 6.4 displays fewer passes from left to right compared to Figure 6.2, as multiple operations can be integrated into a single pass. Given the symmetry of the picture, we observe that the pass with the most operations is the one in the middle. Therefore, we can compute the total number of passes from left to right to be $2 * (n - 1 - 1) + 1$, which simplifies to $2n - 3$. This number is substantially smaller than the n^2 level of number of passes in Figure 6.2.

As a parallel algorithm, it shares common features with various parallel algorithms, which can be summarized as follows.

- *Multiple passes* Even with multiple processors, a parallel algorithm may not have the ideal case that each processor simply completes its work. Instead, the entire algorithm requires multiple sequential passes, and only within each pass can multiple processors work independently.
- *Synchronization and barrier* At the completion of each pass, all processors must reach a barrier that enforces a synchronization point. Only after this point can the next pass commence. Such an operation often constitutes a bottleneck in the execution of the entire algorithm.
- *Load balance* Within each pass, parallel tasks should be assigned to as many available processors as possible, enabling them to carry out their assigned work independently of other processors. Ideally, all processors should operate in a load-balanced manner.

6.2.3   Odd–Even Sort

Based on the parallel bubble sort diagram in Figure 6.4, it is evident that the algorithm suffers from load unbalancing in certain passes. Specifically, in the first pass, the algorithm performs only a single operation – a comparison and swap between the first two elements. This means that even if multiple processors are available, only one processor will be utilized for this operation, while the rest remain idle.

Now, let us assume that the smallest element in the array is the last element. In this case, it is clear that the element can be moved to the head of the array only after multiple passes. However, the question arises as to why we cannot execute a comparison and swap operation between it and its predecessor in the first pass. This comparison could occur simultaneously with the comparison between the first two elements, provided that the array contains at least four elements.

In the parallel bubble sort diagram, it is evident that the comparison and swap operation for the last element can only occur as late as in the $(n-1)$th pass. Actually, the issue with the parallel bubble sort algorithm is that it fails to take advantage of obvious parallelism opportunities in certain passes, resulting in unnecessary processor idleness and additional passes required to complete the sorting process. This, in turn, leads to increased inefficiency throughout the algorithm. As a result, it raises the question of whether a better parallel sorting algorithm can be developed that reduces the number

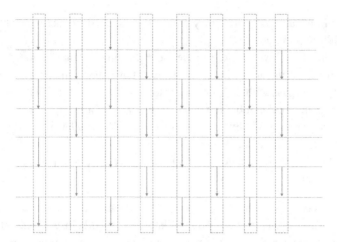

Figure 6.5 Illustration of a parallel odd–even sort algorithm. The algorithm alternatively executes on odd-indexed or even-indexed pairs in two adjacent passes.

of passes while making each pass more load balanced. By addressing this issue, we can improve the efficiency of parallel sorting algorithms and achieve faster and more efficient sorting.

One potential solution to the issues with parallel bubble sort is the odd–even sorting algorithm, as demonstrated in Figure 6.5. Upon comparing the images of parallel bubble sort and odd–even sort, we can see that odd–even sort has more operations occurring within each pass. Additionally, the operations in each pass can be performed in parallel since they involve nonoverlapping pairs.

The odd–even sorting algorithm requires n passes for an input array of size n. Each pass is numbered from 1 to n, and for odd-numbered passes, all comparisons and swaps are performed between an odd-indexed element and its next element. On the other hand, for even-numbered passes, each pair starts from an even-indexed element. It is worth noting that we are using a one-based indexing method, meaning the first element's index is 1 rather than 0.

As demonstrated in Figure 6.5, the odd–even sorting algorithm iteratively executes two types of passes: one for comparisons between odd–even pairs and the other for even–odd pairs. This approach allows for improved load balancing and a reduction in the number of passes required to complete the sorting process.

Figure 6.6 illustrates how the odd–even sorting algorithm can be used to sort eight numbers ranging from 1 to 8. The initial ordering is set to a completely reversed order, from 8 to 1. The figure depicts the array after each pass of execution. While a strict proof is not provided here, we can observe that the algorithm requires eight passes to sort the eight elements. Specifically, the value 8 is moved to its final position after seven passes. In contrast, the value 7 requires eight passes to reach its final position. This is because of the comparison sequence, which causes the value 7 to take two passes to reach and stay at the head of the array and an additional six passes to reach the second-most right position.

Upon comparing the two parallel algorithms so far, namely parallel bubble sort and odd–even sort, it becomes clear that automatic parallelism mining and exploitation approaches may not be the most effective for parallel processing. This is because (1) it is difficult for a compiler to analyze all potential parallelism opportunities in a given sequential program (e.g., from bubble sort to parallel bubble sort), and (2) even if automatic parallelization is successful, its benefits for parallel operations are less than those of new algorithms (e.g., from parallel bubble sort to odd–even sort).

In light of these challenges, it is essential to design parallel algorithms that are explicitly tailored to parallel processing. These algorithms can effectively take advantage of the inherent parallelism in the problem being solved, rather than relying on automatic parallelization techniques that may not be optimized for the specific problem at hand. By developing new parallel algorithms and optimizing existing ones, we can improve the efficiency and effectiveness of parallel processing in a variety of applications.

6.2.4 Batcher's Sorting Networks

The primary limitation of the odd–even sorting algorithm is its high complexity, requiring n passes of comparisons and swaps for n inputs in its corresponding sorting network. This is because the algorithm, much like traditional bubble sort, only executes comparisons and swaps between two neighboring elements whose distance is obviously only 1. As a result, each pass can move an element only one position backward or forward. For instance, in Figure 6.6, a single pass can only move the element 8 backward by one position. As a consequence, at least $n - 1$ passes are necessary to move the largest number from the head of the array to the tail.

pass	8	7	6	5	4	3	2	1
1	7	8	5	6	3	4	1	2
2	7	5	8	3	6	1	4	2
3	5	7	3	8	1	6	2	4
4	5	3	7	1	8	2	6	4
5	3	5	1	7	2	8	4	6
6	3	1	5	2	7	4	8	6
7	1	3	2	5	4	7	6	8
8	1	2	3	4	5	6	7	8

Figure 6.6 Observe the step-by-step sorting process of a reverse-sorted sequence of eight integers using the odd–even algorithm. This illustrative example demonstrates how the algorithm operates on alternating odd–even indexed pairs, resulting in an efficient sorting method for arrays of elements.

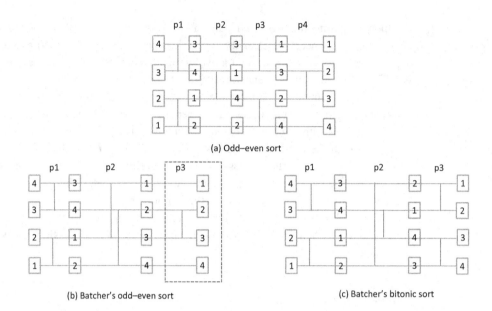

Figure 6.7 Three different sorting networks for the same input array (4,3,2,1) when using (a) the traditional odd–even sorting algorithm, (b) Batcher's odd–even sorting algorithm, and (c) Batcher's bitonic sorting algorithm, respectively.

Increasing the distance of comparisons and swaps is a natural idea that may allow for sorting with fewer passes. However, this approach introduces a new challenge, as the design space of possible algorithms increases significantly, since it is allowable to compare two elements whose distance can be any value instead of only 1. In this section, we provide a simple example with only four elements to illustrate this idea and explain both the simplicity and complexity behind the idea of long-distance comparisons. We begin with an array of four elements (1,2,3,4), with their initial order in the to-be-sorted array set as descending, that is, (4,3,2,1). Our task is to convert this array into ascending order (1,2,3,4).

Figure 6.7 illustrates the example we have provided. Figure 6.7(a) shows the illustration of the odd–even sorting algorithm, followed by Figures 6.7(b) and (c), which are two improved algorithms utilizing the idea of long-distance operations. While we will study these improved algorithms in more detail later in this chapter, here we use this example to explain the main idea. In Figure 6.7, the comparison direction is downward (as the default case, the arrow is not shown). As we discussed previously, odd–even sort requires four passes (p1–p4) to sort this array in (a). However, in both (b) and (c), the sorting networks have fewer passes. Actually, the minimal number of passes for sorting an array of all possible four inputs is 3 [36]. But for a concrete example, it could use even fewer passes. For example, in (b), the third passes (p3) is unnecessary. But this does not represent all the cases. For example, if the inital order is (4,2,3,1), then p3 in (b) is required. It is important to note that p1 is not changed. Its purpose is to create two sorted sequences, that is, (3,4) and (1,2). Therefore, the sorting networks in both (b) and (c) can be seen as different approaches to merge the two sequences.

Actually, both (b) and (c) belong to the category of merge sort algorithms. In (b), the p2 step involves comparing the first element of the two sequences and then comparing the second element of the two sequences. After this step, the minimal value (1) and maximal value (4) have reached their final positions. A final comparison/swap step is then used in p3 to compare the two middle elements (although this final step is unnecessary for this example). In general, this example follows the main idea of Batcher's odd–even merge sort algorithm for merging two sorted sequences: First merging the corresponding odd and even subsequences from the two inputs and then using a final comparison and swap step for some unsorted neighbors. Readers can think about how the algorithm works if we change the initial order to (4,2,3,1) or other ones.

In (c), when merging the two sorted sequences from p1, the p2 step involves comparing the minimal value of one sequence to the maximal value of the other sequence. This process partitions the input values into two halves, where the values of the first half are smaller than the values in the second half. In the figure, we can see that (2) and (1) are in the first half, and (4) and (3) are in the second half. Since the values within each half are not sorted, an additional p3 step is required to sort each half individually. In general, the main idea is to create a sequence split pattern by comparing corresponding elements of two sequences, with one scanning forward and the other scanning backward. This approach allows the merging to be recursively processed in smaller ranges. Owing to the use of two different scanning directions, this algorithm is called Batcher's bitonic merge sort algorithm.

While the main ideas behind Batcher's odd–even merge sort algorithm and Batcher's bitonic merge sort algorithm may sound simple, these algorithms can present a variety of challenges and details to implement effectively on GPUs. Then, readers may wonder why we need to implement them on GPUs? Actually, the reason is that these two algorithms are well suited for execution on a GPU due to their inherent parallelism and regular data access patterns. In the following sections, we will provide a comprehensive introduction and explanation of these algorithms using the PAPA methodology we introduced earlier in this chapter. We will begin by focusing on Batcher's bitonic sort algorithm and provide detailed insights into its implementation and optimization for parallel processing on GPUs.

6.3   Bitonic Sort

In this section, we will use the simple term "bitonic sort" to represent Batcher's bitonic sort algorithm.

6.3.1   Premier

The premier of bitonic sort is to exploit the properties of the so-called "bitonic sequence" to convert sorting into a process of first creating such a sequence and then recursively splitting it. A bitonic sequence is defined as either a sequence of the form

$a_0 <= \cdots <= a_m >= \cdots >= a_{n-1}$, where $0 <= m < n$, or a circular shift of such a sequence.

In a bitonic sequence with $2n$ elements $(a_0, \ldots, a_{2n-1})$, the first half consists of elements a_0 to a_{n-1}, and the second half consists of elements a_n to a_{2n-1}. A bitonic split is a process of partitioning the sequence into two smaller subsequences, each consisting of n elements, denoted as $s1$ and $s2$. This split is achieved by comparing and swapping (if necessary) each element in the first half (e.g., a_x) with its corresponding element a_{x+n} in the second half. After the bitonic split, the sequence $s1$ becomes $(\min(a_0, a_n), \ldots, \min(a_{n-1}, a_{2n-1}))$, and $s2$ becomes $(\max(a_0, a_n), \ldots, \max(a_{n-1}, a_{2n-1}))$.

One of the properties of the bitonic split is that all the elements in the first subsequence $s1$ are less than or equal to the ones in the second subsequence $s2$. Another property is that both newly generated subsequences remain bitonic sequences. This creates the possibility of using recursive bitonic splits to process the subsequences further. During the recursive bitonic splits, the smaller elements are moved towards the sequence head, while the larger ones are moved towards the sequence tail. This gradual movement of the elements ensures that they are sorted in ascending order, in accordance with the comparison and swap operations performed during the bitonic split.

In Figure 6.8, an example of how a bitonic sequence with 16 elements is split into two subsequences, each with eight elements, is shown. As the figure demonstrates, both properties of bitonic split are easily observed. Notably, the second subsequence

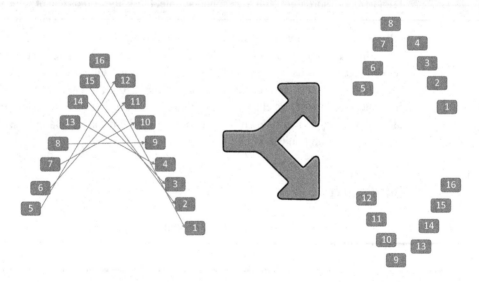

Figure 6.8 An example of a bitonic split. For each sequence, the most-left number is its first one, and the most-right number is its last one. This figure shows how a bitonic sequence on the left side ([5,6,...,16,12,11,...,1]) is split into two bitonic subsequences, and all elements of the first subsequence ([5,6,7,8,4,3,2,1]) is smaller than any element of the second subsequence ([12,11,10,9,13,14,15,16]).

$(12, 11, 10, 9, 13, 14, 15, 16)$ appears to be first descending and then ascending. How-ever, it still qualifies as a bitonic sequence, as it is a circular shift of the bitonic sequence $(13, 14, 15, 16, 12, 11, 10, 9)$ in accordance with the definition.

6.3.2   Algorithm

According to the key idea of bitonic sort, it is straightforward to develop a recursive algorithm for sorting a given input in ascending order. The algorithm begins by assum-ing that the number of elements is a power of 2. Algorithm 6.1 shows the recursive form of the algorithm, which creates a bitonic sequence by first sorting the input's first half in ascending order and the second half in descending order. The input sequence is then split recursively until the sorting process is completed.

To convert the input to a bitonic sequence, the CreateBitonicSequence method recur-sively sorts the first half of the input in ascending order and the second half in descend-ing order. This method can easily create a sequence, as illustrated by the left-hand part of Figure 6.8. In contrast, the SplitBitonicSequence method first executes the bitonic split operation, as illustrated by the right-hand part of Figure 6.8. It then recursively splits the resulting subsequences until the sorting process is complete.

Extending this recursive algorithm (Algorithm 6.1) to a parallel version is not a straightforward task, even though the algorithm's parallelism is hidden since the first half and second half can be processed independently during both the bitonic sequence creation and splitting stages. To create a parallel algorithm, we first need to develop a nonrecursive version of the algorithm, which can be aided by examining the sorting network created by the algorithm.

An example of a bitonic sorting network for an input with $2^4 = 16$ elements, created using the aforementioned recursive algorithm (Algorithm 6.1), is illustrated in Figure 6.9. This network has a two-layer structure that comprises four stages and one to four steps (passes) within each stage. The sorting network clearly demonstrates

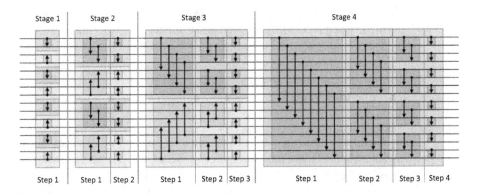

Figure 6.9 An example of the bitonic sorting network for 16 elements (by Wikipedia user Bitonic). The concepts of stage and step are illustrated on the picture. Different arrow directions show the "bitonic" nature of the algorithm.

Algorithm 6.1 A recursive form for the bitonic sort algorithm. We here ignore the details of several trivial assisting functions.

Require: $len(input) = 2^k$

BITONICSORT($input$, "$ascending$")

procedure BITONICSORT($input, direction$)
    CREATEBITONICSEQUENCE($input$)
    SPLITBITONICSEQUENCE($input, direction$)
end procedure

procedure CREATEBITONICSEQUENCE($input$)
    if $len(input) > 1$ **then**
        BITONICSORT($FirstHalf(input)$, "$ascending$")
        BITONICSORT($SecondHalf(input)$, "$descending$")
    end if
end procedure

procedure SPLITBITONICSEQUENCE($input, direction$)
    $n \leftarrow len(input)$
    if $n > 1$ **then**
        for each $i \in [0, n/2 - 1]$ **do**
            COMPAREANDSWAP($FirstHalf(input)[i], SecondHalf(input)[i], direction$)
        end for

        SPLITBITONICSEQUENCE($FirstHalf(input), direction$)
        SPLITBITONICSEQUENCE($SecondHalf(input), direction$)
    end if
end procedure

---

the recursive behaviors that occur within the above algorithm. Stage 4 represents the SplitBitonicSequence method, while stages 1–3 represent the CreateBitonicSequence method, which recursively creates similar subnetworks for smaller element ranges.

The sorting directions in each step of the bitonic sorting network are represented by arrows. If we disregard the original recursive form, we can summarize the sorting network into a nonrecursive logic that possesses the following three primary characteristics. These characteristics can help us develop a nonrecursive bitonic sort algorithm.

- The overall structure implies a double loop for controlling stages and steps.
- An additional inner loop is required to execute the compare and swap operation for pairs in each step.
- Different steps have distinct pair distances and sorting direction switches.

Algorithm 6.2 is the result (we explicitly use ascending order). In each step, the variable *pair_distance* represents the distance of two elements to be compared,

---

Algorithm 6.2 A nonrecursive form of the bitonic sort algorithm for sorting a 2^k-length array. (The sorting direction is explicitly set to ascending order. To sort in descending order, the variable *direction* should be reversed).

Require: $len(input) = 2^k$

> **for** each *stage* $\in [1, k]$ **do**
> > **for** each *step* $\in [1, stage]$ **do**
> > > *pair_block* $\leftarrow 2^{stage}$
> > > *pair_distance* $\leftarrow 2^{stage-step}$
> > > **for** each *element_index* $\in [0, 2^k - 1]$ **do**
> > > > *pair_index* $\leftarrow BitwiseXOR(element\_index, pair\_distance)$
> > > > **if** *pair_index* > *element_index* **then**
> > > > > **if** $BitwiseAND(element\_index, pair\_block) = 0$ **then**
> > > > > > *direction* $\leftarrow$ "ascending"
> > > > > **else**
> > > > > > *direction* $\leftarrow$ "descending"
> > > > > **end if**
> > > > > COMPAREANDSWAP($input[element\_index], input[pair\_index], direction$)
> > > > **end if**
> > > **end for**
> > **end for**
> **end for**

---

while *pair_block* is the number of elements that have the same sorting direction (as shown in Figure 6.9). The algorithm uses bitwise XOR and bitwise AND operations for corresponding calculations, which are familiar to readers with knowledge of C language and binary representation. Here is a simple example to illustrate how the bitwise XOR operation works: If *pair_distance* is 4 (0b1000), elements with indices 1 (0b0001) and 5 (0b1001) will be mutually paired since $0b1000\verb|^|0b0001 = 0b1001$ and $0b1000\verb|^|0b1001 = 0b0001$.

If we combine the concepts of stage and step into a pass, which represents the depth of a sorting network, we can observe that the depth of a bitonic sorting network is $O(k^2)$, where k is the logarithm of the input size $n = 2^k$. Therefore, for an input of size n, the depth of the bitonic sorting network is $O(\log^2 n)$, resulting in an overall time complexity of $O(n \log^2 n)$. When we compare this to the $O(n)$ depth of the previous odd–even sort (as shown in Figure 6.5 and 6.6), we can conclude that bitonic sort is much more efficient than odd–even sort.

For the bitonic sorting algorithm, both the recursive form in Algorithm 6.1 and the nonrecursive form in Algorithm 6.2 are equivalent. However, the nonrecursive form is more suitable for conversion into a parallel algorithm. In the sequential algorithm, the innermost loop is used to process each element, as shown in Algorithm 6.2. However, as there is no dependence between any two elements, they can be processed independently. Therefore, we can convert the algorithm into a parallel one by keeping the first two outer loops while parallelizing the most inner loop.

With the idea of parallelization, Algorithm 6.3 presents a GPU-targeted parallel algorithm for bitonic sort. Each of the n threads launched by the algorithm is responsible for processing one element, as in the innermost loop of Algorithm 6.2. However, this one-to-one mapping between elements and threads has an obvious drawback: The sequential algorithm processes each pair of elements only once, by the element with a smaller index (as indicated by the if condition *pair_index > element_index*), but in the parallel version, half of the threads do not perform any actual work.

Algorithm 6.3 A GPU parallel version of the bitonic sort algorithm for sorting a 2^k-length array in ascending order.

Require: $len(input) = 2^k$

  for each *stage* $\in [1, k]$ **do**
    for each *step* $\in [1, stage]$ **do**
      KERNEL-BITONICSORTSTEP(*input, stage, step*)   ▷ Launch 2^k threads
      ALLTHREADSYNCHRONIZATION
    end for
  end for

  procedure KERNEL-BITONICSORTSTEP(*input, stage, step*)   ▷ a thread
    pair_block $\leftarrow 2^{stage}$
    pair_distance $\leftarrow 2^{stage-step}$
    element_index $\leftarrow$ *thread_index*
    pair_index $\leftarrow BitwiseXOR(element\_index, pair\_distance)$
    if *pair_index > element_index* **then**
      if $BitwiseAND(element\_index, pair\_block) = 0$ **then**
        direction $\leftarrow$ "ascending"
      else
        direction $\leftarrow$ "descending"
      end if
      COMPAREANDSWAP(*input[element_index], input[pair_index], direction*)
    end if
  end procedure

One significant but perhaps hidden difference between the GPU parallel algorithm in Algorithm 6.3 and the sequential algorithm in Algorithm 6.2 is the presence of the *thread_index* variable in the former. In the parallel algorithm, each thread is responsible for processing a single element and therefore can simply use the *thread_index* as the equivalent of *element_index* in the sequential algorithm. This is not possible in the sequential algorithm, which must iterate over all elements using the *element_index* variable. Additionally, if there are not enough hardware threads to handle all elements, a limited number of hardware threads must complete the work in a round-robin fashion.

One important feature of this parallel algorithm (Algorithm 6.3) is its multiple passes of GPU kernel launches. Each pass executes the work required by that pass and is partitioned among multiple threads. At the algorithm level, an explicit barrier is needed to ensure that threads of the next pass cannot be executed until all threads of the previous pass have finished. The synchronization mechanism for this barrier can be either simple or complex depending on the hardware or programming environment. Additionally, some aspects of this parallel algorithm are trivial, such as the fact that the calculation of *pair_block* is the same for all threads, allowing it to be precomputed before kernel launches. These trivial aspects do not significantly impact the correctness or performance of the program.

6.3.3 Program

Simply implementing Algorithm 6.3 using CUDA on Nvidia GPUs is not really challenging even for GPU programming beginners. This algorithm can be used as a means to learn CUDA programming. However, there are three important issues that need to be considered when implementing this algorithm in practice.

Memory management The data structure used in this algorithm is a simple array with a specified data type. The program can either use explicit cudaMemcpy [104] to copy the array allocated in the main memory to the GPU device memory and copy it back after sorting or use the Unified Memory feature [104], which provides a single memory space for both GPU device memory and host main memory. Graphics processing unit memory management is an important topic in CUDA programming, and there is a lot of research work on optimizing memory allocation and usage to improve program performance.

Performance tuning Here we will discuss the block size for the bitonic sorting algorithm. For an input with $n = 2^k$ elements to be sorted, since the algorithm requires one thread for each element, we need to decide the number of threads in each block. The block count is determined by dividing the total number of elements by the number of threads in each block, which is represented by t. In CUDA, the maximum number of threads in a block is 1024, and commonly used values for t are 512 or 256. It is recommended that readers try different values of t for performance tuning.

Synchronization consideration The algorithm requires thread synchronization at the end of each round of GPU threads, which can be a complicated problem related to program correctness in real-world scenarios. However, a single CUDA stream guarantees serial kernel execution. So in this case, there is no explicit synchronization required in the program. It is worth noting that different generations of Nvidia GPU hardware and CUDA programming platforms could provide different supports to thread synchronization. It is the programmer's job to correctly implement any synchronization requirement required by the algorithm in the practical CUDA program.

The three issues discussed above may seem trivial for the bitonic sorting problem. But they are actually crucial in many GPU-based data analytical applications. Memory management is important because it is common for the GPU device memory to be smaller than the data size, and the method chosen for memory management can significantly impact program performance. Performance tuning is important because it is necessary to find the optimal combination of parameters for both the workload and hardware features in order to maximize program performance. Synchronization is critical for program correctness, and incorrect usage of synchronization can be difficult to detect and debug. Therefore, careful attention to these issues is essential in GPU programming.

The following is a reference implementation of the algorithm. In the main function, an array with $2^{10} = 1024$ elements is explicitly used as input for sorting. A thread block size of 512 threads is also explicitly specified. It is important to note that this program is for demonstration purpose only, and does not include any optimizations or supports to other data types and error handling.

```
#include <stdio.h>
#include <stdlib.h>
__device__ void CompareAndSwap(int* input, int x, int y, int direction){
    if (((direction == 0) && (input[x] > input[y])) ||
        ((direction != 0) && (input[x] < input[y])))
    {
        int t = input[y];
        input[y] = input[x];
        input[x] = t;
    }
}
__global__ void KBitonicSortingPass(int* input, int stage, int step){
    int thread_index = blockDim.x * blockIdx.x + threadIdx.x;
    int element_index = thread_index;
    int pair_block = 1 << stage;
    int pair_distance = 1 << (stage - step);
    int pair_index = element_index ^ pair_distance;
    if (pair_index > element_index)
    {
        int direction = (element_index & pair_block);
        CompareAndSwap(input, element_index, pair_index, direction);
    }
}
void GPUBitonicSort(int* input, int k){
    int len = 1 << k;
    size_t lensize = len * sizeof(int);
    int* gpu_input = 0;
    cudaMalloc((void**)&gpu_input, lensize);
    cudaMemcpy(gpu_input, input, lensize, cudaMemcpyHostToDevice);
    dim3 block_size = 512;
    dim3 block_count = (len / 512);
    for (int stage = 1; stage <= k; stage++)
    {
        for (int step = 1; step <= stage; step++)
        {
            KBitonicSortingPass<<<block_count, block_size>>>
                                (gpu_input, stage, step);
        }
    }
    cudaMemcpy(input, gpu_input, lensize, cudaMemcpyDeviceToHost);
    cudaFree(gpu_input);
}
```

```
int main(){
    int k = 10;
    int len = 1 << k;
    int* input = (int*)malloc(len * sizeof(int));
    for (int i = 0; i < len; i++) { input[i] = rand(); }
    GPUBitonicSort(input, k);
    free(input);
    return 0;
}
```

6.4 The Advancement of Bitonic Sort

6.4.1 Advancement 1: Architectural Interactions

After developing a parallel algorithm and program for bitonic sort, it is necessary to consider two aspects of further advancement: architectural interaction and anomaly handling. Architectural interaction aims to improve the performance of the algorithm and program based on the underlying GPU architecture. On the other hand, anomaly handling modifies the algorithm or program to handle cases that are beyond the existing assumptions, such as cases where the number of elements is not a power of two. In the following sections, we will discuss how the algorithm and program can be advanced in these two aspects.

The current algorithm/program is not optimized for architecture as it has a significant locality issue, meaning it performs unnecessary global memory accesses and fails to take advantage of shared memory. In Algorithm 6.3, every time a thread needs to execute

$$CompareAndSwap(input[element\_index], input[pair\_index], direction)$$

it reads the GPU global memory twice, and writes back twice if a swap is necessary since the array being sorted resides in the global memory. To make matters worse, these global memory accesses are repeatedly executed in every sorting pass. This raises a natural question: Is it necessary to write back to global memory after every sorting pass?

6.4.2 Optimization for Memory Hierarchy

The reason why global memory is accessed every pass is that the algorithm uses an oversimplified abstraction for the underlying GPU architecture. Figure 6.10 illustrates two abstractions of the GPU architecture with the purpose of introducing shared memory. Before we dive into the performance problem of our algorithm, let us first provide a general introduction to the GPU architecture. Figure 6.10(a) shows that a GPU is abstracted into a number of parallel threads and a global memory, which implies that all parallel threads can access any memory location at the same fixed cost. This abstraction is often referred to as the "PRAM-CREW" model in conventional parallel computing domain, which stands for "Parallel Random-Access Machine – Concurrent

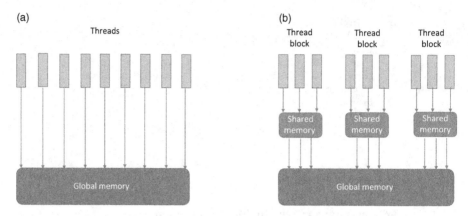

Figure 6.10 Comparison of two abstractions for programming GPU devices: (a) shows a basic threading approach, while (b) introduces thread block organization with shared memory as a cache for global memory.

Read Exclusive Write" [61]. Such an abstract provides a foundation to design and implement parallel algorithms without considering the real memory hierarchy in practical parallel computing hardware. So far, our bitonic sorting algorithm has essentially been designed for this abstraction, focusing on parallelism only.

Figure 6.10(b) presents a more realistic abstraction of the GPU architecture, which incorporates two changes. First, multiple threads are organized into a thread block. Second, a thread block can use a shared memory between the hardware threads (i.e., the cores) and the global memory. However, different thread blocks do not have any shared memory between them. From the perspective of traditional CPU memory hierarchy, a shared memory can be considered as a cache between the CPU and memory, with a higher degree of software-based management. As the shared cache is on-chip, its access latency is approximately 100 times lower than uncached global memory latency. Thus, an efficient way to sort the data is to first bring the data from global memory to shared memory and perform fast sorting within the shared memory. The challenge, however, is that shared memory has only limited capacity (e.g., for Nvidia ADA GPUs, a streaming multiprocessor, on which one or more thread blocks will be executed, has 128 KB shared memory [107]). Therefore, any algorithm aiming to utilize shared memory must be well tuned based on the size limitation.

Historically, thread synchronization was only supported within a thread block. However, with advancements in GPU hardware and software, synchronization across thread blocks can also be achieved using the concept of *cooperative groups* programming. Nevertheless, a memory-optimized GPU program typically enables shared memory and thread synchronization within a thread block.

One way to optimize shared memory usage is to keep a thread alive after it brings an element from global memory to shared memory, rather than simply executing a compare and swap operation and writing back to global memory before termination. By doing so, the thread can continue to execute more operations on the element without

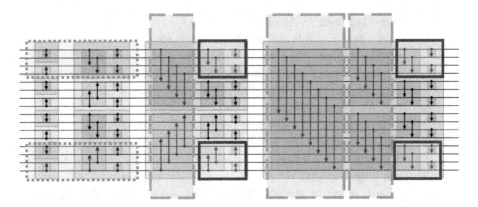

Figure 6.11 Mapping operations to fit shared memory: An example illustrating how the size of shared memory (assumed to be four) can impact the mapping of operations. Local operations within the shared memory are depicted with dot-line and solid-line boxes, while global operations that extend beyond the shared memory size are indicated with dash-line boxes.

the need for global memory accesses. However, this strategy is only effective for pairs of elements that can fit in shared memory. For pairs whose elements cannot fit in shared memory, this strategy cannot be applied due to the limited size of shared memory.

Figure 6.11 illustrates an example of utilizing shared memory (with an assumed capacity of four elements) for the bitonic sorting algorithm. Here, we partition the network into three different types of boxes. But before introducing them, we re-examine the logic of the bitonic sorting algorithm in this example. With a total of 16 elements, the sorting process can be thought of as consisting of two phases. The first phase is "partial sorting," which yields four four-element short sequences with different orders according to the bitonic sorting requirement. The second phase is "bitonic merging," which first yields two eight-element sorted sequences and then finalizes a 16-element sequence. These two phases result in three different types of boxes in the figure.

First, during the "partial sorting" phase, the 16-element bitonic sorting network is divided into four dot-line boxes, each of which contains all three steps to sort four elements. Since the shared memory can hold four elements, once the first four elements are brought into shared memory, the subsequent two steps can be executed without any global memory accesses. Second, during the "bitonic merging" phase, there are two different kinds of boxes. The dash-line box represents a step that cannot benefit from shared memory because the two elements being compared cannot be placed into shared memory together due to their distance being greater than or equal to the shared memory size. As the merging steps move forward, the distance between the pairs shrinks. Then, the solid-line box represents a merging operation that can be fully executed in shared memory, and contains multiple steps.

To execute the different types of boxes, each box requires a unique GPU kernel. The dot-line and solid-line boxes contain multiple steps for the elements they cover. For instance, a dot-line box contains three steps, which correspond to three times of kernel launching in Algorithm 6.3. Therefore, if a thread is assigned to an element in a dot-line box, the thread's work should include a double loop for the three steps. This is different from Algorithm 6.3, where the double loop is on the CPU side. Instead, the new approach requires each kernel to execute the double loop. Typically, a GPU program consists of different kernels, each of which is only responsible for a specific part of the whole program.

Ignoring how the concrete GPU kernels are implemented, the following algorithm for bitonic sort is shown in Algorithm 6.4. The algorithm uses a variable *SharedMemLimit* to set the limit of the number of elements that shared memory can contain (a safe value is 1024). It is also the work that a thread block needs to process by all its threads. Therefore, the block count is determined by *len(input)/SharedMemLimit*. Additionally, this algorithm allows one thread to be responsible for two elements. So the thread count within a thread block is *SharedMemLimit*/2. The purpose of this strategy is to avoid over-launched idle threads in Algorithm 6.3. This algorithm requires explicit kernel launching parameters *BC* and *TC*.

Algorithm 6.4 A GPU parallel version of the bitonic sort algorithm that uses shared memory. Kernel functions will be shown in separate algorithms.

Require: $len(input) = 2^k$
Require: $SharedMemLimit = 2^s (s < k)$

$BC \leftarrow len(input)/SharedMemLimit$ ▷ Block Count
$TC \leftarrow SharedMemLimit/2$ ▷ Thread Count

GSHAREDMEMSORTING[BC,TC](input)

$MergeSize \leftarrow 2 \times SharedMemLimit$
while $MergeSize \leq len(inpt)$ **do**
    $CompareSize \leftarrow \dfrac{MergeSize}{2}$

    while $CompareSize \geq 1$ **do**
        if $CompareSize \geq SharedMemLimit$ **then**
            GGLOBALMERGING[BC,TC](input, MergeSize, CompareSize)
        else
            GSHAREDMEMMERGING[BC,TC](input, CompareSize)
            BREAK
        end if
        $CompareSize \leftarrow \dfrac{CompareSize}{2}$
    end while

    $MergeSize \leftarrow 2 \times MergeSize$
end while

The main logic of this algorithm is illustrated in Figure 6.11, and can be broken down into two steps. The first step involves creating multiple sorted sequences of size *SharedMemLimit* using the GPU kernel *GSharedMemSorting*. The block count is determined by the size of the input and the shared memory limit. Each block is assigned a set of elements to sort, with one thread responsible for sorting two elements to avoid over-launched idle threads.

The second step involves merging the sorted sequences according to the bitonic merging approach, using a double loop. If the merging operation can be done within a shared memory, the GPU kernel *GSharedMemMerging* is used. This kernel executes the loop inside the kernel (the solid-line boxes in Figure 6.11). If the merging operation cannot be done within a shared memory, the GPU kernel *GGlobalMerging* is used, which does not utilize shared memory at all. The launching parameters *BC* and *TC* can be the same for all three kernels, or different for *GGlobalMerging*.

Now the question arises as to how to implement the three different kernels in Algorithm 6.4. *GSharedMemSorting* and *GSharedMemMerging* are similar because they both use shared memory. Thus, their main logic consists of three steps: (1) copying data from global memory to shared memory, (2) executing the required tasks within shared memory, and (3) copying the results from shared memory back to global memory. However, *GSharedMemMerging* is similar to the kernel in the previous Algorithm 6.3 with the exception that each thread must process two elements because it uses *BC* and *TC* of the other kernels.

Corresponding to the above three steps, the *GSharedMemSorting* kernel's algorithm is shown in Algorithm 6.5 (sorting in ascending order). We will first examine how data are transferred between global memory and shared memory (steps 1 and 3), and then analyze its main logic for sorting within shared memory (step 2). But before that, we have to explain two important variables: *local_thread_index* and *block_index*. The existence of these two variables is due to the fact that all threads are grouped into a set of thread blocks, so that each thread has a block index and a thread index, corresponding to the two variables, respectively. Based on these two variables, a thread's global index *global_index* can be calculated using the formula $block\_index \times \frac{SharedMemLimit}{2} + local\_thread\_index$, because a thread block has $\frac{SharedMemLimit}{2}$ threads. For convenience, we use another variable, *global_addr*, which equals to $block\_index \times SharedMemLimit + local\_thread\_index$, to indicate the starting address in global memory that a thread will access. Note that this variable is not a global thread index.

The algorithm requires allocating a continuous memory space from shared memory of each thread block, whose size depends on the variable *SharedMemLimit*. In the actual CUDA program, the function *AllocSharedMemoryForElements* is implemented using the "__shared__" directive before an array declaration, as follows, for example.

$$\_\_shared\_\_ \ int \ sminput[SharedMemLimit]$$

The directive signifies that all threads within a block share the *sminput* array, rather than each thread creating its own array. After the array creation, $\frac{SharedMemLimt}{2}$ threads must copy *SharedMemLimit* elements from global memory into this array, so that each

---

Algorithm 6.5 GPU kernel *GSharedMemSorting* for Algorithm 6.4.

Require: $len(input) = 2^k$
Require: $SharedMemLimit = 2^s (s < k)$
   procedure GSHAREDMEMSORTING(*input*)
       GET(*local_thread_index*)   ▷ thread index inside its thread block
       GET(*block_index*)   ▷ block index
       $global\_index \leftarrow block\_index \times \dfrac{SharedMemLimit}{2} + local\_thread\_index$
       $h \leftarrow SharedMemLimit/2$
       $sminput \leftarrow$ ALLOCSHAREDMEMORYFORELEMENTS(*SharedMemLimit*)

                 ▷ Step 1: Copy two elements from global memory to shared memory
       $global\_addr \leftarrow block\_index \times SharedMemLimit + local\_thread\_index$
       $sminput[local\_thread\_index] \leftarrow input[global\_addr]$
       $sminput[local\_thread\_index + h] \leftarrow input[global\_addr + h]$
       BLOCKTHREADSYNCHRONIZATION

                ▷ Step 2: Execute the bitonic sorting within shared memory
       for each *stage* $\in [1, s]$ **do**   ▷ $SharedMemLimit = 2^s$
          $pair\_block \leftarrow 2^{stage}$
          if $BitwiseAND(global\_index, pair\_block/2) = 0$ **then**
             $direction \leftarrow$ "ascending"
          else
             $direction \leftarrow$ "descending"
          end if

          for each *step* $\in [1, stage]$ **do**
             $pair\_distance \leftarrow 2^{stage-step}$
             $backd \leftarrow BitwiseAND(local\_thread\_index, pair\_distance - 1)$
             $small\_index \leftarrow 2 \times local\_thread\_index - backd$
             $big\_index \leftarrow small\_index + pair\_distance$
             COMPAREANDSWAP(*sminput*[*small_index*], *sminput*[*big_index*], *direction*)
             BLOCKTHREADSYNCHRONIZATION
          end for
       end for
                       ▷ Step 3: Copy back sorted result
       $input[global\_addr] \leftarrow sminput[local\_thread\_index]$
       $input[global\_addr + h] \leftarrow sminput[local\_thread\_index + h]$
   end procedure

---

thread copies two elements. In Algorithm 6.5, the two elements of one thread have a gap of $h = SharedMemLimit/2$. The main purpose of such copying is to best utilize the global memory bandwidth by creating a coalesced memory access pattern, which we will explain extensively later.

Algorithm 6.5 involves executing bitonic sorting within shared memory, as described in step 2. The primary logic employed is similar to that of Algorithms 6.2 and 6.3.

However, there are some notable differences. For instance, a single thread is responsible for comparing both elements, as opposed to two separate threads. As a result, when determining the sorting direction, the thread utilizes *pair_block*/2 rather than *pair_block* in order to switch sorting directions. This is because the former algorithm utilizes only half of the number of threads. In addition, when determining the two elements to be sorted, a thread uses $2 \times$ *local_thread_index* $-$ *BitwiseAND*(*local_thread_index*, *pair_distance* $-$ 1) to ascertain the index of the element with the smaller index.

6.4.3   Global Memory Accesses

Another significant difference between this kernel and the ones in previous algorithms is that explicit thread synchronization is required, which is expressed by the form of the *BlockThreadSynchronization* command. This command ensures that all threads within a thread block are synchronized after the initial shared memory loading and each step of compare and swap operation. Without such a barrier, there is no guarantee that the parallel threads can deliver correct results. In actual CUDA programs, the *BlockThreadSynchronization* command can be implemented using either the __syncthreads() function, which provides block-level thread synchronization, or the Cooperative Group APIs to synchronize a thread block group.

Let us now discuss the issue of global memory access in step 1 and step 3, which is a crucial factor affecting the performance of GPU programming. When a thread performs a global memory access, such as *input*[*global_addr*], how does the memory reference actually occur? In reality, the memory references of multiple threads are directly influenced by how the threads are organized and executed in a batch mode within the GPU. As a result, instead of individual memory accesses by each thread, the GPU hardware combines memory accesses among a set of concurrent threads into combined memory transactions.

Nvidia GPUs organize 32 threads with consecutive thread indexes into a unit known as a *warp* [104]. When a warp is executed by a GPU core, all 32 threads are executed simultaneously with the same instruction stream in lock-step, although they can access different datasets. This execution style is known as *single-instruction, multiple-thread (SIMT)*. In a GPU kernel, both computing instructions and memory access instructions must be executed in this warp-based fashion. There are many research and development challenges associated with optimizing how branch-rich programs should be optimized in this SIMT manner. However, in this book, for the purpose of explaining the importance of how a set of threads should access data in a coordinated way, we will focus only on the aspect of memory accesses.

Within a warp, a memory reference in a kernel implies that 32 memory references are executed concurrently (assuming no branching occurs). However, depending on how these 32 memory accesses are related to one another, they can be grouped into a varying number of memory transactions. It is worth noting that different generations of Nvidia GPU/CUDA platforms may have distinct capabilities for defining, executing, and optimizing memory transactions.

For instance, with recent Nvidia GPUs, if (1) each thread accesses a 4-byte word, (2) all 32 threads access a total of 128-byte contiguous memory segment, and (3) such a segment is aligned with 32-byte segments, then the 32 thread memory references are coalesced into four 32-byte transactions. However, if the memory accesses are not aligned or span across a large memory range, more transactions are required, which can waste memory bandwidth and cause a reduction in performance.

Let us return to Algorithm 6.5 and use it as an example to illustrate the significance of coalesced memory accesses in GPUs. Recall that the kernel requires one thread to be responsible for two elements that must be loaded and stored between a partition of global memory and shared memory corresponding to a thread block. In the algorithm, we can use $block\_addr = block\_index \times SharedMemLimit$ as the starting address of the partition for a block. Intuitively, the problem would be straightforward if one thread is responsible for one element. In this case, the number of threads is equal to the size of both shared memory and the partition of the global memory, so the loading statement (ignoring storing for the moment due to similarity) is as follows.

$$sminput[local\_thread\_index] = input[block\_addr + local\_thread\_index]$$

Clearly, $block\_addr + local\_thread\_index$ is equivalent to $global\_addr$. The issue now is: Which two elements should be assigned to each thread? It is worth considering this issue because the above warp mechanism, which combines 32 threads into grouped memory transactions, can result in varying performance behaviors based on different assignments of elements-to-threads. Before we explain the memory accesses in Algorithm 6.5, we first present an alternative assignment. If we assign two consecutive elements to each thread in the following manner, we can create a memory access pattern as illustrated in Figure 6.12.

$$sminput[local\_thread\_index \times 2] = input[block\_addr + local\_thread\_index \times 2]$$

$$sminput[local\_thread\_index \times 2 + 1] = input[block\_addr + local\_thread\_index \times 2 + 1]$$

In the image, we have depicted only 16 threads (actually 32 threads in a single warp) due to page limitations. Each thread loads two elements using the two statements mentioned above. We have used dark grayscale to represent the loading of the first

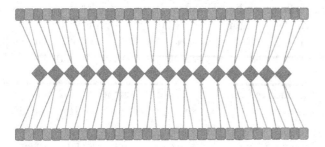

Figure 6.12 Illustration of strided memory accesses. The central idea is that one thread t is responsible for two elements at $2t$ and $2t + 1$.

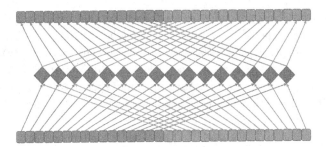

Figure 6.13 Illustration of coalesced memory accesses. The central idea is that one thread t is responsible for two elements at t and $t + n$, where n is the number of the total threads.

element and light grayscale for the second one. This assignment represents a typical data partitioning strategy among multiple threads in traditional CPU scenarios. With a total of N threads, the target dataset is partitioned into N consecutive subsets, and each thread processes each subset independently. However, as can be seen from the figure, when all threads process the first element (the dark grayscale one), a strided memory access pattern is formed (*stride* $= 2$). Therefore, the total memory access range of the 32 threads is $32 \times (4 + 4) = 256$ bytes. When each thread processes the first element, it would create $256/32 = 8$ memory transactions. Correspondingly, when each thread processes the second element, another 8 memory transactions are executed. Thus, a total of 16 memory transactions are executed.

The issue with the above strided accesses is that each memory transaction has to load 50 percent unnecessary data because the addressed memory in a warp is not dense. To create a pattern where a single memory transaction can serve all the memory references of the threads in a warp, we can switch to a new assignment strategy where two adjacent threads process two adjacent elements. Figure 6.13 illustrates such an arrangement, which essentially reflects the memory access pattern implied in Algorithm 6.5. Still, one thread is responsible for two elements, with $h = \frac{SharedMemLimit}{2}$, as shown in the following.

$$sminput[local\_thread\_index] = input[block\_addr + local\_thread\_index]$$

$$sminput[local\_thread\_index + h] = input[block\_addr + local\_thread\_index + h]$$

The benefits of this assignment strategy can be analyzed as follows. As shown in Figure 6.13, for both the first and second elements that each thread must process, a continuous segment is formed so that there is no gap in the memory between two threads of a warp. For the first element, all 32 elements form a continuous $32 \times 4 = 128$-byte segment, which equals to four memory transactions. The same holds for the second element, resulting in a total of eight memory transactions. Compared to the 16 transactions in the previous assignment, Figure 6.13 demonstrates that coalesced memory accesses can achieve a $2\times$ speedup by reducing the number of memory transactions.

In addition to the *GSharedMemSorting* kernel in Algorithm 6.4, there are two other kernels for different steps of bitonic merging: *GGlobalMerging* and *GSharedMem Merging*. We will not provide details of these two kernels here since they are relatively easier than the *GSharedMemSorting* kernel. Clearly, *GGlobalMerging* does not use shared memory at all, and *GSharedMemMerging* is only a part of *GSharedMemSorting*. We encourage readers to implement the two kernels as exercises to gain a better understanding of the architectural interactions involved.

6.4.4   A Summary of Architectural Interactions of Bitonic Sort

The previous content has illustrated a typical example of how GPU computing is utilized to solve a real problem (sorting). The main point is that a parallel algorithm should not only focus on how its parallelism can be revealed and utilized, but also consider important architectural factors that determine how to best map the algorithm to the hardware features. We have highlighted three major advancements in GPU computing environments compared to the original algorithm.

- **Reduce latency** The aim is to make the best use of on-chip shared memory to avoid unnecessary and expensive device memory accesses. In the example above, the improved algorithm maximizes the use of shared memory by partitioning the sorting process into different steps and resorts to device memory only when the comparing stride is out of reach of shared memory.
- **Improve bandwidth** The objective is to make optimal data-to-thread mapping to maximize hardware bandwidth usage. In the earlier example, the solution avoids the issue of strided memory accesses by assigning two consecutive data accesses to each thread, thereby creating coalesced memory access.
- **Avoid overhead** The goal is to organize work into only the necessary threads to minimize overhead and maximize performance. The improved algorithm avoids launching a half of the total threads using the old approach. Carefully arranged thread indexing calculations are essential and even challenging due to the thread coordination required among the targeted datasets.

Indeed, these architectural improvements are limited in scope. The main purpose of the example is to help readers understand the difficulty and importance of implementing an algorithm in a specific parallel computing hardware and environment, such as Nvidia GPUs. However, achieving optimal performance on modern hardware requires much more than the optimizations discussed above.

Achieving optimal performance on hardware requires a much deeper understanding than what we have discussed so far, unless an application is specifically tailored to a particular hardware device. The factors presented in this chapter cannot account for many of the hidden performance factors in GPU hardware. For instance, how can we adapt branch-intensive programs for efficient GPU processing? Returning to the example of bitonic sort, is it possible to assign threads and elements in a more optimal way such that threads executed within the same warp follow the same execution path?

Furthermore, while we did not delve into the problem of transferring data between host memory and GPU device memory, it is evident that this transfer is a crucial performance factor for many GPU-based data analysis applications.

While it is essential to optimize an algorithm for a specific hardware environment, such performance improvement must be grounded in functionality that not only assumes the algorithm's correctness but also accounts for its adaptability to other applications. As such, a significant challenge arises as we seek to determine how an algorithm can be used effectively in practical scenarios.

6.4.5   Advancement 2: Anomaly Handling

The second area of advancement pertains to anomaly handling. The algorithms discussed earlier are only equipped to handle scenarios where the number of elements to be sorted is a power of 2. Naturally, one may wonder how to extend these algorithms to more general cases with arbitrary lengths. However, before delving into this question, a prior question must be considered: Is it truly imperative to undertake such an extension? While such an expansion may be essential for a general-purpose sorting algorithm, it may not be necessary if bitonic sort is exclusively employed for inputs with a power-of-2 length. In this regard, we do not attempt to answer the necessity question but instead focus on the methodology for resolving the challenge of arbitrary input length.

Suppose that the input array's length is denoted by N, where $2^{k-1} < N < 2^k$. A straightforward idea is to utilize the bitonic sorting algorithm to sort the first 2^{k-1} elements, followed by the use of an insertion sort to insert each of the remaining elements into the sorted result, provided that $N - 2^{k-1}$ is relatively small. Alternatively, the array can be extended to a length of 2^k by appending $2^k - N$ elements, each of which is larger than any element in the input array. Subsequently, the newly augmented array can be sorted with utilizing the existing bitonic algorithm, thus enabling the direct sorting of the initial N elements. However, despite the feasibility of these approaches, they are not efficient.

A correct approach to extending bitonic sorting to arbitrary lengths is through the utilization of a technique called "virtual padding." The aforementioned padding technique has a significant drawback in that the padded numbers, while irrelevant for obtaining the actual result, must be moved up and down during the bitonic sorting process (as demonstrated in Figure 6.9), since the two-directional comparison and swap operation inevitably causes the largest numbers to be moved to the middle area (via stages 1–3) before they are returned to their original positions (via stage 4). In contrast, virtual padding seeks to prevent the unnecessary movements of these padded elements by employing one-directional comparisons throughout the entire bitonic sorting process.

Algorithm 6.1 constructs a bitonic sequence by sorting the first half of the input in ascending order and the second half in descending order, after which a bitonic splitting is applied to divide the sequence into two subsequences. Nevertheless, this creation and partition of bitonic sequences is not the only means of implementing bitonic sorting.

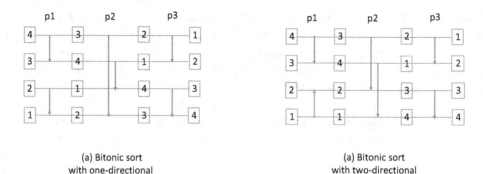

(a) Bitonic sort
with one-directional
comparison/swap

(a) Bitonic sort
with two-directional
comparison/swap

Figure 6.14 An example to illustrate (a) one-directional and (b) two-directional comparison and swap operations when implementing bitonic sort using four numbers (4,3,2,1).

As shown in Figure 6.8, the actual comparison pattern for splitting involves comparing the smallest element in the first half to the largest element in the second half, the second-smallest element in the first half to the second-largest element in the second half, and so forth. Such a comparison pattern can also be effectively and equivalently employed if the second half is sorted in ascending order. In this case, the element with index 0 is compared to the element with index $2^k - 1$ instead of 2^{k-1}, and other elements are paired correspondingly. Once the splitting is completed, the same two subsequences as in the original method are obtained. Consequently, the recursively applied further splitting actions for the two subsequences follow the conventional bitonic splitting as in the original method.

Figure 6.14 illustrates two different ways of implementing bitonic sort for an input of four elements (4,3,2,1). Figure 6.14(a) depicts the scenario of one-directional comparison, which has already been demonstrated in Figure 6.7. Figure 6.14(b) corresponds precisely to one component of the two-directional bitonic sort for four elements displayed in Figure 6.9. The crucial point to note is that both sorting networks represent equivalent implementations of bitonic sort for four elements. In both networks, the p2 step necessitates comparing the value 3 to the value 2 and the value 4 to the value 1, although the indices of 1 and 2 differ owing to the different sorting direction in p1. This elementary example reveals that we can utilize only ascending order while creating bitonic sequences, but we must adjust the indices of the compared pairs when executing bitonic splitting.

Figure 6.15 portrays the bitonic sorting network for 16 elements when employing one-directional comparisons. Readers can compare this to Figure 6.9. Two major disparities are apparent. Firstly, in step 1 of every stage, the comparison has been altered to conform to the principle of one-directional comparison. Secondly, the remaining steps of each stage still follow the same comparison patterns but with differing sorting directions.

One significant benefit of this one-directional bitonic sorting implementation is that it facilitates the use of virtual padding. Since every comparison and swap aims to

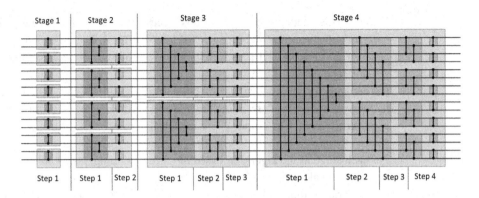

Figure 6.15 Illustration of bitonic sorting of 16 elements using one-directional comparisons. This figure is an adaptation of the original image by Wikipedia user Bitonic, with added visual aids to depict the stages and steps.

move the larger element downward, if an existing element is compared to a padded element with a greater value, the two elements will not be swapped. As a result, such a comparison can be disregarded entirely. This is referred to as virtual padding. We now present a nonrecursive algorithm for this virtual padding-based, one-directional bitonic sorting process in Algorithm 6.6.

Algorithm 6.6 A nonrecursive form of the bitonic sort algorithm for sorting an arbitrary-length array.

Require: $2^{k-1} < len(input) < 2^k$

for each $stage \in [1, k]$ **do**
    for each $step \in [1, stage]$ **do**
        if $step = 1$ **then**
            $pair\_distance \leftarrow 2^{stage} - 1$
        else
            $pair\_distance \leftarrow 2^{stage-step}$
        end if
        for each $element\_index \in [0, len(input) - 1]$ **do**
            $pair\_index \leftarrow BitwiseXOR(element\_index, pair\_distance)$
            if $pair\_index < len(input) \wedge pair\_index > element\_index$ **then**
                COMPAREANDSWAP($input[element\_index], input[pair\_index], direction$)
            end if
        end for
    end for
end for

When comparing the new Algorithm 6.6 for arbitrary input length with the old Algorithm 6.1 for "power of 2" input length, we observe that they have a very similar core logic, yet differ in three significant aspects.

- In the virtual padding approach, it is necessary that both *element_index* and *pair_index* be restricted in the range of $[0, len(input) - 1]$. Therefore, if a comparison between an element and a padded element is required, the comparison will not actually take place.

- It is apparent that the comparison direction in the algorithm based on virtual padding is consistently set to "ascending," while the variable *pair_block* in the original algorithm, which was employed to switch the comparison direction, no longer exists.

- For each stage in the algorithm based on virtual padding, step 1 follows a distinct approach to calculating *pair_distance*, as previously described. Readers can compute several examples to understand how utilizing $2^{stage} - 1$ produces the effect of each step 1 in Figure 6.15.

We encourage readers to undertake exercises to create their own parallel and GPU-optimized algorithms based on Algorithm 6.6. Once readers comprehend how Algorithm 6.2 can be parallelized into Algorithm 6.3 and subsequently optimized in Algorithm 6.4 and Algorithm 6.5, it is relatively easy to parallelize and optimize Algorithm 6.6. We also encourage readers to implement these algorithms into actual GPU programs using CUDA and then evaluate and analyze the performance of their programs.

Thus far, we have illustrated how the initial bubble sort has been progressively expanded and optimized into GPU-optimized, parallel bitonic sorting algorithms. This evolutionary path employs the PAPA methodology, as introduced at the outset of this chapter, and we have emphasized the importance of the advancement component. However, it is worth noting that in Figure 6.7(a), there is another path in the algorithm extension journey: Batcher's odd–even sorting algorithm, which we will elaborate on in the next section (Section 6.5).

6.5   Batcher's Odd–Even Sorting Algorithm

Recall that in Figure 6.7, we demonstrated that Batcher's odd–even sorting algorithm (we simply call it BOES in this book) is essentially an approach for merging two sorted sequences. By combining Figure 6.7(b) and Figure 6.14(b), we can create a new illustration that highlights the structural distinctions between two-directional bitonic sort and BOES for four elements (see Figure 6.16).

The first notable difference between the two algorithms is that in p1, BOES utilizes only one-directional comparison. The second distinction is that in p3, BOES compares only the pair of the second and third elements. However, the significant difference between the two algorithms lies in the actual purpose of p2, although they function identically in this case. In bitonic sort, p2 executes a bitonic splitting to produce disjoint subsequences for p3. In contrast, in BOES, p2 merges the odd-subsequence (elements 2 and 1) and the even-subsequence (elements 4 and 3), while p3 executes remedial comparisons for the final sorting outcome.

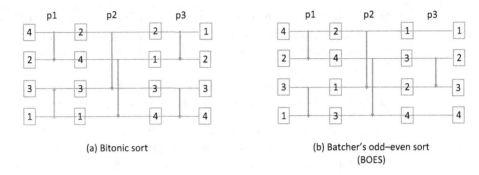

Figure 6.16 Illustration of structural differences between (a) bitonic sort and (b) Batcher's odd–even sorting algorithm (BOES) for four numbers with the initial order (4,2,3,1).

step	8	7	6	4	5	3	2	1
1	4	6	7	8	1	2	3	5
2	1	2	3	5	4	6	7	8
3	1	2	3	4	5	6	7	8

Figure 6.17 Sorting eight elements using BOES algorithm.

6.5.1   Premier

In essence, to merge two sorted sequences, BOES, like bitonic sort, employs a partitioning-based approach to divide the input sequences into smaller subsequences and gradually perform the sorting. However, unlike bitonic sort, BOES partitions an input sequence into one odd-indexed sequence and one even-indexed sequence.

The premier of BOES is the fact that the following steps can be used to sort $n = 2^k$ numbers $X_0, X_1, \ldots, X_{n/2-1}, X_{n/2}, \ldots, X_{n-2}, X_{n-1}$.

- **Step 1: Creating the to-be-merged sequences** Sort the first half sequence $X_0, X_1, \ldots, X_{n/2-1}$ and the second half sequence $X_{n/2}, \ldots, X_{n-2}, X_{n-1}$.
- **Step 2: Odd–even merging** Sort the even-indexed subsequence $X_0, X_2, \ldots, X_{n-2}$ and the odd-indexed subsequence $X_1, X_3, \ldots, X_{n-1}$.
- **Step 3: Final remedy** Compare and swap $[X_i, X_{i+1}]$ for all $i \in 1, 3, \ldots, n - 3$.

Figure 6.17 illustrates the three steps of BOES when sorting eight elements. The input sequence is (8,7,6,4,5,3,2,1). The steps are as follows.

1. Step 1 involves creating two sorted halves, which is a straightforward process. After step 1, the sequence becomes (4,6,7,8,1,2,3,5).

2. Step 2 is to separately sort the even-indexed subsequence (4,7,1,3) and the odd-indexed subsequence (6,8,2,5). The subresults are (1,3,4,7) and (2,5,6,8), respectively. The sequence after step 2 is (1,2,3,5,4,6,7,8). Note that this sequence is not fully sorted.

3. Step 3 is used to remedially compare adjacent elements starting from the second one, and finally exchange 4 and 5 to get the final sorted sequence.

Since BOES is a recursive process, its correctness relies on the correctness of the base case and the validity of the induction, which are the steps above. We do not provide a formal proof of the correctness of the BOES algorithm, but instead offer an explanation of why the steps constitute a valid induction and ensure the correctness of the algorithm. In the given example, the elements 4 and 5 need to be exchanged in the final step. However, after executing step 1 and step 2, we can deduce that (5,4) must come after 3 and before 6. Examining the result of step 2, which is (1,2,3,5,4,6,7,8), we can see that (1) the first and second halves are sorted and (2) the odd and even halves are also sorted. We can explain the relationship between the four elements 3, 4, 5, and 6. Firstly, we know that $4 > 3$ because they are already sorted in the subsequence (1,3,4,7) in step 2. Secondly, we know that $5 > 3$ because they are already sorted in the subsequence (1,2,3,5) in step 1. Similarly, we can prove that 6 is greater than both 5 and 4. Therefore, given that $3 < (4,5) < 6$, the only question that remains is the order of 5 and 4, which cannot be determined without a direct comparison between them.

The combination of step 1 and step 2 eliminates the possibility of unsorted pairs that are not adjacent. This is why step 3 is necessary to perform a final comparison between adjacent neighbors for the final sorting. These adjacent neighbors are for pairs $[X_i, X_{i+1}]$ for $i \in 1, 3, \ldots, n - 3$. For example, the pair (5,4) whose indices after step 2 are actually (3,4) (using 0-based indexing).

We must note that the comparison is not conducted for $[X_i, X_{i+1}]$ for $i \in 0, 2, \ldots, n - 2$. Readers should carefully confirm the indices of elements that should be compared by referring to Figure 6.17. Actually, the first element (1) after step 2 is guaranteed to be the smallest one in the whole sequence, because it is the smaller one from the two leading elements after step 1 (1 and 4). Similarly, the last element (8) is also guaranteed to be the largest one in the sequence.

The final point regarding the premier of BOES is that its step 2, which involves sorting the odd/even-indexed subsequence, is actually a merging of two smaller odd/even-indexed subsequences taken from the first and second halves of the sequence. As the first and second halves are already sorted, their odd/even-indexed subsequences are also sorted. In the example we discussed earlier, when we sorted the even-indexed subsequence (4,7,1,3), we were actually merging (4,7) from the first half with (1,3) from the second half. Consequently, it is equivalent to saying that sorting the odd/even-indexed subsequence involves merging two smaller, sorted odd/even-indexed subsequences. Moreover, the merging operation can be recursively performed on smaller subsequences, and when only two elements remain, a simple compare and swap is carried out.

6.5.2 Algorithm

A recursive algorithm for BOES can be written based on the aforementioned analysis, as shown in Algorithm 6.7. Once the two halves are sorted, BOESMerge is called to merge the two sorted sequences. BOESMerge recursively calls itself to merge even-indexed subsequences and odd-indexed subsequences until the subsequence has only two elements. The final step of BOESMerge is to compare and swap all odd–even adjacent pairs.

Algorithm 6.7 A recursive form for the BOES algorithm. We here ignore the details of several trivial assisting functions.

Require: $len(input) = 2^k$

BATCHERODDEVENSORT(*input*)

procedure BATCHERODDEVENSORT(*input*)
　　BOESHALFSORT(*input*)
　　BOESMERGE(*input*)
end procedure

procedure BOESHALFSORT(*input*)
　　if $len(input) > 1$ **then**
　　　　BATCHERODDEVENSORT(*FirstHalf*(*input*))
　　　　BATCHERODDEVENSORT(*SecondHalf*(*input*))
　　end if
end procedure

procedure BOESMERGE(*input*)
　　if $len(input) = 2$ **then**
　　　　COMPAREANDSWAP(*input*[0], *input*[1], *direction*)
　　else
　　　　evenseq ← *ExtractEvenSequence*(*input*)
　　　　BOESMERGE(*evenseq*)
　　　　oddseq ← *ExtractOddSequence*(*input*)
　　　　BOESMERGE(*oddseq*)

　　　　for $i \in (1, 3, ..., len(input) - 3)$ **do**　　　　　　　　▷ Remedy
　　　　　　COMPAREANDSWAP(*input*[*i*], *input*[*i* + 1], *direction*)
　　　　end for
　　end if
end procedure

Like bitonic sort, parallelizing the recursive version of BOES is not straightforward without first transforming it into a nonrecursive form based on its sorting network

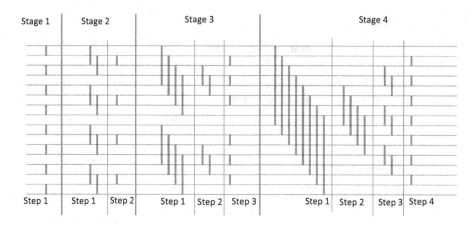

Figure 6.18 A sorting network for 16 elements using the BOES algorithm.

structure. Figure 6.18 displays a sorting network for 16 elements based on BOES. By comparing it to Figure 6.9, we can identify key characteristics of the BOES sorting network and highlight the main differences between the two networks. These differences provide us with insights into how we can modify the nonecursive algorithm of bitonic sorting to suit BOES.

- *Overall structure* The BOES sorting network has the same overall structure as the bitonic sorting network. For an input with 2^k elements, the sorting network requires k stages and the xth stage requires x steps.
- *First step* The first step in each phase of the BOES sorting network is similar to the first step in each phase of the two-directional bitonic sorting network. However, BOES takes only one-directional comparison and swap.
- *Pass through* In the BOES sorting network, elements that do not participate in any comparison and swap operations are passed through in all steps except the first step of each phase. The specific elements that are passed through depend on the stage and step of the sorting network.

All of the above characteristics can be explained by the recursive structure of Algorithm 6.7. Based on these characteristics, we can write a nonrecursive algorithm for BOES, which is shown in Algorithm 6.8. Like the nonecursive algorithm for bitonic sort in Algorithm 6.2, Algorithm 6.8 also requires that the length of the input must be a power of 2, and its main body is also a triple loop. Within the innermost loop, the core task is to find the pairing element with the index *pair_index* for each element with index *element_index*.

For the first step of each phase, finding the comparison and swap pairs is easy because *pair_index*'s value is the same as in Algorithm 6.2. However, for the rest of the steps in each stage, the element pairs involved in a comparison and swap are more complicated to be determined because not all elements participate in the remedy step.

Algorithm 6.8 A nonrecursive form of the BOES algorithm for a 2^k-length array.

Require: $len(input) = 2^k$
  for each $stage \in [1, k]$ **do**
    for each $step \in [1, stage]$ **do**
      $pair\_distance \leftarrow 2^{stage-step}$
      for each $element\_index \in [0, 2^k - 1]$ **do**
        if $step = 1$ **then**
          $pair\_index \leftarrow BitwiseXOR(element\_index, pair\_distance)$
        else
          $dist\_seg \leftarrow \dfrac{element\_index}{pair\_distance}$
          $pair\_block \leftarrow 2^{step}$
          $pair\_local \leftarrow dist\_seg - \dfrac{dist\_seg}{pair\_block} \times pair\_block$
          if $(pair\_local = 0) \vee (pair\_local = (pair\_block - 1))$ **then**
            $pair\_index \leftarrow element\_index$
          else
            if $(pair\_local \mod 2) = 0$ **then**
              $pair\_index \leftarrow element\_index - pair\_distance$
            else
              $pair\_index \leftarrow element\_index + pair\_distance$
            end if
          end if
        end if
        if $pair\_index > element\_index$ **then**
          CompareAndSwap($input[element\_index], input[pair\_index], direction$)
        end if
      end for
    end for
  end for

To determine the value of *pair_index* for each *element_index*, several auxiliary variables are used Algorithm 6.8, including *dist_seq*, *pair_block*, and *pair_local*. Essentially, *pair_local* is used to indicate the relative index of an element in its corresponding sequence relative to the execution of *BOESMerge*. In the remedy step of *BOESMerge*, the first and last elements are just passed through, so the algorithm filters out these two elements using the condition $(pair\_local = 0) \vee (pair\_local = (pair\_block - 1))$. Additionally, the two neighboring elements (with distance *pair_distance*) of each pair must set each other as their paired elements, which is accomplished by the conditional statement inside the if statement $(pair\_local \mod 2 = 0)$. It is worth noting that the algorithm does not have a directionality issue.

Extending the aforementioned algorithm into a parallel version for GPU is a straightforward process. The extension process would be identical to the one from Algorithm 6.2 to Algorithm 6.3. The GPU parallel version would preserve the two outer loops and parallelize the third loop by launching n threads, where each thread is responsible for a single element from 0 to $n - 1$. Algorithm 6.9 illustrates such an algorithm.

Algorithm 6.9 A GPU parallel version of the BOES algorithm for sorting a 2^k-length array.

Require: $len(input) = 2^k$

   for each $stage \in [1, k]$ **do**
      for each $step \in [1, stage]$ **do**
         GPUKERNELSORTING($input, stage, step$)   ▷ Launch 2^k threads
         ALLTHREADSYNCHRONIZATION
      end for
   end for

   procedure GPUKERNELSORTING($input, stage, step$)   ▷ a thread
      $pair\_distance \leftarrow 2^{stage-step}$
      $element\_index \leftarrow thread\_index$
      if $step = 1$ **then**
         $pair\_index \leftarrow BitwiseXOR(element\_index, pair\_distance)$
      else
         $dist\_seg \leftarrow \dfrac{element\_index}{pair\_distance}$
         $pair\_block \leftarrow 2^{step}$
         $pair\_local \leftarrow dist\_seg - \dfrac{dist\_seg}{pair\_block} \times pair\_block$
        if $(pair\_local = 0) \vee (pair\_local = (pair\_block - 1))$ **then**
           $pair\_index \leftarrow element\_index$
        else
           if $(pair\_local \bmod 2) = 0$ **then**
              $pair\_index \leftarrow element\_index - pair\_distance$
           else
               $pair\_index \leftarrow element\_index + pair\_distance$
           end if
        end if
      end if
      if $pair\_index > element\_index$ **then**
         COMPAREANDSWAP($input[element\_index], input[pair\_index], direction$)
      end if
   end procedure

As we discussed when introducing bitonic sort, we should have a beginning algorithm that must finish the important first step for efficient GPU computing – expressing the parallelism inside the computation. Any further more architecture-oriented optimization techniques, such as locality utilization and coalesced global memory accesses, must start from the determining effect of parallelism. So far, Algorithm 6.9 has implemented the goal of parallelism.

6.5.3   Program

Implementing Algorithm 6.9 in the Nvidia CUDA programming environment is no different to implementing the one for bitonic sort. There is no special consideration for this BOES case. The main logic of an implementation program is as follows. (1) We first allocate an array in the host memory for input elements, and then copy them to the GPU device memory. (2) Then the sorting algorithm operates on the elements and writes the sorted elements back to the GPU memory. (3) Finally, the sorted elements are transferred back the host memory.

In the case of using one thread per element, the number of thread blocks will be equal to the number of elements divided by the number of threads per block, which can be expressed as $\frac{n}{x}$. It is essential to experiment with different block sizes to find the optimal configuration for the GPU device being used, which can maximize the parallelism of the computation and minimize memory accesses, leading to better performance.

6.5.4   Advancement

Similar to the previous case of bitonic sort, the above parallel algorithm for BOES on the GPU has several efficiency issues. Firstly, in the parallel version of Algorithm 6.9, half of the threads are redundant as each comparison pair only requires a single thread. Secondly, the algorithm does not make use of shared memory, which results in lower performance. Building upon the idea of advancing the naive bitonic sorting GPU algorithm to an advanced algorithm, we can enhance Algorithm 6.9 to Algorithm 6.10 which represents only the CPU-side work of the new algorithm but does not include the algorithms for the two GPU kernels involved.

Algorithm 6.10 A GPU parallel version of the BOES algorithm using shared memory.

Require: $len(input) = 2^k$
Require: $SharedMemLimit = 2^s (s < k)$
   $BC \leftarrow len(input)/SharedMemLimit$ ▷ Block Count
   $TC \leftarrow SharedMemLimit/2$ ▷ Thread Count
   GSHAREDMEMSORTING[BC,TC](input)
   $MergeSize \leftarrow 2 \times SharedMemLimit$
   while $MergeSize \leq len(inpt)$ **do**
      $CompareSize \leftarrow \dfrac{MergeSize}{2}$
      while $CompareSize \geq 1$ **do**
         GGLOBALMERGING[BC,TC](input, MergeSize, CompareSize)
         $CompareSize \leftarrow \dfrac{CompareSize}{2}$
      end while
      $MergeSize \leftarrow 2 \times MergeSize$
   end while

When compared to Algorithm 6.4, the main difference in Algorithm 6.10 is that it does not use shared memory-based merging. This means that regardless of the value of *CompareSize*, the algorithm still utilizes *GGlobalMerging*. The reason behind this is that comparison pairs can cross the boundary of *SharedMemLimit*, as illustrated in Figure 6.18. Assuming that shared memory can only hold four elements, then for every four elements in stage 1 and stage 2, the kernel method *GSharedMemSorting* can be executed. However, starting from stage 3, all steps are carried out by the kernel *GGlobalMerging*. As shown in Figure 6.18, it is evident that in stages 3 and 4, if we group four elements together, cross-group comparisons are inevitable in all steps. This is why it is difficult to use shared memory for merging in these stages.

Algorithm 6.11 depicts the kernel *GSharedMemSorting* algorithm. It has the same structure as its counterpart for bitonic sort, so the details of step 1 and step 3, which involve data loading and writing between global memory and device memory, are not shown. These parts are similar to those in Algorithm 6.4. The critical part is step 2, which explains how to perform BOES sorting within shared memory with n threads handling $2n$ elements.

In general, step 2 of Algorithm 6.11 can be easily understood through two observations. Firstly, when $step = 1$, it uses the same method as Algorithm 6.4 to determine the comparing pair (*small_element, big_element*). Secondly, the other steps' calculations are based on the first step, which employs the same approach for determining *base_index*. However, two modifications have been made: (1) It utilizes a condition (*offset* $\geq$ *pair_distance*) to identify certain elements (or pairs), and (2) it uses *base_index* as the *big_index* and *base_index* − *pair_distance* as the *small_index* accordingly. To elaborate on these two modifications, let us revisit the sorting network example in Figure 6.18. Consider the comparison between Step 2 of stage 2 and step 1 of stage 1, and we can understand why the algorithm works in this way.

Here, we haven't included the algorithm for the GGlobalMerging kernel. However, readers should be able to write one based on the existing knowledge we have covered thus far. Additionally, we have not demonstrated how BOES can be extended to handle input lengths that are not a power of 2. This is because the one-directional nature of BOES makes it easy to extend it in a similar manner to one-directional bitonic sort.

6.6   Summary and Exercise Projects

We have successfully completed a sorting journey, which began with the sequential bubble sorting algorithm and progressed to two complex GPU parallel sorting algorithms. Throughout the journey, we emphasized the necessity of algorithm evolution in both logical and physical aspects. However, it is important to note that the chapter does not provide concrete performance numbers to determine which algorithm is faster, nor does it explain how these algorithms are practically used. Actually, both algorithms can be used as components in a practical sorting implementation that executes merging on sorted segments. Rather than focusing solely on the algorithms themselves, the chapter

---

Algorithm 6.11 GPU kernel *GSharedMemSorting* in Algorithm 6.10.

Require: $len(input) = 2^k$
Require: $SharedMemLimit = 2^s (s < k)$
  procedure GSHAREDMEMSORTING(*input*)
      GET(*local_thread_index*)   ▷ thread index inside its thread block

                 ▷ Step 1: Copy two elements from global memory to shared memory
      LOADELEMENTSFROMGLOBALTOSHARED
      BLOCKTHREADSYNCHRONIZATION

                 ▷ Step 2: Execute BOES sorting within shared memory
      offset ← −1
      for each *stage* ∈ [1, s] **do**   ▷ *SharedMemLimit* = 2^s
         for each *step* ∈ [1, *stage*] **do**
            pair_distance ← $2^{stage−step}$
            backd ← *BitwiseAND*(*local_thread_index*, *pair_distance* − 1)
            base_index ← 2 × *local_thread_index* − *backd*
            small_index ← *big_index* ← 0
            if *step* = 1 **then**
               offset ← *backd*
               small_index ← *base_index*
               big_index ← *base_index* + *pair_distance*
            else
               if *offset* ≥ *pair_distance* **then**
                  small_index ← *base_index* − *pair_distance*
                  big_index ← *base_index*
               end if
            end if
            if *small_index* < *big_index* **then**
               COMPAREANDSWAP(*sminput*[*small_index*], *sminput*[*big_index*], *direction*)
            end if
            BLOCKTHREADSYNCHRONIZATION
         end for
      end for
                 ▷ Step 3: Copy back sorted result
      STOREELEMENTSFROMSHAREDTOGLOBAL
  end procedure

---

highlights the use of sorting as a main thread to introduce various critical factors for GPU computing.

    Beyond the sorting task itself, our primary objective was to provide readers with a holistic experience in building parallel programs in the modern computing era. This journey encompassed both parallelism-oriented algorithm design thinking and hardware architecture-based implementation and optimization skills, which are essential to achieving high-performance computing in sophisticated accelerators like GPUs.

Parallel programming remains a dynamic and active research domain due to its diverse practical applications and the continuously evolving hardware devices. This requires parallel programmers to possess both domain-specific knowledge and hardware programming skills. The feasibility of machine learning-based auto-programming, auto-parallelization, and auto-optimization techniques, for example those based on large language models (LLMs) such as ChatGPT, is an open question that remains to be explored. Interested readers can find further related work on this topic through a search or by engaging in a conversation with ChatGPT.

At the conclusion of this chapter, we present three exercise projects to provide readers with firsthand experience in utilizing the PAPA methodology in GPU parallel programming. These projects necessitate genuine Nvidia CUDA programming to achieve the desired final programs. While there are numerous available educational resources such as tutorials, research papers, and code samples, we strongly encourage readers initially to devise their own solutions before delving into those references. The three exercise projects, categorized as easy, medium, and hard, are as follows.

- Project 1 (*easy*) As we introduced three premiers for generating the Fibonacci sequence earlier in this chapter, this project entails implementing three GPU CUDA programs each of which effectively leverages one of the premiers. By comparing the execution times of the programs for varying Fibonacci lengths, readers will gain a profound appreciation for the pivotal role of a premier in GPU programming.
- Project 2 (*medium*) This project entails implementing GPU CUDA versions of both one-directional bitonic sort and BOES algorithms for inputs of arbitrary lengths. The implementation should incorporate the performance optimization techniques we have examined, such as shared memory utilization and coalesced memory access. Furthermore, for input lengths that are powers of 2, it is necessary to implement the two-directional bitonic sort as well. A comprehensive performance comparison and analysis report should be prepared, considering various input lengths.
- Project 3 (*hard*) Although the primary focus of this chapter revolves around the case study of Batcher's two sorting network algorithms, it is worth noting that the PAPA principle and GPU performance tuning strategies are applicable to various GPU computing tasks. This project necessitates the implementation of two conventional sequential sorting algorithms, namely radix sort and quicksort. While these sorting algorithms were not covered in detail within this chapter, it is the implementer's responsibility to design and develop their GPU parallel versions, exploring diverse optimization possibilities for both algorithms and programs. Ultimately, the project entails comparing and analyzing the performance of these two algorithms on GPU against the aforementioned bitonic sort and BOES algorithms.

7 GPU for Structured Data

> Everything should be made as simple as possible, but not simpler.
>
> Albert Einstein, *one of the greatest scientists of all time.*

This chapter provides an introduction to leveraging GPUs for executing SQL queries in structured data analysis. The abbreviation SQL, which stands for "structured query language," is the widely adopted language for analyzing data stored in relational database systems. In the realm of databases, when we refer to structured data, we typically mean data that has been organized into a relational format and can be efficiently stored and analyzed using relational database management systems (DBMSs). In fact, contemporary relational DBMSs, including prominent commercial products like Oracle and open-source alternatives like PostgreSQL, play a crucial role in practical data management applications across diverse industries.

Moreover, in the era of big data that has transpired over the past decade, contemporary analytical systems such as Apache Hive, Spark, and Presto persist in employing SQL as the language of choice for analyzing structured data. These datasets are often stored in widely adopted formats like RCFile and Apache ORC. The essence of managing structured or relational data lies in the fact that both the user interface, represented by SQL, and the data storage format, such as RCFile, adhere to standardized conventions. This standardized approach allows implementers of intermediate systems to possess maximum flexibility in selecting hardware and software combinations for their specific solutions.

As a result, GPU-accelerated database systems have experienced a surge in popularity within the database industry over the past decade, particularly for large-scale deployments of mission-critical applications. The rise of GPU database systems can be attributed to their ability to meet real-world application requirements. A key requirement that these systems address is the need for users to extract dynamic business insights by analyzing data that is continuously updated in real time. Consequently, the utilization of GPUs to execute complex SQL queries has emerged as a prominent research area in high-performance database systems.

7.1   Introduction to Primitives for GPU-Based SQL Processing

When it comes to executing SQL queries using GPUs, there are more technical challenges compared to simple tasks like executing bitonic sort, as we discussed in the previous chapter. Let us begin by summarizing two fundamental characteristics of bitonic sort: (1) the parallel threads only require synchronization without any additional information exchange, and (2) the behavior of each parallel thread is independent of the specific data it needs to process. However, GPU-based SQL executions are inherently data dependent, giving rise to two additional types of coordination among threads.

- **Collective decision-making** Parallel threads need to collect information from all the peers to make a global decision. Though it may sound straightforward, this operation actually entails multiple challenges associated with parallel computing, including thread synchronization, parallel information passing, and rapid decision-making.
- **Resource competition** Parallel threads must resolve conflicts when accessing a shared resource. Here, the term "resource" can refer to various concepts, including a variable in code or a memory location. The crucial point is that when such a resource is shared by multiple users, conflicts are inevitable and therefore must be controlled.

While there are other types of coordination necessary for more complex parallel algorithms, for GPU SQL engines, solving the two coordination challenges described above is essential. An example of the first challenge is determining where a thread should write its output or which memory address to use. For the second challenge, consider the scenario where two threads need to write to the same memory address. These questions do not arise in bitonic sort, as each thread has its own predetermined writing address. However, as this section will explain, the "data-dependent" behavior of threads necessitates dynamic coordination during their execution.

While "collective decision-making" and "resource competition" represent the general coordination required for GPU-based SQL executions, concrete forms of coordination could be diverse in various different computer algorithms and programs. In this chapter, we introduce a vital parallel computing primitive called "prefix sum" as one such algorithm for collective decision-making. Additionally, we discuss the use of atomic operations in CUDA programs, which provide a concrete solution for supporting resource competition on Nvidia GPUs.

7.1.1   Prefix Sum

The prefix sum of a sequence of n numbers $(x_0, x_1, \ldots, x_{n-1})$ is a second sequence of n numbers $(y_0, y_1, \ldots, y_{n-1})$ in which each y_i equals the sum of x_0 through x_i, inclusive. In other words, the prefix sum of a number is the cumulative sum of all its preceding numbers, including itself. Depending on whether the number itself is included in the result, the prefix sum can be either "inclusive" or "exclusive."

In the general domain of computer science, prefix sum is often referred to as "scan." However, in the database domain, "scan" typically denotes "table scan," an operation that iteratively goes through every row of a table. To avoid confusion, we use the term prefix sum instead of scan throughout this book.

Prefix sum is particularly important for parallel threads to calculate their writing addresses in a continuous memory space. For instance, suppose we have five threads $(T_1, \ldots, T_5)$, each of which needs to output several elements. If the number of output elements for each thread is $(2, 1, 4, 3, 2)$, then the writing address of the threads is an exclusive prefix sum of $(0, 2, 3, 7, 10)$. Using this information, the five threads can write to their designated spaces independently, avoiding conflicts. This example is a typical scenario of collective decision-making for parallel threads.

A sequential algorithm to calculate the prefix sum for a sequence with n numbers takes $O(n)$ time, while a parallel algorithm that utilizes n processors can do so in $O(\log n)$ time. While this book does not cover the implementation of prefix sum using GPUs, readers who are interested in detailed algorithms and implementations can refer to Chapter 39 of the book *GPU Gems 3* [85]. The CUB and Thrust libraries offer prefix sum implementations for both inclusive and exclusive cases, although they use the term "scan."

7.1.2 Atomic Operations

Atomic operations are essential for parallel threads that need to access shared resources. Consider the previous example where five threads need to output several elements individually. The question then becomes: How many elements were output in total? It is a simple and obvious answer, 12, to sum all the numbers $(2, 1, 4, 3, 2)$, where each number represents the count of elements that a thread has output. A sequential summation $2 + 1 + 4 + 3 + 2 = 12$ is simple. However, the problem becomes tricky when multiple threads are used for the computation, as each needs to add their respective number to the final sum, or to write to a shared resource.

Suppose the final sum is stored in the global memory address *result* with the initial value 0, then the logic of each thread with its own a_count is shown as follows.

```
int x = *result;
x += a_count;
*result = x;
```

Suppose there are only two threads, and one thread needs to add 2 and the other needs to add 3 to *result*. The code given in the previous example can easily produce an incorrect result of 2 or 3 instead of the correct result of 5. This is because when the two threads simultaneously execute the code, they are likely to execute the following three steps at the same time: (1) read the initial value 0 of *result* and set x to it, (2) update their own x to 2 or 3, and (3) update *result* with their own x, resulting in *result* being set to 2 or 3 depending on who writes first. Different from this lockstep execution, other execution sequences could be also possible: The two threads simultaneously execute their (1), then the first thread executes its own (2) and (3), and finally the second thread executes its own (2) and (3). In this scenario, the second thread's result becomes the final answer, leading to an incorrect result.

Note that these two kinds of wrong executions are essentially not related to whether the temporary variable x is introduced or involved. Without such an x, the code can be simply written as

```
*result += a_count
```

but the mistakes can still happen. Actually, to ensure the correct execution of the given code, the actions inside it should be treated as an atomic operation. This can be achieved using Nvidia CUDA's atomicAdd [104] function, which is defined for integers as follows.

```
int atomicAdd(int* address, int val)
```

The function is an uninterruptible read–modify–write memory operation. It reads the value of *address* into the variable *old*, updates *address* with $old + val$, and returns *old*. When multiple threads use this function to update the final result, the summation is executed sequentially, ensuring the correctness of the result.

In addition to the atomicAdd operation, Nvidia CUDA provides other atomic operations against a memory location, including subtraction, minimum/maximum, and bitwise operations such as AND/OR/XOR. One particularly important operation is atomicCAS, which stands for atomic compare and swap. It is defined for integers as follows,

```
int atomicCAS(int* address, int compare, int var)
```

The operation is to atomically execute (1) reading the value of *address* into *old*, (2) if $old = compare$, then writing *var* to *address*, and (3) returning *old*. We will explain how atomicCAS can be used to implement a lock-free hash table in this chapter.

7.2   An Overview of the GPUDB SQL Engine

At the core of a GPU database system is its SQL engine, which leverages GPUs to execute a query plan tree composed of relational operators such as table scans, selections, joins, and aggregations. In GPUDB [139], an early experimental GPU database system, the SQL engine dynamically generates a complete GPU program to execute a SQL query. This program can be based on either Nvidia CUDA or OpenCL [100], a parallel programming framework similar to CUDA. Alternatively, some other GPU engines may only dynamically generate partial code.

In this book, we primarily use GPUDB as a foundation to explain how to implement a GPU-based SQL engine. Figure 7.1 illustrates the overall structure of GPUDB and its SQL engine. It is worth noting that a GPU SQL engine can also be integrated into a traditional database system, such as PostgreSQL, working with other existing components including SQL parser, query optimizer, and storage manager.

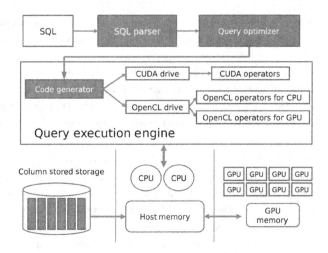

Figure 7.1 An overview of GPUDB's SQL engine. Essentially, an SQL query is translated into a C++ program that uses a set of operators implemented in CUDA or OpenCL.

The internal design and working mechanism of a SQL engine need to address the following points.

- **Data storage** Data storage refers to the underlying format or representation of data (e.g., whether it is compressed), its layout (e.g., row-wise or column-wise), and/or its access method (e.g., the indexing structures used to access it). While many SQL engines can process data stored in nonnative formats, such capabilities often require additional components for data format conversion.
- **Execution model** A SQL query is represented by a query plan tree, where each node represents a relational operation. An execution model is the way of scheduling the executions of all the nodes in the tree and arranging the data and control flows among them.
- **Operator implementations** The aforementioned execution model focuses primarily on how operators are connected, rather than how a given operator is implemented. For instance, a hash join operator may execute only a join or may perform multiple operations in a batched manner. The latter approach can be considered as an optimization technique for operator implementations, but initially, the focus should be on leveraging GPUs to execute a single relational operation.

7.2.1   Data Storage

Relational databases store data using tables as the fundamental unit, which is a two-dimensional data organization. Therefore, there are two fundamental ways to store a table.

- **Row-store** In this approach, a table is stored as a set of rows, with each row stored as a continuous space that contains values from each column.

- **Column-store** In contrast, a table is stored as a set of columns in this approach, with each column stored as a continuous space that contains values from each row.

Traditional database systems, such as PostgreSQL, use row-store because it is more suitable for transactional workloads that involve more write operations such as Insert, Delete, and Update. Because all data items of each row are stored together, it only takes one write to insert a row. On the other hand, column-store requires multiple writes for a single record as its data items are stored separately. However, row-store is not well-suited for analytical SQL or online analytical processing (OLAP) workloads that primarily involve read operations on specific columns. In this scenario, column-store can have a distinct advantage by allowing unnecessary columns to be skipped.

As GPUDB is specifically designed to accelerate OLAP workloads it uses a column-store to store each column of a table in a separate file on disk. When the query engine initiates a query, the files for the relevant columns are read into main memory and then copied into the GPU device memory for subsequent operations. The storage format for intermediate results during query execution is determined by the execution model of the query engine.

7.2.2   Execution Model

Traditional database systems use the iterator model to execute a query plan tree, and PostgreSQL is a typical example of this approach. The iterator model can be summarized into the following three characteristics.

- **Standard interface** Under the iterator model, each operator must implement several functions such as Open/GetNext/Close, which form a standard interface to connect operators. This allows all operators to be integrated into a tree in a way that is independent of how each individual operator was implemented.
- **Pulling-based data flow** The execution of the whole plan tree is a recursive GetNext call from a parent operator to its one or more child operators in the query plan tree. Each GetNext call is a pulling action that makes the child operator output a record. In this way, the query plan tree's execution becomes pipelined.
- **Row-oriented intermediate data** The output of each GetNext call is essentially a row of the total output table of a child operator. However, the operator does not need to first calculate and store all of its output and then serve one row whenever it receives a GetNext call.

The iterator model is considered the gold standard for relational database systems. However, it is not a right choice for GPU SQL engines for two key reasons. Firstly, it is designed for row-stores, while GPUDB uses a column-store which makes operators generate results (with values of multiple rows) in a batched mode instead of the pipelined mode. Secondly, it is designed for sequential computing, while GPUs excel at massively parallel computing. As a result, GPUDB uses a new execution model, often referred to as an "operator-at-a-time" or "operator-based, pushing model."

The execution model for a given query plan tree involves executing all operators using a postorder traversal. Each operator is executed once its child operator(s) have finished execution and its output results are available as input. A unique characteristic of a GPU SQL engine is its effort to keep intermediate data in GPU device memory for as long as possible until all subsequent operations on the data are completed.

The operator-at-a-time model of a GPU SQL engine processes all the rows from its input using the GPU's massive parallelism, which is a departure from the iterator model's one-row-at-a-time processing. One disadvantage of this model is that intermediate results must be stored. Since the data are stored in a column-store format, intermediate data are also stored as columns. However, since a row-store query result is expected, the issue of *materialization* arises [2], which is about when and how to execute *tuple construction* that combines separated columns together to form the final output. The query optimizer determines whether to use *early materialization* or *late materialization* based on estimated execution cost.

7.2.3 Operator Implementation Using Selection as an Example

The implementation of an operator is influenced by two factors – the operation that it is intended to perform (such as joining two tables) and the algorithm that can effectively carry out the operation (such as a hash join algorithm). It is common for an operation to have multiple algorithms, and it is the responsibility of database system developers to determine which algorithm is best suited for a particular operation. This section will delve into GPU-based operator implementation, starting with the selection operation. This is an excellent starting point because it is the most fundamental operation for almost any SQL query, and it is uncomplicated, requiring no sorting or hashing-based algorithms.

Let us consider an example SQL query that involves only a selection operation on a table T, which contains 26 integer columns named from a to z.

```
select x,y,z from T where a + b * c > d;
```

The intent of this query is apparent – to select the x, y, and z columns from the rows that satisfy the specified WHERE condition. To perform this selection, a sequential algorithm iteratively goes through each row of the table, executing the WHERE condition test for each row. If the condition passes, the data items from the x, y, and z columns are outputted as the result of a single GetNext call. The crux of the computation lies in the evaluation of the expression $a + b * c > d$ for each row, where a, b, c, and d represent the values in the corresponding columns.

For a GPU SQL engine that employs a column store and an operator-at-a-time model, the selection operator can utilize the GPU to parallelize the selection process by capitalizing on the parallelism that can be achieved by processing each row independently. The basic steps involved in this parallelization process are as follows.

- **Step 1: Expression evaluation** The first step is to use a GPU program to test each row's ability to satisfy the WHERE condition by evaluating the expression ($a + b *$ $c > d$), resulting in a 0-1 vector where each element represents the test result for a specific row.
- **Step 2: Result positioning** Next, each thread counts the number of rows that pass the WHERE condition, and then a prefix sum is performed to compute the cumulative index of the output range for all threads in the total output.
- **Step 3: Column scanning** Finally, for each column that needs to be outputted (x, y, z), allocate the corresponding space and use a GPU program to scan the original column data. For each row that satisfies the WHERE condition (i.e., its corresponding element in the 0-1 vector is 1), copy the item to the newly allocated space.

Step 2 involves a typical collective decision-making coordination to determine the position for each thread to write results. This ensures that there is no interthread synchronization required, as each thread has its own allocated space for writing. Additionally, the total number of output records, which is used to determine the required space for the result columns, can be obtained by using the last item in the prefix sum result if it is inclusive. If the prefix sum is exclusive, then the total count must be obtained by adding the last thread's count to the last item in the prefix sum. This approach obviates the need to use an atomic operation to compute the total count independently.

Overall, the GPU-based approach to execute selection is relatively straightforward. However, it has two challenging issues that merit further study – *thread management* and *code generation*.

7.2.4   Thread Management

In step 1 above, a natural question arises when processing n rows: How many threads should be employed? As previously discussed in Chapter 6, the strategy employed involves assigning one thread to handle one element, or two elements (which can be thought of as one pair of elements for comparison and swap). Therefore, in essence, the number of threads required is fundamentally determined by the problem size, that is, the number of input elements.

Certainly, we can implement selection using a *one-thread–one-element* model. For n input elements, we can launch n threads (for instance, using 256 threads per block, and $\lceil \frac{n}{256} \rceil$ blocks). In this scenario, the kernel for step 1 (where the expression is $a + b * c > d$) will resemble the following.

```
__global__ void kernel_expression_evaluation_1(
    int* ret_01_v, int* a, int* b, int* c, int* d)
{
    int tid = blockIdx.x * blockDim.x + threadIdx.x;
    ret_01_v[tid] = (a[tid] + b[tid] * c[tid] > d[tid]);
}
```

However, in practice, a more-efficient approach is to use a *grid-stride loop* model that employs a fixed number of threads to process more elements. The central idea is that if there are n threads in the grid, then thread 0 will process the elements indexed by $(0, n, 2n, \ldots)$, thread 1 will handle elements $(1, n+1, 2n+1, \ldots)$, and so on, with thread $n-1$ processing elements $(n-1, 2n-1, 3n-1, \ldots)$. Each thread will thus process a series of grid-stride elements using an explicit loop in their kernel. In this scenario, the corresponding kernel is as follows.

```
__global__ void kernel_expression_evaluation_2(
    int* ret_01_v, int* a, int* b, int* c, int* d)
{
    int tid = blockIdx.x * blockDim.x + threadIdx.x;
    int stride = blockDim.x * gridDim.x;
    for(int i = tid; i < n; i += stride)
    {
        ret_01_v[i] = (a[i] + b[i] * c[i] > d[i]);
    }
}
```

In the code, $blockDim.x * gridDim.x$ is precisely the number of total threads, which is referred to as a thread grid in the Nvidia GPU ecosystem. This approach offers two advantages over the previous one. Firstly, it eliminates the overhead associated with launching too many threads, since creating and destroying threads incurs unavoidable costs, as does data initialization. By reusing threads to process more elements, these costs can be significantly reduced. Secondly, the code can work with any number of block counts and thread counts. For instance, if both values are set to 1, a sequential version of the code is executed. Thus, the code makes it simpler to perform performance debugging and tuning.

Furthermore, like the one-thread–one-element model, this grid-stride loop approach also ensures that threads have a coalesced memory access pattern. This can greatly enhance the performance of global memory access.

Given these reasons, the grid-stride loop is a widely adopted approach in GPUDB's source code to organize threads for various kernels, even though the actual work inside the for loop may differ. For instance, in step 3, the kernel remains the same, with the actual work being the only difference. In this case, assuming we want the x column, the kernel would be as follows.

```
__global__ void kernel_scan_x_column(
    int* ret_x, int* ret_01_v, int* x, int* psum)
{
    int tid = blockIdx.x * blockDim.x + threadIdx.x;
    int stride = blockDim.x * gridDim.x;
    int localcount = psum[tid];
    for(int i = tid; i < n; i += stide)
    {
        if(ret_01_v[i] == 1)
        {
```

```
                        ret_x[localcount++]  =  x[i];
              }
          }
      }
```

7.2.5　Code Generation

In the aforementioned code, the core of the operation is testing the WHERE condition $(a + b * c > d)$ for each row. However, connecting the expression in the original SQL query to the actual expression evaluation in the GPU CUDA programs can be a complex issue. Let us compare two situations. The first scenario assumes a very simple expression $a = b$ used as the WHERE condition in a SQL query. When the database system executes the query, it can simply call a preimplemented kernel that is specifically designed to compare two columns. When it calls the kernel, it merely uses a and b as the two inputs. In this situation, the expression evaluation problem $(a = b)$ can be readily solved because a kernel exists that is precisely suited for the expression.

Now let us consider the second situation, which involves the complex expression $a + b * c > d$ that we have been using as an example. It is evident that a database system may not have a preimplemented kernel for this expression, which involves four columns with $+$, $*$, $>$ operators. Additionally, we need to address the question: How should a GPU database system execute an arbitrary expression in a SQL query if there is no predefined kernel available for it?

Before we can answer this question, we need to examine how a traditional database system, such as PostgreSQL, handles expression evaluation problems. The traditional approach is to use a general-purpose, object-oriented class to represent an expression, which results in an expression evaluation that becomes a series of recursive calls to subroutines for child expressions. For example, $a + b * c > d$ becomes an expression tree, with the root operation being $>$, the left child tree being $a + b * c$, and the right child tree being d. This approach is general purpose and can execute arbitrary expressions.

However, this traditional approach is not suitable for GPU SQL engines, for two reasons.

- *Limited hardware and software support* GPUs are designed for massive parallelism between simple and flat computation kernels, although later generations of the CUDA platforms can support recursive kernel calls.
- *Unnecessary costs for general purpose* Although it is possible to use a nonrecursive form of general-purpose expression evaluation, it will inevitably involve costs of stack operations and branch operations due to dynamically determining branches of various operations (e.g., $+ - * /$).

Since a general-purpose expression class or object is not feasible, a GPU SQL engine can use an alternative way to execute arbitrary expressions by using a hybrid approach that involves (1) driving the execution of an expression tree on the CPU side and (2) executing each basic operation on the GPU side. For instance, in the case of the $a + b * c < d$ expression, assuming there are three predefined kernels for the $+ * <$ operations, the engine would first call the kernel for $x = b * c$, then call the kernel for $y = a + x$, and finally call the kernel for $y < d$. Clearly, this approach incurs overheads related to storing intermediate results (e.g., x, y) and launching multiple kernels.

The ideal solution to this expression evaluation problem is based on code generation. In the earlier kernel examples, the expression in the original SQL query $a + b * c < d$ is expressed as $a[i] + b[i] * c[i] > d[i]$ in the CUDA program. This approach is fundamentally different from the traditional approach of using a general-purpose expression class. Instead, for each expression, the system dynamically generates code that is specific to that expression. This approach does not have any unnecessary branch code to execute other cases because it is 100 percent fixed to one expression.

If dynamic code generation is the best approach for a GPU SQL engine, the next question is: How to implement it? The answer depends on the programming language used for generating the code. Since code generation is a complex topic in GPU programming and other domains, we will provide a simple demonstration here. Interested readers can learn more about it from reading papers from proceedings of the CGO conferences (*IEEE/ACM International Symposium on Code Generation and Optimization*).

The code used in the earlier kernels is written in the C language. Nvidia CUDA provides a facility called NVRTC that can compile a string to PTX code (Nvidia's GPU assembly language) and then link/execute the code. With this feature, when the query engine needs to execute an expression (e.g., $a + b * c > d$), it can dynamically generate a kernel for that expression and then execute it.

Another possibility for code generation is to use a low-level language such as LLVM, an intermediate representation between high-level languages and assembly language [84] instead of a high-level language like C/C++. Using low-level languages can result in more programming difficulties but can reduce the time required for the compilation and linking of dynamically generated C/C++ code. In practice, there exist different code generation approaches with various optimization techniques.

Overall, the implementation of dynamic code generation in a GPU SQL engine requires a deep understanding of the programming language and tools used, as well as the ability to design and implement the code generation process for each expression.

7.3 Hashing-Based Operators on GPUs

In this section, we will introduce two hashing-based operators: hash join and hash aggregation. Join and aggregation (or Group By) are two critical operations in SQL. For both operations, there are hashing-based and sorting-based solutions, and there has been a long debate about which approach is better. In the era of GPU databases, this debate continues, and there is not a single solution that is perfect for all cases. It is the responsibility of a query optimizer to determine which operators should be used for a given SQL query in a database.

7.3.1   Hash Join

Join is one of the fundamental operations in relational databases to match and connect records from two tables. Equijoin is the most commonly used join which essentially selects those matching pairs according to an equal condition. In fact, when we use the term join, we usually mean equijoin, and other join forms require special terms, such as semijoin. Join performance is a critical factor for almost all database systems.

To execute a join $T_1 \bowtie T_2$, the naive approach is to perform a selection on top of the Cartesian product of the two tables. However, this algorithm has a complexity of $O(n^2)$, supposing each table has n rows. Another way to think of this approach is that for each row in T_1, we compare it to all rows in T_2. Intuitively, there is significant room for performance improvement if we can eliminate unnecessary comparisons. Based on this idea, hashing-based and sorting-based join algorithms have been developed.

Suppose we want to execute a join with the condition $T_1.f_1 = T_2.f_2$. The fundamental idea behind hash join is to preload the rows into corresponding hash buckets, where each bucket contains only rows whose hash values are equal to the bucket number. This approach ensures that when we need to compare a pair of rows, each from one table, their hash values must be the same, that is, $h(T_1.f_1) = h(T_2.f_2)$, where h is the hash function. By avoiding unnecessary comparisons, we can significantly improve performance. Row comparisons are only necessary within each bucket since cross-bucket comparisons cannot generate any results.

The above idea may sound simple. However, it involves three complex factors.

- **Hash function choice** A good hash function is crucial for calculating a hash value for a given input key, which is the foundation for hash table design and hash join execution.
- **Hash table design** The design of a hash table is critical for handling collisions when two different keys produce the same hash value, a common problem that hash functions cannot always avoid.
- **Hash join algorithm** Determining how to use one or more hash tables to execute the join requires considering various performance factors, such as parallelism, locality, load balance, and more.

Before we introduce good hash functions, let us consider an extremely underperforming and unrealistic case where the hash function always returns 1 for any input, that is, $h(x) \equiv 1$. If such a function was used for hash join, all elements would be placed in bucket 1, rendering it ineffective for solving the join problem. However, despite its impracticality, such a function has its feasible advantage of being computationally fast, as the result is always 1.

Therefore, this example highlights two important goals that a good hash function should achieve: first, uniform distribution of values across the output space, which helps minimize hash collisions; and second, fast computation, as the hash function should not be too complex and time-consuming to build and probe, diverting resources from the actual task the application needs to solve (e.g., join).

The code provided next is an implementation of Thomas Wang's hash function [130] for a 32-bit integer. This hash function takes in a 32-bit integer and returns another 32-bit integer that can be used as a hash value. The function first performs a series of bit manipulation operations on the input key, such as left and right shifting, XOR, and addition/subtraction with complemented values. These operations are designed to achieve a uniform distribution of hash values across the entire output space. This hash function is widely used and has been tested for quality and performance in various applications.

```
int inthash(int key)
{
  key += ~(key << 15);
  key ^=  (key >>> 10);
  key +=  (key << 3);
  key ^=  (key >>> 6);
  key += ~(key << 11);
  key ^=  (key >>> 16);
  return key;
}
```

Although there exists the so-called "perfect hash function" approach [123], it is not suitable for being used in database systems due to the dynamic nature of data changes. Instead, hash collisions are often inevitable and become a crucial issue for the design and implementation of hash tables for databases. There are two main categories of collision resolution mechanisms.

The first category involves accepting multiple keys with the same hash value to occupy the same position in the hash table. In this case, a separate data structure is used to store the keys with the same hash value, and any key lookup requires an additional search in that data structure. This type of hash table is commonly referred to as separate chaining.

The second category aims to avoid multiple keys with the same hash value occupying the same position in the hash table. When a new key is assigned to a position already occupied by another key, various strategies are employed to adjust the position. Examples of algorithms include cuckoo hashing [112] and hopscotch hashing [65].

Hash join operations can be divided into two steps: building hash tables and probing hash tables. The decision on which table to use, or whether to use both tables, for building hash tables is up to the hash join algorithm. If the hash table is built on top of the left table, a hash probe is required for each row of the right table. This approach implies that hash probes must be efficient. In disk-based database systems, efficiency means that the hash table should stay in the main memory; otherwise, a disk access will be needed, which can cause disk seeks due to random accesses. In memory-based database systems, efficiency often means the best use of on-chip CPU caches. To achieve efficiency, improved hash joins use hash functions to partition both tables and create smaller but more efficient hash tables [22, 120].

In general, the three issues mentioned above – hash function choice, hash table design, and hash join algorithm – are closely related. However, there is no one-size-fits-all solution for all cases. A comprehensive solution must make tradeoffs among multiple factors, taking into account the specific requirements and constraints of each use case. When it comes to GPU-based hash joins, this book provides an introduction to the hash join algorithm and implementation in GPUDB, offering insights into how to optimize performance and balance memory and processing requirements.

7.3.2   GPUDB's Hash Join Implementation

The GPUDB hash join is specifically designed to execute typical star-schema data warehouse joins, where a large fact table needs to be joined with one or more smaller-dimension tables [53]. The hash join operator in GPUDB is implemented as a binary join operator, which can handle the join between the fact table and one dimension table. However, it is also possible to implement a special operator that can join the fact table with multiple dimension tables simultaneously, as is the case with RateupDB [88].

When performing a join between the fact table T_f and the dimension table T_d, GPUDB's hash join builds a hash table on T_d using a conventional separate chain-similar approach to handle conflicts. The probing phase involves executing a hash table lookup for each row of T_f. While the main logic is simple, parallelizing the hash join using GPUs introduces two key differences from the sequential version, which are the focus of this book.

- GPUDB's hash table uses a continuous memory space rather than separate chains.
- GPUDB's hash table building and probing requires a *double execution* strategy.

Figure 7.2 illustrates how GPUDB stores a hash table. Conventional methods that use a separate chain to store elements in a bucket rely on dynamic memory allocation. Since the number of elements a bucket can contain is unknown, when a new element is added to a bucket, the bucket must be expanded to a larger size. Higher-level object-oriented languages such as C++ (e.g., using std::vector) can conceal this dynamic memory allocation requirement. However, this requirement is not ideal for GPU kernels as each thread requires a predetermined memory access address. Instead, GPUDB's hash table employs a single continuous memory space to store all buckets and uses additional arrays to store the starting address and number of elements within each bucket.

Although using a continuous memory space eliminates the need for dynamic memory allocations, it requires a two-step process for building the hash table. In the first step, the underlying table is scanned to determine the number of elements each bucket will have. And in the second step, the table is scanned again to fill each bucket. This double execution approach is common in GPU data processing for many tasks and is also used in the hash table probing phase of hash join. The purpose of this approach is to let each thread predetermine where it should write before the actual output, which is essential for efficient GPU processing.

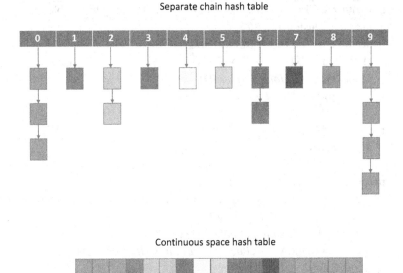

Figure 7.2 A demonstration of organizing hash table using separate chains and continuous memory space.

Algorithm 7.1 GPUDB's hash join algorithm 1: overall.

Require: Probing Table T_p (fact able or a join result)
Require: Dimension Table T_d

▷ Building Hash Table

$BucketSize \leftarrow KCalculateBucketSize(T_d)$
$BucketAccuAddress \leftarrow PrefixSum(BucketSize)$
$HashTable \leftarrow KCalculateBucket(T_d)$

▷ Probing Hash Table

$(DimRowID, ThreadCount) \leftarrow KCalcuateJoinResult(T_p, HashTable)$
$ThreadAddress \leftarrow PrefixSum(ThreadCount)$
for $Column \in OutputColumns$ **do**
    KGETJOINRESULT($Column, ThreadAddress, DimRowID$)
end for

Algorithms 7.1, 7.2, and 7.3 outline the main logic of GPUDB's hash join algorithm. In Algorithm 7.1, we can see that both hash table building and probing require two steps (as shown in the other algorithms). Between these steps, a prefix sum operation, also known as collective decision-making coordination, is performed. We did not show the memory allocation step after the prefix sum. The functions starting from K are all GPU kernels. For simplicity, we only show the work needed for each row. In reality, the kernel should be written using a grid-stride loop where one thread is responsible for multiple rows.

Algorithm 7.2 GPUDB's hash join algorithm 2: building hash table.

Require: Dimension Table T_d
   procedure KCALCULATEBUCKETSIZE(*input*)
      PARALLEL EXECUTION FOR EACH ROW: ▷ Each row has its RowID
      JoinKey ← *GetJoinKey(RowID)*
      BucketID ← *HashFunction(JoinKey)*
      ATOMICADD(&*num[BucketID]*, 1)
   return *num[BucketID]*
   end procedure

   procedure KCALCULATEBUCKET(*input*)
      PARALLEL EXECUTION FOR EACH ROW: ▷ Each row has its RowID
      JoinKey ← *GetJoinKey(RowID)*
      BucketID ← *HashFunction(JoinKey)*
      pos ← ATOMICADD(&*BucketAccuAddress[BucketID]*, 1) × 2
      HashTablet[pos] ← *JoinKey*
      HashTable[pos + 1] ← *RowID*
   return *HashTable*
   end procedure

In Algorithm 7.2, the function KCalcuateBucketSize is used to calculate the size of each bucket, while KCalculateBucket is used to fulfill the buckets. As the hash table is shared by threads, atomic operations (atomicAdd) are needed to execute concurrent updating. The quality of the HashFunction plays a crucial role in determining the degree of hash conflicts.

In Algorithm 7.3, the focus is on hash probing, which is typically the dominant operation in hash join. KCalculateJoinResult is responsible for finding the corresponding row ID from the dimension table for each row of the probing table, while also counting the number of row matches in each thread. KGetJoinResult is then used to assemble the result column based on the row IDs. Neither of these functions require atomic operations, allowing for high parallelism and efficient execution. This parallel execution is the key to achieving good performance in hash join.

Improving the performance of hash join requires the development of better algorithms and optimization techniques that are tailored to the GPU architecture. For instance, the use of shared memory with partitioned hash tables can lead to significant performance gains. However, achieving these gains can be a challenging task as it often requires a comprehensive consideration of multiple factors. In some cases, the adoption of certain techniques that appear to have performance advantages may actually lead to performance degradation. For example, while cuckoo hashing is known to offer performance advantages in many scenarios, it can cause performance degradation when a hash join has a low selectivity. This is because cuckoo hash requires more key comparisons than chained hash when there is no match for the key in the hash table.

Algorithm 7.3 GPUDB's hash join algorithm 3: probing hash table.

Require: Probing Table T_p (fact able or a join result)
Require: Dimension Table T_d
   procedure KCALCUATEJOINRESULT(*input*, *HashTable*)
      PARALLEL EXECUTION FOR EACH ROW: ▷ Each row has its RowID
      FactKey ← GETJOINKEY(ROWID)
      BucketID ← *HashFunction*(*FactKey*)
      for *aKey* ∈ *AllKeysInThisBucket*(*BucketID*) **do**
         if *Factkey* = *aKey* **then**
            LCount ← *LCount* + 1   ▷ Thread variable, not per row
            fvalue ← GETROWIDHERE
            BREAK
         end if
      end for
      factFilter[*RowID*] ← *fvalue*
      ThreadCount[*ThreadID*] ← *LCount*   ▷ Thread variable, not per row
   return (*factFilter*, *ThreadCount*)
   end procedure

   procedure KGETJOINRESULT(*Column*, *ThreadAddress*, *DimRowID*)
      address ← *ThreadAddress*[*ThreadID*]
      PARALLEL EXECUTION FOR EACH ROW: ▷ Each row has its RowID
      if *DimRowID*[*RowID*] ≠ 0 **then**
         address ← *address* + 1
         Column[*address*] ← *DimRowID*[*RowID*]
      end if
   end procedure

Interested readers can explore related papers in the database research domain for more insights.

7.3.3   Hash Aggregation

The term "aggregation" usually refers to both Group By and Aggregation functions. For example, the following SQL query uses both the two concepts.

```
Select SUM(salary)
From employee
Group By employeeID
```

The logic behind aggregation is straightforward: It involves grouping all the rows for each employee and then performing the sum within each group. However, aggregation without Group By is also possible, where all rows belong to the same group.

Intuitively, the sequential algorithm for executing aggregation appears to be simple: Scan all the rows, and for each row, (1) update the aggregation result of an existing group if it belongs to that group (according to Group By), or (2) create a new group if it does not belong to an existing one. However, this algorithm has a time complexity of $O(n^2)$ as each row needs a $O(n)$ search for its matching group. To avoid unnecessary search, similar to join, hashing-based or sorting-based approaches can be used. In this section, we discuss hash aggregation.

Certainly, when using a hash table, it allows for efficient group searching by directing the search to a specific bucket, thereby skipping unnecessary searches. However, this introduces the challenge of hash conflicts, where a single bucket may contain multiple distinct keys. On the other hand, if all elements within a single bucket belong to the same group, this simplifies the situation. Additionally, there is a concurrency issue when multiple threads are employed to execute an aggregation that necessitates accurate updating of the hash table. Ensuring the correctness of the hash table updates becomes a critical concern in such scenarios.

The hash table introduced earlier for hash join can also be utilized for hash aggregation. The algorithm can be summarized into two steps: partitioning the input tables into multiple buckets using a hash function, and then performing aggregation inside each bucket. In the hash table structure shown in Figure 7.2, one thread can be assigned to each bucket, and a simple aggregation algorithm can be executed naively within that bucket, with a $O(n^2)$ complexity. However, because of the possibility of hash conflicts, aggregation functions cannot be executed on all elements of a bucket.

The GPU solution for hash aggregation is functional, but it faces a significant issue that could result in overly large buckets. This happens because, before aggregation, each bucket has to store all its elements. However, this storage is unnecessary as the primary goal of aggregation is to calculate the final aggregated value, not to store the raw data. Essentially, when a row is inserted into a bucket, our main goals are: (1) if the row is new to the bucket, we create a new value for its aggregation, and (2) if the row is not new, it should update an existing value accordingly.

In the aforementioned SQL query, the aggregation function utilized is *SUM(salary)*. Consequently, within each bucket, there are two sets of data: one consisting of unique *employeeID* values and the other comprising corresponding aggregated results. During the execution of a hash aggregation for a row, should we be able to locate an existing *employeeID* through a scan of the bucket, we can then ascertain the memory address of the aggregated value for this *employeeID* (subject to the manner in which the two sets are physically stored within the bucket). We employ a variable, *sum_address*, to hold this address, which should be updated through an atomic addition operation as follows.

```
atomicAdd(sum_address, salary);
```

The challenge, however, presents itself when a new item is inserted into the bucket. When using the hash table for a hash join, the atomicAdd function is utilized to perform the insert operation. However, this method is not suitable for hash aggregation. We must ensure the uniqueness of each item within a bucket, a fundamental prerequisite for the Group By operation. The use of atomicAdd could potentially lead to a situation where two threads write duplicate items, given that there is no executed comparison between items.

The proper solution necessitates that when a thread needs to insert a new *employeeID*, and consequently create a new SUM value in the bucket, it should first locate an available address (perhaps where the existing value is 0) to store the new *employeeID*. This can be accomplished by utilizing an *available_ID_address* variable. However, the issue arises when multiple threads attempt to write to this same address simultaneously. In such a scenario, atomicCAS can be employed, which executes an atomic compare and swap operation that conditionally sets a new value for a memory address. The following code illustrates the logic of inserting a new *employeeID* into the bucket.

```
old_value = atomicCAS(available_ID_address, 0, employeeID);
if(old_value == 0)
{
    // this thread win
    // execute the updating for aggregation
    get sum_address
    atomcAdd(sum_address, salary)
}
else if (old_value == employeeID)
{
    // another thread win, but it has the same employeeID
    // execute the updating for aggregation
    get sum_address
    atomcAdd(sum_address, salary)
}
else
{
    try the next available address
}
```

The code leverages atomicCAS to make an attempt at writing the *employeeID* value to the *available_ID_address* address, provided that the current value at that address is 0. If this attempt proves successful, atomicCAS returns the old value at the *available_ID_address*, which is 0, signifying that the current thread has emerged as a winner in the contest to utilize the address. As a result, the thread can proceed to perform the update aggregation using atomicAdd on the corresponding *sum_address*.

If the old value returned by atomicCAS is not 0, it implies that the thread didn't prevail in the competition amongst threads. Under these circumstances, the thread should try again, attempting to secure the next available address. However, if the old value matches the *employeeID* that this thread was aiming to write, the thread can still carry out the updating operation. This is because the winning thread wrote the same *employeeID* as this thread. This process ensures that only unique items are inserted into the bucket, while simultaneously facilitating efficient updates of existing items.

The above text outlines the essential step for hash aggregation, which involves creating a hash table with unique keys for each bucket. The remaining steps, such as memory allocation and final result formation, are similar to those in hash join. With this approach, readers can create their complete implementation.

7.4   Sorting-Based Operators on GPUs

In this section, we will introduce sorting-based join and aggregation operators that can be executed efficiently using GPUs. These operators tackle two critical challenges: (1) optimizing the execution of sorting operations and (2) effectively performing join and aggregation operations using sorted data on GPU-based operators. Among various types of sorting-based or sorting-involved queries, the simplest one is when the user query only requires sorted rows from a table, as exemplified by the following SQL query.

```
Select * From employee Order By salary;
```

Suppose the table has two columns: employeeID and salary; then the sorting result is a sorted array of salary and corresponding row IDs. Since the query needs to return materialized results with both columns, for each row a read to the corresponding employeeID item according to the row ID is needed. Such an operation is often called a *gather*. With its reverse operation *scatter*, gather/scatter is a commonly used primitive in the parallel computing domain, including GPU computation.

7.4.1   GPU Sorting: Practical Choices

The premier challenge with sorting-based join and aggregation is how to execute the sorting itself. As we have introduced in Chapter 6, two popular sorting algorithms for GPUs are bitonic sort and Batcher's odd–even sorting, which are often used as building blocks for hybrid sorting algorithms. While these algorithms have a time complexity of $O(n \log^2 n)$, making them slow for very large n, they are well suited for sorting the number of elements equal to the thread count, which can fit in shared memory within a thread block (e.g., 512 threads). Once many small sorted blocks are created, a merging algorithm can be used to get the final sorted result. Different merging algorithms exist, and this chapter introduces the merge path algorithm [58], which can also be used for executing sort-merge join, a widely used join algorithm in database systems.

Radix sort [117] is a highly efficient sorting algorithm when the input elements are integers, or when they can be sorted lexicographically. This is because of its non-comparative nature, which means it is not limited by the $O(n \log n)$ bound that applies to comparison-based sorting algorithms. For example, in the case of 32-bit integers, radix sort can execute 32 rounds of sorting operations, each of which is responsible for sorting based on a single bit. On GPUs, each round of radix sorting can be viewed as a scatter operation that writes each element into its corresponding location. More-efficient implementations can use shared memory to avoid extensive GPU device memory accesses. Generally speaking, radix sort is the fastest sorting algorithm to execute on GPUs, provided that the input is suitable for this algorithm. Otherwise, a hybrid approach that combines bitonic sort and merge sort can be used, as it is a general-purpose solution.

In addition, there are also GPU versions of traditional sorting algorithms such as quicksort [30] and sample sort [89]. However, they are not as widely used as radix sorting and the hybrid sorting algorithms included in the Nvidia Thrust and CUB libraries. Further research and study on the implementation, optimization, and comparison of these algorithms may be of interest. Nonetheless, for the purpose of this book, we will focus on how join and aggregation operations can be executed on top of sorted data.

7.4.2   Sort-Merge Join

Sort-merge join is a widely used join algorithm in most database systems. To execute a join $T_1 \bowtie T_2$ with the condition $T_1.f_1 = T_2.f_2$, the algorithm first sorts the two inputs T_1 and T_2 using their columns f_1 and f_2, respectively. Then, a merge-like operation, which we call a *merge join*, is executed to select all the equal pairs from the two sorted inputs according to the join condition. Consider the following example.

```
2  2  4  5  5  7
1  2  2  3  5  6
```

A merge join will generate the result of equal pairs.

```
(2,2),  (2,2),  (2,2),  (2,2),  (5,5),  (5,5)
```

The sequential execution of merge join is straightforward, as the two inputs are already sorted. The algorithm involves iterating through the two inputs from start to end, using two pointers, p_1 and p_2, to indicate the current element of each input. We then compare $*p_1$ and $*p_2$. If they are not equal, we move the pointer of the smaller element to the next element. If they are equal, we move both pointers to their next different elements and output all the cross-product pairs of the same elements. In the example provided, the result contains four pairs of (2,2).

To parallelize the merge join algorithm ($T_1 \bowtie T_2$) efficiently, we can approach the problem in two ways. Firstly, for each element of T_1, a binary search can be used to find its matching elements from T_2, as T_2 is already sorted. This reduces the time complexity to $O(\log n)$ for each search. Secondly, there is no dependency between the elements of T_1, so the search operation can be performed in parallel using n processors, resulting in a parallel time complexity of $O(\log n)$ for the entire process. Thus, the parallel algorithm offers significant improvements over the sequential algorithm, which has a time complexity of $O(n)$.

A naive GPU implementation of this parallel algorithm would store both T_1 and T_2 in the global memory and have each thread execute a binary search in T_2 for an element of T_1. However, this approach would not be efficient due to the large number of random global memory accesses required by the binary search. To improve the performance, we can partition T_2 into multiple small chunks, each of which can be fully stored in the shared memory. This way, a binary search to a T_2 chunk will not cause any slow global memory access.

For instance, in the previous example, if the shared memory can only hold two elements, we can split T_2 (1,2,2,3,5,6) into three partitions: (1,2), (2,3), and (5,6). Consequently, a binary search on T_2 can be broken down into three separate binary searches on the three partitions, as for $R \bowtie S$, we have

$$R \bowtie (S_1 \vee S_2 \vee \cdots \vee S_n) = (R \bowtie S_1) \vee (R \bowtie S_2) \vee \cdots \vee (R \bowtie S_n).$$

As each partition is also sorted, we can easily determine its minimum and maximum values, which define the range of the probing elements. For instance, for the partition (2,3), we can eliminate any element in R outside of the range defined by the minimum and maximum values of the partition. In this way, when we perform $R \bowtie S_i$, we can quickly discard any irrelevant elements of R.

The aforementioned algorithm represents a typical GPU-based sort-merge join algorithm. When executing $R \bowtie S$, the overall structure is as follows.

```
Step 1: Partition R into multiple chunks;
Step 2: Load each chunk into shared memory;
Step 3: For each chunk, extract its min and max values;
Step 4: For each chunk, identify the starting and ending indexes
        of S's elements;
Step 5: For each corresponding S's element, do a binary search
        in the chunk.
```

The entire procedure can be conceptualized as a copartitioning strategy, based on ranges, which restricts elements capable of yielding final results to their corresponding ranges. In this context, the range-based partitioning approach bears considerable similarity to the hash-value-based partitioning method employed in hash joins. The performance comparison between sort-merge join and hash join has sparked multiple decades of debate, with discussions centered around which technique proves faster under varying scenarios. This topic has been the subject of numerous research papers (e.g., [10, 56, 81, 88]), with analysts dissecting the advantages and disadvantages of the two algorithms across a spectrum of workloads and hardware configurations. Interested readers can make further study by reading those related papers.

Merge Path

The sort-merge join algorithm we have described can suffer from a load imbalance problem when there is significant data skew. Although input table R is equally partitioned, the sizes of the chunks of table S are not guaranteed to be the same due to data dependence. As a result, this can lead to a load imbalance among threads, causing performance degradation and low GPU efficiency.

Merge Path is a merge algorithm that partitions two inputs into equal-sized chunks, allowing each thread to merge the same amount of data. Although Merge Path is originally designed as a merge algorithm, its partitioning step is also useful for merge-join algorithms to address the load unbalance problem. To demonstrate the main idea, consider the following example.

Suppose we need to merge the following two sequences.

```
1  2  3  8
4  5  6  7
```

If we partition the first sequence into two subsequences, $(1,2)$ and $(3,8)$, we will create two different workloads for merging: $[(1,2), null]$ and $[(3,8),(4,5,6,7)]$. This partitioning can be thought of as using 2 as a boundary to split the inputs. However, the fundamental reason for the resulting load imbalance is that the partitioning approach is input oriented, rather than output oriented. If we instead choose a pivotal point that creates two identical workloads, we should use 4 as the number. This would result in two workloads: $[(1,2,3),(4)]$ and $[(8),(5,6,7)]$. In this way, each workload will process four elements, which is exactly half of the total workloads required to merge the eight numbers. This raises the following questions. Why is 4 the number that evenly divides the workloads? And how can we generate the pivotal number for any workload?

Merge Path provides an answer to the questions raised in the previous paragraph. Its main idea can be demonstrated through a visualized picture, as shown in Figure 7.3.

The demonstration of Merge Path involves several key features.

- *Comparison matrix* We use a matrix to represent the comparison results of all pairs of the two inputs (with each cell containing either 0 or 1).
- *Merge path* We draw a merge path through the matrix to determine which element should be picked during the merging process.
- *Intersection point* We calculate the intersection point of the merge path and a diagonal line in the matrix.

In Figure 7.3, the number at the intersection point is 4, which is the pivotal point that can divide the merging into two equal-sized workloads. Moreover, if we need to partition the merging into n workloads, then we need to use $n - 1$ diagonal lines. For

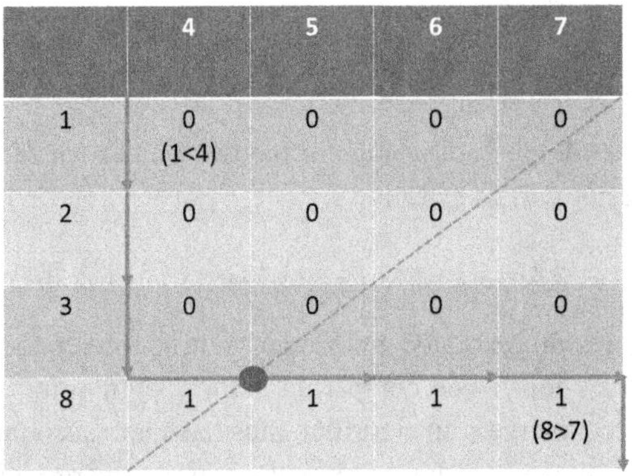

Figure 7.3 A demonstration of Merge Path. The core idea is to use 4 as a pivotal to divide eight numbers (on one side is 1,2,3,8, and on the other side is 4,5,6,7) into two equal-size subsets. The figure shows the core idea of how Merge Path can find the pivotal number, that is, 4.

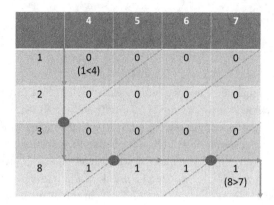

Figure 7.4 A demonstration of Merge Path for more parititions.

instance, Figure 7.4 shows how the merge can be partitioned into four equal-sized workloads: [(1,2), null], [(3), (4)], [null, (5,6)], and [(8), (7)].

The merge path in Figures 7.3 and 7.4 represents the boundary between 0 and 1 elements. To calculate the intersection point for a given diagonal line, a binary search can be used with a time complexity of $O(n)$. Moreover, there is no dependency between any two diagonals, so the partitioning process can be parallelized. In the implementation, it is unnecessary to store the matrix as its elements are only comparison results. After partitioning, inside each workload, that is, between two adjacent diagonal lines, a merge can be executed by an independent GPU thread. It is worth noting that better GPU implementation strategies are possible, as described in related papers.

Note that Merge Path was originally designed for merge instead of merge-join. Therefore, when using Merge Path to execute merge-join, it is not possible to simply execute the merge-join inside each partition. To illustrate this problem, let us use the previous example again. Suppose we need to perform the join operation $R \bowtie S$ with the following two tables.

```
2  2  4  5  5  7
1  2  2  3  5  6
```

Figure 7.5 illustrates the Merge Path results for the two sequences. If we generate four partitions, then the result will be as follows.

```
[null,(1,2,2)],  [(2,2),(3)],  [(4,5),(5)],  [(5,7),(6)]
```

While the partitioning result generated by Merge Path is correct for merging, it is not appropriate for merge-join since comparing across neighboring partitions is required. Therefore, a correct merge-join algorithm must take into account the joining across neighbor partitions. One approach is to reuse the previous merge-join algorithm and use only the partitions generated by Merge Path. For example, we can use only [(1,2,2),(3),(5),(6)] as the partitions of R and apply the same steps as in steps 2–5 for the merge-join.

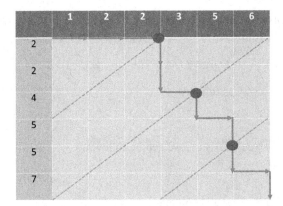

Figure 7.5 A demonstration of the Merge Path for two sequences containing repeated numbers. In this example, there are four instances of the number 2. However, these four instances will not be placed in the same partition.

7.4.3   Sort Aggregation

We now study how to execute Group By and aggregations on sorted data. When executing a Group By operation, the elements with the same value are grouped together for further aggregations. Sorting is an effective solution for Group By as it ensures that elements with the same value are physically stored together. This way, we can efficiently perform aggregations on these groups.

Considering the following SQL query.

```
Select EmpID, sum(EmpSalary)
From Employee
Group By EmpID;
```

A sorting-based aggregation algorithm needs to take the following six steps.

- *Step 1* Sort the table by the EmpID column. This produces two arrays: a sorted EmpID array and an array of corresponding row IDs.
- *Step 2* Create a new array by going through each element in the sorted EmpID array. If the element is different from its next element, set it to 1; otherwise, set it to 0.
- *Step 3* Execute an exclusive prefix sum on the 0-1 array so that we have a new array that contains the group ID for each element in EmpID (or for each row ID).
- *Step 4* Allocate memory for two output columns (i.e., one for EmpID and one for the aggregation SUM(EmpSalary)) according to the total number of result groups.
- *Step 5* For each element in the sorted EmpID array, if its corresponding value in the 0-1 array is 1, write the EmpID to the EmpID output array at the position indexed by the corresponding value in the prefix sum array.
- *Step 6* For each element in the sorted EmpID array, get the corresponding row ID and the value of EmpSalary. Finally, use atomicAdd to add the value to the aggregation output array at the same position as in step 5.

In the example, suppose all the EmpSalary value is 1.0, and suppose we have the sorted EmpID column as follows.

```
['X1', 'X2', 'X2', 'Y1', 'Y1', 'Z1', 'Z2', 'Z2']
```

Then, we can get the 0-1 array as follows.

```
[1,0,1,0,1,1,0,1]
```

After executing an exclusive prefix sum, we get the following.

```
[0,1,1,2,2,3,4,4]
```

Finally, we can get the output EmpID column as

```
['X1','X2','Y1','Z1','Z2']
```

and we can get the output Sum(EmpSalary) column as follows.

```
[1.0, 2.0, 2.0, 1.0, 2.0].
```

The high efficiency of the whole process on GPUs is the result of the high optimization of both sorting and prefix sum, which are basic primitives of GPU computation. The performance bottleneck occurs in the last step (step 6), where atomic operations are used for aggregation, similar to hashing-based aggregation. Further improvements in performance can be achieved by optimizing the execution of atomic operations. For instance, using thread local aggregation can reduce unnecessary atomic operations Readers interested in the subject can explore further related work (e.g., [88]).

7.5   Subquery Processing on GPUs

Nested queries play a vital role in SQL as they enable users to express complex-use cases by linking the output of a subquery (the inner query block) as input to the outer query block. Subqueries can be nested within different clauses such as SELECT, FROM, WHERE, or HAVING, and they can involve expression operators like <, >, or =, among others. Additionally, subqueries can be utilized in UPDATE or DELETE statements, as well as in SQL views. In essence, subqueries offer a flexible and powerful approach to working with relational data, empowering users to write more efficient and intricate queries.

7.5.1   An Introduction to Subquery Processing

In SQL, there are two main categories of subqueries: uncorrelated subqueries and correlated subqueries. In the case of an uncorrelated subquery, the nested query block is executed once, and the results are subsequently used by the outer query block. Execution of such subqueries is similar to flat queries. On the other hand, in a correlated subquery, the inner query block contains parameters that are resolved from a relation of the outer block. Correlated subqueries are the most widely used and cannot be executed in a straightforward manner.

Query 1 provides a typical example of a correlated subquery that is embedded in the WHERE condition of another query.

```
Query 1:
SELECT R.col1, R.col2
FROM R
WHERE R.col2 = (
    SELECT min(S.col2)
    FROM S
    WHERE R.col1 = S.col1);
```

Despite its simple structure, the nested method executes correlated subqueries in an algorithmically inefficient way. In essence, the subquery must be reevaluated for each tuple of the referenced column from the outer query block, resulting in high computation complexity. Typically, when evaluating such a subquery, the execution engine analyzes the query plan trees for the outer and inner query blocks separately, and utilizes a syntax like the Subplan of PostgreSQL to connect them. For instance, in Query 1's nest subquery, the engine evaluates the subquery for each tuple of the column R.col1 and accesses the relation S multiple times.

One common approach to reduce the complexity of the nested method is to unnest the nested loops. By using JOIN and GROUP BY operations, the correlated subquery can be merged into its upper level query block. To unnest Query 1 and obtain the equivalent Query 2 (as shown next), one can use the "first-aggregation-then-join" algorithm. This algorithm first precomputes all possible results due to the execution of the correlated subquery and then uses a join to match the rows for the outer table.

```
Query 2:
SELECT R.col1, R.col2
FROM R, (
    SELECT min(S.col2) as t1_min_col2,
    S.col1 as t1_col1
    FROM S
    GROUP BY S.col1) T1
WHERE
    R.col1 = T1.t1_col1 AND
    R.col2 = T1.t1_min_col2;
```

Query 2 is essentially a flat query. During the execution, a derived table T1, which is the outcome of grouping S.col1 and then aggregating on S.col2, is first generated. The final result is projected by performing a join between the relation R and the derived table T1 with the conditions $R.col1 = t1\_col1$ and $R.col2 = t1\_min\_col2$. Figure 7.6 illustrates the query plan trees of Query 1 and Query 2, where we can observe that the query plan tree of Query 2 is not different from a normal query without any subqueries. However, for Query 1, each row of Relation R will cause an execution of the subquery.

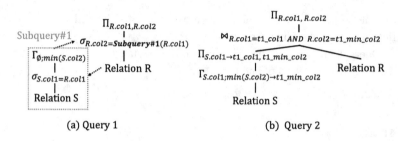

Figure 7.6 Query plan trees of (a) Query 1 and (b) Query 2.

Despite the apparent simplicity of the subquery unnesting approach we have just shown, efficiently executing various arbitrary subqueries can be a challenging problem in traditional database systems. This is because different subquery forms may require different unnest approaches and may pose tricky issues under many conditions, such as when column values could be NULL. As a result, existing database systems cannot unnest arbitrary correlated subqueries by following general rules, and significant engineering effort is required to implement unnesting strategies into a database engine.

However, with the advent of GPU databases, a new situation has emerged, which presents both unique challenges and novel opportunities to solve the subquery problem. This has been the focus of much recent research, and promising results have been achieved using various techniques and strategies that are tailored to the GPU architecture. Overall, the emergence of GPU databases has opened up new possibilities for solving the subquery problem and improving the efficiency and effectiveness of SQL query execution.

7.5.2   NestGPU: Opportunities and Challenges

We first present an overview of the NestGPU solution [52], which is a GPU-based subquery execution framework introduced in a research paper published in *IEEE 37th International Conference on Data Engineering (ICDE 2021)*. NestGPU aims to provide a universal method for processing nested queries on a GPU without having to unnest them. Such an approach is based on the rationale that the high computational complexity of the nested method can be counterbalanced by optimized parallel processing on a GPU, and its low memory usage can make the nested method feasible within the limited GPU memory capacity. This makes the nested method for executing correlated subqueries a viable option on a GPU. However, implementing such a method on a GPU presents several challenges. On a CPU, the nested method requires little engineering effort since recursively executing a subquery in a predicate of an operator (e.g., selection and join) is feasible and efficient, naturally following the same way of processing flat queries.

In contrast, implementing a recursive method on a GPU is complicated and inefficient. The relational operators on a GPU are typically implemented as GPU kernels. Recursively calling GPU kernels with dynamic parallelism, which is the only way for recursive kernel execution on GPU, not only results in significant runtime overhead, but also complicates the system design, where different GPU kernels must be generated in advance for different subqueries or the execution control flow, that is, analyzing the whole query plan tree, has to be offloaded to the GPU. To address this structural issue, a solution is to use a code-generation framework for the nested query processing on a GPU. This method generates code to iteratively evaluate a subquery for all correlated tuples before evaluating the predicate containing the subquery, so that we can realize the subquery execution by manipulating preimplemented and highly optimized GPU kernels in an iterative manner.

NestGPU offers unique benefits for GPU-accelerated nested query processing. Firstly, certain nested queries cannot be algorithmically unnested, making the nested method of NestGPU the only viable solution on a GPU. Secondly, owing to high memory-capacity requirements, certain algorithmically unnested workloads are unable to complete execution on a GPU. Conversely, these workloads run effectively on NestGPU by leveraging the GPU device memory. Thirdly, our experiments indicate that the execution performance of representative workloads by NestGPU and the unnested method are very comparable, and in some cases, NestGPU outperforms the unnested approach. Lastly and perhaps most importantly, NestGPU is general purpose and does not require complex unnesting efforts. This greatly encourages the design and implementation of the nested method on a GPU for practical purposes.

7.5.3 Code-Generation Techniques

To represent a subquery, NestGPU introduces a new operator, SUBQ, into the query plan tree. When the parser of NestGPU detects a subquery, it will insert a SUBQ into the predicate that contains the subquery. Eventually, the SUBQ will be substituted with an iteration loop of the execution code. Since a subquery is itself a complete query block, it will be parsed into another query plan tree. Moreover, since a subquery may contain another subquery, the NestGPU parser will generate a tree-of-trees structure. In our implementation, all query plan trees except for the outermost one are stored in a list, allowing any of them to be located by their indices while traversing the tree during code generation.

The operator SUBQ has varying operands, including the subquery index and the correlated columns. Figure 7.7 provides an example of a three-level query plan tree that includes two subqueries. The first subquery is located in the predicate on the right table of the join operator at Level 0, while the second one is in the selection operator at Level 1.

Through traversal of the query plan tree, NestGPU generates a driver program that is subsequently compiled and linked to preimplemented relational operators. The code generator commences from the outermost query plan tree, moving from the leaves towards the root. For any node, that is, a query operator, in the query plan tree that has a subquery as an operand of its predicate, the code generator generates code to evaluate the subquery for all correlated values passed from the outer loop, and prepares the

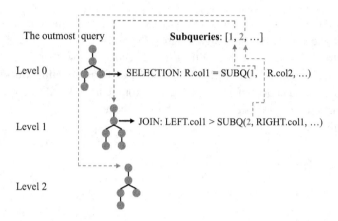

Figure 7.7 A query plan tree with two correlated subqueries.

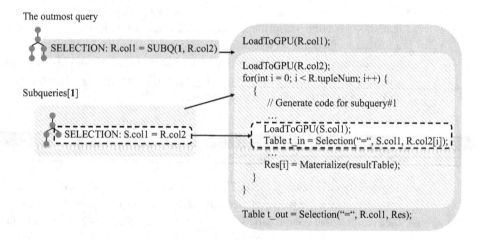

Figure 7.8 Generating code for a subquery in Selection.

results as a vector. Following this, the operator containing the subquery is evaluated with the result vector as input.

Selection operators that contain correlated subqueries are processed by NestGPU as shown in Figure 7.8, which provides a pseudocode example in the drive program. Normally, a selection operator loads all operands, such as a constant or a column, into GPU memory before running GPU kernels to perform the selection operation. The output is then used as input for the next operator. However, if one of the selection's operands is a subquery, the code generator must produce code to process the subquery.

As demonstrated in Figure 7.8, the correlated columns (R.col2) are loaded into a GPU device memory. An iterative loop is then generated to process the subquery, with the loop size set to the number of tuples in the input table of the selection operator (i.e., the tuple count of R). Within the loop, the generated code uses each correlated value (i.e., R.col2[i]) to perform the selection. The results may serve as input for the following operator in the subquery, and the final results are stored in the vector according to the current iteration number (Res[i]). Following the loop, an upper-level selection is used to evaluate the predicate containing the subquery, which involves the selection on R.col1 and Res. In this way, the code generator recursively traverses the query plan tree but produces iterative code for the subquery in the selection operator.

Processing join operators that contain correlated subqueries in NestGPU differs from that of selection operators, as the code generator must determine the iteration number for the subquery. There are two cases to consider. First, if correlated tuples come from one of the two tables of the join, the iteration number is equal to the corresponding table size. Second, if correlated tuples come from both tables, the iteration number is the Cartesian product of the two tables.

Figure 7.9 illustrates the code generated for these two cases. Apart from the code generated for the subquery, the code for the join operator containing the subquery also differs. For the second case, the join operator that follows the loop must use both the left and right tuple IDs to locate the subquery result in Res. If the join operator containing correlated subqueries is a natural join with all its predicates connected by AND, the query can be optimized by first joining the two tables with predicates that do

```
LoadToGPU(LEFT.col1);
                                    JOIN: LEFT.col1 = SUBQ(2, RIGHT.col1)

LoadToGPU(RIGHT.col1);
for(int i = 0; i < RIGHT.tupleNum; i++) {
    {
        // Generate code for subquery#2
        ...
        Res[i] = Materialize(resultTable);
    }
}

Table t_out = JOIN("=", LEFT.col1, Res);
```

```
LoadToGPU(LEFT.col1);
                          JOIN: LEFT.col1 = SUBQ(3, LEFT.col2, RIGHT.col1)
LoadToGPU(LEFT.col2);
LoadToGPU(RIGHT.col1);
for(int i = 0; i < LEFT.tupleNum * RIGHT.tupleNum; i++) {
    {
        // Generate code for subquery#3
        // LEFT.col2[i / LEFT.tupleNum] and RIGHT.col1[i % LEFT.tupleNum]are
used in current iteration
        ...
        Res[i] = Materialize(resultTable);
    }
}

// The value in Res used to join is at left_idx * RIGHT.tupleNum + right_idx
Table t_out = JOIN("=", LEFT.col1, Res);
```

Figure 7.9 Generating code for a subquery in Join.

not contain correlated subqueries, and then performing a selection on the result table for predicates containing the subqueries. This optimization can effectively reduce the iteration numbers required to call subqueries, thus improving performance.

The code-generation framework in NestGPU is capable of handling queries with arbitrary levels of correlated subqueries. Figure 7.10 illustrates the complete workflow to generate the drive program for the three-level query plan tree shown in Figure 7.7, where both subqueries are correlated with their upper-level query block. In Figure 7.10, code blocks marked by different grayscale correspond to subqueries at different levels. At each level, the generated code evaluates the subquery and stores its results in a vector that is then fed back to the operator at the upper level. In this way, NestGPU can handle nested subqueries by recursively traversing the query plan tree on the CPU and generating iterative code blocks in a nested loop with the push mode.

Some types of correlated subqueries return a scalar result for each subquery evaluation, and the result size is fixed. In this case, the results can be organized as a vector residing in a space of continuous memory, much like any table columns. However, some correlated subqueries are different because their results have variable lengths. For example, a typical subquery with an IN operator, such as "R.col1 IN (...)" can return variable-length results. To handle such subqueries, a solution is to use a two-level array to store the results of subquery evaluations. The first level stores the lengths of variable results for each subquery evaluation, while the second level stores the results themselves. This allows for efficient storage and retrieval of variable-length results, which can be critical for achieving high performance in subquery execution.

7.5.4   Memory Management Techniques

Memory management is a critical component of NestGPU because frequent calls to raw system interfaces like malloc can result in inefficient memory management due to the iterative execution of subqueries. To address this issue, NestGPU builds memory pools for efficient management of memory towards various aspects such as table columns, metadata, intermediate tables, and interkernel results. By utilizing memory pools, NestGPU can avoid the overhead associated with frequent calls to malloc and efficiently manage memory usage in the execution of iterative subqueries.

Memory pools are designed to contain data that needs to be frequently allocated and freed on both the host and device memory. There are three types of data that are suitable for memory pools, including meta data, intermediate tables, and interkernel results. The meta data contains information such as column types and the number of tuples in a table, which is used on the host side. The intermediate tables are composed of column data that are produced by an operator and serve as input for the next operator. As an operator may consist of several GPU kernels, the interkernel results are temporary data on the GPU that are passed from one kernel to the next, such as a 0-1 vector generated by the prefix sum kernel that is used as input for a materialization kernel to determine which tuples should be written to device memory. By utilizing memory pools, NestGPU can efficiently manage the allocation and deallocation of

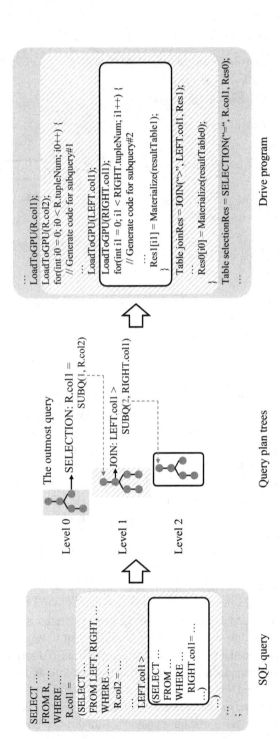

Figure 7.10 The work flow eventually generating a drive program for a three-level correlated nested query.

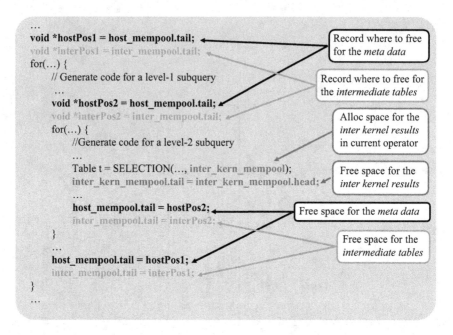

Figure 7.11 The use cases of memory pools for three types of data: metadata, intermediate tables, and interkernel results.

data, resulting in improved memory usage and performance for the iterative execution of subqueries.

Each of these three types of data has its own memory pool, and memory is linearly allocated by moving the tail pointers forward. When deallocating memory, tail pointers are moved backward. Setting the tail pointer to the head of a memory pool releases all the allocated memory in it. For interkernel results, NestGPU clears the memory pool after the execution of an operator. For meta data and intermediate tables, tail positions are recorded before the subquery execution. After each iteration of the subquery, the tail pointer position is recovered, allowing the space allocated in the previous iteration to be reused. This approach avoids frequent system calls to raw interfaces like malloc, leading to more efficient memory management. Figure 7.11 shows how the memory pools are used in a drive program generated for a three-level subquery.

To minimize data loading overhead, NestGPU adopts a column-preloading strategy. Specifically, the required columns are loaded onto a GPU device memory before the subquery loop is executed, and then released after all iterations are completed. In cases where the device memory is insufficient to hold all required columns, the memory is divided into two parts, with one part used to store preloaded columns and the other for on-demand loading. Two principles are followed when preloading columns: (1) columns used by subqueries at inner levels have higher priority, and (2) for columns at the same level, smaller tables are given higher priority as sequential reads tend to be more efficient. These principles help to ensure that the most critical data are preloaded onto GPU device memory, while reducing unnecessary data transfers and memory usage.

7.5.5 Summary

NestGPU is a GPU-based approach to executing subquery processing in nested structures. Unlike customized unnesting methods, NestGPU is a general-purpose approach that requires minimal development effort while still delivering high performance. To achieve this, NestGPU employs a new code-generation framework optimized for GPU processing and a series of optimizations for improved performance. With NestGPU, nested queries that cannot be unnested algorithmically and queries that cannot be processed on GPUs due to memory constraints can be processed efficiently. Additionally, in representative cases, NestGPU performs comparably to unnesting methods while outperforming them when the outer table is relatively small. For more detailed information and performance evaluation results, readers can refer to the related paper [52].

7.6 Concluding Remarks and Exercise Projects

The realm of GPU-accelerated database system research is a dynamic and active area of investigation, spanning a broad spectrum of topics that encompass algorithm design, system building, and beyond. It is worth noting that this chapter does not purport to provide an exhaustive tutorial on the implementation of GPU database systems. Rather, its primary objective is to elucidate how traditional SQL concepts can be effectively mapped to novel GPU devices. This mapping entails grappling with more-complex challenges such as synchronizations and atomic operations, as opposed to the relatively simpler sorting problems tackled in Chapter 6.

Furthermore, it is important to acknowledge that there exist a multitude of optimization techniques for GPU databases that fall beyond the scope of this book, such as data compression, kernel fusing, memory management, complex code generation, and so forth.

It is important to note that, regardless of the complexity or intricacy of a given concept or optimization technique, its performance benefits can be fully realized only through careful management of several key aspects, including data locality, parallelism exploitation, load balancing, and avoidance of unnecessary or redundant operations, among others. The crux of the matter is that the benefits of any optimization technique must be weighed against the costs of its implementation, and thus, determining when to employ an optimization instead of simply implementing it can be a critical problem. As such, it is vital to identify the common requirements for the most-frequently encountered performance problems.

Fortunately, the robust database community offers a wide range of applications and industrial standard benchmarks, including the renowned TPC benchmarks. These benchmarks serve as invaluable resources for database implementers, enabling them to identify and rectify performance issues effectively. This advantage extends to builders of GPU-based databases as well, as they can leverage these benchmarks to pinpoint and overcome performance bottlenecks with precision.

The current challenge in structured data management lies in determining whether it is necessary or feasible to utilize a unified SQL database system to manage ad-hoc data types, regardless of whether they are structured or unstructured. From a theoretical perspective, modern SQL is Turing complete [20], and advanced database systems, such as PostgreSQL, can incorporate various extension solutions to implement virtually any functionality within a database. Despite these features that make database systems general purpose for managing ad-hoc data, the industry has still opted to utilize specific data management systems for managing specific types of unstructured data. In Chapter 8, we will delve into the world of unstructured data and explore how GPUs can interact with them.

This chapter has three exercise projects as follows.

- Project 1 (*easy*) The project mandates the implementation of a selection operator targeting a specific table composed of 26 integer columns, each labeled from "a" to "z." The operator employs a user-provided string as the selection criterion, strictly constrained to a comparative expression that contrasts two arithmetic expressions (only +−*/) derived from the aforementioned columns. An example of such an expression would be "a+b*c=d/e". The format in which the table is stored remains flexible; however, it is essential that the operator generates a new table that adheres to the same format as the input.
- Project 2 (*medium*) The primary objective of this project is to implement two distinct join operators: a sort-merge join operator and a hash join operator. Once implemented, a comparative analysis of their performance is required, taking into consideration varying data sizes and distributions. The input data, which can be in any given format, must be identical for both operators. Correspondingly, the output generated by these operators should also adhere to a uniform format. For each operator, the selection of specific sorting or hashing algorithms remains at the implementer's discretion.
- Project 3 (*hard*) The objective of this project is to construct a bespoke SQL engine capable of successfully executing Query 1 from the TPC-H benchmark. The query does not necessitate the use of a join operation; however, it does involve extensive aggregations on a singular table. The implementer is afforded the flexibility to select the type of aggregation algorithms they deem most suitable. An integral feature of the engine is an SQL parser, which is required to accurately parse the SQL syntax for the query. Both the target table and the query results can be stored in a format chosen by the implementer.

8 GPU for Spatial Data: A Case Study in Pathology Imaging Applications

> The exploration of space will go ahead, whether we join in it or not, and it is one of the great adventures of all time.
>
> John F. Kennedy, *the 35th US president, September 12, 1962.*

In this chapter, we embark on an exploration of a case study that harnesses GPU technology to accelerate a computational task of spatial data processing. The term "spatial data" refers to information about objects situated in different spaces, ranging from two-dimensional surfaces to three-dimensional environments. Although geographic data related to Earth's topography, such as maps, are commonly used examples of spatial data, we shift our focus here to pathology imaging data. These data are pivotal in clinical diagnostics, contributing significantly to the advancement of human healthcare. Our discussion will cover a computational task associated with this data, starting with traditional CPU-based processing methods. Subsequently, we will delve into the development and benefits of GPU-based solutions, highlighting their remarkable capacity for massive parallelism. This juxtaposition of CPU and GPU methodologies exemplifies the overarching theme of this book – *interactions between data management applications and the underlying hardware and systems.*

8.1 An Introduction to Spatial Data Processing

According to the Oxford English Dictionary, the term "spatial" is defined as

```
having extension in space; occupying or taking up space;
consisting of or characterized by space.
```

Thus, when we discuss spatial data, we refer to any information related to a variety of objects, events, and relationships within a given space. The concept of space, intricate in both mathematics and physics, remains one of the most enigmatic aspects of human understanding. Fortunately, in the realm of computer science, the concept of space for spatial data is primarily confined to the familiar three-dimensional Euclidean space, a concept we're acquainted with from high school and experience in everyday life. Within this space, a location or point is typically defined by its Cartesian coordinates

(x, y, z), and the distance between two points can be efficiently calculated using the Pythagorean theorem.

With an understanding of space, we can begin to define and describe a range of spatial objects, starting from the simplest forms like a single point, a line, and a triangle, to more-complex shapes. This leads us to explore the relationships between these objects – for instance, determining if two lines intersect or calculating attributes like the area of a triangle or the volume of a three-dimensional sphere. In practical applications of spatial data, the core tasks often encompass data representation, storage, indexing, searching, and various forms of data analysis. These tasks mirror those found in conventional structured data management, as discussed in Chapter 7. However, given their spatial orientation, these tasks present unique technical challenges, which we will delve into in this chapter.

8.1.1   Spatial Data Representation: Vector and Raster

The foundational step in any spatial data processing application is determining how to represent the data within a computer system. One common method involves representing spatial data using geometric objects within a coordinate system. This method is called the *vector data model* approach. The Open Geospatial Consortium (OGC) has established a standard markup language for this purpose, known as Well-Known Text (WKT). Well-Known Text allows for the representation of various geometric objects, defining several basic shapes such as points, linestrings, and polygons. It also introduces the concept of a "GeometryCollection," which can encompass multiple geometric primitives. For instance, Figure 8.1 illustrates how three geometric primitives can be represented in an X–Y plane.

Well-Known Text simplifies the definition of a geometric primitive by first specifying its type, followed by the coordinates of its constituent points. The most basic

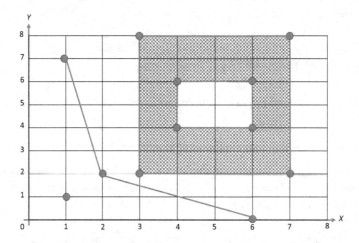

Figure 8.1 An example of using WKT to define geometric objects: a point, a linestring, and a polygon with a hole.

example is a point. As shown in Figure 8.1, a point located at (1,1) is defined as "POINT (1 1)." Next, a linestring represented in the figure can be described as "LINESTRING (6 0, 2 2, 1 7)," which connects three points in sequence. Additionally, the figure includes a polygon, deliberately designed with a hole for demonstration purposes. This polygon is defined as "POLYGON ((7 2, 7 8, 3 8, 3 2, 7 2), (4 4, 4 6, 6 6, 6 4, 4 4))." The definition starts with the outer boundary of the polygon, traversing the points in a counter-clockwise direction, followed by the hole's boundary, traced in a clockwise direction. It is worth noting that for polygons without holes, only the outer boundary is necessary. Furthermore, WKT supports the definition of a collection of objects. For instance "GEOMETRYCOLLECTION(POINT(1 1),LINESTRING(6 0, 2 2, 1 7))" can be used to group two primitives into a cohesive structure.

Let us reconsider the relationship between the linestring definition "LINESTRING (6 0, 2 2, 1 7)" and its corresponding geometric representation in Figure 8.1. If we view the point coordinates and the visual depiction of the geometric object in the figure as equivalent, it leads us to an alternative representation method. This method, known as the *raster data model* approach, is particularly effective for representing real-world geographic images, such as satellite imagery. The essence of raster image data lies in its structure: a grid or matrix of cells, often referred to as pixels. These are organized in rows and columns, with each cell representing a specific value that corresponds to certain properties (such as color) of the associated location or area.

Figure 8.2 demonstrates the representation of "LINESTRING(6 0, 2 2, 1 7)" using the raster data model. This figure is divided into two subfigures, showcasing the image at two different resolutions: 8×8 and 16×16. It is evident that increasing the number of cells or pixels enhances the clarity of the representation, but this also results in a corresponding increase in the storage space required for the data. Thus, raster data

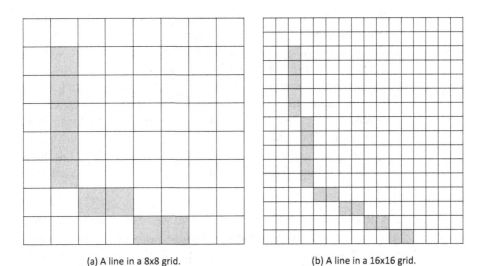

(a) A line in a 8x8 grid.   (b) A line in a 16x16 grid.

Figure 8.2 Two examples of using the raster data model to represent the same line with two resolutions.

inherently grapples with resolution issues due to its pixel-based structure. However, a significant advantage of the raster data model lies in its suitability for depicting raw digital image data, such as aerial photographs or medical scan images. These forms of data are often foundational in various spatial data applications.

In this section, we have provided a concise overview of both the vector and raster data models to give readers a foundational understanding of spatial data management in computer systems. It is essential to recognize that the field of spatial data processing is rife with complex challenges, and an exhaustive exploration of all related concepts falls outside the scope of this book. For example, in the realm of vector data, while WKT offers a human-readable format, its binary equivalent, Well-Known Binary (WKB), is tailored for better machine efficiency. Additionally, the task of efficiently converting between raster and vector data in various applications presents its own set of challenges. For those seeking deeper insights into these topics, we recommend consulting specialized Geographic Information Systems (GIS) literature.

8.1.2   Spatial Data Applications

Spatial data applications are indispensable tools in numerous industries and fields. Broadly, we can categorize these applications into two categories, based on the nature of the space they represent.

The first, and perhaps more prevalent, category encompasses applications dealing with data from our real-world three-dimensional space or the Earth's surface. These applications typically revolve around geographic data and are often built on the framework of GIS. The range of GIS-based spatial data applications is vast, including the following.

- *Map services* Utilizing GIS technology, these services offer detailed and accurate maps, fundamental in tools like Google Maps, Bing Maps, or OpenStreetMap.
- *Navigation* Relying on GIS for routing and real-time traffic updates, navigation systems analyze spatial data such as road networks and traffic patterns.
- *Location-based services (LBS)* Central to apps like ride-sharing services and local business finders, LBS use GIS data to leverage the user's geographic context.
- *Urban planning* They help in designing city layouts, considering things like traffic flow, zoning, and public ransportation.
- *Environmental and disaster management* GIS plays a crucial role in mapping areas at risk for natural disasters, combining different data types to identify vulnerable regions.

A pivotal process in the GIS applications we've discussed is georeferencing. This involves aligning geographic data – such as maps, aerial photographs, or satellite images – with a known coordinate system. By doing so, these data can be accurately viewed, queried, and analyzed in conjunction with other geographic information. The necessity for a standard coordinate system is clear, and here, the World Geodetic System of 1984 (WGS 84) emerges as a critical global standard. Published and maintained by the United States National Geospatial-Intelligence Agency, WGS 84 serves as a comprehensive datum and geographic coordinate system. It is instrumental not only for mapping and navigation but also forms the backbone of Global Positioning System (GPS) technology. As such, WGS 84 is one of the most universally adopted reference systems for representing the Earth's surface.

The second category of spatial data applications pertains to local or virtual spaces. These applications are evident in various innovative fields.

- *Three-dimensional (3D) printing* Here, spatial data processing is pivotal for storing and managing intricate 3D models and geometries, crucial for the accurate rendering of objects in 3D printing, including their dimensions and spatial relationships.
- *Computer-aided design (CAD)* In engineering, architecture, and construction, CAD systems heavily rely on spatial data to manage design elements. This includes the precise storage and retrieval of detailed models, whether they are of buildings, machinery, or other structures.
- *Building information modeling (BIM)* BIM utilizes spatial data processing to handle and analyze the spatial aspects of building data, from the layout of rooms to the positioning of structural components.
- *Virtual reality (VR) and augmented reality (AR)* In these immersive fields, managing spatial data is essential to create interactive virtual environments.
- *Advanced manufacturing* Industries such as aerospace or automotive benefit from spatial data in designing and manufacturing processes, particularly in managing complex geometries and spatial relationships within parts and assemblies.

In these applications, users have the flexibility to define their own coordinate systems to suit specific project needs. The most prevalent approach involves adopting a basic Cartesian coordinate system, comprising X-, Y-, and Z-axes. Measurements within this system are tailored to the project's requirements, using units that are most relevant, such as millimeters or inches. This customization allows for precision and relevance in a wide array of spatially oriented projects.

8.1.3 Spatial Data Analysis

In typical spatial data applications, a diverse array of tasks is involved, encompassing data storage, indexing, searching, querying, analysis, and visualization. Each of these tasks poses greater challenges compared to those encountered with relational data, primarily due to the unique characteristics of spatial data. One particularly demanding aspect is spatial data analysis, which requires specialized calculations that take into account the properties of spatial objects and their interrelationships. This analysis often necessitates a deep understanding of computational geometry, along with a thorough grasp of the intricate details involved in various scenarios.

A plethora of spatial functions has been integrated into SQL for spatial data analysis, standardized by the OGC Simple Feature Access. These functions are implemented by various spatial database systems, such as PostGIS, which extends PostgreSQL with spatial capabilities. While a comprehensive overview of all these functions is beyond our scope here, we will focus on two essential categories that are particularly relevant to our upcoming case study on pathology data analysis.

The first category involves calculating the area of a polygon, which can also be adapted to determine the length of a linestring or the volume of a 3D object. The second category deals with assessing the relationships between two spatial objects. This includes determining whether they interact and, if so, defining the geometry of their intersection (or union). These functions are unique to spatial data and pose significant challenges in the development and optimization of algorithms and programs for their execution.

As an illustration, let us examine the description of *ST_Intersection* in PostGIS, as found in their documentation (https://postgis.net/docs/manual-1.5/ST_Intersection .html).

```
geometry ST_Intersection( geometry geomA , geometry geomB );

Returns a geometry that represents the point set intersection
of the Geometries. In other words - that portion of geometry A
and geometry B that is shared between the two geometries. If
the geometries do not share any space (are disjoint), then
an empty geometry collection is returned.
```

In this function, the "geometry" object is an abstract class capable of representing diverse forms such as 1D lines, 2D polygons, and 3D objects. To many, the concept of calculating the intersection of two lines may recall middle school or high school geometry lessons. However, the challenge escalates considerably when dealing with 2D or 3D shapes, especially given the vast array of shapes and interaction possibilities. In the context of pathology imaging processing, we will delve into relevant algorithms and their implementations later in this chapter, presenting a concrete case study that illustrates the complexities involved.

8.2 Spatial Data Analysis for Pathology Imaging Data

According to the Oxford English Dictionary, the word "pathology" is defined as follows.

> The study of disease; the branch of science that deals with
> the causes and nature of diseases and abnormal anatomical and
> physiological conditions...

This definition underscores the vital role of pathology in understanding human health and diseases. The analysis of pathology imaging data is particularly crucial in advancing the field of pathology. In this section, we will provide a succinct overview of pathology imaging analysis and subsequently outline a computational task that poses a significant challenge in this domain, which will be the primary focus of this chapter.

8.2.1   Introduction to Pathology Imaging Analysis

Digital pathology marks a significant evolution in the field, moving from traditional microscopy to an advanced, image-based approach. This progress enables the acquisition, management, and interpretation of pathology data through digitized glass slides. Departing from the conventional microscopy where physical slides are scrutinized under a microscope, digital pathology utilizes high-resolution imaging technologies. These technologies facilitate the scanning of slides, leading to the creation of digital representations that are more manageable in terms of storage, retrieval, and analysis. Furthermore, this digital format encourages global collaboration among pathologists and integrates effectively with artificial intelligence (AI), enhancing both diagnostic accuracy and research capabilities.

Central to digital pathology is whole-slide imaging (WSI), a technique that scans traditional glass pathology slides to produce detailed digital images (e.g., shown in Figure 8.3). These high-resolution raster images capture the full extent of the tissue sample on a slide, preserving essential microscopic details for accurate diagnoses. The technique of WSI allows pathologists to inspect slides as thoroughly as with traditional microscopy, but with added advantages such as enhanced detail through magnification, simultaneous comparison of multiple slides, and the convenience of sharing images for consultation or educational purposes. The digital format of WSI is especially suited for integration with computational tools, opening new avenues for automated analysis and machine learning applications.

A key element in pathology imaging analysis is the extraction of spatial locations and boundaries of microanatomic structures from digital slide images (e.g., shown in Figure 8.3), typically represented by polygons and identified using segmentation algorithms [38]. The effectiveness of these algorithms depends on a range of factors, including the quality of staining machines, the peculiarities of tissue structures, and the staining techniques used. Even minor adjustments in algorithm parameters can significantly alter segmentation outcomes, thus making the evaluation of their effectiveness

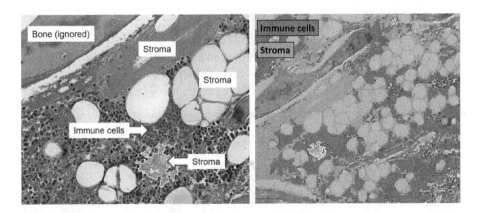

Figure 8.3 An example of using Pathology segmentation techniques to extract various tissue structures. (Public domain image courtesy of Mikael Häggström, MD.)

and sensitivity a central aspect of pathology imaging studies. Emphasizing iterative validation and study of parameter sensitivity in these algorithms is crucial, especially when the task involves efficiently comparing millions of spatial boundaries of segmented microanatomic objects.

Developing high-performance tools for cross-comparison poses a significant challenge, largely due to the vast amount of data generated in pathology imaging analysis. Whole-slide images, which result from scanning microscope slides at a diagnostic resolution, are extremely large, often containing more than $100{,}000 \times 100{,}000$ pixels and featuring millions of objects like cells or nuclei. A single study might include hundreds of such images from a large subject cohort, and in large-scale, interconnected analyses, numerous algorithms with varying parameters might generate multiple sets of results that require comparison and consolidation. Consequently, the data derived from a single study's images can reach tens of terabytes and is expected to grow even larger in future clinical settings.

8.2.2   Problem Identification: Spatial Cross-Comparison

The pathology segmentation process described above can essentially be viewed as a raster-to-vector conversion operation. A fundamental technique in this process is the cross-comparison of two sets of polygons, which may have been segmented by different algorithms or by the same algorithm with varying parameters. The objective of this comparison is to ascertain the degree of similarity between these polygon sets. To this end, the Jaccard similarity index is widely employed in the field of pathology due to its simplicity and its meaningful geometric interpretation. This measure has become a standard tool for quantifying the similarity between sets of polygons, thereby providing valuable insights into the effectiveness of different segmentation approaches.

Suppose P and Q are two sets of polygons representing the spatial boundaries of objects generated by two methods from the same image. Their Jaccard similarity is defined as

$$J(P,Q) = \frac{\|P \cap Q\|}{\|P \cup Q\|},$$

where $P \cap Q$ and $P \cup Q$ denote the intersection and the union of P and Q, and $\|\cdot\|$ is defined as the area of one or multiple polygons in a polygon set. To further simplify the computation, researchers in digital pathology use a variant definition of Jaccard similarity: Let $r(p,q) = \frac{\|p \cap q\|}{\|p \cup q\|}$, then

$$J'(P,Q) = \langle\{r(p,q) : p \in P, q \in Q, \|p \cap q\| \neq 0\}\rangle,$$

in which $\langle\cdot\rangle$ represents the average value of all the elements in a set. The greater the value of J' is, the more likely P and Q resemble each other. Compared with J, J' does not consider missing polygons that appear in one polygon set but have no intersecting counterpart in the other. Missing polygons can be easily identified by comparing the number of polygons that appear in the intersection with the number of polygons in each polygon set. Other additional measurements of similarity, such as distance of centroids, are omitted in our discussion, as their computational complexity is low.

The computation of J' is highly challenging due to the massive amount of polygons involved in spatial cross-comparison. In medical analysis, a considerable amount of dependability is required, which necessitates a sufficiently large image base – hundreds of whole slide images are typical, with each image generating millions of polygons. Since a single image contains numerous objects, the average size of polygons extracted from pathology images is typically very small.

To expedite both segmentation and comparison, large image files are typically prepartitioned into many small tiles to fit into memory and allow for parallel segmentations. The resulting polygon files for each whole image also reflect the structure of such partitioning: Polygons extracted from a single tile are contained in a single polygon file. A group of polygon files constitutes the segmentation result for a whole image, and different segmentation results for the same image are represented with different groups of polygon files. These groups of polygon files are cross-compared with each other for the purpose of algorithm validation or sensitivity studies.

For the sake of simplicity, in the rest of this chapter, we will refer to the area of the intersection of two polygons as the "area of intersection," and the area of the union of two polygons as the "area of union."

8.3   Spatial Database Solution

Pathologists primarily rely on spatial database management system (SDBMS) to execute spatial cross-comparisons [129]. However, performing cross-comparisons on a massive amount of polygons is time consuming using SDBMS, which cannot fully utilize the rich parallel resources of modern hardware. That is the reason why we will develop a GPU-accelerated solution for the problem, as we will explain in the next sections. But in this section, we will first give a brief introduction to spatial database systems, and then explain how spatial cross-comparison can be implemented by a spatial database system, and finally we will discuss possible performance optimization results for the database solution.

8.3.1   An Introduction to Spatial Database Systems

A spatial database management system can be conceptualized as an extension of a conventional relational database system, enriched with spatial capabilities. These enhancements include the definition of spatial data types, specialized methods for spatial data storage and indexing, and an array of spatial functions for various calculations, among other features. This integration ensures maximum compatibility with existing database ecosystems and a wide range of tools, facilitating the rapid development of diverse spatial data applications. Numerous established database systems, encompassing both commercial offerings like Oracle and IBM DB2, and open-source systems such as

PostgreSQL and MySQL, offer spatial extensions. For the purposes of this section, we will focus on PostGIS, the spatially extended version of PostgreSQL.

At its core, PostGIS adds support for geographic objects to the PostgreSQL database, effectively transforming it into a spatial database for GIS operations. This extension allows users to store, query, and manipulate spatial data within the PostgreSQL framework. PostGIS complies with the OGC standards, ensuring compatibility and interoperability with a wide range of GIS software. It supports a variety of spatial data types, including points, lines, polygons, and geometry collections, making it a versatile tool for a broad spectrum of spatial data applications.

The strength of PostGIS lies in its comprehensive suite of functions for spatial querying and analysis. These functions enable users to perform sophisticated spatial operations like measuring distances and areas, finding nearest neighbors, and conducting spatial joins and overlays. PostGIS also integrates seamlessly with other PostgreSQL features, such as robust indexing, query optimization, and transaction management, ensuring efficient and secure handling of large-scale spatial data. Its ability to handle complex spatial queries and integrate with other PostgreSQL functions makes PostGIS an indispensable tool for developers, researchers, and organizations dealing with large volumes of geographic data. From urban planning and environmental monitoring to logistics and location-based services, PostGIS provides the necessary functionality to manage and analyze spatial data effectively.

To demonstrate clearly the effectiveness of PostGIS in addressing spatial data requirements, we present a straightforward example. For those wishing to follow along, there are two options: installing PostGIS on a personal computer or using an online PostgreSQL service that includes PostGIS extensions, such as dbfiddle.uk (https://dbfiddle.uk/). In this example, we pose a question to explore spatial querying capabilities: *"What is the distance between the White House in Washington DC, USA, and the Eiffel Tower in Paris, France?"*. This query not only showcases the functionality of PostGIS but also provides an engaging way to understand spatial data operations.

To address our query, the first step is to ascertain the geographic coordinates of the White House and the Eiffel Tower. These can be easily obtained using Google Maps: simply search for the location and right-click to copy the latitude and longitude coordinates from the pop-up menu. The coordinates for these landmarks are as follows.

- White House: Latitude: 38.89785996953108, Longitude: −77.0366049056195
- Eiffel Tower: Latitude: 48.858444059707985, Longitude: 2.29460150279015766

With these coordinates, we can create two points in PostGIS to represent each location. As discussed earlier, spatial data here are tied to real geographic locations, so we utilize the standard WGS84 coordinate system. The SQL script below demonstrates how to create a table with two columns: one for the place name and another for the geometry object. Each record inserted corresponds to one of the two places. It is important to note that in PostGIS, the SRID (an ID for a spatial reference system) 4326 refers to the WGS84 standard. Without specifying a coordinate system, spatial data values would be ambiguous. In PostGIS, the geometry is defined using the WKT format, and for the POINT object, longitude corresponds to x, and latitude to y.

```
CREATE TABLE my_geotable
(
place TEXT,
geom geometry(Geometry, 4326) -- Specify WGS84 SRID
);

INSERT INTO my_geotable  VALUES
(
'White House',
ST_GeomFromText('POINT(-77.0366049056195 38.89785996953108)', 4326)
);

INSERT INTO my_geotable VALUES
(
'Eiffel Tower',
ST_GeomFromText('POINT(2.2946015027901576 48.858444059707985)', 4326)
);
```

This script, now in place with the necessary data structure and location inputs, sets the stage for executing spatial queries and analyses in PostGIS. To calculate the distance between the White House and the Eiffel Tower, the following SQL query is used.

```
SELECT place1, place2,
       ST_Distance(geom1, geom2), ST_DistanceSphere(geom1, geom2)
FROM
    (SELECT place AS place1, geom AS geom1 FROM my_geotable
    WHERE place = 'White House') AS t1,
    (SELECT place AS place2, geom AS geom2 From my_geotable
    WHERE place = 'Eiffel Tower') AS t2;
```

This query utilizes two PostGIS functions: *ST_Distance* and *ST_DistanceSphere*. *ST_Distance* calculates the minimum Cartesian distance between two geometries in a planar projection, while *ST_DistanceSphere* estimates the minimum spherical distance between points on a sphere – more appropriate for geographic distances on the Earth's surface. The query fetches both distance measurements between the specified locations, providing a comprehensive understanding of the spatial relationship between the White House and the Eiffel Tower.

Before we delve into the results, it is crucial to reiterate the importance of coordinate systems in spatial data applications, a feature that distinctly characterizes this field. The function *ST_Distance* calculates distances based on the units of the input geometries (in this case, longitude and latitude degrees). As a result, the output is also in degrees, which may not be immediately meaningful for readers. In contrast, *ST_DistanceSphere* provides results in meters, offering a more tangible measure of distance. With this understanding, we can now examine the query results presented in Table 8.1.

Readers have the option to independently verify the distance measurement using Google Maps. This can be accomplished by selecting the "Measure Distance" option from the right-click pop-up menu. As illustrated in Figure 8.4, the distance measured

Table 8.1 Spatial query results: Distance between the White House and the Eiffel Tower.

place1	place2	st_distance	st_distancesphere
White House	Eiffel Tower	79.95407147626182	6161451.91389163

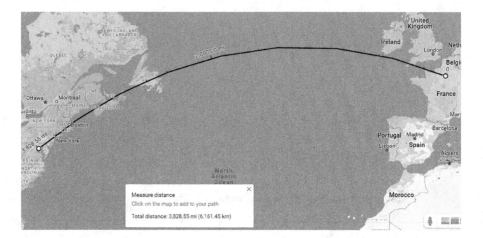

Figure 8.4 The distance between the White House and the Eiffel Tower on Google Maps. (A screenshot of Google Maps in the Chrome browser.)

on Google Maps is 6161.45 km. This figure aligns closely with our query result from *ST_DistanceSphere*, which is 6,161,451 m. Such a cross-verification confirms the accuracy of our results, providing assurance that the spatial data analysis conducted is indeed correct. Note that, when performing the "Measure Distance" operation on Google Maps, the method of selecting a destination by "Clicking on the map" can easily lead to minor shifts away from the exact target location, potentially resulting in slight numerical discrepancies in the measurement.

This example serves to illustrate the ease and effectiveness of spatial database systems in addressing real-world spatial data challenges. It is worthwhile to summarize the key advantages that make these systems particularly appealing to pathologists for their applications. Firstly, the use of SQL language and standard spatial functions provides a straightforward interface for a range of tasks, from data definition to complex analysis expressions. Secondly, spatial capabilities are seamlessly integrated into the database environment, allowing the use of various existing features, such as the subqueries employed in our example, which are a staple of traditional SQL. These advantages contribute to the popularity of database solutions in spatial data applications. Consequently, there arises a need to assess their performance and explore optimization strategies for these applications, which will be the primary focus of the subsequent sections in this chapter.

8.3.2   Implementing Cross-Comparison in PostGIS

Recalling our previous discussion, we identified that the key to calculating the Jaccard similarity for our pathology imaging analysis task lies in determining the ratio of the intersection area to the union area of two polygons. Let us now explore how this can be implemented using PostGIS. Figure 8.5 demonstrates two intersecting polygons. In PostGIS, these polygons can be defined using the WKT format. It is important to note that, as the polygons in this example represent locally defined data, we use an SRID of 0. This indicates an undefined spatial reference system, implying a simple 2D Cartesian plane (x–y plane).

The following SQL script sets up two tables, each containing a polygon, and then inserts the polygon data.

```
CREATE TABLE t1 (
     geom geometry(Polygon, 0)
);

CREATE TABLE t2 (
     geom geometry(Polygon, 0)
);

INSERT INTO t1 (geom) VALUES
     ('POLYGON((1 1, 1 4, 4 4, 4 1, 1 1))');
INSERT into t2 (geom) VALUES
     ('POLYGON((3 3, 3 6, 6 6, 6 3, 3 3))');
```

To calculate the intersection of the two polygons defined in our PostGIS tables, we utilize the *ST_Intersection* function in the following SQL query.

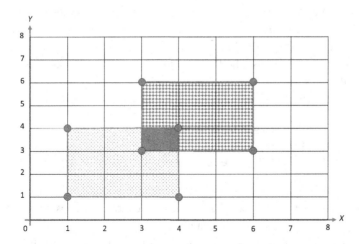

Figure 8.5 An example to demonstrate the intersection and union of two polygons.

```
SELECT
    ST_AsText(ST_Intersection(a.geom, b.geom))
FROM
    t1 a, t2 b;
```

This query is straightforward: The *ST_AsText* function is used to convert the geometric object resulting from the intersection into a text format. Executing this query in our test environment yields the following.

```
POLYGON((4 4,4 3,3 3,3 4,4 4))
```

Readers can easily recognize this polygon as corresponding to the intersection of the two input polygons depicted in Figure 8.5. However, observant readers may notice that the points in the resulting polygon are not ordered counter-clockwise, differing from the order in which the input polygons were defined. Importantly, PostGIS does not guarantee the orientation of polygons resulting from the *ST_Intersection* function. The orientation will conform to standard geometry rules but will vary based on the geometries involved and the function's processing. If maintaining a counter-clockwise orientation is essential, the *ST_ForcePolygonCCW* function can be used. This function ensures that the polygon's points are ordered counter-clockwise, as shown in the following query.

```
SELECT
    ST_AsText(ST_ForcePolygonCCW(ST_Intersection(a.geom, b.geom)))
FROM
    t1 a, t2 b;
```

Executing this revised query produces the following result with the points in reverse order.

```
POLYGON((4 4,3 4,3 3,4 3,4 4))
```

This adjustment demonstrates the flexibility of PostGIS in handling specific requirements related to the orientation of polygons resulting from spatial operations. However, we are actually more interested in the area of the intersection polygon instead of the polygon itself, so we can use the *ST_Area* to calculate the area, as shown in the following SQL query.

```
SELECT
    ST_Area(a.geom),
    ST_Area(a.geom),
    ST_Area(ST_Intersection(a.geom, b.geom))
FROM t1 a, t2 b;
```

No surprisingly, the result will be 9, 9, 1, for the three polygons, respectively.

Carrying out experiences with spatial operations in SQL, we can now logically progress to calculating the ratio of the intersection area to the union area of two polygons. This can be achieved using the following SQL query in PostGIS.

```
SELECT
    ST_Area(ST_Intersection(a.geom, b.geom)) /
    ST_Area(ST_Union(a.geom, b.geom))
FROM t1 a, t2 b;
```

This query utilizes the *ST_Area* function to compute the areas of the intersection and the union of the two polygons. By dividing these two values, we obtain the desired ratio. Executing this query yields a result of 1/17, or approximately 5.88 percent. This percentage represents the proportion of the intersection area relative to the total area covered by both polygons combined.

In finalizing our approach to calculate the Jaccard similarity for the pathology imaging application, we begin with the SQL query and then address two key points for consideration. The SQL query is as follows.

```
SELECT AVG(ratio)
FROM (
    SELECT
        ST_Area(ST_Intersection(a.geom, b.geom)) /
        ST_Area(ST_Union(a.geom, b.geom)) AS ratio
    FROM t1 a, t2 b
    WHERE
        ST_Intersects(a.geom, b.geom)
    ) AS tmp
WHERE ratio > 0;
```

Firstly, in our simplified example, we haven't specified a join condition between the two tables, as each table contains only one record. However, in practical applications with n records per table, this would result in n^2 pairs for ratio calculations. To manage this, it is essential to include a WHERE clause that filters out unnecessary pairs. This is achieved using the *ST_Intersects* function, which determines whether a pair of geometries (a.geom, b.geom) is relevant for further calculations. Secondly, since our focus is on pairs that actually intersect (i.e., where the ratio is greater than 0), the query is wrapped in an outer query. This structure filters out pairs with no intersection, thus focusing on meaningful Jaccard similarity calculations.

Up to this point, readers should now understand the distinction between *ST_Intersects* and *ST_Intersection*, both of which have been utilized in our previous example. The difference between these two functions is straightforward yet significant. *ST_Intersects* returns a Boolean value indicating whether two polygons intersect with each other. In contrast, *ST_Intersection* actually computes and returns the intersecting polygon created from the two input polygons.

Having established this, we have now reached a stage where we possess a functional SQL query capable of executing the Jaccard similarity test between two sets of polygons. In Section 8.3.3, we will shift our focus to analyzing the performance of this query. Subsequently, we will explore optimized solutions to enhance its efficiency.

8.3.3   Performance Profiling and Optimization

Can We Optimize the Query?
The SQL query discussed earlier presents two key opportunities for optimization.

- *Efficient area calculation* By leveraging the formula $\|p \cup q\| = \|p\| + \|q\| - \|p \cap q\|$, we can streamline the query. Instead of directly calculating the area of the union, we can focus on executing the *ST_Intersection* operator for each pair of intersecting polygons. The area of the union can then be deduced indirectly through this formula, reducing the computational workload.
- *Faster test of polygon intersects* The current use of *ST_Intersects* can be optimized, considering that we are primarily interested in records where *ratio* > 0. Given that the intersection of two polygons can be inferred from the area of their intersection, we can replace *ST_Intersects* with the && operator. This operator tests the intersection of the minimum bounding rectangles (MBRs) of the polygons, offering a faster alternative for determining polygon intersections.

By applying the aforementioned optimizations, we can significantly enhance the query's performance. This is achieved by simplifying the area calculations and accelerating the intersection tests. The optimized SQL query is as follows.

```
SELECT AVG(ratio)
FROM (
    SELECT ai / (ap + aq - ai) AS ratio
    FROM (
        SELECT
            ST_Area(ST_Intersection(a.geom, b.geom)) AS ai,
            ST_Area(a.geom) AS ap,
            ST_Area(b.geom) AS aq,
        FROM
            t1 a, t2 b
        WHERE a.geom && b.geom
        ) AS tmp1
    WHERE ai > 0
    ) AS tmp2;
```

In this query, the && operator plays a critical role. According to PostGIS documentation, the && operator returns TRUE if the 2D bounding box of geometry A intersects the 2D bounding box of geometry B. This means that with the condition a.geom && b.geom, we can swiftly exclude pairs whose objects cannot possibly intersect, as nonintersecting objects would not have overlapping bounding boxes. While this approach may initially include some false positives – pairs whose bounding boxes intersect but the objects themselves do not – the subsequent condition that the intersection area must be greater than zero effectively filters out these cases. Thus, the query becomes more efficient by quickly eliminating nonintersecting pairs and focusing only on those with meaningful intersections.

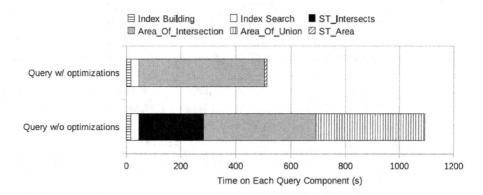

Figure 8.6 Execution time decomposition of cross-comparing queries in PostGIS on a single core.

Performance Profiling

To test the real performance of the aforementioned queries, we conducted a series of experiments with PostGIS. We used a real-world dataset extracted from a brain tumor slide image. The total size of the dataset in raw text format is approximately 750 MiB, with two sets of polygons (representing tumor nuclei) each containing over 450,000 polygons, and over 570,000 pairs of polygons with MBR intersections.

We divided the query execution into separate components and profiled the time spent by the query engine on each component during single-core execution. The results are presented in Figure 8.6 for both the unoptimized and optimized queries. "Index Search" refers to the testing of MBR intersections based on the built indexes. "Area Of Intersection" and "Area Of Union" represent computing the areas of intersection and union, which correspond to the two combined operators, $ST\_Area(ST\_Intersection())$ and $ST\_Area(ST\_Union())$. ST_Area denotes the other two stand-alone ST_Area operators in the optimized query.

For the unoptimized query, $ST\_Intersects$ (21.8 percent), "Area Of Intersection" (37.4 percent), and "Area Of Union" (36.7 percent) take the highest percentages of execution time, representing the bottlenecks of the query execution. For the optimized query, since $ST\_Intersects$ and "Area Of Union" are removed from the SQL statement, "Area Of Intersection" becomes the sole performance bottleneck, capturing almost 90 percent of the total query execution time. As shown in the left two bars of the figure, very little time (less than 6 percent) was spent on index building and index search in both queries. The bar for ST_Area indicates that the time to compute polygon areas is negligible and further suggests that the high overhead of "Area Of Intersection" and "Area Of Union" comes from spatial operators $ST\_Intersection$ and ST_Union.

The Unveiled Optimization Direction

The profiling results explain the low performance of spatial databases in supporting cross-comparing queries. Computing the intersection/union of polygons is too costly as the number of polygon pairs is large. The SDBMSs usually rely on some geometric computation libraries, such as GEOS in PostGIS, to implement spatial operators. Designed to be general purpose, the algorithms used by these libraries to compute the intersection and union of polygons are compute intensive and very difficult to parallelize.

We analyzed the source codes of the respective functions for computing polygon intersection and union in GEOS and another popular geometric library, CGAL, and found that only a few sections of the codes can be parallelized without significantly changing algorithm structures. Both GEOS and CGAL use generic sweepline algorithms, which are not built for computationally intensive queries and thus lead to limited performance in SDBMSs.

Using a large computing cluster can certainly improve system performance. However, unlike in many high-performance computing applications, pathologists can hardly afford expensive facilities in real clinical settings [22]. Therefore, a cost effective and highly productive solution is greatly desired. This motivates us to design a customized solution to accelerate large-scale spatial cross-comparisons. To eliminate the performance bottleneck, our solution needs an efficient GPU algorithm for computing the areas of intersection and union, as will be introduced in the next section.

8.4   Sweep Line: A Conventional Solution to Polygon Intersection

In this section, we delve into the mechanics of how the PostGIS solution operates behind the scenes. Our analysis indicates that while calculating a polygon's area is relatively quick, the true performance bottleneck lies in the computation of polygon intersections. This is understandable, as the area of a polygon can be efficiently calculated using a mathematical formula known as the "shoelace formula" or "Gauss's area formula." Given a polygon with n vertices, where the coordinates of the ith vertex are (x_i, y_i), the formula for the area of the polygon is:

$$A = \frac{1}{2} \left| \sum_{i=1}^{n} (x_i y_{i+1} - x_{i+1} y_i) \right|.$$

Here, (x_{n+1}, y_{n+1}) are taken to be the same as (x_1, y_1), essentially closing the loop of the polygon by connecting the last vertex back to the first one, as we have introduced in Section 8.3. This formula allows for the rapid calculation of polygon areas, highlighting why the area computation is not the limiting factor in performance. Instead, the more-complex process of determining polygon intersections demands greater computational resources, thereby becoming the focal point of optimization efforts in spatial data processing.

Now, let us consider the task of calculating the intersection polygon for the two polygons depicted in Figure 8.7. The polygon on the left can be defined as "POLYGON(3 1, 6 4, 3 7, 0 4, 3 1)," while the polygon on the right as "POLYGON(5 1, 8 4, 5 7, 2 4, 5 1)." As illustrated, it is relatively straightforward to visually determine

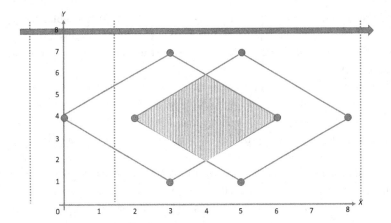

Figure 8.7 An illustration of the sweep line algorithm. We draw three vertical sweep lines and we use the arrow to indicate the sweep direction (from the left to the right).

the intersection area of these two polygons. We can define the intersection polygon as "POLYGON (4 2, 6 4, 4 6, 2 4, 4 2)." It is important to note that all three polygons are defined with their vertices in a counter-clockwise orientation.

We are now poised to explain how this visual judgment can be translated into a systematic and step-by-step computational process. This process will enable us to calculate the intersection of these polygons accurately. The challenge lies in converting our intuitive understanding of spatial overlap into a reliable algorithmic operation that can be executed within a computational environment.

In Figure 8.7, we observe that the resultant intersection polygon includes two new intersection points: one at $(4, 2)$ and the other at $(4, 6)$. These points are the intersections of corresponding line segments from the two polygons. This observation leads us to deduce that an effective algorithm for polygon intersection should encompass two primary steps.

- *Intersection point identification* This crucial first step involves calculating all the intersection points between the line segments of the two polygons. It requires an algorithmic approach that systematically evaluates each segment pair to determine their points of intersection, if any.
- *Final polygon formation* Once the intersection points are identified, the next step is to construct the final intersection polygon. This involves integrating these newly identified intersection points with the existing vertices of the original polygons. The challenge here is to determine the correct sequence of points, including both the original vertices and the intersection points, to accurately represent the area of overlap.

Considering the problem of calculating the intersection points of two polygons, a straightforward approach might involve comparing each line segment of one polygon with every segment of the other. Determining whether and how two line segments intersect is a basic mathematical problem. This method resembles the brute-force approach used in database joins, as discussed in Chapter 7. However, such an approach inevitably leads to $O(n^2)$ complexity since it requires examining all possible pairs of line segments.

The key question is whether we can develop a more-efficient algorithm to reduce this complexity, much like employing a sort-merge join in databases to avoid brute-force methods. The **sweep line** algorithm offers a solution to this challenge. As depicted in Figure 8.7, imagine a vertical line sweeping from the leftmost edge of the plane to the rightmost edge of the plane, scanning the entire area. As this scanning line moves across the plane, it encounters various points of the polygons. The fundamental principle of the sweep line algorithm lies in orchestrating specific actions when the line intersects different types of points. By employing this algorithm, we can efficiently identify intersection points without exhaustively comparing every pair of line segments. The sweep line moves systematically, only focusing on relevant segments at each position, thereby reducing the overall computational load and enhancing the efficiency of the intersection calculation.

The sweep line algorithm utilizes advanced data structures to efficiently handle events (such as vertices and intersections) and manage the current state of the sweep line (the active edges). Below is a high-level overview of these data structures and the algorithm's workflow.

- **Event queue (EQ)** This is a priority queue used to manage events, which include the start and end vertices of edges from both polygons, as well as intersection points. Events in the EQ are primarily sorted by their x-coordinates and secondarily by their y-coordinates.
- **Sweep line status (SLS)** This data structure, often implemented as a balanced binary tree, maintains the order of edges as they intersect with the sweep line. It allows for efficient querying and updating of edges and their neighboring relationships.
- **Main algorithm steps**

  1. Initialize the EQ with all the vertices of both polygons.
  2. While the EQ is not empty, process each event.
     - If the event is a start vertex, insert the corresponding edge into the SLS. Then, check for intersections with neighboring edges.
     - If the event is an end vertex, check for intersections between the neighbors of this edge. Afterwards, remove the edge from the SLS.
     - If the event is an intersection, swap the intersecting edges in the SLS and check for further intersections with their new neighbors.
  3. Collect and return all identified intersection points.

The sweep line algorithm, as depicted in Figure 8.7, methodically processes relevant events, ensuring the accurate identification of intersection points while optimizing the computational load. This figure provides a clear visual representation of the algorithm in action. As the sweep line moves from left to right, its position along the

x-axis increases, triggering specific actions upon encountering certain points. When the sweep line is at $x = 0$, it results in the addition of two edges to the SLS. At $x = 2$, two more edges are added; however, as the figure illustrates, they do not create intersection points. The critical moment occurs at $x = 3$, where two edges are removed and two new edges are introduced, leading to the creation of two intersection points: (4, 6) and (4, 2). These points are subsequently added to the event queue for later processing. As the sweep line crosses positions $x = 4, 5, 6$, and 8, the calculation comes to completion. A key aspect to note is that at $x = 3$, the newly added edges are not compared against all existing edges in the SLS but only against their immediate neighbors. This selective comparison is crucial for avoiding redundant calculations and hinges on maintaining the y-order of the edges. While this example is relatively straightforward, it aptly demonstrates the sequential nature of the sweep line algorithm, highlighting the necessity for edge processing to adhere to an ordered structure along both the x-axis and y-axis.

After identifying all intersection points between two polygons, the next step is to construct the final intersection polygon, or polygons, as the case may be. The basic approach involves tracing the edges of one polygon starting from an intersection point. When another intersection point is reached, the traversal switches to the other polygon. This process continues until a closed loop is formed, returning to the starting point, thereby completing an intersection polygon. In scenarios with multiple intersection polygons, this process is repeated for other unprocessed intersection points until all intersection polygons are identified.

To illustrate a more-complex scenario, consider Figure 8.8, where the polygon on the right side has a hole, as described in Section 8.3 on the WKT language. This figure further elucidates the logic of forming intersection polygons in situations with more complex polygon shapes, including those with holes. The traversal logic adapts to these complexities, ensuring accurate formation of intersection polygons regardless of the intricacies of the original shapes.

Determining the correct path to follow at an intersection point of two polygons is crucial when constructing their intersection polygon. This decision point often presents two options: following an edge from either of the intersecting polygons. To illustrate, consider an example where (4, 6) is an intersection point. At this juncture, we face the following choice.

- Following the edge from the right-side polygon towards point (2, 4), or
- following the edge from the left-side polygon towards point (3, 7).

The correct choice for building the intersection polygon depends on which edge lies inside the other polygon. Visually, it is evident that the first option is correct, as the edge from the right-side polygon resides within the left-side polygon, making the intersection possible. Conversely, the second choice leads us outside the right-side polygon, and thus, is not part of the intersection.

To systematically determine the correct path, two techniques are commonly employed.

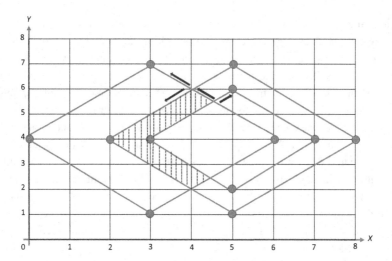

Figure 8.8 An illustration of building the intersection polygon between two polygons: One is the left polygon, and the other one is the right polygon which has a hole inside. The result intersection polygon is represented by the hatched area.

- *Cross product of vectors* This approach utilizes the cross product of two vectors to determine which direction maintains the traversal within the intersection area. In Figure 8.8, we illustrate two scenarios: one at point (4, 6) and another at point (4.5, 5.5). The latter appears more complex due to the presence of a hole. By applying the right-hand rule, which aligns with the fact that the outer boundary of a polygon is defined in a counter-clockwise direction and holes in the reverse, we can discern the correct edge to follow at these points. As depicted, the correct edges are those that encircle the intersection area.
- *Point-in-polygon (PIP) tests* This technique involves testing a point on an edge (excluding the endpoints) to determine if it resides within the other polygon. If the point is inside, the edge is part of the intersection area and should be pursued. The PIP problem is a fundamental question in computational geometry, often solved using the ray casting or even–odd rule algorithm. This method involves extending a ray from the test point to infinity and counting the number of times it intersects with the polygon's edges. An odd number of intersections indicates the point is inside the polygon. This concept can be visually verified in the figure and will be further explored in the next section, as it forms the basis of our GPU-accelerated solution.

In practice, a combination of these two methods can be utilized for accuracy, especially in complex scenarios with numerous edges and intersections. The underlying principle is to ensure that the chosen path aligns with the boundary of the intersected area, thereby accurately constructing the intersection polygon.

Summarizing the major points regarding the unsuitability of sweep-line-based polygon intersection algorithms for parallelization on GPUs, we can highlight several key aspects.

1. **Inherent sequential nature** The sweep line algorithm fundamentally relies on a sequential process. It involves a *sweep line* moving across the plane, handling geometric events (like vertex encounters and edge intersections) in a specific order determined by their X-coordinates. This sequential progression is crucial for the algorithm's correctness, as the state of the algorithm at any point is dependent on the order in which these events are processed. However, GPUs are designed for massively parallel tasks where many operations can be carried out simultaneously and independently. The dependent and sequential nature of the sweep line algorithm does not align well with this parallel processing paradigm.

2. **Branch-intensive executions and diverse case handling** The algorithm involves numerous conditional branches to handle various geometric scenarios, such as overlapping edges, intersecting vertices, and different types of intersections. Each of these scenarios requires specific logic and decision-making paths. GPU architectures excel in scenarios where the execution path is uniform and predictable across multiple threads. However, the diverse and branch-intensive nature of the sweep line algorithm leads to a divergence in execution paths, which can significantly reduce the efficiency and effectiveness of parallel execution on GPUs.

3. **Dynamic state management and dependencies** A key component of the algorithm is the dynamic management of the SLS, which tracks the ordering and intersection of edges as the sweep line progresses. This state is continuously updated based on the events processed, creating dependencies between sequential operations. In a parallel processing environment like a GPU, managing these dependencies efficiently is challenging, as it often requires synchronization and communication between threads, which can be a major bottleneck.

4. **Irregular memory access patterns** Efficient GPU computation also relies heavily on regular and predictable memory access patterns. The sweep line algorithm, however, utilizes data structures like priority queues (for event processing) and balanced binary trees (for the SLS), which have irregular and dynamic memory access patterns. Such patterns are not well suited for the memory architecture of GPUs and can lead to inefficient memory usage and increased latency.

5. **Overhead of synchronization and communication** In any attempt to parallelize the sweep line algorithm on a GPU, significant overhead would be incurred due to the need for synchronization and communication between threads. This is particularly true in the context of handling the SLS and resolving intersections, where the outcomes of certain operations are directly dependent on others. The overhead can often negate the benefits of parallel processing, making GPUs an unsuitable platform for this algorithm.

In conclusion, while GPUs offer powerful parallel processing capabilities, their architecture and operational characteristics are not conducive to the efficient implementation of sweep-line-based polygon intersection algorithms. The sequential nature, branch-intensive logic, dynamic state management, irregular memory access patterns, and synchronization overhead inherent in these algorithms make them better suited for processing on CPUs or other architectures that can effectively handle sequential and state-dependent operations.

8.5   GPU Solution: The PixelBox Algorithm

We are now poised to discuss the use of GPU technology to address our core problem: computing the Jaccard similarity between two polygons. It is crucial to reiterate that our focus is on the area of the intersection between two polygons, rather than on the intersection polygon itself. Traditional spatial database solutions, which rely on standard functions, often unnecessarily compute the intersection polygon first (using *ST_Intersection*) before calculating its area (using *ST_Area*). This approach, while standard, involves an avoidable computational step.

In this section, we introduce PixelBox, a GPU-based algorithm designed to compute the areas of intersection and union for an array of polygon pairs. PixelBox is tailored to address three primary challenges.

- *Parallelizing the computation* Developing a strategy to parallelize the computation of intersection and union areas on GPUs, leveraging their capability to handle multiple operations concurrently.
- *Handling large polygon pairs* Finding ways to minimize computational intensity, particularly when dealing with large polygon pairs, to ensure efficiency and speed.
- *Optimizing GPU implementation* Crafting an efficient implementation of the algorithm on GPUs, focusing on maximizing the architectural strengths of these processors.

While our explanation uses Nvidia CUDA terminology, the principles behind PixelBox's design are universally applicable across various GPU architectures and programming models. This universality makes PixelBox a versatile solution, adaptable to different hardware and software environments.

8.5.1   Pixelization of Polygon Pairs

Polygons extracted from pathology images exhibit a distinct characteristic: Their vertices are integer valued, and their edges are aligned either horizontally or vertically. This specific attribute classifies these polygons as a type of "rectilinear" polygons. As depicted in Figure 8.9, this characteristic arises because medical images are typically raster images. Consequently, the boundaries of the segmented polygons adhere to the regular grid lines of the image, corresponding to pixel-level granularity.

This conformity to grid lines at a pixel level is significant, as it simplifies the geometric complexity of the polygons. In the context of GPU-based calculations, such as those performed by PixelBox, these rectilinear properties allow for more-efficient processing. The integer-valued coordinates and the alignment of edges along the grid make it easier to parallelize computations and optimize the algorithm for the unique structure of these medical image-derived polygons.

By utilizing this property, PixelBox considers a polygon as a continuous region that is surrounded by its spatial boundary on a pixel map. As depicted in Figure 8.10(a), pixels within the minimum bounding rectangle (MBR) of polygons p and q can be classified into three categories:

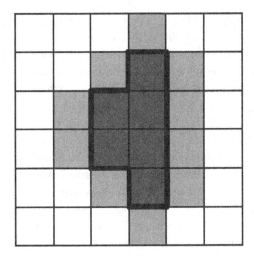

Figure 8.9 Polygons extracted from medical images have axis-aligned edges and integer-valued vertices.

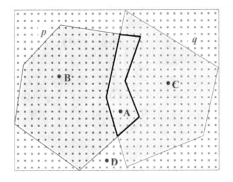

(a) A pixelized view of polygon intersection and union.

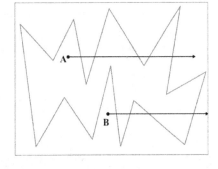

(b) Determination of a pixel's position relative to a polygon.

Figure 8.10 The principle of the PixelBox algorithm is to use (a) a pixelized view of polygon and (b) the ray-casting approach for point-in-polygon determination.

1. pixels (e.g., A) that are located inside both p and q,
2. pixels (e.g., B and C) that are situated inside one polygon but not the other, and
3. pixels (e.g., D) that are outside both polygons.

The area of intersection $\|p \cap q\|$ can be determined by counting the number of pixels belonging to the first category. The area of union $\|p \cup q\|$ corresponds to the number of pixels in the first and second categories. Finally, pixels in the third category do not contribute to either $\|p \cap q\|$ or $\|p \cup q\|$. The pixel-based approach for computing polygon intersection and union eliminates the need for boundary computations, and more importantly, provides an excellent opportunity for leveraging fine-grained data parallelism that is hidden in the cross-comparison computation.

In our analysis, we encounter the point-in-polygon (PIP) problem once again. This problem is crucial for determining whether a specific pixel falls within or outside a polygon. A common method to resolve this involves casting a ray from the pixel and counting how many times this ray intersects with the polygon's boundary. This technique is effectively demonstrated in Figure 8.10(b). According to this method, the position of a pixel relative to the polygon is determined by the parity of its ray's intersections with the polygon's edges. If the ray from a pixel, such as pixel A in the figure, intersects the polygon's boundary an odd number of times, the pixel is located inside the polygon. Conversely, if the ray intersects an even number of times, as is the case with pixel B, the pixel is outside the polygon. This method, based on the even–odd rule, provides a straightforward and reliable means to classify pixels in relation to the polygon.

The pixelization approach is highly suitable for GPU execution. Since checking the position of one pixel is completely independent of another, we can parallelize the computation by employing multiple threads to process the pixels in parallel. Furthermore, as the positions of different pixels are calculated against the same pair of polygons, the operations carried out by different threads follow the SIMT fashion, which is required by GPUs. Lastly, the area of intersection and area of union can be computed simultaneously during a single traversal of all pixels, with almost no additional overhead, because the criteria for testing intersection (which uses a Boolean AND operation) and union (which uses a Boolean OR operation) both depend on each pixel's position relative to the same pair of polygons. Since the number of input polygon pairs is typically large, we can assign them to multiple thread blocks. For each polygon pair, all threads within a thread block can compute the contributions of all pixels within the MBR in parallel.

8.5.2   Reduction of Compute Intensity

The pixelization method described above has a weakness, which is that the compute intensity increases rapidly as the number of pixels within the MBR grows. Although polygons are typically small in pathology imaging applications, as the resolution of the scanner lens increases, the sizes of polygons may also increase to capture more object details. There may also be situations where the areas of intersection and union are computed between a small group of relatively large polygons and numerous small polygons, such as when processing an image with a few capillary vessels surrounded by many cells. Additionally, even when polygons are small, it is still possible to reduce further the compute intensity and enhance performance.

To decrease the intensity of computation and improve the algorithm's scalability, PixelBox employs another technique known as sampling boxes. The concept of this technique is similar to the adaptive mesh refinement method [9] used in numerical analysis. Owing to the continuity of the interior of a polygon, the positions of pixels exhibit spatial locality. If a pixel is located inside (or outside) a polygon, it is probable that other pixels in its vicinity also lie inside (or outside) the polygon, with exceptions near the polygon's boundary. By utilizing this property, we can compute the areas of

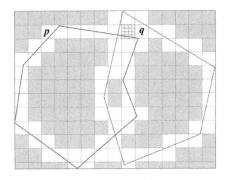

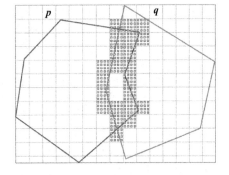

(a) Using sampling boxes to reduce compute intensity.

(b) Using both pixelization and sampling-box approaches.

Figure 8.11 The optimization principles of PixelBox: Using sampling boxes to reduce unnecessary calculations in the hybrid pixelBox approach.

intersection and union region by region, instead of pixel by pixel, so that all pixels within a region can contribute to the computation simultaneously.

This technique is demonstrated in Figure 8.11(a). The MBR of a pair of polygons is partitioned into sampling boxes recursively, initially at a coarser granularity (as shown by the large grid cells in the figure), then progressively finer within selected subregions (e.g., as depicted by the small boxes near the top) that require further exploration. For instance, while computing the area of intersection, if a sampling box is entirely inside both polygons, the contribution of all pixels within the sampling box can be obtained simultaneously, which equals the size of the sampling box. If the sampling box is not entirely inside both polygons, it must be partitioned into smaller subsampling boxes and tested further. In Figure 8.11(a), the gray sampling boxes do not require further partitioning since their contributions to the areas of intersection and union have already been determined.

Similar to the pixelization method, the sampling-box approach necessitates calculating a sampling box's position relative to a polygon, which has three possible values: Inside – every pixel within the box lies inside the polygon; outside – every pixel within the box lies outside the polygon; and hover – some pixels lie inside the polygon, while others lie outside it.

Lemma 8.1 *A sampling box's position relative to a polygon is determined by three conditions: (i) none of the sampling box's four edges crosses the polygon's boundary; (ii) none of the polygon's vertices lies inside the sampling box; (iii) sampling box's geometric center lies inside the polygon. The sampling box lies inside the polygon if all three conditions are true; it lies outside the polygon if the first two conditions are true but the last is false; it hovers over the polygon in all other cases, when either condition (i) or (ii) is false.*

Lemma 8.1 outlines the criteria for determining the position of a sampling box, which is further illustrated in Figure 8.12. For each sampling box, its four edges are

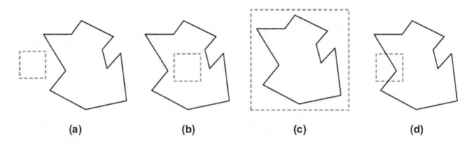

Figure 8.12 A sampling box's position relative to a polygon: (a) outside; (b) inside; (c, d) hover.

tested against the polygon's boundary. If there are edge-to-edge crossings, the sampling box must hover over the polygon (case (d) in Figure 8.12). If any of the polygon's vertices lies inside the sampling box, the entire polygon must be contained within the sampling box due to the continuity of its boundary. In this case, the position is also hover (case (c) in Figure 8.12). If none of the polygon's vertices are inside the sampling box, the sampling box may either be completely inside (case (b) in Figure 8.12) or entirely outside (case (a) in Figure 8.12) the polygon, in which case the position of the sampling box's geometric center provides the final answer. If the sampling box's four edges overlap with the polygon's boundary, its position can be considered either inside or outside. The next level of partitioning will differentiate the contribution of each subsampling box to the areas of intersection and union.

The process of testing the position of a sampling box is more expensive than doing so for a pixel. When the granularity of a sampling box is coarse, the additional overhead is offset by the reduction in per-pixel computations. However, as the sampling boxes become more fine grained, the cost of computing their positions becomes more significant. Furthermore, the use of sampling boxes necessitates synchronization between cooperative threads – the examination of one sampling box cannot begin until all threads have finished partitioning its parent box. Frequent synchronizations result in low utilization of computing resources and have been one of the primary barriers to improving performance on GPUs.

To maintain the advantages of both efficient data parallelization and low compute intensity, PixelBox combines pixelization with sampling-box techniques. As shown in Figure 8.11(b), sampling boxes are initially employed to rapidly complete testing for a vast number of regions. When the size of a sampling box becomes smaller than a threshold, T, the pixelization method takes over and completes the remainder of the computation.

In contrast to the pixelization-only approach, computing the area of intersection and the area of union simultaneously will result in additional overhead when using sampling boxes. For example, if a sampling box hovers over one polygon but is outside the other, its contribution is evident to the area of intersection but unclear to the area of union. In this instance, more fine-grained partitioning is required until the area of union is determined, or the pixelization threshold is met. To minimize the number of sampling box partitionings and further enhance the algorithm's performance, the area of union is not calculated simultaneously with the area of intersection in PixelBox.

Instead, similar to the query optimization we introduced in the previous section, we compute the areas of polygons, and use the formula $\|p \cup q\| = \|p\| + \|q\| - \|p \cap q\|$ to derive the areas of union indirectly. Computing the area of a simple polygon is very easy to implement on GPUs. With formula $A = \frac{1}{2} \sum_{i=0}^{n-1} (x_i y_{i+1} - x_{i+1} y_i)$, in which (x_i, y_i) is the coordinate of the ith vertex of the polygon, we can let different threads compute different vertices and sum up the partial results to get the area.

8.5.3   Optimized Algorithm Implementation

Algorithm 8.1 presents the pseudocode for PixelBox. Sampling boxes are generated and analyzed recursively – one region is examined from coarser to finer granularities before moving on to the next one. A shared stack is utilized to store the sampling box coordinates and flags indicating whether each sampling box requires further partitioning. For each polygon pair assigned to a thread block, its MBR is added to the stack as the first sampling box (line 13). All threads pop the topmost sampling box from the stack for examination (line 18). If the sampling box does not need further probing, all threads proceed to pop the next sampling box (lines 19–20) until the stack is empty, and the computation for the polygon pair is finished. For a sampling box that requires further examination, if its size is less than threshold T, the pixelization process is utilized (lines 22–28). Otherwise, the sampling box is partitioned into subsampling boxes, and new sampling boxes are pushed onto the stack by all threads in parallel after further processing (lines 30–39).

In the algorithm, PolyArea computes the partial area of a polygon assigned to a thread; BoxSize returns the number of pixels within a sampling box; PixelInPoly (m, i, p) computes the position of the ith pixel in sampling box m with respect to polygon p; SubSampBox(b, i) partitions a sampling box b and returns the ith subbox for a thread to process; BoxPosition(b, p) determines the position of sampling box b relative to polygon p; BoxContinue determines whether a sampling box requires further partitioning based on its positions with respect to two polygons; and BoxContribute determines whether a sampling box contributes to the area of intersection based on its position.

The use of a stack to store sampling boxes saves lots of memory space and makes testing sampling box positions and the generation of new sampling boxes parallelized. A synchronization is required before popping a sampling box (line 17) to ensure that thread 0 or the last thread in the thread block has pushed the sampling box to the top of the stack. When threads push new sampling boxes to the stack, they do not overwrite the old stack top (line 37); otherwise, an extra synchronization would be required before pushing new sampling boxes to ensure that the old stack top has been read by all threads. In the current design, the old stack top is marked as "no further probing" (line 38), and will be omitted by all threads when being popped out again.

Algorithm 8.1 The PixelBox GPU algorithm.

1: $\{p_i, q_i\}$: the array of input polygon pairs
2: $\{m_i\}$: the MBR of each polygon pair
3: N: total number of polygon pairs
4: stack[]: the shared stack containing sampling boxes
5: I[N][blockDim.x]: partial areas of intersections
6: A[N][blockDim.x]: partial summed areas of polygons
7:
8: **procedure** KERNEL_SAMPBOX
9:    tid ← threadIdx.x
10:    **for** i = blockIdx.x to N **do**
11:        A[i][tid] ← A[i][tid] + PolyArea(p_i)
12:        A[i][tid] ← A[i][tid] + PolyArea(q_i)
13:        Thread 0: stack[0] ← $\{m_i, 1\}$
14:        top ← 1
15:        **while** top > 0 **do**
16:            top ← top − 1
17:            SYNCTHREADS
18:            {box, c} ← stack[top]
19:            **if** c = 0 **then**
20:                **continue**
21:            **else**
22:                **if** BoxSize(box) < T **then**
23:                    **for** j ← tid to BoxSize(box) **do**
24:                        φ_1 ← PixelInPoly(box, j, p_i)
25:                        φ_2 ← PixelInPoly(box, j, q_i)
26:                        I[i][tid] ← I[i][tid] + ($\varphi_1 \wedge \varphi_2$)
27:                        j ← j + blockDim.x
28:                    **end for**
29:                **else**
30:                    subbox ← SubSampBox(box, tid)
31:                    φ_1 ← BoxPosition(box, p_i)
32:                    φ_2 ← BoxPosition(box, q_i)
33:                    c ← BoxContinue(φ_1, φ_2)
34:                    t ← BoxContribute(φ_1, φ_2)
35:                    a ← $(1 - c) \times t \times$ BoxSize(subbox)
36:                    I[i][tid] ← I[i][tid] + a
37:                    stack[top + 1 + tid] ← {subbox, c}
38:                    Thread 0: stack[top].c ← 0
39:                    top ← top + 1 + blockDim.x
40:                **end if**
41:            **end if**
42:        **end while**
43:        i ← i + gridDim.x
44:    **end for**
45: **end procedure**

The GPU kernel only computes the partial areas of intersections and the partial summed areas of polygons accumulated per thread (lines 5–6), which will be reduced later on the CPU to derive the final areas of intersection and union. Reduction is not performed on the GPU because the number of partial values for each polygon pair is relatively small (equal to the thread block size), which makes it not very efficient to execute on the GPU. We measured the time take by the reductions on a CPU core; the cost is negligible compared to other operations on the GPU.

8.5.4   The PixelBox System Framework

After presenting the core GPU algorithm for computing areas of intersection and union, we can now explain how the entire workflow for spatial cross-comparison is implemented and optimized in a CPU–GPU hybrid environment. The workflow involves multiple logical stages, starting with the input of raw text data for polygons and ending with the output of final results. To fully exploit the abundant resources of the underlying CPU/GPU hardware, these stages must be executed in a controllable and dynamically adaptable way. In order to achieve this goal, the system framework must address three challenges.

1. Since the GPU has a disconnected memory space from the CPU, input data batching for the GPU is necessary to compensate for the long latency of host–device communication.
2. The GPU is an exclusive, nonpreemptive compute device, which means uncontrolled kernel invocations may cause resource contention and low execution efficiency on the GPU.
3. Task executions have to be balanced between CPUs and GPUs to maximize system throughput.

The entire workload is executed by a pipelined structure, which allows for task productions and consumptions to overlap through interstage buffers, thereby improving resource utilization and system throughput. As shown in Figure 8.13, the cross-comparing pipeline consists of four stages.

1. The parser loads polygon files and converts the format of polygons from text to binaries. This stage is executed on CPUs with multiple worker threads.

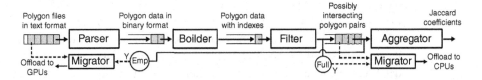

Figure 8.13 A cross-comparing pipeline with dynamic task migrations.

2. The builder creates spatial indexes on the converted polygon data. Since polygons are small, Hilbert R-tree [78] is used to speed up index building. This stage is executed on CPUs in a single thread because it already operates very quickly.
3. The filter performs a pairwise index search on the polygons parsed from each pair of polygon files and generates an array of polygon pairs with intersecting MBRs. Similar to the builder stage, this stage also executes on CPUs with a single worker thread.
4. The aggregator calculates the areas of intersection and union for each polygon array using the PixelBox algorithm. The area ratios are then aggregated to obtain the Jaccard similarity for an entire image. Polygon pairs that do not actually intersect, that is, with an area of intersection of zero, will not be considered.

A computation task at each pipeline stage is defined at the image tile scale. For example, an input task for the parser is to parse two polygon files segmented from the same image tile; an input task for the builder is to build indexes on the two sets of polygons parsed by a single parser task. In practice, a digital image slide may contain hundreds of small image tiles; each tile may contain thousands of polygons. The granularity of tasks defined at the image tile level matches the image segmentation procedure, and allows the workload to propagate through the pipeline in a balanced way.

Using such a pipelined framework is essential for addressing the challenges mentioned earlier. Firstly, the work buffers between pipeline stages provide natural support for GPU input data batching. For instance, since the number of polygon pairs filtered may vary significantly from tile to tile, the aggregator must group multiple small tasks in its input buffer and send them to the GPU in a batch all at once. Secondly, with a pipelined framework, a single instance of the aggregator consolidates all kernel invocations to the GPUs, which considerably reduces unnecessary contentions and increases the execution efficiency. Finally, the pipelined framework creates a convenient environment for load balancing between CPUs and GPUs.

8.6   Concluding Remarks and Exercise Projects

In this chapter, we have detailed a GPU-accelerated approach for efficiently cross-comparing analytical pathology imaging data. Our analysis began with a thorough profiling of a spatial database solution, which revealed a significant bottleneck in computing the areas of intersection and union of polygon sets. Addressing this, we introduced the PixelBox algorithm, optimized for GPU execution. This solution not only alleviates the bottleneck but also achieves a substantial performance enhancement – over 18 times faster than a parallelized PostGIS implementation when applied to real-world pathology data. This case study underscores the critical importance of effective parallelization strategies on GPUs, leveraging the specific characteristics of the problem and the strengths of GPU architecture. For instance, PixelBox's focus on data parallelism rather than compute efficiency aligns perfectly with GPU capabilities. Developing such parallelism-oriented approaches is essential in contemporary high-performance computing.

As we conclude this chapter, it is important to highlight that specialized data processing tasks are a hallmark of today's data-centric computing era. While this book primarily uses case studies to impart an understanding of GPU-oriented problem-solving paradigms, our focus here has been on a specific case with unique attributes that still follows a broader pattern of practical GPU utilization. This pattern involves three crucial factors.

- **Know where time goes** It is vital to perform detailed performance measurement and profiling to identify and understand performance bottlenecks.
- **See the whole picture** A holistic understanding of potential solutions is necessary. This involves assessing whether massive parallelism can significantly contribute to performance improvement and ensuring no overwhelming obstacles exist within the solution pipeline.
- **Never ignore details** In a highly parallelized environment, even minor issues can escalate into major performance impediments. This includes challenges such as synchronization costs, data skew, and global data sharing.

Given the current state of technology, particularly the lack of AI-based auto-parallelization, the responsibility for crafting high-performance solutions remains with parallel programmers. These professionals must skillfully navigate these three factors, hand-coding solutions as needed. While the case studies in this book provide patterns and insights from real-world applications, they are not meant to be universally applicable algorithms. They serve instead as valuable guidance for developers facing similar challenges. It is also worth noting that this book focuses on specific case studies and does not encompass a broad spectrum of data types like genetic, textual, or multimedia data. Readers seeking information on these topics may find domain-specific journals or machine-learning literature more suitable.

This chapter has three exercise projects, as follows.

- Project 1 (*easy*) This project involves implementing a function in C, akin to the "ST_Area" function in spatial database systems, to calculate the area of a polygon defined in WKT format, a concept we have explored in this chapter. The function must accurately handle polygons that may include one or more holes. Additionally, the accuracy of the C implementation will be validated by comparing its output with results from the "ST_Area" function in PostGIS.
- Project 2 (*medium*) The objective of this project is to implement the Jaccard similarity measure for two sets of randomly generated polygons, which do not contain any holes, using PostGIS. This builds on concepts introduced earlier in the chapter. The project will involve writing both unoptimized and optimized SQL queries. A detailed performance analysis will be conducted to evaluate the queries' efficiency. This project includes PostGIS installation, data loading, query execution, and thorough performance measurement.
- Project 3 (*hard*) This project requires implementing two variants of the Jaccard similarity measure. The first variant involves creating a sequential version in C, utilizing the sweep line algorithm for polygon intersection and the area calcula-

tion function from Project 1. The second variant entails using Nvidia CUDA for a GPU-accelerated parallel implementation of the PixelBox algorithm. The outcomes of both versions will be validated against the results obtained from PostGIS in Project 2, using identical polygon sets. Comprehensive performance comparisons should be conducted and reported among the three versions: the PostGIS version, the sequential C version, and the GPU parallel version.

9 Ray Tracing Hardware in GPUs for Accelerated Computation

> Thus, the photons which constitute a ray of light behave like intelligent human beings: out of all possible curves they always select the one which will take them most quickly to their goal.
>
> Max Planck, *the pioneer of quantum mechanics and the winner of the 1918 Nobel Prize in Physics.*

As we step into an era defined by specialized computing, the landscape of computational hardware is undergoing a significant transformation. The focus is shifting toward domain-specific architectures, which are tailored to efficiently handle specific types of computational tasks. This trend marks a departure from the one-size-fits-all approach of traditional general-purpose computing. Accelerators, designed to optimize particular operations, are becoming increasingly prevalent, offering enhanced performance and efficiency for targeted applications. Their emergence is reshaping how we approach complex computing challenges, paving the way for innovations across various fields, from artificial intelligence and big data analytics to high-performance computing.

In the midst of this architectural evolution, ray tracing hardware emerges as a notable example of such specialized technology. This chapter delves into the intricate world of ray tracing hardware, a cutting-edge component predominantly recognized for its role in rendering photorealistic graphics. However, its utility extends far beyond mere graphical applications. We explore the architectural nuances of ray tracing hardware embedded in modern GPUs, uncovering its potential to revolutionize not just how we render images but also how we process and analyze data.

The prospect of harnessing ray tracing hardware for tasks beyond its traditional scope is both challenging and promising. This chapter aims to demystify this potential, presenting how ray tracing hardware can be adeptly repurposed for various computational tasks. While the integration of such specialized hardware into nontraditional domains presents its own set of challenges, including the need for specialized knowledge and programming techniques, the rewards could be substantial. By the end of this chapter, readers will gain insights into the innovative applications of ray tracing hardware, illustrating its versatility and the promising future it holds in the realm of domain-specific computing.

9.1   Introduction to Ray Tracing

This chapter begins by providing an insightful overview of ray tracing, a sophisticated rendering technique known for its ability to produce highly realistic lighting and
shadows.

9.1.1   What Is Ray Tracing?

Ray tracing stands as a pivotal graphic rendering technology, utilized in both software
and hardware implementations to create stunningly realistic effects in 3D scenes on
computer screens. Its unique approach to image creation marks a significant advancement in the realm of digital graphics, offering an unprecedented level of realism in
visual simulations.

   The core principle of ray tracing lies in its methodical approach to calculating each
pixel's color. This is achieved by casting rays from the viewer's eye to various objects
in the scene, tracing the paths of these rays as they intersect with different surfaces.
The interaction of these rays with light sources and objects determines the final color
and intensity of each pixel, accounting for shadows, reflections, and refractions, and
thereby contributing to the image's overall realism.

   Figure 9.1 illustrates the main idea of ray tracing. We summarize the main concepts
and processes in the figure as follows.

- **Camera/eye** The starting point for the view ray, representing the viewer's perspective or the camera lens.
- **View ray** A line (or path) drawn from the camera to the object, representing the line
  of sight. This is used to determine which objects or parts of objects are visible from
  the camera's perspective.
- **Object** In this case, a sphere that the view ray intersects. The point of intersection
  is where calculations are made to determine the color and shading of that point on
  the object's surface based on lighting and material properties.

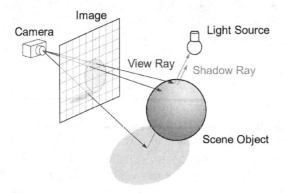

Figure 9.1 A visual representation of the ray tracing process (© Henrik / Wikimedia Commons /
CC BY-SA 4.0).

- **Light source** The origin of light in the scene, which is used to calculate how the light interacts with objects.
- **Shadow ray** From the point where the view ray intersects the object, a shadow ray is cast towards the light source. If this ray reaches the light without intersecting any other objects, the original point is lit. If another object blocks the shadow ray, it means the original point is in shadow.

Ray tracing is characterized by several key features that set it apart from other rendering methods. One such feature is backward tracing, where rays are traced from the camera rather than the light source, significantly reducing the number of rays required. Additionally, ray tracing adeptly handles complex interactions like reflections and refractions, accurately simulating the behavior of light as it interacts with different surfaces and materials. This capability allows for the realistic portrayal of a wide array of visual effects, from the subtle nuances of lighting to the intricate patterns of shadows.

Today, ray tracing has gained immense popularity and is increasingly becoming a standard in graphic rendering, especially in high-end applications. Its ability to produce images of exceptional quality and realism has made it a preferred choice in fields ranging from film production and video game development to architectural visualization and virtual reality experiences. This surge in popularity is also attributed to advancements in hardware capabilities, making ray tracing more accessible and feasible for a broader range of applications.

9.1.2   Ray Tracing vs. Rasterization

Again, we meet the word "rasterization" which we first introduced in Chapter 8. Rasterization has long been the cornerstone of rendering techniques in computer graphics, particularly before the widespread adoption of ray tracing. This method involves converting 3D objects into a 2D image by projecting each object onto the screen's plane, primarily focusing on the object's vertices and edges. Rasterization efficiently handles these conversions, making it highly effective for real-time rendering applications.

In the evolving landscape of graphic rendering, understanding the differences and relative strengths of rasterization and ray tracing is crucial. While both techniques aim to produce high-quality images, their approaches and outcomes vary significantly. If we were to highlight the key difference in one sentence, it would be: Ray tracing calculates color for each pixel when viewing an object, whereas rasterization simply projects that object onto the screen. This comparison will delve into the pros and cons of each method, offering insights into their optimal applications.

Rasterization excels in its speed and efficiency. Its ability to process and render scenes rapidly makes it ideal for real-time applications, such as video games and interactive simulations. The technique is less computationally intensive, allowing for higher frame rates and responsiveness, which are critical in dynamic environments.

The primary limitation of rasterization lies in its struggle with complex lighting and shadow effects. It often requires additional algorithms to simulate these effects, which can still fall short of achieving the realism seen in ray tracing. Rasterization also faces challenges in accurately rendering reflections, refractions, and subtle light interactions.

Ray tracing, in contrast, excels at producing highly realistic images with intricate lighting and shadow effects. Its ability to accurately trace the path of light and simulate its interactions with objects results in images with stunning realism, including realistic reflections, refractions, and subtle lighting nuances.

However, ray tracing is computationally more demanding than rasterization. This higher computational load translates to slower rendering times, which has historically limited its use in real-time applications. The complexity of ray tracing algorithms also requires more robust hardware and specialized optimization techniques.

The contrasting strengths and weaknesses of rasterization and ray tracing underscore the need for specialized hardware to optimize their performance. Particularly for ray tracing, the advent of GPUs equipped with dedicated ray tracing cores has been a game-changer, making it feasible for real-time applications and broadening its practical use beyond high-end, noninteractive applications.

9.1.3   Ray Tracing Hardware

Ray tracing, at its core, is an algorithmic technique for rendering images by simulating the behavior of light interacting with objects within a virtual environment. Fundamentally, this technique can be executed on a variety of hardware platforms, ranging from general-purpose CPUs to specialized GPUs. The essence of ray tracing doesn't inherently require specialized hardware; however, the computationally intensive nature of the process often makes dedicated hardware advantageous, particularly when performance and real-time rendering are key considerations. This distinction underscores that while ray tracing can technically be executed on standard computing hardware, the drive for efficiency, speed, and higher-quality renders has led to the development and adoption of specialized ray tracing hardware.

Ray tracing, as a rendering technique, possesses distinct characteristics that make the development and use of customized hardware both feasible and desirable.

1. **High computational demand** Ray tracing involves a significant amount of computation, particularly because of its detailed and realistic rendering process. This includes calculating light paths, reflections, refractions, and shadows for each pixel, which can be challenging for processing speed, especially in complex scenes or high-resolution outputs.
2. **Consistent calculation patterns** The process of handling ray–object intersections follows relatively fixed patterns. This consistency in calculation allows for the design of specialized hardware components that are optimized specifically for these types of operations, leading to more-efficient processing compared to general-purpose hardware.
3. **Rich parallelism** A key feature of ray tracing is its inherent parallelism. Since each ray is traced independently and the calculations for one ray generally do not depend on others, this allows for parallel processing of multiple rays simultaneously.

Custom hardware can leverage this parallelism to a greater extent than general-purpose CPUs, significantly speeding up the rendering process.

4. **Real-time rendering demand in interactive applications** In applications like video gaming, where real-time interaction is crucial, the demands for real-time ray tracing are high. Customized hardware that can handle ray tracing efficiently makes it possible to achieve the desired level of realism without compromising on performance, which is essential for maintaining user engagement and experience in interactive environments.

The synthesis of the aforementioned characteristics of ray tracing has fueled a multidecade journey towards hardware acceleration, stretching back to the 1980s. This pursuit has been marked by numerous milestones, each contributing to the gradual realization of efficient, hardware-accelerated ray tracing. Early efforts often involved specialized rendering machines (e.g., the LINKS-1 computer graphics system [103]), and progress continued through the 1990s and 2000s with advancements in various ASIC/FPGA-based systems (e.g., VIZARD II [79]) or ray processing units (RPUs) [136], leading to more-sophisticated and faster ray tracing techniques.

A significant leap occurred with the introduction of GPUs with dedicated ray tracing cores, such as Nvidia's RTX series, which emerged as a pivotal development. These specialized cores are tailored to handle the computationally intensive tasks of ray tracing, harnessing the inherent parallelism and consistent calculation patterns to deliver unprecedented rendering speeds. As a result, real-time ray tracing, once a distant dream, has become a tangible reality, particularly evident in the realm of video gaming and interactive media. This evolution has reached a point where GPU ray tracing cores have become a standard configuration in modern GPUs, for example, three popular GPU cards (all released in Q4 of 2022) as shown in Table 9.1, symbolizing the culmination of years of dedicated research and development in this field.

As we delve deeper into the realm of ray tracing, this chapter will specifically utilize the Nvidia RT Core and its associated programming platforms, CUDA and OptiX, as primary examples and case studies to elucidate the core concepts and applications of this technology. While Nvidia's solutions will serve as our reference, it is important to recognize that other vendors offer fundamentally similar ray tracing solutions, albeit with different software environments and system support capabilities. The field of ray tracing is characterized by its highly dynamic and rapidly evolving nature. As such, new advancements in hardware capabilities, alongside the introduction of novel APIs and software enhancements, are constantly reshaping the landscape. This ongoing

Table 9.1 Comparison of Nvidia 4090, AMD 7900 XTX, and Intel Arc A770 GPUs.

GPU model	Codename	Ray tracing hardware
Nvidia GeForce RTX 4090	AD102	128 third generation RT Cores
AMD Radeon RX 7900 XTX	Navi 31	96 ray tracing accelerators
Intel Arc A770	ACM-G10	32 ray tracing units (RTUs)

evolution underscores the need for adaptability and continuous learning to stay abreast of the latest developments in ray tracing technology.

9.2   Ray Tracing in GPUs: A Case Study of Nvidia's RT Core

In this section, we embark on a detailed exploration of ray tracing within the GPU landscape, focusing on Nvidia's pioneering RT Core technology. The journey from the inception of real-time ray tracing to its current state of widespread implementation is both fascinating and instructive. We'll begin with a historical overview, tracing Nvidia's path through the development and refinement of RT Cores, which have played a pivotal role in bringing ray tracing to the forefront of graphics technology. Following this, we'll delve into the precise operations of the RT Core hardware, demystifying how it accelerates the complex computations involved in ray tracing. Complementing the hardware's capabilities, we'll examine Nvidia's OptiX, the dedicated software environment designed to maximize the potential of RT Cores. By understanding both the hardware and software aspects of this technology, we'll gain comprehensive insights into the inner workings and the transformative impact of Nvidia's RT Core on the realm of computer graphics and beyond.

9.2.1   A Brief History of Nvidia RT Core

Since the introduction of ray tracing hardware acceleration, Nvidia has been at the forefront, continually evolving its RT Core technology. This has resulted in three distinct generations of RT Cores, each marking a significant leap forward in ray tracing capabilities.

- **First generation: Turing architecture [105]** The first generation of RT Cores was introduced with Nvidia's Turing architecture. These were groundbreaking at the time, representing the first dedicated hardware for ray tracing acceleration in consumer graphics cards. Turing RT Cores brought real-time ray tracing into the realm of possibility, allowing for reflections, refractions, and shadows to be rendered with a level of realism far beyond what had been possible with traditional rasterization techniques. This first iteration set the foundation, handling the intensive computations for ray-triangle intersection tests which are central to the ray tracing process.
- **Second generation: Ampere architecture [106]** The second generation of RT Cores came with the Ampere architecture, which built upon the strengths of the Turing cores. Ampere's RT Cores were designed to be more efficient and powerful, offering up to double the throughput. This meant faster performance and the ability to handle more complex scenes and lighting effects. The second-generation cores also introduced hardware support for ray traced motion blur, significantly enhancing the visual fidelity of moving objects in real-time applications.
- **Third generation: Ada Lovelace architecture [107]** The latest, third generation of RT Cores is found in the Ada Lovelace architecture. These cores are even more

efficient and feature improvements in concurrency, enabling them to perform ray tracing tasks alongside traditional shading. This allows for an even more seamless integration of ray tracing into games and applications, pushing the boundaries of what's achievable in terms of photorealism and complex lighting effects.

In Chapter 6, we presented a detailed illustration of how RT Cores are woven into the GPU's architecture (see Figure 6.1 in Chapter 6). Readers are encouraged to revisit this diagram to better understand the strategic placement of an RT Core within each streaming multiprocessor (SM), alongside the CUDA cores. This architectural design has remained consistent across all three generations of Nvidia's RT Cores. With each successive generation, Nvidia has made significant strides in the realm of graphics technology, inching ever closer to achieving real-time photorealistic rendering. As Nvidia continues to advance its RT Core technology, these cores are poised to become increasingly instrumental in shaping the future of gaming, cinematic production, and immersive virtual reality experiences.

9.2.2   What Does the Hardware Do, Exactly?

Modern computing systems are best characterized by their hybrid nature, seamlessly blending hardware and software to create comprehensive solutions. In these systems, hardware serves as the backbone, performing core operations with speed and efficiency, while software constructs the environment within which these operations take place. This symbiosis of software and hardware is not just an engineering feat but also an intricate dance of art and science, unfolding within a vast design space of possibilities. The evolution of computers alongside the development of reduced instruction set computing (RISC) chips exemplifies this codesign approach, where hardware efficiency and software capabilities mutually enhance each other. Similarly, the function of hardware RT Cores in supporting ray tracing applications epitomizes this philosophy. By handling the computationally demanding tasks of ray tracing, RT Cores allow the software to fully harness the realism and precision of this rendering technique, creating a unified and potent graphical computing platform.

So, what does the hardware do, exactly? To answer this, we must delve into the intricacies of ray tracing technology and the role of RT Cores within it. This chapter will unravel three fundamental components: Firstly, the core process of ray tracing itself, which is the essence of what RT Cores are designed to accelerate. Secondly, we will examine the concept of bounding volume hierarchy (BVH), a crucial data structure that RT Cores utilize for efficiently managing complex scenes. And thirdly, the entire ray tracing pipeline will be dissected to understand how software and hardware responsibilities are distributed and coordinated. By dissecting these elements, we can appreciate how hardware RT Cores and software algorithms come together to form a cohesive and efficient ray tracing system.

At the heart of ray tracing lies a deceptively simple yet complex process, primarily concerned with two key determinations (as shown in Figure 9.1): (1) whether a ray intersects with any object in the scene, and (2) the subsequent action based on whether there's a hit or a miss. The first aspect revolves around calculating if and where a ray, emanating from the camera or eye, intersects objects in the virtual environment. This intersection is crucial as it lays the groundwork for how light behaves in the scene. The second aspect delves into the response to these intersections. When a ray hits an object, the software must decide the ray's next course – whether it reflects, refracts, or gets absorbed, depending on the surface's properties or material characteristics. On the other hand, a miss generally results in the ray capturing the background or environment lighting.

These seemingly straightforward steps give rise to recursive ray tracing, where initial rays can spawn secondary rays to simulate complex light interactions like reflections and refractions. This recursive nature not only contributes to the realism in the rendered image but also adds to the computational complexity, necessitating sophisticated programming to accurately depict various surface materials and their interaction with light. Therefore, while the fundamental principles of ray tracing might appear basic, the myriad of permutations and interactions they enable, and the necessity for precise programming of material behaviors, make it an intricate and nuanced process.

In the realm of ray tracing, the generation of countless ray-to-object intersection calculations is inevitable, especially given the high-resolution outputs, scenes rich with diverse objects, and the complex interactions arising from recursive ray shooting. Each ray potentially interacts with every object in the scene, leading to a staggering number of calculations. The naive approach to this problem would be a brute-force method, where each ray is compared against every object to determine intersections. However, as we have seen in previous discussions, such as with hash join techniques, there are often more efficient methods than brute-force comparisons. This is where the concept of BVH comes into play; BVH is a tree structure that organizes objects in a scene in such a way that it significantly reduces the number of comparisons needed to determine ray–object intersections. By hierarchically segmenting the space, BVH allows the ray tracing algorithm to quickly eliminate large groups of objects that a particular ray cannot possibly intersect, thereby streamlining the intersection testing process and dramatically enhancing efficiency.

To illustrate how BVH streamlines ray tracing, consider a scene composed of several polygons. These polygons can be organized into a hierarchical tree structure, where each node of the tree represents a group of polygons, and each group is enclosed within a bounding volume. A common type of bounding volume used in BVH is the axis-aligned bounding box (AABB). An AABB is a box that completely encloses a group of objects (like polygons) and is aligned with the coordinate axes, which simplifies the mathematics required to test for intersections. When a ray is traced through the scene, the ray tracing algorithm first checks for intersections with these AABBs, starting from the root of the tree and moving down. If a ray intersects an AABB, there is a possibility that it might intersect the polygons within it, prompting further checks. However, if there's no intersection with an AABB, the algorithm can immediately discard all the polygons inside that box, significantly reducing the number of intersection tests. This hierarchical culling process makes it much more efficient to determine which polygons a ray interacts with, particularly in complex scenes with a large number of objects.

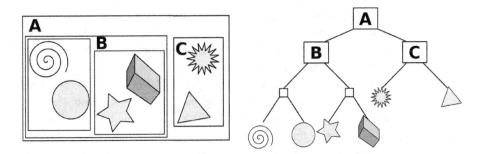

Figure 9.2 Example of a BVH demonstrating how multiple geometric objects are organized into a tree structure, akin to an R-tree (or its variants) in database terminology (© Schreiberx / Wikimedia Commons / CC BY-SA 3.0).

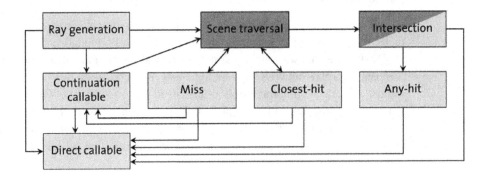

Figure 9.3 The ray tracing pipeline in Nvidia OptiX as per the programming guide [108]. It highlights that hardware executes the dark area parts, including the entire Scene traversal and half the Intersection box. The other areas represent user-provided callback functions. The Intersection box is partially shaded to indicate that hardware only supports triangle-based ray–object intersections, while custom intersection functions are needed for other geometric objects. This distinction emphasizes the hybrid nature of ray tracing in OptiX, blending hardware acceleration with software customization.

Figure 9.2 shows an example BVH structure that can let readers have a quick picture in mind how the above process works.

In the intricate dance of ray tracing, the specific tasks delegated to hardware are crucial for understanding the overall process. The core operations the hardware performs are BVH traversal and triangle hit testing, as outlined in Nvidia's OptiX framework depicted in Figure 9.3. The operation of BVH traversal allows the hardware to efficiently navigate through the scene's hierarchy to identify potential ray intersections, a process that reduces the computational load by quickly discarding irrelevant areas. The subsequent operation, triangle hit testing, determines precise intersections between the rays and the scene's geometry. These operations are fundamental to accelerating the ray tracing process, offloading the most computationally demanding tasks from the software.

The intricacies of ray interactions are managed by user programming, which defines how rays respond upon intersection with objects. This is where the ray generation, scene traversal, and intersection stages, as seen in the flow chart, come into play. The user program dictates actions for various ray events, such as a miss, closest-hit, or any-hit—terms that correspond to different potential outcomes of a ray's journey through the scene. For instance, a "miss" program handles the scenario where a ray does not intersect with any object, while "closest-hit" and "any-hit" programs define shading behaviors for rays that do intersect with objects. The upcoming subsection will delve into these user-defined aspects, explaining how they contribute to the final rendered image and providing a deeper understanding of the ray tracing pipeline's customizable nature.

9.2.3   Nvidia OptiX: The Software Environment

After examining the pivotal role of hardware in the ray tracing process, we now shift focus to the software that unleashes the full power of this profound technology. Nvidia OptiX stands as the software foundation, a critical environment that orchestrates the complex interplay between rays of light and the geometries they encounter. This sophisticated ray tracing framework offers developers a robust set of GPU-accelerated library functions and APIs designed to work in concert with Nvidia's RT Cores. OptiX simplifies the complexities of the underlying hardware, providing developers with a more accessible and versatile platform for crafting advanced ray tracing applications.

While Nvidia GPUs are tailored for their proprietary CUDA and OptiX platforms, they represent just one avenue in the broader landscape of ray tracing technology. The industry has also embraced standards like Vulkan [119] and DirectX on Windows [93], both of which provide robust support for ray tracing across a range of hardware, including GPUs from Intel and AMD. These competitors offer their own specific APIs to harness the capabilities of their hardware. Although the implementations and APIs provided by different vendors may vary, the core principles of ray tracing remain constant across platforms. This universality echoes the hardware segment, where despite differences in architecture or design, the foundational elements of ray tracing – such as efficient handling of intersections and lighting calculations – hold true industry-wide, ensuring a cohesive approach to rendering lifelike scenes.

In this subsection, we will use a program example to explore how OptiX enables developers to build customizable programs for the various stages of ray processing. While ray tracing and computer graphics are complex subjects, fully explaining their intricacies is beyond the scope of this book. Instead, we will focus on providing a clear and accessible overview of how OptiX supports the essential components of the ray tracing pipeline. Figure 9.3 has already introduced the concept of what the user needs to program: implementing various callback functions. These functions form the backbone of user-defined behavior in the ray tracing process and will be our focus as we examine how OptiX empowers developers to harness the full potential of GPU-accelerated ray tracing.

At its core, a ray tracing application hinges on three fundamental requisites.

- **Scene** It necessitates the design of a spatial scene populated with a set of objects to define the virtual environment. This scene is the canvas upon which light and geometry interact.
- **Ray** A ray shooting framework is essential; it determines the origin, direction, and other properties of the rays that will traverse the scene. This framework governs how rays are cast from the camera or light sources and is critical in simulating how light behaves in the real world.
- **Action** Designing corresponding actions for when rays intersect with objects is paramount. These actions, which include "hit" or "miss" behaviors, dictate the resulting visual effects, such as reflections, refractions, or shadows, contributing to the realism and aesthetic of the rendered image.

Together, these elements form the triad that underpins any ray tracing application, each playing a pivotal role in the algorithm's ability to simulate lifelike lighting and shadows. Within a ray tracing application, several critical functions must be implemented to handle different aspects of ray and object interactions.

- **Intersection** This function is responsible for determining the point at which a ray intersects with an object in the scene. For nontriangle primitives, users need to provide a custom implementation that defines how these intersections are calculated.
- **Miss** The miss function defines what happens when a ray does not intersect with any object. This typically involves setting the background color or environment effects that the ray would capture in the absence of other objects.
- **Any-hit** This function is invoked when a ray potentially intersects with multiple objects, and any intersection is sufficient for the application's requirements. It is often used for shadow rays or transparency effects, where finding just one blocker or refractor is enough.
- **Closest-hit** The closest-hit function is crucial for determining the nearest intersection point along the ray's path. This function calculates the exact color, texture, and shading based on the material properties of the object that the ray hits first.

These functions are integral to the ray tracing pipeline, each serving a unique purpose that contributes to the final rendered scene's complexity and depth. Equipped with an understanding of these essential functions within the ray tracing pipeline, we are now well prepared to embark on explaining our first ray tracing program. This initial example, sourced from the Nvidia OptiX 7.0 SDK, will be kept simple to illustrate the fundamental process of rendering an image that includes a single triangle as shown in Figure 9.4. The simplicity of this example serves to clarify the core concepts of ray tracing without the complexity of a more-intricate scene, laying the groundwork for more-advanced programming and rendering techniques that will be explored later.

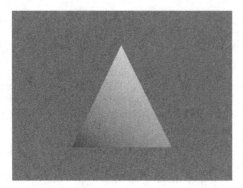

Figure 9.4 A triangle rendered using ray tracing in a background, originally produced in color by the Nvidia OptiX program. This image is presented in grayscale in this book, yet still effectively distinguishes the brightness between the triangle's interior and its surrounding background.

9.3   An Image Rendering Example Based on Ray Tracing

As we approach the task of rendering a simple triangle image through ray tracing, it is crucial to keep in mind that ray tracing is fundamentally a tool for simulating a 3D world on a 2D screen. This requires us to adopt a 3D perspective right from the outset. Recall the three fundamental elements we previously outlined: the scene, the rays, and the actions. For our triangle rendering task, we must devise a strategy that leverages ray tracing to effectively generate the desired image within this 3D context.

It is important to understand that there is considerable design flexibility in how one can implement a given task using ray tracing. The approach we introduce here is crafted for educational purposes, to illustrate the basic principles and mechanics of the process. However, this is not the only solution; the field of ray tracing offers a vast design space, allowing for various innovative implementations.

9.3.1   The Logical Part

Our exploration will begin with an overview of the logical workflow required to render the triangle. Following this, we will delve into the specifics of how this process is implemented in the Nvidia OptiX environment. This step-by-step approach will not only demystify the fundamental operations of ray tracing but also provide a practical example of how these concepts are translated into OptiX code.

Figure 9.5 provides a comprehensive visual representation of the process to generate the targeted triangle image within a 3D space. Taking into account the three fundamental elements of ray tracing, we can summarize the approach as follows.

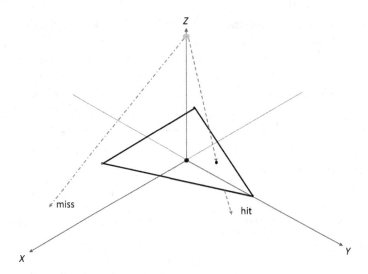

Figure 9.5 Illustrating the concept of image rendering for Figure 9.4, this image depicts a triangle placed on the *XY* plane, observed from a camera positioned along the Z-axis and directed downwards towards the triangle. This perspective effectively highlights the rendering process and the spatial arrangement of the objects in the scene.

- **Scene** The scene is set within a 3D coordinate system, where a triangle is placed on the *XY* plane. The coordinates of the triangle's vertices are designated as $(-0.5, -0.5, 0)$, $(0.5, -0.5, 0)$, and $(0, 0.5, 0)$, respectively.
- **Ray** Positioned at $(0, 0, 2)$, the eye or camera is strategically located to ensure that the rays it emits encompass the area of the triangle. This setup, as illustrated in the figure, ensures optimal ray coverage of the target object.
- **Action** In terms of rendering actions, rays that miss the triangle result in a background color being generated, representing the miss event. Conversely, rays that successfully intersect with the triangle produce a color based on the specific point of impact.

This organized breakdown offers a clear understanding of how each element – scene, ray, and action – plays a vital role in constructing the image, laying the foundation for the subsequent explanation of the rendering process.

9.3.2 Scene

We first introduce how the scene is implemented in Nvidia OptiX. Of course, simply defining a triangle is easy, as the following code shows.

```
const std::array<float3, 3> vertices =
    { {
            { -0.5f, -0.5f, 0.0f },
            {  0.5f, -0.5f, 0.0f },
            {  0.0f,  0.5f, 0.0f }
    } };
```

However, to integrate this defined triangle into the ray tracing pipeline effectively, it is necessary to execute three major operations to construct a geometry acceleration structure (GAS) for it. It is important to note that the subsequent code snippet serves primarily as a demonstration. While it may not provide exhaustive explanations, readers with a background in C and CUDA should be able to grasp the essential aspects of the code. This snippet illustrates the foundational steps required to translate the triangle's geometrical definition into a format that the ray tracing pipeline can utilize effectively.

1. Allocate memory on the GPU to hold this triangle.

```
const size_t vertices_size = sizeof( float3 )*vertices.size();
CUdeviceptr d_vertices=0;
CUDA_CHECK( cudaMalloc( reinterpret_cast<void**>( &d_vertices ),
                   vertices_size ) );
CUDA_CHECK( cudaMemcpy(
                       reinterpret_cast<void*>( d_vertices ),
                       vertices.data(),
                       vertices_size,
                       cudaMemcpyHostToDevice
                       ) );
```

2. Define an OptixBuildInput object for that triangle.

```
const uint32_t triangle_input_flags[1] = { OPTIX_GEOMETRY_FLAG_NONE };
OptixBuildInput triangle_input = {};
triangle_input.type                         =
                            OPTIX_BUILD_INPUT_TYPE_TRIANGLES;
triangle_input.triangleArray.vertexFormat   =
                            OPTIX_VERTEX_FORMAT_FLOAT3;
triangle_input.triangleArray.numVertices    =
        static_cast<uint32_t>( vertices.size() );
triangle_input.triangleArray.vertexBuffers = &d_vertices;
triangle_input.triangleArray.flags         = triangle_input_flags;
triangle_input.triangleArray.numSbtRecords = 1;
```

3. Call optixAccelBuild to create the acceleration structure.

```
OPTIX_CHECK( optixAccelBuild(
                   context,
                   0,                   // CUDA stream
                   &accel_options,
                   &triangle_input,
                   1,                   // num build inputs
                   d_temp_buffer_gas,
                   gas_buffer_sizes.tempSizeInBytes,
                   d_buffer_temp_output_gas_and_compacted_size,
                   gas_buffer_sizes.outputSizeInBytes,
                   &gas_handle,
                   &emitProperty,   // emitted property list
                   1                // num emitted properties
       ) );
```

9.3.3 Ray

Having established the scene with our target triangle positioned on the *XY* plane, we now shift our focus to the generation of rays. The ray generation process in this context can be thought of as comprising two fundamental subprocesses: the definition of the camera, which serves as the origin point for all rays, and the method for systematically generating a ray corresponding to each pixel in the target image. Let us begin by delving into the first subprocess, which involves setting up the camera.

Configuring a camera in Nvidia OptiX involves more than just defining its position, although for our current setup, the camera is fixed at (0,0,2), directly above the triangle. A comprehensive camera setup in OptiX requires several additional parameters and the establishment of a UVW Frame. The following code snippet provides an illustration of this process.

```
Camera cam;
cam.setEye( {0.0f, 0.0f, 2.0f} );
cam.setLookat( {0.0f, 0.0f, 0.0f} );
cam.setUp( {0.0f, 1.0f, 3.0f} );
cam.setFovY( 45.0f );
cam.setAspectRatio( (float)width / (float)height );
```

This code configures the camera, or "eye," at the position (0,0,2), with its gaze directed towards the origin (0,0,0). Understanding the remaining parameters requires an immersive 3D perspective. The "up" vector of the camera is set to (0,1,3), analogous to identifying the direction of the sky when looking straight ahead. "FovY" stands for the field of view in the *Y*-axis, indicating the breadth of the camera's observational angle. Lastly, the aspect ratio is set based on the image width and height, preserving the proportions of the rendered image. Each parameter plays a crucial role in defining how the camera perceives and captures the 3D scene, ultimately influencing the final rendered output.

With these parameters, we can generate the camera's UVW frame. In 3D rendering, cameras are often represented by a coordinate system defined by three orthogonal vectors: U (right), V (up), and W (forward). This coordinate system is crucial for defining the camera's orientation and perspective in the scene. In OptiX, you typically set up the camera's UVW frame in the ray generation program. This setup involves calculating the U, V, and W vectors based on the camera's position, target, and up vector, and then using these vectors to generate rays for each pixel in the image.

To gain a deeper understanding of how the UVW frame is established in the camera setup, let us examine the following C++ code snippet. In this context, "this" refers to the pointer to the object that the function belongs to, and the attributes referenced after "this" can be interpreted based on our earlier discussion of camera parameters.

```
void Camera::UVWFrame(float3& U, float3& V, float3& W) const
{
    W = this.Lookat - this.Eye;
    float wlen = length(W);
    U = normalize(cross(W, this.Up));
```

```
V = normalize(cross(U, W));

float vlen = wlen * tanf(0.5f * this.FovY * M_PIf / 180.0f);
V *= vlen;
float ulen = vlen * this.AspectRatio;
U *= ulen;
}
```

In this function, UVWFrame, we calculate the vectors U, V, and W, which constitute the camera's coordinate frame. The vector W is determined as the direction from the camera's eye position ("this.Eye") to the lookat point ("this.Lookat"). U and V are then computed as orthogonal vectors to W, forming a basis for the camera's viewing plane. The length of V is adjusted according to the camera's field of view ("this.FovY") and the distance to the lookat point ("wlen"), while U's length is scaled based on the aspect ratio ("this.AspectRatio"). This function effectively sets up the camera's view frame, aligning it with the desired orientation and perspective within the 3D scene.

Figure 9.6 shows an 3D coordinate system that illustrate the relationships of these concepts. To understand the figure, we begin by noticing that the eye is at (0,0,2) and the lookat position is the original (0,0,0). So, with the above code, we know W (lookat − eye = (0, 0, −2)) is a vector pointing downward. Then, we can calculate U,V, before scaling, are actually (1,0,0) and (0,1,0), according to the cross production results, which can also follow the right-hand rule. The lengths of the three vectors are not normalized. The length of V can be determined by the tangent function of the angle of field of view,

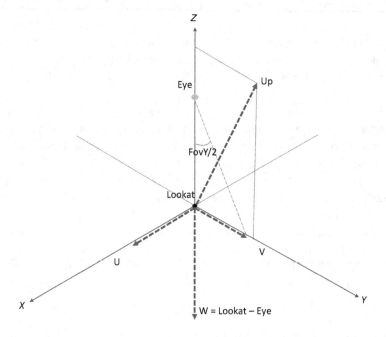

Figure 9.6 An illustration of how the camera UVW frame is made. Note that the camera is located at the eye position.

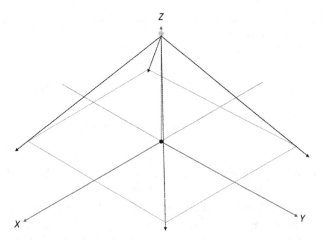

Figure 9.7 An illustration of rays that cover the area for the image to be generated. The triangle in the image is ignored.

as illustrated in Figure 9.6 and shown by the earlier code. Correspondingly, the length of U is determined further by the AspectRatio.

Having configured the camera, our next task is to generate the rays. Figure 9.7 provides an illustration of rays originating from the camera and extending into the 3D space. In this depiction, the focus is on the rays themselves and the boundaries they form based on their corresponding pixels in the image, rather than on the triangle within the scene. This visualization aids in understanding the ray generation within the OptiX programming framework.

In OptiX, the user is required to specify the dimensions of the pixels to be rendered, which in our case are the width and height of the target image. The OptiX Runtime then automatically launches GPU threads, with each thread dedicated to executing the ray tracing function for its assigned pixel. Essentially, the user must implement a specialized kernel function that corresponds directly to a pixel in the image and, consequently, to the index of the thread. The following pseudocode snippet illustrates how this process is set up.

```
extern "C" __global__ void __raygen__rg()
{
    const uint3 idx = optixGetLaunchIndex();
    const uint3 dim = optixGetLaunchDimensions();

    const float3    U       = Get(U);
    const float3    V       = Get(v);
    const float3    W       = Get(w);
    const float2    d = 2.0f * make_float2(
            static_cast<float>( idx.x ) / static_cast<float>( dim.x ),
            static_cast<float>( idx.y ) / static_cast<float>( dim.y )
            ) - 1.0f;

    const float3 origin     = Get(cam_eye);
    const float3 direction  = normalize( d.x * U + d.y * V + W );
```

```
float3        payload_rgb;
optix_trace( params.handle,
        origin,
        direction,
        0.00f,   // tmin
        1e16f,   // tmax
        &payload_rgb );

final_image[idx.y * image_width + idx.x] = make_color( payload_rgb );
}
```

The provided code example, derived from the Nvidia OptiX SDK 7.0, conveys several critical pieces of information in a simplified format. Firstly, at its core, the code represents a CUDA kernel function. This function is capable of determining the thread index and the corresponding pixel's position within the entire image. Secondly, based on this information, each thread computes the specific ray that needs to be generated for the pixel it is assigned to render. Finally, once the color of each pixel is established, the composite image can be assembled.

The pivotal question then becomes: what specific ray should a thread generate for its assigned pixel? The function initially retrieves the UVW frame of the camera, setting the stage for the subsequent calculations. It then proceeds to compute the value of "d" for each pixel in both the "x" and "y" directions within the range of $(-1, 1)$. This step is crucial for directing each pixel's ray within the predetermined range. With this information, the direction of each ray is determined. Given that the ray's origin is fixed, we now possess all the necessary data to define each ray's trajectory. The process then advances with the invocation of the OptiX trace function, initiating the ray tracing operation. From this point onward, the execution of callback functions for either hit or miss events during the ray tracing process is automatic.

9.3.4   Action

As we shift our focus to the "action" aspect of ray tracing, several considerations come into play. Firstly, since our object of interest in this case study is a triangle, the hardware itself automatically handles the determination of whether a ray intersects with it. This means there is no need for us to implement a customized intersection function for this purpose. Secondly, in our example with only one object (the triangle), there is no practical distinction between any-hit and closest-hit scenarios. Therefore, we only need to implement one of these functions. Finally, we must address the situation where rays miss the triangle, which is a critical part of the rendering process.

Considering these factors, the following code snippets represent the "action" component for our ray tracing application. The "__miss__ms" function defines the behavior for rays that do not intersect the triangle, setting a background color. The "__closesthit__ch" function calculates the color at the point of intersection based on the barycentric coordinates of the hit. Additionally, the setPayload function is used to set the color payload that will be returned to the ray generation program. The following shows how these components are implemented.

```
extern "C" __global__ void __miss__ms()
{
    setPayload( backgroundcolor );
}
extern "C" __global__ void __closesthit__ch()
{

    const float2 barycentrics = optixGetTriangleBarycentrics();
    setPayload( make_float3( barycentrics, 1.0f ) );
}
static __forceinline__ __device__ void setPayload( float3 p )
{
    optixSetPayload_0( float_as_int( p.x ) );
    optixSetPayload_1( float_as_int( p.y ) );
    optixSetPayload_2( float_as_int( p.z ) );
}
```

An essential aspect to highlight in our ray tracing example is the functionality of the closest-hit action. In the provided code, when a hit occurs, the primary objective of the hit function is to ascertain the color at the point of intersection. However, since our object is a triangle, a primitive type inherently supported by the hardware, the user's program doesn't manipulate the intersection point directly. Instead, it relies on retrieving the corresponding payload information.

A key function here is optixGetTriangleBarycentrics, which warrants further explanation. OptiX doesn't directly provide the coordinates of the intersection point between the ray and the triangle. Rather, it offers the barycentric coordinates of the intersection point relative to the triangle's vertices within the 3D environment. These coordinates are crucial as they allow the program to interpolate properties like color, texture coordinates, or normals at the point of intersection, based on the attributes of the triangle's vertices. Understanding this subtlety is vital for comprehending how OptiX handles ray–triangle intersection tests and how it facilitates the rendering process in a 3D space.

9.4   RTSort: A Ray-Tracing-Based Sorting Algorithm

In this section, we embark on an exploration of "RTSort," a novel sorting algorithm that leverages the unique capabilities of ray tracing hardware. Traditionally associated with graphical rendering, ray tracing hardware possesses untapped potential in a variety of computational tasks, sorting being a particularly intriguing application. This section will first extend our understanding of ray tracing beyond its conventional use in rendering, illustrating its versatility. We will then provide an introduction to counting sort, a fundamental sorting technique, to lay the groundwork for understanding RTSort. Following this, we will delve into the conceptual framework of RTSort, examining how it synergizes the methodologies of counting sort with ray tracing technology. Finally, we will analyze RTSort's performance, offering insights into its efficiency and potential impact on the future of computational tasks. This journey from theory to practice will not only highlight the innovative use of ray tracing hardware but also open up possibilities for its application in areas previously unexplored.

9.4.1   Beyond Rendering: Extending the Usage of Ray Tracing

While image rendering, as exemplified in the aforementioned triangle example, is a specialized application, the functionality of RT Cores is fundamentally rooted in BVH traversal and triangle hit testing. These capabilities, though initially conceived for rendering purposes, are not inherently limited to just that. They hold the potential for broader applications beyond their original design scope. However, to leverage these hardware features effectively in nonrendering contexts, any application must be adeptly translated into a ray tracing scene, as required by frameworks like OptiX. This translation is key to unlocking the versatility of RT Cores, allowing them to extend their utility beyond the conventional bounds of image rendering and into new computational domains.

The previous example, featuring a solitary triangle, does not fully showcase the strengths of RT Cores or the acceleration structures that are adept at organizing numerous geometric objects. However, it effectively illustrates the fundamental elements of ray tracing: scene, ray, and action. When considering applications that could be adapted to a ray-tracing-based framework, it is imperative for designers to thoughtfully conceptualize these three aspects. Designing a scene in a ray tracing context, determining how rays interact within it, and defining the corresponding actions, require careful deliberation. The complexity lies in the vast array of possibilities that a 3D space offers, making the design process both challenging and rich with potential. Each decision in this process can significantly influence the efficiency and effectiveness of leveraging ray tracing hardware for applications beyond traditional rendering.

When contemplating the adaptation of computation tasks to ray tracing, two critical questions arise. The first, an enabling question, asks whether a specific computational task can feasibly be converted into a ray tracing problem. The second, a question of performance, considers whether a ray-tracing-based solution offers any performance advantages over traditional GPU parallel implementations or even over original CPU versions. Addressing these questions is not straightforward; there is no universal guideline or automated mechanism to seamlessly translate computational tasks into ray tracing solutions. Performance considerations, in particular, are complex and multifaceted. They depend on a myriad of factors including the inherent complexity of the algorithm, the intricacies involved in converting it to a ray tracing framework, the capabilities of the hardware, and the breadth of optimization possibilities. Moreover, the rapid evolution of RT hardware adds a dynamic element to this equation, constantly shifting the boundaries of what is possible and advantageous in the realm of ray tracing applications.

Having explored the broader potential of ray tracing hardware beyond rendering, we now turn our attention to a practical case study: employing ray tracing for sorting. The choice of sorting as our focal task is strategic and purposeful. Sorting is not only a fundamental cornerstone of computer science but has also been a recurring theme in this book, as evidenced by our previous discussion on bitonic sorting to introduce GPU capabilities. Using sorting to demonstrate the extension of ray tracing hardware into general data management tasks offers a clear and relatable example. It provides readers with an intuitive framework to visualize how familiar data management challenges can be innovatively addressed using ray tracing technology. This case study aims to bridge the conceptual gap between well-known computational tasks and the novel application of ray tracing hardware, offering insights into its versatile utility.

9.4.2   An Introduction to Counting Sort

As our readers are already familiar with the concept of sorting, it is clear that the essence of any sorting process is to determine the correct position for each element in a sorted sequence. Traditional sorting algorithms, like the bitonic sorting algorithm discussed in previous chapters, typically achieve this through a process of continuous adjustment, with elements gradually finding their final positions. This raises an intriguing question: *Is it possible to calculate the final position of each element directly, without iterative adjustments?* Counting sort [41] answers this question affirmatively. Unlike conventional algorithms that rely on comparisons and swaps, counting sort uniquely calculates the final position of each element based on the frequencies of elements. This simple yet powerful idea forms the cornerstone of counting sort, distinguishing it from other sorting methodologies.

Though less renowned than some of its counterparts, counting sort has a rich history in computer science, invented by Harold H. Seward in 1954. It is a noncomparison-based sorting technique, falling under the category of radix sort algorithms due to its method of sorting based on the digits or units of numbers. This approach stands in stark contrast to comparison-based methodologies. Counting sort's mechanism, which focuses on element frequency rather than direct comparisons, sets it apart both historically and operationally, making it particularly efficient in scenarios where input values have a limited and well-defined range.

For example, consider an array of integers ranging from 1 to 10. Counting sort first tallies each integer's frequency in the array, creating a count array. It then uses this count array to determine each element's position in the sorted output. For instance, if "3" appears twice, the count array will reflect this, placing "3" accordingly in the sorted array.

Fundamentally, counting sort can be distilled into three major steps.

1. **Step 1: Frequency indication array** Create a frequency indication array for the input array, spanning the domain between the minimum and maximum values. Record each element's frequency, indicating its occurrences.
2. **Step 2: Prefix sum calculation** Perform a prefix sum on the frequency array to calculate the cumulative frequency, representing each element's final position in the sorted array.
3. **Step 3: Copying elements to sorted positions** Use the cumulative frequency data to correctly place each input element in the sorted array, copying them to specific indices as determined by the prefix sum results.

The combination of steps 1 and 2 effectively creates an indication array that delineates the final destination of each element in the sorted array. When we connect this concept to ray tracing, it becomes apparent how counting sort's process could be adapted to the operations of ray tracing hardware. The challenge lies in translating the combinational effect of these steps into an operation that can be efficiently executed by RT Cores, with their specialized capabilities in managing spatial data. In the following paragraphs, we will explore how this translation can be realized, laying the groundwork for a ray-tracing-based implementation of counting sort.

9.4.3   RTSort: An Idea of Bridging Sorting and Ray Tracing

We venture into a groundbreaking territory where the principles of sorting algorithms intersect with the advanced capabilities of ray tracing hardware. RTSort represents a novel approach, transcending traditional boundaries to harness the power of ray tracing for sorting data. This idea is not just an experimental fusion of disparate computing fields; it is a testament to the evolving versatility of ray tracing technology. Here, we will explore the conceptual framework of RTSort, examining how the essential operations of a counting sort-like algorithm can be reimagined and executed within a ray tracing environment. Our discussion will delve into the intricacies of mapping sorting tasks onto ray tracing processes, addressing the challenges and innovations this unique combination presents. By bridging sorting and ray tracing, RTSort opens a new avenue for computational efficiency and expands the application scope of ray tracing hardware beyond its traditional graphical domain.

Now that we have distilled the essence of counting sort into determining the precise position of each element in the sorted result, let us consider the next critical step. For any given element, its rightful place in the sorted array is fundamentally dictated by the quantity of elements that are smaller than it. The challenge, and indeed the crux of transforming this problem into a ray tracing paradigm, lies in conceptualizing a scenario where a ray influences only those objects that are logically smaller than a given value, while remaining theoretically unaffected by its target. This notion forms the cornerstone of our approach: devising a method within the ray tracing framework where rays can simulate this counting and positioning process. By reimagining the elements of the array as objects in a 3D space, we can explore how a ray's interaction with these objects can be used to deduce their order, akin to counting how many elements are smaller, thereby mapping the counting sort logic onto ray tracing operations.

Figure 9.8 offers a visual representation of the RTSort algorithm. Although the figure depicts a 2D X–Y coordinate system, it is important to note that there is also a Z-axis, which is used to orient triangles perpendicular to the X-axis. For the sake of simplicity, let us consider that the numbers to be sorted are positive integers and unique. Given an input array, $input = v_0, v_1, \ldots, v_{n-1}$, RTSort arranges a ray and a triangle for each $v_i \in input$ according to the following rules.

- **Triangle** Place a triangle along the X-axis at the position corresponding to v_i. If we disregard the Z-axis for a moment, this can be visualized as placing a vertical line. The triangle's height, h, should exceed the maximum number in $input$, positioning the top vertex of the triangle at $(v_i, h, 0)$. Considering the Z-axis, the triangle extends

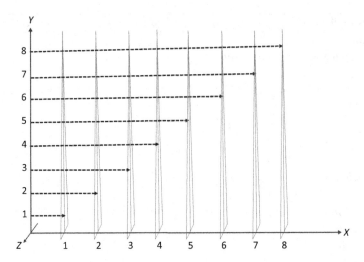

Figure 9.8 An illustration of RTSort.

along it, with its two bottom vertices defined at $(v_i, 0, -z)$ and $(v_i, 0, +z)$, where z is an arbitrary value.

- **Ray** For each v_i, generate a ray originating from the Y-axis at the location v_i, extending along the X-axis. The ray's origin is $(0, v_i, 0)$, and it extends to $(v_i, v_i, 0)$. As illustrated, this ray will intersect the triangle corresponding to v_i, cross over some, and not reach others. Obviously, the ray travels only on the X–Y plane.

In this ray tracing scenario, the number of triangles intersected by a ray corresponding to an element v_i directly indicates the element's position in the final sorted array. Along with the scene and ray setup as depicted in Figure 9.8, the action component is straightforward: For each intersection ("hit") encountered by a ray, we increment a hit counter for that ray by one. This approach, though seemingly simple, effectively leverages ray tracing technology to determine the sorted order of elements in an array. By counting the intersections each ray makes, we can map these counts to the positions of the elements, thereby translating the ray tracing interactions into a sorted sequence.

Algorithm 9.1 outlines the core framework of the RTSort algorithm, focusing on its logical structure while abstracting away the intricate details of ray tracing and the Nvidia OptiX specifics. This algorithm is divided into three distinct phases, each represented by a for loop in the framework. The first phase is dedicated to scene construction, where the necessary elements and their spatial relationships are established. The second phase involves ray shooting, during which the any-hit function is automatically invoked to track the interactions between rays and scene elements. The final phase compiles the output results, effectively sorting the elements based on the ray interactions. A key aspect of RTSort's design is its inherent parallelizability: Each for loop can be executed concurrently without any interelement dependencies. This parallel structure allows RTSort to leverage the full computational power of ray tracing hardware, showcasing its potential for general computational tasks beyond traditional rendering applications.

Algorithm 9.1 RTSort algorithm for a set of positive and unique numbers.

1: $input \leftarrow \{v_1, \ldots, v_n\}$
2: **for** each element i in $input$ **do**
3:     $x \leftarrow input[i]$
4:     PUTTRIANGLE$((x, h, 0), (x, 0, -z), (x, 0, z))$ ▷ h and z parameters
5: **end for**
6: **for** each element i in $input$ **do**
7:     $x \leftarrow input[i]$
8:     RAYTRACE$((0, x, 0)- > (x, x, 0))$
9: **end for**
10: **for** each element i in $input$ **do**
11:     $position \leftarrow hitCounter[input[i]]$
12:     $output[position] \leftarrow input[i]$ ▷ Place element at its sorted position
13: **end for**
14: **function** ANYHIT
15:     $hitCounter[ray] \leftarrow hitCounter[ray] + 1$ ▷ ray payload
16: **end function**

9.4.4   Performance and Insight Analysis

In our exploration of the RTSort algorithm, it is important to note that its application extends beyond just sorting positive integers. With efficient encoding strategies, RTSort can be adapted to support a variety of data types. Additionally, the algorithm can handle duplicated data by employing an extension of nested triangles at the same X-axis location. In cases of duplicates, elements can be relocated to the next available slots to resolve conflicts. However, these modifications, while showcasing the algorithm's flexibility, are secondary to the primary goal of RTSort. The principal aim is to demonstrate the feasibility of utilizing ray tracing technology for general computational tasks, rather than just for rendering purposes. As we will see in the following analysis, despite its innovative approach, RTSort may not be the most practical or fastest solution owing to a combination of factors. These include its inherent complexity and the specific ways in which ray tracing hardware is employed within the algorithm, among others.

As we delve into the complexity analysis of RTSort, it is crucial to recognize that it diverges from the conventional counting sort algorithm. Unlike counting sort's linear complexity, RTSort inherently exhibits a quadratic time complexity, $O(n^2)$, in its basic form. This increased complexity arises because, in the worst-case scenario, each ray in RTSort may potentially interact with every other element in the input set. A clear example of this is the longest ray in the illustrative figure, which traverses the entire span of elements. However, it is important to note that RTSort's design allows for significant parallelization. With a sufficient number of processors, the algorithm can achieve parallel complexity of $O(n)$. This is possible because each element, and consequently each ray, operates independently, enabling concurrent processing. Thus, while RTSort's base complexity might be higher than traditional counting sort, its parallel nature aligns well with the capabilities of ray tracing hardware, offering potential efficiency gains in appropriately equipped computational environments.

While RTSort serves as an illustrative example of applying ray tracing hardware to a well-known task like sorting, it is not necessarily an ideal-use case for this technology. The choice to explain RTSort is primarily the result of the universal familiarity of the sorting task, making it a suitable introductory case. However, there are other more-complex data processing tasks where ray tracing hardware can be more effectively utilized; this will be explored in Section 9.5. Specifically, RTSort encounters two major mismatches with the optimal use of ray tracing hardware as per Nvidia's performance optimization guidelines. Firstly, the requirement to create a triangle for each element leads to an excessive number of triangles, especially for large input sizes (N). This abundance of triangles results in extended times for building the BVH, diminishing efficiency. Secondly, and more critically, the ray–object interaction in RTSort does not leverage the inherent advantage of the hardware's tree structure. The real performance benefits of ray tracing hardware stem from its ability to rapidly traverse and disregard irrelevant objects. Unfortunately, RTSort's design fails to capitalize on this, as its rays interact with nearly all objects in the worst-case scenario. While RTSort successfully transforms the sorting problem into a ray tracing scenario, it does not align well with the hardware's strengths, highlighting the importance of matching algorithm design with the capabilities of the underlying technology.

As we reflect on the implementation of the RTSort algorithm, it becomes evident that the callback programming mechanism, integral to ray tracing technology, introduces certain performance overheads, especially for straightforward computational tasks like sorting. This mechanism, where the hardware executes predefined operations and the software is responsible for complex event-driven logic, can be less efficient for tasks that do not inherently require such intricate interaction. While this programming model is a cornerstone of ray tracing's versatility and power, it is important to recognize that its application to simpler tasks may not always yield optimal performance. The use of ray tracing hardware for data processing involves a delicate balance of leveraging its strengths while being mindful of potential inefficiencies. Moving forward, our discussion will focus on understanding these dynamics and identifying scenarios where ray tracing can be most effectively utilized, particularly in contexts that extend beyond straightforward computational tasks like sorting.

9.5 An Introduction to Ray-Tracing-Accelerated Applications

In this section, we turn our attention to the innovative and burgeoning field of applying ray tracing hardware to diverse computational tasks. These applications, documented in recent academic research, transcend the traditional confines of image rendering, showcasing the versatile capabilities of ray tracing technology. Unlike RTSort, which offers limited performance advantages for simple sorting, these applications demonstrate tangible and significant improvements in efficiency. It is important to note, however, that a detailed explanation of each task is beyond the scope of this book. Instead, our focus will be on providing a high-level overview for each application by addressing three key aspects: (1) the nature of the computational task, (2) the mechanics of the proposed ray-tracing-based solution, and (3) the observed performance speedup. We will explore several intriguing applications, including nearest neighbor search, density-based spatial clustering of applications with noise (DBSCAN), and database indexing. Each of these case studies exemplifies how ray tracing hardware can be repurposed to solve complex, nongraphical problems, opening new horizons in computational efficiency and application.

9.5.1   Nearest Neighbor Search

Nearest neighbor search (NNS) is a fundamental algorithm used in various domains such as machine learning, computer vision, and data retrieval. It involves finding the closest or most similar data points in a dataset to a given query point. This task is particularly challenging in high-dimensional spaces, where the search becomes computationally intensive due to the "curse of dimensionality."

In applying ray tracing to NNS, we introduce a paper [146] titled "RTNN: Accelerating neighbor search using hardware ray tracing," authored by Yuhao Zhu, published in the *Proceedings of the 27th ACM SIGPLAN Symposium on Principles and Practice of Parallel Programming (PPoPP'22)*.

The paper presents a novel approach where data points are treated as objects in a 3D space, and rays are used to search for the nearest neighbors. Specifically, each data point in the dataset is represented as a geometric object in a ray tracing scene. When a query for a nearest neighbor is made, a ray is cast into this scene. The ray tracing hardware then computes intersections of this ray with the geometric representations of the data points, effectively identifying the closest points to the query. This method transforms the NNS problem into a spatial search problem, well suited to the strengths of ray tracing hardware.

The paper further introduces optimizations to enhance this process. One key optimization is the strategic placement and structuring of data points in the 3D space to minimize search times. Another involves fine tuning the ray traversal algorithm to quickly and efficiently navigate through the data points. These optimizations are crucial for leveraging the high-speed intersection testing capabilities of ray tracing hardware, thereby ensuring that the nearest neighbor search is conducted as swiftly and accurately as possible.

The research paper presents significant performance improvements for nearest neighbor search using ray tracing. The experimental results show speedups ranging from 2.2× to 65.0× over existing neighbor search libraries on GPUs. This includes comparisons with both optimized and unoptimized CUDA neighbor search methods. These speedups demonstrate the effectiveness of ray tracing hardware in accelerating the neighbor search process, providing substantial efficiency gains over traditional methods.

9.5.2   DBSCAN

Density-based spatial clustering of applications with noise (DBSCAN) is a popular clustering algorithm [51]. It identifies clusters in a dataset based on the density of data points, allowing it to form clusters of arbitrary shape and handle noise effectively; and it operates on the principle of identifying "core points" with a minimum number of neighbors within a given radius and grouping reachable points into clusters.

In applying ray tracing to DBSCAN, we introduce a paper [101] titled "RT-DBSCAN: Accelerating DBSCAN using ray tracing hardware," authored by Vani Nagarajan and Milind Kulkarni, published in the *Proceedings of 2023 IEEE International Parallel and Distributed Processing Symposium (IPDPS'23)*.

The technique of RT-DBSCAN innovatively applies ray tracing hardware to the neighbor search component of the DBSCAN algorithm. The core idea is to transform the problem of finding neighbors within a certain radius into a ray tracing query. This is achieved by representing data points as spheres in a 3D space. Through ray tracing, intersections with these spheres are detected, efficiently identifying neighboring points, thereby enhancing the clustering process of DBSCAN.

In RT-DBSCAN, specific optimizations are applied to improve efficiency. The representation of data points as spheres allows for an intuitive spatial interpretation of neighbor relationships. The ray tracing query, optimized for spatial data, quickly identifies potential neighbors by checking for intersections. This method capitalizes on the strengths of ray tracing hardware, particularly its high-speed spatial data processing capabilities, thus streamlining the clustering mechanism in DBSCAN.

A significant performance improvement is demonstrated by RT-DBSCAN over traditional GPU-based DBSCAN implementations. The research shows speedups ranging from $1.3\times$ to $4\times$, depending on various factors like dataset size and the complexity of the data. This speedup is attributed to the efficient handling of neighbor search queries by the ray tracing hardware, which excels in spatial data processing.

9.5.3   Database Indexing

Database indexing is a technique used to speed up data retrieval from a database. It involves creating an index, which is a data structure that improves the speed of data retrieval operations on a database table at the cost of additional writes and storage space to maintain the index.

In applying ray tracing to database indexing, we introduce a paper [63] titled "RTIndeX: Exploiting hardware-accelerated GPU raytracing for database indexing," authored by Justus Henneberg and Felix Schuhknecht, published in the *Proceedings of the VLDB Endowment*, volume 16, issue 13, 2023.

The RTIndeX approach revolutionizes database indexing by utilizing hardware-accelerated GPU ray tracing. It reimagines database indexing as a ray tracing problem. In this innovative method, the dataset to be indexed is visualized as objects within a 3D scene. Index lookups are then executed as intersection tests conducted by the ray tracing cores. This technique effectively harnesses the spatial data processing capabilities of ray tracing hardware, tailor-made for efficient intersection testing.

Key optimizations are introduced by RTIndeX to enhance the efficiency of database indexing. By representing data as 3D objects and employing ray tracing cores for intersection tests, it optimizes the indexing process. This method not only improves the speed but also the accuracy of database queries. The utilization of ray tracing for spatial data handling in this context demonstrates a significant advancement in database management technology, leveraging the inherent strengths of ray tracing hardware for optimized data retrieval.

Considerable performance improvements are shown by RTIndeX over traditional GPU-based indexing methods. The paper [63] highlights speedups in various scenarios, demonstrating that this approach can effectively leverage ray tracing hardware for database indexing, resulting in faster and more efficient data retrieval.

9.5.4   Summary

This section provides a concise overview of research papers exploring ray tracing-based tasks, aligning them with the RTSort algorithm. A key theme is constructing a 3D ray tracing scenario encompassing scene, ray, and action, as previously introduced. The efficacy of these applications in utilizing hardware capabilities, specifically BVH traversal and triangle intersection tests, is pivotal. Adherence to principles like maximizing parallel ray tracing, targeting rays for efficient BVH acceleration, and utilizing triangles (being hardware-supported) is crucial. For further exploration, readers are encouraged to consult Nvidia's online programming guidance, "Best Practices for Using Nvidia RTX Ray Tracing." However, this guidance primarily focuses on image rendering – the original purpose of ray tracing – and might not directly answer how to convert problems into ray tracing scenarios. Future technological advancements may yield automatic tools for this purpose.

9.6   Concluding Remarks and Exercise Projects

In this chapter, we have embarked on an enlightening journey through the realm of ray tracing, exploring its concepts, hardware and software environments, and applications in data management. We began with an introduction to ray tracing, delved into image rendering applications, and ventured into general data management tasks such as sorting. This progression demonstrates the potential of ray tracing cores in GPUs to accelerate various data management tasks. The educational focus has been on understanding the methodology of applying ray tracing to problem solving, employing a scene–ray–action approach. Through examples from both traditional graphics applications and extended nongraphics workloads like sorting, this chapter aims to impart an understanding of the main concepts and principles of accelerated computing in the era of domain-specific architecture. It has emphasized the foundational ideas over detailed algorithmic and programming specifics, which can be constrained by product version specifics, such as Nvidia OptiX 7.

As we conclude this chapter, it is important to acknowledge the dynamic and rapidly evolving nature of ray tracing technology, both in hardware features and software APIs. The advent of new hardware like ray tracing cores demands a reimagining of traditional problems, urging a mindset that bridges seemingly disparate concepts and domains. This new era requires not just innovative thinking but also meticulous coding practices, detailed performance measurement, and a thorough analysis of how algorithms map onto specific architectures. Achieving tangible acceleration in real-world applications hinges on a deep understanding of these elements, ensuring that the full potential of ray tracing hardware is harnessed effectively.

This chapter has three exercise projects, as follows.

- Project 1 (*easy*) This project involves using Nvidia OptiX to develop a rendering application akin to the triangle picture example discussed in this chapter. However, the application will render a circle instead of a triangle. This modification necessitates the creation of a user-defined object intersection function, as circles are not inherently supported by hardware. With this specific alteration, a significant portion of the code from the Nvidia OptiX SDK example can be repurposed for this project.

- Project 2 (*medium*) This project calls for the implementation of the RTSort algorithm using Nvidia OptiX, as introduced in this chapter. While the algorithm's introduction primarily focuses on triangles in a 3D space, implementers are encouraged to creatively design their ray tracing scenes with different object shapes and explore how varying object shapes impact performance. The project culminates with a comprehensive performance test and analysis, comparing the implementation with standard sorting algorithms from the C library and the GPU-accelerated Thrust library. These findings must be thoroughly documented and reported.

- Project 3 (*hard*) This project involves the implementation and comparison of three distinct database indexes for integers: (1) a multicore-oriented in-memory B-tree index, (2) a GPU-oriented B-tree index, and (3) an index similar to RTindeX [63], utilizing ray tracing hardware with Nvidia OptiX. All three versions must support point queries, range queries, and updates. Implementers are required to conduct thorough performance tests and analyses under various workloads, considering factors such as data size and the ratio of read to write operations. The insights and outcomes from these evaluations should be detailed in the final report.

10 The Future of Computing: Synergies in Data Management and System Architecture

> The best way to predict the future is to invent it.
>
> Alan Kay, *the recipient of the Turing Award in 2003.*

As we reach the culmination of our exploration, this book now turns towards synthesizing the wealth of knowledge presented, casting an eye towards the future of the intricate interplay between data management, computer hardware architecture, and software systems. In this final chapter, we delve into key points poised to significantly influence the computing landscape in the near future, shaping the dynamic relationship between applications and their underlying platforms. Our aim is not only to present these emerging trends and concepts but also to inspire deeper contemplation and innovative thinking among our readers. It is our hope that these discussions will serve as a catalyst, sparking new ideas and perspectives within the ever-evolving ecosystem of computing and data processing.

Embracing Domain-Specific Architecture in Data Management In the realm of data management, the advent of domain-specific architectures represents a paradigm shift. These architectures, tailored for specific types of data processing, exemplify the seamless integration of hardware design with the unique demands of data handling tasks. For instance, architectures optimized for high-throughput streaming data differ markedly from those best suited for large-scale batch processing tasks. This differentiation not only enhances efficiency but also underscores the importance of context in system design. By aligning hardware capabilities with specific data management requirements, these architectures offer nuanced solutions that traditional general-purpose systems cannot match. This focus on specialization not only improves performance but also drives innovation in developing new data processing methodologies.

The impact of these architectures extends beyond mere performance gains; they also influence the development of algorithms and software. A poignant example is the rise of specialized processors for machine learning tasks, such as TPUs. These processors are designed to accelerate machine learning algorithms, offering a stark contrast to traditional CPUs in terms of both architecture and performance. This shift highlights the growing need for hardware and software to evolve in tandem, a trend that is particularly pronounced in the field of data management.

Parallelism and GPUs: A New Era in Data Processing The exploration of parallelism, especially through the lens of GPU technology, has dramatically transformed the landscape of data processing. Initially designed for rendering graphics, GPUs have found a new calling in accelerating data-intensive tasks. Their architecture, inherently suited for parallel processing, makes them ideal for handling large-scale datasets and complex computations. This adaptability is best illustrated in applications like deep learning and high-performance computing, where GPUs significantly outpace traditional CPUs in both speed and efficiency. The transition to GPU-accelerated data processing is not merely a technological advancement; it represents a fundamental shift in how we approach data management. This shift is evident in the growing popularity of CUDA and OpenCL, programming frameworks that allow developers to harness the power of GPUs for general-purpose computing.

The impact of GPUs extends to various facets of data management, including data analytics, machine learning, and scientific simulations. For example, in the field of bioinformatics, GPU-accelerated tools have enabled researchers to analyze large genomic datasets much faster than was previously possible. This acceleration has profound implications for fields like personalized medicine, where the ability to quickly process vast amounts of data can lead to more timely and accurate diagnoses. The role of GPUs in these applications underscores the importance of parallel processing in modern data management, highlighting the symbiotic relationship between hardware advancements and software innovation.

End-to-End Application Optimization for Data Efficiency In the quest for optimal data management, the focus has shifted from isolated improvements to end-to-end application optimization. This holistic approach involves fine tuning every component of the computing stack – from hardware to software – ensuring that they work in concert to achieve maximum efficiency. A prime example is the optimization of database systems, where adjustments at the hardware level (like custom storage solutions) are coupled with software enhancements (like optimized query processing algorithms) to improve overall performance. This strategy is particularly crucial in an era characterized by explosive data growth and varied data types, where traditional one-size-fits-all solutions fall short.

The importance of this approach is exemplified in real-time analytics, where the need to process and analyze data swiftly is paramount. In such scenarios, every millisecond counts, and a system that is cohesively optimized can significantly outperform one where components are optimized in isolation. This optimization extends beyond traditional computing environments to encompass emerging technologies like edge computing, where data is processed closer to its source. In edge environments, the optimization of both hardware (like low-power, high-performance processors) and software (like lightweight, efficient algorithms) is critical to ensure timely data processing and decision-making.

Algorithm Analysis in Data Management Systems Algorithm analysis is at the heart of efficient data management. By dissecting and understanding algorithms, we can tailor them to leverage the strengths of the underlying hardware, thereby achieving optimal performance. This analysis goes beyond theoretical efficiency; it involves practical considerations like memory usage, parallelizability, and scalability. For instance, the choice between different sorting algorithms (like quicksort, mergesort, or heapsort) in database systems is not just a matter of theoretical complexity; it also depends on factors like data distribution, available memory, and the architecture of the underlying hardware.

The role of algorithm analysis is also crucial in the field of big data analytics. Here, the ability to process vast amounts of data quickly and accurately is dependent on the choice and optimization of algorithms. Algorithms like MapReduce and its derivatives (e.g., Apache Hadoop and Spark) are designed to process large datasets distributed across clusters of machines. The efficiency of these algorithms is heavily influenced by the way they handle data distribution, fault tolerance, and parallel processing. By analyzing and optimizing these algorithms, we can significantly enhance the performance of big data systems.

Customized Solutions in Data Systems The era of customized solutions in data management reflects the diverse and ever-evolving nature of data itself. Tailoring solutions to specific data scenarios ensures the optimal use of computing resources, whether it is in the form of specialized data storage formats or bespoke data processing techniques. This customization is a response to the varied nature of data – from structured data in traditional databases to unstructured data in big data applications. For instance, the design of a data warehouse for business intelligence requires a different approach compared to a system designed for streaming analytics.

The emergence of NoSQL databases like MongoDB and Cassandra exemplifies this trend towards customization. These databases are designed to handle large volumes of unstructured data, offering flexibility in data modeling that traditional relational databases do not. Similarly, the rise of time-series databases for IoT applications reflects a customization of data management solutions to meet the specific needs of time-sensitive data generated by sensors and devices. This trend towards customized solutions is not just a matter of efficiency; it is a necessity in a world where the one-size-fits-all approach is increasingly inadequate.

AI-Generated Content as a Data Management Solution The integration of AI in generating and processing content represents a significant leap forward in data management. With their ability to learn and adapt, AI technologies offer innovative methods to handle, analyze, and generate data. This integration is particularly impactful in areas like content recommendation systems, predictive analytics, and natural language processing. For example, AI algorithms can analyze user behavior and content preferences to provide personalized recommendations, enhancing user experience and engagement.

The role of AI in data management extends to more complex tasks like predictive maintenance and fraud detection. Here, AI algorithms can sift through vast amounts of data to identify patterns and anomalies that would be impossible for humans to detect in a timely manner. This capability not only improves efficiency but also opens up new possibilities for proactive problem solving. As we integrate AI more deeply into data management systems, we are witnessing a transformation in how data is processed, analyzed, and utilized. This convergence of AI with traditional computing paradigms is redefining the boundaries of data management, promising a future where AI is not just a tool but a fundamental component of data systems.

Concluding Thoughts on Data Management and System Interplay As we conclude our journey through the multifaceted world of data management and system architecture, it is clear that the field is defined by constant evolution and adaptation. The synergy between hardware advancements, software innovations, and algorithmic refinements has propelled us into a new era of computing. The future, as outlined in this book, is one where the boundaries between data management, computer architecture, and systems are increasingly blurred, leading to more integrated and efficient solutions.

The landscape of computing is no longer static; it is a dynamic interplay of various components, each evolving and influencing the other. The convergence of domain-specific architecture, parallelism, GPU capabilities, AI-generated content, and customized solutions is not just a technological advancement; it is a paradigm shift in how we approach data and computing. This book is a testament to that shift – a narrative that captures the essence of modern computing and offers a glimpse into its future – a future where data management is not just about storing and retrieving data, but about understanding, optimizing, and leveraging it in ways we are only beginning to imagine.

References

[1] Daniel Abadi, Peter Boncz, Stavros Harizopoulos Amiato, Stratos Idreos, and Samuel Madden. *The Design and Implementation of Modern Column-Oriented Database Systems*. Now, 2013.

[2] Daniel J. Abadi, Daniel S. Myers, David J. DeWitt, and Samuel R. Madden. Materialization strategies in a column-oriented DBMS. In *2007 IEEE 23rd International Conference on Data Engineering*, pages 466–475. IEEE, 2007.

[3] Trilok Acharya and Meggie Ladlow. Cache replacement algorithms in hardware. Technical report, Swarthmore College, 2008.

[4] Alfred V. Aho, Peter J. Denning, and Jeffrey D. Ullman. Principles of optimal page replacement. *Journal of the ACM (JACM)*, 18(1):80–93, 1971.

[5] Anastassia Ailamaki, David J. DeWitt, Mark D. Hill, and Marios Skounakis. Weaving relations for cache performance. In *VLDB*, volume 1, pages 169–180, 2001.

[6] John D' Ambrosia and Mark Nowell. IEEE P802.3df 200 Gb/s, 400 Gb/s, 800 Gb/s, and 1.6 Tb/s Ethernet Task Force, 2022. www.ieee802.org/3/df/index.html.

[7] Owen Astrachan. Bubble sort: An archaeological algorithmic analysis. *ACM Sigcse Bulletin*, 35(1):1–5, 2003.

[8] Manos Athanassoulis, Michael S. Kester, Lukas M. Maas, et al. Designing access methods: The RUM conjecture. In *EDBT*, volume 2016, pages 461–466, 2016.

[9] M. N. Baibich, J. M. Broto, A. Fert, et al. Giant magnetoresistance of (001)Fe/(001)Cr magnetic superlattices. *Physical Review Letters*, 61:2472–2475, Nov. 1988. https://doi.org/10.1103/PhysRevLett.61.2472.

[10] Cagri Balkesen, Gustavo Alonso, Jens Teubner, and M. Tamer Özsu. Multi-core, main-memory joins: Sort vs. hash revisited. *Proceedings of the VLDB Endowment*, 7(1): 85–96, 2013.

[11] Luiz André Barroso, Jimmy Clidaras, and Urs Hölzle. *The Datacentre as a Computer: An Introduction to the Design of Warehouse-Scale Machines*, 2nd ed. Synthesis Lectures on Computer Architecture. Morgan & Claypool Publishers, 2013.

[12] Kenneth E. Batcher. Sorting networks and their applications. In *Proceedings of the April 30–May 2, 1968, Spring Joint Computer Conference*, pages 307–314, 1968.

[13] Rudolf Bayer. Symmetric binary B-trees: Data structure and maintenance algorithms. *Acta Informatica*, 1(4):290–306, 1972.

[14] Rudolf Bayer and Edward McCreight. Organization and maintenance of large ordered indexes. In *Software Pioneers*, pages 245–262. Springer, 2002.

[15] Norbert Beckmann, Hans-Peter Kriegel, Ralf Schneider, and Bernhard Seeger. The R*-tree: An efficient and robust access method for points and rectangles. In

Proceedings of the 1990 ACM SIGMOD International Conference on Management of Data, pages 322–331, 1990.

[16] Laszlo A. Belady. A study of replacement algorithms for a virtual-storage computer. *IBM Systems Journal*, 5(2):78–101, 1966.

[17] Brian N. Bershad, Dennis Lee, Theodore H. Romer, and J. Bradley Chen. Avoiding conflict misses dynamically in large direct-mapped caches. In *Proceedings of the Sixth International Conference on Architectural Support for Programming Languages and Operating Systems*, pages 158–170, 1994.

[18] Kristof Beyls and Erik D'Hollander. Reuse distance as a metric for cache behavior. In *Proceedings of the IASTED Conference on Parallel and Distributed Computing and Systems*, volume 14, pages 350–360. Citeseer, 2001.

[19] Andrew D. Birrell and Bruce Jay Nelson. Implementing remote procedure calls. *ACM Transactions on Computer Systems (TOCS)*, 2(1):39–59, 1984.

[20] Mark Blacher, Joachim Giesen, Sören Laue, Julien Klaus, and Viktor Leis. Machine learning, linear algebra, and more: Is SQL all you need? *CIDR*. www. cidrdb. org, pages 1–6, 2022.

[21] Geoffrey Blake, Ronald G. Dreslinski, and Trevor Mudge. A survey of multicore processors. *IEEE Signal Processing Magazine*, 26(6):26–37, 2009.

[22] Peter A. Boncz, Stefan Manegold, and Martin L. Kersten. Database architecture optimized for the new bottleneck: Memory access. In *Proceedings of the 25th International Conference on Very Large Data Bases*, pages 54–65, 1999.

[23] David C. Brock and Gordon E. Moore. *Understanding Moore's Law: Four Decades of Innovation*. Chemical Heritage Foundation, 2006.

[24] Alice R. Burks and Arthur Walter Burks. *The First Electronic Computer: The Atanasoff Story*. University of Michigan Press, 1989.

[25] Arthur W. Burks and Alice R. Burks. Atanasoff–Berry computer. In *Encyclopedia of Computer Science*, pages 108–109, 2003.

[26] Idan Burstein. Nvidia data center processing unit (DPU) architecture. In *2021 IEEE Hot Chips 33 Symposium (HCS)*, pages 1–20. IEEE, 2021.

[27] Ali R. Butt, Chris Gniady, and Y. Charlie Hu. The performance impact of kernel prefetching on buffer cache replacement algorithms. In *Proceedings of the 2005 ACM SIGMETRICS International Conference on Measurement and Modeling of Computer Systems*, pages 157–168, 2005.

[28] Francois Caen and Christopher Negus. *BSD Unix® Toolbox: 1000+ Commands for FreeBSD®, OpenBSD, and NetBSD®*. John Wiley & Sons, 2008.

[29] Cosmin Cartas. Rust – the programming language for every industry. *Academy of Economic Studies. Economy Informatics*, 19(1):45–51, 2019.

[30] Daniel Cederman and Philippas Tsigas. GPU-quicksort: A practical quicksort algorithm for graphics processors. *Journal of Experimental Algorithmics (JEA)*, 14:1–4, 2010.

[31] Paul E. Ceruzzi. The early computers of Konrad Zuse, 1935 to 1945. *Annals of the History of Computing*, 3(3):241–262, 1981.

[32] Fay Chang, Jeffrey Dean, Sanjay Ghemawat, et al. BigTable: A distributed storage system for structured data. *ACM Transactions on Computer Systems (TOCS)*, 26(2): 1–26, 2008.

[33] Feng Chen, David A. Koufaty, and Xiaodong Zhang. Hystor: Making the best use of solid state drives in high performance storage systems. In *Proceedings of the International Conference on Supercomputing*, pages 22–32, 2011.

[34] Feng Chen, Rubao Lee, and Xiaodong Zhang. Essential roles of exploiting internal parallelism of flash memory based solid state drives in high-speed data processing. In *2011 IEEE 17th International Symposium on High Performance Computer Architecture*, pages 266–277. IEEE, 2011.

[35] Ching-Hsiang Chu, Sreeram Potluri, Anshuman Goswami, et al. Designing high-performance in-memory key–value operations with persistent gpu kernels and openshmem. In *Workshop on OpenSHMEM and Related Technologies*, pages 148–164. Springer, 2018.

[36] Michael Codish, Luís Cruz-Filipe, Thorsten Ehlers, Mike Müller, and Peter Schneider-Kamp. Sorting networks: To the end and back again. *Journal of Computer and System Sciences*, 104:184–201, 2019.

[37] Douglas Comer. Ubiquitous B-tree. *ACM Computing Surveys (CSUR)*, 11(2):121–137, 1979.

[38] Lee A. D. Cooper, Jun Kong, David A. Gutman, et al. Integrated morphologic analysis for the identification and characterization of disease subtypes. *Journal of the American Medical Informatics Association*, 19(2):317–323, 2012.

[39] George P. Copeland and Setrag N. Khoshafian. A decomposition storage model. *ACM Sigmod Record*, 14(4):268–279, 1985.

[40] Fernando J. Corbato. A paging experiment with the Multics system. Technical report, Massachusetts Institute of Technology, Cambridge, Project MAC, 1968.

[41] T. H. Cormen, C. E. Leiserson, R. L. Rivest, and C. Stein. *Introduction to Algorithms*, 2nd ed. The MIT Press, 2001.

[42] Asit Dan and Don Towsley. An approximate analysis of the LRU and FIFO buffer replacement schemes. In *Proceedings of the 1990 ACM SIGMETRICS Conference on Measurement and Modeling of Computer Systems*, pages 143–152, 1990.

[43] Robert H. Dennard. How we made DRAM. *Nature Electronics*, 1(6):372–372, 2018.

[44] Peter J. Denning. The working set model for program behavior. *Communications of the ACM*, 11(5): 323–333, 1968.

[45] Peter J. Denning. The locality principle. *Communications of the ACM*, 48(7): 19–24, 2005.

[46] Chen Ding and Yutao Zhong. Predicting whole-program locality through reuse distance analysis. In *Proceedings of the ACM SIGPLAN 2003 Conference on Programming Language Design and Implementation*, pages 245–257, 2003.

[47] Xiaoning Ding, Song Jiang, Feng Chen, Kei Davis, and Xiaodong Zhang. Diskseen: Exploiting disk layout and access history to enhance I/O prefetch. In *USENIX Annual Technical Conference*, volume 7, pages 261–274, 2007.

[48] Aleksandar Dragojević, Dushyanth Narayanan, Miguel Castro, and Orion Hodson. Farm: Fast remote memory. In *11th USENIX Symposium on Networked Systems Design and Implementation (NSDI 14)*, pages 401–414, 2014.

[49] Nicola Dragoni, Saverio Giallorenzo, Alberto Lluch Lafuente, et al. Microservices: yesterday, today, and tomorrow. *Present and Ulterior Software Engineering*, pages 195–216, 2017.

[50] Gil Einziger, Roy Friedman, and Ben Manes. TinyLFU: A highly efficient cache admission policy. *ACM Transactions on Storage (ToS)*, 13(4):1–31, 2017.

[51] Martin Ester, Hans-Peter Kriegel, Jörg Sander, and Xiaowei Xu. A density-based algorithm for discovering clusters in large spatial databases with noise. In *Proceedings*

of the Second International Conference on Knowledge Discovery and Data Mining, KDD'96, page 226–231. AAAI Press, 1996.

[52] Sofoklis Floratos, Mengbai Xiao, Hao Wang, et al. NestGPU: Nested query processing on GPU. In *2021 IEEE 37th International Conference on Data Engineering (ICDE)*, pages 1008–1019. IEEE, 2021.

[53] William A. Giovinazzo. *Object-Oriented Data Warehouse Design: Building a Star Schema*. Prentice Hall PTR, 2000.

[54] GitHub. RDMA core userspace libraries and daemons, 2022. `https://github.com/linux-rdma/rdma-core`.

[55] Google. Introducing GRPC, a new open source http/2 RPC framework, 2015. `https://developers.googleblog.com/2015/02/introducing-grpc-new-open-source-http2.html`.

[56] Goetz Graefe. Sort-merge-join: An idea whose time has (h) passed? In *Proceedings of 1994 IEEE 10th International Conference on Data Engineering*, pages 406–417. IEEE, 1994.

[57] Jim Gray and Franco Putzolu. The 5 minute rule for trading memory for disc accesses and the 10 byte rule for trading memory for CPU time. *ACM SIGMOD Record*, 16(3), 1987. `https://doi.org/10.1145/38714.38755`.

[58] Oded Green, Robert McColl, and David A. Bader. GPU merge path: A GPU merging algorithm. In *Proceedings of the 26th ACM International Conference on Supercomputing*, pages 331–340, 2012.

[59] A. Nico Habermann. *Parallel Neighbor-Sort (or the Glory of the Induction Principle)*. Defense Technical Information Center, 1972.

[60] Richard A. Hankins and Jignesh M. Patel. Data morphing: An adaptive, cache-conscious storage technique. In *Proceedings of the 2003 VLDB Conference*, pages 417–428. Elsevier, 2003.

[61] Tim J. Harris. A survey of PRAM simulation techniques. *ACM Computing Surveys (CSUR)*, 26(2):187–206, 1994.

[62] Yongqiang He, Rubao Lee, Yin Huai, et al. RCFile: A fast and space-efficient data placement structure in MapReduce-based warehouse systems. In *2011 IEEE 27th International Conference on Data Engineering*, pages 1199–1208. IEEE, 2011.

[63] Justus Henneberg and Felix Schuhknecht. RTIndeX: Exploiting hardware-accelerated GPU raytracing for database indexing. *Proceedings of the VLDB Endowment*, 16(13): 4268–4281, Sept. 2023. `https://doi.org/10.14778/3625054.3625063`.

[64] John L. Hennessy and David A. Patterson. *Computer Architecture: A Quantitative Approach*. Elsevier, 2011.

[65] Maurice Herlihy, Nir Shavit, and Moran Tzafrir. Hopscotch hashing. In *Distributed Computing: 22nd International Symposium, DISC 2008, Arcachon, France, September 22–24, 2008. Proceedings 22*, pages 350–364. Springer, 2008.

[66] Mark D. Hill. A case for direct-mapped caches. *Computer*, 21(12):25–40, 1988.

[67] Mark D. Hill and Alan Jay Smith. Evaluating associativity in CPU caches. *IEEE Transactions on Computers*, 38(12):1612–1630, 1989.

[68] A. F. Horadam. A generalized Fibonacci sequence. *The American Mathematical Monthly*, 68(5):455–459, 1961.

[69] Yin Huai, Siyuan Ma, Rubao Lee, Owen O'Malley, and Xiaodong Zhang. Understanding insights into the basic structure and essential issues of table placement methods in clusters. *Proceedings of the VLDB Endowment*, 6(14):1750–1761, 2013.

[70] Bruce Jacob, David Wang, and Spencer Ng. *Memory Systems: Cache, DRAM, Disk.* Morgan Kaufmann, 2010.

[71] H. V. Jagadish, P. P. S. Narayan, Sridhar Seshadri, S. Sudarshan, and Rama Kanneganti. Incremental organization for data recording and warehousing. In *VLDB*, volume 97, pages 16–25. Citeseer, 1997.

[72] Aamer Jaleel, Kevin B. Theobald, Simon C. Steely Jr., and Joel Emer. High performance cache replacement using re-reference interval prediction (RRIP). *ACM SIGARCH Computer Architecture News*, 38(3):60–71, 2010.

[73] Song Jiang and Xiaodong Zhang. LIRS: An efficient low inter-reference recency set replacement policy to improve buffer cache performance. *ACM SIGMETRICS Performance Evaluation Review*, 30(1):31–42, 2002.

[74] Song Jiang, Feng Chen, and Xiaodong Zhang. Clock-pro: An effective improvement of the clock replacement. In *USENIX Annual Technical Conference, General Track*, pages 323–336, 2005.

[75] Song Jiang, Xiaoning Ding, Feng Chen, Enhua Tan, and Xiaodong Zhang. DULO: an effective buffer cache management scheme to exploit both temporal and spatial locality. In *Proceedings of the 4th Conference on USENIX Conference on File and Storage Technologies*, volume 4, page 8, 2005.

[76] Theodore Johnson, Dennis Shasha, et al. 2Q: A low overhead high performance buffer management replacement algorithm. In *Proceedings of the 20th International Conference on Very Large Data Bases*, pages 439–450. Citeseer, 1994.

[77] Norman P. Jouppi, Cliff Young, Nishant Patil, et al. In-datacenter performance analysis of a tensor processing unit. In *Proceedings of the 44th Annual International Symposium on Computer Architecture*, pages 1–12, 2017.

[78] Ibrahim Kamel and Christos Faloutsos. Hilbert R-tree: An improved R-tree using fractals. In *Proceedings of the 20th International Conference on Very Large Data Bases*, pages 500–509, 1994.

[79] Urs Kanus, Gregor Wetekam, Johannes Hirche, and Michael Meißner. VIZARD II: An FPGA-based interactive volume rendering system. In *Field-Programmable Logic and Applications: Reconfigurable Computing Is Going Mainstream: 12th International Conference, FPL 2002 Montpellier, France, September 2–4, 2002 Proceedings 12*, pages 1114–1117. Springer, 2002.

[80] Richard E. Kessler and Mark D. Hill. Page placement algorithms for large real-indexed caches. *ACM Transactions on Computer Systems (TOCS)*, 10(4):338–359, 1992.

[81] Changkyu Kim, Tim Kaldewey, Victor W. Lee, et al. Sort vs. hash revisited: Fast join implementation on modern multi-core CPUs. *Proceedings of the VLDB Endowment*, 2 (2):1378–1389, 2009.

[82] David B. Kirk and Wen-mei W. Hwu. *Programming Massively Parallel Processors: A Hands-On Approach*. Morgan Kaufmann, 2012.

[83] Anthony LaMarca and Richard E. Ladner. The influence of caches on the performance of sorting. *Journal of Algorithms*, 31(1):66–104, 1999.

[84] Chris Lattner and Vikram Adve. LLVM: A compilation framework for lifelong program analysis & transformation. In *International Symposium on Code Generation and Optimization, 2004, CGO 2004*, pages 75–86. IEEE, 2004.

[85] Hubert Nguyen. *GPU Gems 3*. Addison-Wesley Professional, 2007.

[86] Donghee Lee, Jongmoo Choi, Jong-Hun Kim, et al. On the existence of a spectrum of policies that subsumes the least recently used (LRU) and least frequently used (LFU)

policies. In *Proceedings of the 1999 ACM SIGMETRICS International Conference on Measurement and Modeling of Computer Systems*, pages 134–143, 1999.

[87] Rubao Lee, Xiaoning Ding, Feng Chen, Qingda Lu, and Xiaodong Zhang. MCC-DB: Minimizing cache conflicts in multi-core processors for databases. *Proceedings of the VLDB Endowment*, 2(1):373–384, 2009.

[88] Rubao Lee, Minghong Zhou, Chi Li, et al. The art of balance: A RateupDB™ experience of building a CPU/GPU hybrid database product. *Proceedings of the VLDB Endowment*, 14(12):2999–3013, 2021.

[89] Nikolaj Leischner, Vitaly Osipov, and Peter Sanders. GPU sample sort. In *2010 IEEE International Symposium on Parallel & Distributed Processing (IPDPS)*, pages 1–10. IEEE, 2010.

[90] Charles E. Leiserson, Neil C. Thompson, Joel S. Emer, et al. There's plenty of room at the Top: What will drive computer performance after Moore's law? *Science*, 368(6495), 2020.

[91] Bojie Li, Zhenyuan Ruan, Wencong Xiao, et al. KV-Direct: High-performance in-memory key-value store with programmable NIC. In *Proceedings of the 26th Symposium on Operating Systems Principles*, pages 137–152, 2017.

[92] Jiang Lin, Qingda Lu, Xiaoning Ding, et al. Gaining insights into multicore cache partitioning: Bridging the gap between simulation and real systems. In *2008 IEEE 14th International Symposium on High Performance Computer Architecture*, pages 367–378. IEEE, 2008.

[93] Frank Luna. *Introduction to 3D Game Programming with DirectX 11*. Mercury Learning and Information, 2012.

[94] Chen Luo and Michael J. Carey. LSM-based storage techniques: A survey. *The VLDB Journal*, 29(1):393–418, 2020.

[95] Richard L. Mattson, Jan Gecsei, Donald R. Slutz, and Irving L. Traiger. Evaluation techniques for storage hierarchies. *IBM Systems Journal*, 9(2):78–117, 1970.

[96] Wolfgang Mauerer. *Professional Linux Kernel Architecture*. John Wiley & Sons, 2010.

[97] Keith McLuckie and Angus Barber. Tournament sort. In *Sorting Routines for Microcomputers*, pages 68–86. Springer, 1986.

[98] Nimrod Megiddo and Dharmendra S. Modha. Arc: A self-tuning, low overhead replacement cache. In *Fast*, volume 3, pages 115–130, 2003.

[99] Ulrich Meyer, Peter Sanders, and Jop Sibeyn (eds.). *Algorithms for Memory Hierarchies: Advanced Lectures*, volume 2625. Springer Science & Business Media, 2003.

[100] Aaftab Munshi. The OpenCL specification. In *2009 IEEE Hot Chips 21 Symposium (HCS)*, pages 1–314. IEEE, 2009.

[101] Vani Nagarajan and Milind Kulkarni. RT-DBSCAN: Accelerating DBSCAN using ray tracing hardware. In *Proceedings of 2023 IEEE International Parallel and Distributed Processing Symposium (IPDPS'23)*, pages 963–973. IEEE, 2023.

[102] John Nickolls and William J. Dally. The GPU computing era. *IEEE Micro*, 30(2):56–69, 2010.

[103] Hitoshi Nishimura, Hiroshi Ohno, Toru Kawata, Isao Shirakawa, and Koichi Omura. LINKS-1 – a parallel pipelined multimicrocomputer system for image creation. *ACM SIGARCH Computer Architecture News*, 11(3):387–394, 1983.

[104] Nvidia. CUDA toolkit documentation. 2018.

[105] Nvidia. Nvidia Turing GPU architecture. 2018.

[106] Nvidia. Nvidia Ampere ga102 GPU architecture. 2021.

[107] Nvidia. Nvidia Ada GPU architecture. 2022.

[108] Nvidia. Nvidia Optix 8.0 programming guide. 2023.

[109] Elizabeth J. O'Neil, Patrick E. O'Neil, and Gerhard Weikum. The LRU-K page replacement algorithm for database disk buffering. *ACM Sigmod Record*, 22(2): 297–306, 1993.

[110] Patrick O'Neil, Edward Cheng, Dieter Gawlick, and Elizabeth O'Neil. The log-structured merge-tree (LSM-tree). *Acta Informatica*, 33(4):351–385, 1996.

[111] John Ousterhout, Arjun Gopalan, Ashish Gupta, et al. The RAMCloud storage system. *ACM Transactions on Computer Systems*, 33(3), 2015. https://doi.org/10 .1145/2806887.

[112] Rasmus Pagh and Flemming Friche Rodler. Cuckoo hashing. *Journal of Algorithms*, 51 (2):122–144, 2004.

[113] Markus Pilman, Kevin Bocksrocker, Lucas Braun, Renato Marroquin, and Donald Kossmann. Fast scans on key–value stores. *Proceedings of the VLDB Endowment*, 10 (11):1526–1537, 2017.

[114] An Qin, Mengbai Xiao, Jin Ma, et al. Directload: A fast web-scale index system across large regional centers. In *2019 IEEE 35th International Conference on Data Engineering (ICDE)*, pages 1790–1801. IEEE, 2019.

[115] Scott Rixner, William J. Dally, Ujval J. Kapasi, Peter Mattson, and John D. Owens. Memory access scheduling. *ACM SIGARCH Computer Architecture News*, 28 (2):128–138, 2000. https://doi.org/10.1145/342001.339668.

[116] John T. Robinson and Murthy V. Devarakonda. Data cache management using frequency-based replacement. In *Proceedings of the 1990 ACM SIGMETRICS Conference on Measurement and Modeling of Computer Systems*, pages 134–142, 1990.

[117] Nadathur Satish, Mark Harris, and Michael Garland. Designing efficient sorting algorithms for manycore GPUs. In *2009 IEEE International Symposium on Parallel & Distributed Processing*, pages 1–10. IEEE, 2009.

[118] Jiri Schindler, John Linwood Griffin, Christopher R. Lumb, and Gregory R. Ganger. Track-aligned extents: Matching access patterns to disk drive characteristics. In *FAST*, volume 2, pages 259–274, 2002.

[119] Graham Sellers and John Kessenich. *Vulkan Programming Guide: The Official Guide to Learning Vulkan*. Addison-Wesley Professional, 2016.

[120] Ambuj Shatdal, Chander Kant, and Jeffrey F. Naughton. Cache conscious algorithms for relational query processing. In *Proceedings of the 20th International Conference on Very Large Data Bases*, pages 510–521, 1994.

[121] Konstantin Shvachko, Hairong Kuang, Sanjay Radia, and Robert Chansler. The Hadoop distributed file system. In *2010 IEEE 26th Symposium on Mass Storage Systems and Technologies (MSST)*, pages 1–10. IEEE, 2010.

[122] Yannis Smaragdakis, Scott Kaplan, and Paul Wilson. EELRU: simple and effective adaptive page replacement. *ACM SIGMETRICS Performance Evaluation Review*, 27(1): 122–133, 1999.

[123] Renzo Sprugnoli. Perfect hashing functions: A single probe retrieving method for static sets. *Communications of the ACM*, 20(11):841–850, 1977.

[124] Dejun Teng, Lei Guo, Rubao Lee, et al. A low-cost disk solution enabling LSM-tree to achieve high performance for mixed read/write workloads. *ACM Transactions on Storage (TOS)*, 14(2):1–26, 2018.

[125] Rik van Riel. Towards an O (1) VM: Making Linux virtual memory management scale towards large amounts of physical memory. In *Proceedings of the Linux Symposium*, 2003.

[126] Hans Vandierendonck and Koenraad De Bosschere. XOR-based hash functions. *IEEE Transactions on Computers*, 54(7):800–812, 2005.

[127] John Von Neumann. First draft of a report on the EDVAC. *IEEE Annals of the History of Computing*, 15(4):27–75, 1993.

[128] Carl Waldspurger, Trausti Saemundsson, Irfan Ahmad, and Nohhyun Park. Cache modeling and optimization using miniature simulations. In *2017 USENIX Annual Technical Conference (USENIX ATC 17)*, pages 487–498, 2017.

[129] Fusheng Wang, Jun Kong, Lee Cooper, et al. A data model and database for high-resolution pathology analytical image informatics. *Journal of Pathology Informatics*, 2(1):32, 2011.

[130] Thomas Wang. Integer hash function, 1997. https://web.archive.org/web/20071223173210/http://www.concentric.net/~Ttwang/tech/inthash.htm

[131] R. Clinton Whaley and Jack J. Dongarra. Automatically tuned linear algebra software. In *SC'98: Proceedings of the 1998 ACM/IEEE Conference on Supercomputing*, page 38. IEEE, 1998.

[132] Gio Wiederhold. *Database Design*, volume 1077. McGraw-Hill, 1983.

[133] Maurice V. Wilkes. Slave memories and dynamic storage allocation. *IEEE Transactions on Electronic Computers*, 14(2):270–271, 1965.

[134] Niklaus Wirth. *Algorithms & Data Structures*. Prentice-Hall, Inc., 1985.

[135] Theodore M. Wong and John Wilkes. My cache or yours?: Making storage more exclusive. In *USENIX Annual Technical Conference, General Track*, pages 161–175, 2002.

[136] Sven Woop, Jörg Schmittler, and Philipp Slusallek. RPU: A programmable ray processing unit for realtime ray tracing. *ACM Transactions on Graphics (TOG)*, 24(3):434–444, 2005.

[137] Li Xiao, Xiaodong Zhang, and Stefan A Kubricht. Improving memory performance of sorting algorithms. *Journal of Experimental Algorithmics (JEA)*, 5:3–es, 2000.

[138] Yong Yan and Xiaodong Zhang. Cacheminer: A runtime approach to exploit cache locality on SMP. *IEEE Transactions on Parallel and Distributed Systems*, 11(4):357–374, 2000.

[139] Yuan Yuan, Rubao Lee, and Xiaodong Zhang. The yin and yang of processing data warehousing queries on GPU devices. In *PVLDB*, pages 817–828, 2013.

[140] Chenxi Zhang, Xiaodong Zhang, and Yong Yan. Two fast and high-associativity cache schemes. *IEEE Micro*, 17(5):40–49, 1997.

[141] Kai Zhang, Kaibo Wang, Yuan Yuan, et al. Mega-KV: A case for GPUs to maximize the throughput of in-memory key-value stores. *Proceedings of the VLDB Endowment*, 8 (11):1226–1237, 2015.

[142] Zhao Zhang, Zhichun Zhu, and Xiaodong Zhang. A permutation-based page interleaving scheme to reduce row-buffer conflicts and exploit data locality. In

Proceedings of the 33rd Annual ACM/IEEE International Symposium on Microarchitecture, pages 32–41, 2000.

[143] Kai Zhao, Wenzhe Zhao, Hongbin Sun, et al. LDPC-in-SSD: Making advanced error correction codes work effectively in solid state drives. In *11th USENIX Conference on File and Storage Technologies (FAST 13)*, pages 243–256, 2013.

[144] Chen Zhong, Xingsheng Zhao, and Song Jiang. LIRS2: an improved lirs replacement algorithm. In *Proceedings of the 14th ACM International Conference on Systems and Storage*, pages 1–12, 2021.

[145] Yuanyuan Zhou, James Philbin, and Kai Li. The multi-queue replacement algorithm for second level buffer caches. In *USENIX Annual Technical Conference, General Track*, pages 91–104, 2001.

[146] Yuhao Zhu. RTNN: Accelerating neighbor search using hardware ray tracing. In *Proceedings of the 27th ACM SIGPLAN Symposium on Principles and Practice of Parallel Programming (PPoPP'22)*, pages 76–89, 2022.

[147] Zhichun Zhu, Zhao Zhang, and Xiaodong Zhang. Fine-grain priority scheduling on multi-channel memory systems. In *Proceedings of the Eighth International Symposium on High Performance Computer Architecture*, pages 107–116. IEEE, 2002.

Index

Printed in the United States
by Baker & Taylor Publisher Services